Study Guide to

CLARENCE BYRD
Athabasca University

IDA CHEN
Clarence Byrd Inc.

Byrd & Chen's
Canadian
Tax
Principles
2005-2006
Edition

PEARSON

Prentice
Hall

Toronto

0-13-201637-0
This ISBN is shared with the text (*Byrd & Chen's Canadian Tax Principles*, 2005–2006 Edition).

Acquisitions Editor and Executive Marketing Manager: Cas Shields
Developmental Editor: Paul Donnelly
Production Editor: Marisa D'Andrea
Production Coordinator: Deborah Starks

1 2 3 4 5   10 09 08 07 06

Printed and bound in Canada.

PEARSON
Prentice
Hall

Preface

Content

Your textbook is accompanied by this Companion Study Guide. Solutions to both the Exercises and the Self Study Problems and Cases will be found in this Guide. While other tax texts, such as those by Beam and Laiken and Denhamer, include a limited amount of such material as an appendix to a single volume, we believe that having these solutions available in a separate Guide will greatly facilitate your use of this material. An important result of this decision is that it provides for a more conveniently sized basic text.

Additional features of the Companion Study Guide that have been well received by our users are detailed guidance on how to work through each Chapter (the How To Work Through The Chapter lists) and a guide for reviewing the basic concepts that you should have mastered on completion of each Chapter (the list of Objectives). Further review opportunities are made available in the PowerPoint slide presentations found on the Companion CD-ROM and the web site for the text.

Using The Solutions

With respect to the problem solutions that are included in this book, the header at the top of each page identifies the solution on the page. The page numbers in this Companion Study Guide have been numbered with the prefix "S-" to distinguish them from the page numbers of the text. As always, we encourage you to attempt to solve each Exercise or Self Study Problem prior to consulting these solutions. It is our opinion that one of the most unfortunate misconceptions that many students have, is the belief that simply reading through a solution is a learning experience. It is not!

Web Site

The web site for this book can be found at:

www.pearsoned.ca/byrdchen/ctp2006/

This web site contains updates and corrections to the text that are available to all users. Please check the web site for additions or corrections to the text before using this book.

We welcome any corrections or suggestions for additions or improvements. These can be sent to us at:

Clarence Byrd Inc.
139 Musie Loop Road, Chelsea, Quebec   J9B 1Y6
e-mail address: ichen@byrdinc.ca

August, 2005

Clarence Byrd, Athabasca University
Ida Chen, Clarence Byrd Inc.

Table Of Contents

Introduction

Web Site

The web site for this book can be found at:

www.pearsoned.ca/byrdchen/ctp2006/

Here you will find

- Updates and corrections to the textbook
- Links to other web sites
- A "Guide to Using Your Companion CD-ROM"
- A short on-line survey ($100 cash prize available)
- When the updated Intuit GreenPoint software is available in January, 2006, a download site for the updated software program and updated sample tax returns and Cases using ProFile software

Study Guide On Companion CD-ROM

For your convenience, we have included the Study Guide for Chapters 1 to 14 on the Companion CD-ROM in PDF format. To assist you in navigating through the electronic version of this Study Guide, we have provided bookmarks that are set to automatically show when you first open the file. You will be able to expand or collapse the table of contents branches and jump to any solution by clicking on the solution number with your mouse. For example, by clicking on " Solution To Self Study Problem Two-3" in the expanded CHAPTER 2 Table of Contents, you will jump to the solution for Self Study Problem Two-3.

To hide the bookmarks, choose the "Hide Bookmarks" option under the Window menu (Hotkey is F5).

CHAPTER ONE

How To Work Through Chapter One

Web Site

As a reminder, the web site for this book can be found at:

www.pearsoned.ca/byrdchen/ctp2006/

Here you will find

- Updates and corrections to the textbook
- Links to other websites
- A "Guide to Using Your Companion CD-ROM"
- A short on-line survey ($100 cash prize available)
- When the updated ProFile software is available in January, 2006, a download site for the updated software program and updated sample tax returns and Cases using ProFile software

We recommend the following approach in dealing with the material in this chapter:

The Canadian Tax System

☐ Read pages 1 through 3 (through paragraph 1-8) of the text.

☐ Complete Exercise One-1. The Exercise is on page 3 of the text. The solution is on page S-2 of this Study Guide.

☐ Read pages 3 (from paragraph 1-9) and 4 (through paragraph 1-14) of the text.

☐ Complete Exercise One-2. The Exercise is on page 4 of the text. The solution is on page S-2 of this Study Guide.

☐ Read pages 4 (from paragraph 1-15) through 6 (through paragraph 1-23) of the text.

☐ Complete Exercise One-3. The Exercise is on page 6 of the text. The solution is on page S-2 of this Study Guide.

☐ Read pages 6 (from paragraph 1-24) through 11 (through paragraph 1-41) of the text.

Introduction To The Income Tax Act And Its Structure

☐ Read pages 11 (from paragraph 1-42) through 18 of the text.

To Complete This Chapter

☐ Review the Key Terms Used In The Chapter on page 18 of the text. Consult the Glossary for the meaning of any key terms you do not know.

☐ Review the Learning Objectives of the Chapter found on page S-3 of this Study Guide.

☐ As a review, we recommend that you view the PowerPoint Slides for Chapter One that are on your Companion CD-ROM. If you do not have access to the Microsoft PowerPoint program, the PowerPoint Viewer program can be installed from the Companion CD-ROM.

Unlike the other Chapters in this book, there are no Self Study Problems to be completed.

Solution to Chapter One Exercises

Exercise One - 1 Solution

Income tax returns would have to be filed by Max Jordan, the Jordan family trust, and Jordan Enterprises Ltd.

Exercise One - 2 Solution

Federal Tax Payable [(16%)($27,000)]	$4,320
Provincial Tax Payable [(7.5%)($27,000)]	2,025
Total Tax Payable [(16% + 7.5%)($27,000)]	$6,345

Exercise One - 3 Solution

Margie's GST and provincial sales tax paid total $25,800 [(7% + 8%)($172,000)]. Based on her Taxable Income of $895,000, this would represent an effective rate of 2.9 percent ($25,800 ÷ $895,000).

Jane's GST and provincial sales tax paid total $4,125 [(7% + 8%)($27,500)]. On her Taxable Income of $18,000, this would be an effective rate of 22.9 percent ($4,125 ÷ $18,000).

Chapter One Learning Objectives

After completing Chapter 1, you should be able to:

1. List some of the different bases that can be used by the various levels of government to assess taxes (paragraphs 1-1 through 1-4).

2. List all of the types of entities that are subject to paying federal income taxes (paragraphs 1-5 through 1-8).

3. Explain the relationship between the assessment of income taxes at the federal level and the assessment of income taxes at the provincial level (paragraphs 1-9 through 1-20).

4. List some of the ways that taxation is used to achieve economic objectives (paragraph 1-21).

5. Describe the differences between progressive, regressive, and flat tax systems, including some of the advantages and disadvantages of each system (paragraphs 1-22 through 1-31).

6. Discuss the issue of who ultimately pays the cost of various types of taxes (paragraphs 1-32 and 1-33).

7. Explain the nature of tax expenditures (paragraphs 1-34 through 1-38).

8. Evaluate issues in tax policy on the basis of the qualitative characteristics of tax systems (paragraphs 1-39 through 1-41).

9. Describe the general structure of the *Income Tax Act* (paragraphs 1-46 through 1-56).

10. List and explain the nature of other sources of income tax legislation (paragraphs 1-57 through 1-65).

11. Describe other sources of income tax information (paragraphs 1-66 through 1-70).

CHAPTER TWO

How To Work Through Chapter Two

We recommend the following approach in dealing with the material in this chapter:

Introduction To Procedures And Administration

☐ Read pages 23 through 28 (through paragraph 2-33) of the text.

☐ Complete Exercise Two-1. The Exercise is on page 28 of the text. The solution is on page S-7 of this Study Guide.

☐ Read page 28 (paragraphs 2-34 through 2-36) of the text.

☐ Complete Exercise Two-2. The Exercise is on page 29 of the text. The solution is on page S-7 of this Study Guide.

Instalment Payments For Individuals

☐ Read pages 29 (from paragraph 2-37) through 31 (through paragraph 2-48) of the text.

☐ Complete Exercises Two-3 through Two-5. The Exercises are on page 31 of the text. The solutions are on page S-7 of this Study Guide.

☐ Complete Self Study Problem Two-1. The Self Study Problem is on page 50 of the text. The solution is on page S-8 of this Study Guide.

Interest And Penalties For Individuals

☐ Read pages 31 (from paragraph 2-49) through 33 (through paragraph 2-57) of the text.

☐ Complete Exercise Two-6. The Exercise is on page 33 of the text. The solution is on page S-7 of this Study Guide.

☐ Read page 33 (paragraphs 2-58 and 2-59) of the text.

Returns And Payments For Corporations

☐ Read pages 34 (from paragraph 2-60) and 35 (through paragraph 2-63) of the text.

☐ Complete Exercises Two-7 and Two-8. The Exercises are on page 35 of the text. The solutions are on page S-7 of this Study Guide.

☐ Complete Self Study Problems Two-2 and Two-3. The Self Study Problems are on pages 50 and 51 of the text. The solutions are on pages S-8 and S-9 of this Study Guide.

Due Date For Balance Owing For Corporations

☐ Read page 35 (paragraph 2-64) of the text.

☐ Complete Exercise Two-9. The Exercise is on page 35 of the text. The solution is on page S-7 of this Study Guide.

☐ Complete Self Study Problem Two-4. The Self Study Problem is on page 51 of the text. The solution is on page S-10 of this Study Guide.

Interest And Penalties For Corporations

☐ Read pages 35 (from paragraph 2-65) and 36 (through paragraph 2-66) of the text.

Returns And Payments For Trusts

☐ Read page 36 (paragraphs 2-67 through 2-70) of the text.

General Administrative Issues

☐ Read pages 36 (from paragraph 2-71) through 40 (through paragraph 2-92) of the text.

☐ Complete Self Study Problem Two-5. This Self Study Problem is on page 51 of the text. The solution is on page S-10 of this Study Guide.

Appeals

☐ Read pages 40 (from paragraph 2-93) and 41 (through paragraph 2-104) of the text.

☐ Complete Exercise Two-10. The Exercise is on page 41 of the text. The solution is on page S-8 of this Study Guide.

☐ Read pages 41 (from paragraph 2-105) and 42 (through paragraph 2-112) of the text.

Tax Evasion, Avoidance, And Planning

☐ Read pages 42 (from paragraph 2-113) through 45 (through paragraph 2-129) of the text.

Collection And Enforcement

☐ Read pages 45 (from paragraph 2-130) through 47 (through paragraph 2-141) of the text.

Fairness Package

☐ Read pages 47 (from paragraph 2-142) and 48 (through paragraph 2-148) of the text.

To Complete This Chapter

☐ Review the Key Terms Used In The Chapter on page 49 of the text. Consult the Glossary for the meaning of any key terms you do not know.

☐ Review the Learning Objectives of the Chapter found on pages S-11 and S-12 of this Study Guide.

☐ As a review, we recommend that you view the PowerPoint Slides for Chapter Two that are on your Companion CD-ROM. If you do not have access to the Microsoft PowerPoint program, the PowerPoint Viewer program can be installed from the Companion CD-ROM.

Solution to Chapter Two Exercises

Exercise Two - 1 Solution

While Mr. Katarski's 2005 tax return does not have to be filed until June 15, 2006, his tax liability must be paid by April 30, 2006 in order to avoid the assessment of interest.

Exercise Two - 2 Solution

Ms. Sally Cheung's 2005 tax return must be filed by the later of six months after the date of her death and her normal filing date. As she has business income, her normal filing date is June 15. The later of the two dates would be August 15, 2006, six months after the date of her death. Her final return for 2006 would be due on June 15, 2007.

Exercise Two - 3 Solution

She is not required to make instalment payments as long as her actual 2005 net tax owing is less than $2,000.

Exercise Two - 4 Solution

As his net tax owing in the current year and one of the two preceding years is in excess of $2,000, he is required to make instalment payments. The minimum amount would be based on the preceding taxation year's net tax owing of $1,500, and would be $375 per quarter.

Exercise Two - 5 Solution

Use of the estimate for the current year of $32,000 would provide the lowest total instalments for the year. The required payments would be $8,000 in each quarter. While the second preceding year has the lowest net tax owing, if this were used for the first two quarters, the third and fourth quarter payments would have to bring the total amount to the net tax owing for the first preceding year, a total of $37,000. If $37,000 in instalments had been paid, the CRA would not pay interest on the overpayment of $5,000 ($37,000 - $32,000).

Exercise Two - 6 Solution

Given the size of her net tax owing, ITA 163.1 will not be applicable and there will be no penalties for late instalments. However, a penalty of 7 percent of taxes payable will be assessed for filing two months late (5 percent, plus 1 percent per month). If, in one of the three preceding taxation years she has committed a similar offence, the penalty would be 14 percent (10 percent, plus 2 percent per month).

Exercise Two - 7 Solution

The first two instalments would be based on the second preceding year and would be $4,333 each ($52,000 ÷ 12). The remaining 10 instalments would be based on the preceding year, less the $8,666 paid in the first two instalments. The amount would be $8,033 [($89,000 - $8,666) ÷ 10].

Exercise Two - 8 Solution

The minimum instalments would be based on the estimated taxes payable for the current year. The amount would be $5,583 ($67,000 ÷ 12). Note that, if the estimate for 2005 is too low, interest will be assessed on the deficiency.

Exercise Two - 9 Solution

Radco Inc.'s tax return is due six months after their year end, on July 31, 2005. Unless Radco is able to claim the small business deduction, the final payment on their taxes must be made two months after their year end, on March 31, 2005. If they are eligible for the small business deduction, they can defer the final payment for an additional month, to April 30, 2005.

Exercise Two - 10 Solution

The notice of objection must be filed by the later of:

- 90 days after the date of mailing of the reassessment (August 13, 2007); or
- one year after the due date for filing the return that is being reassessed (April 30, 2007).

The later of these two dates is August 13, 2007.

Solution to Self Study Problem Two - 1

Need For Instalments Instalments are required when an individual's "net tax owing" exceeds $2,000 in the current year and in either of the two preceding years. In somewhat simplified terms, "net tax owing" is defined as the combined federal and provincial taxes payable, less amounts withheld under ITA 153. Mr. Gore's net tax owing for 2005 is $4,000 ($17,000 - $13,000). In addition, the amount for 2003 is $2,500 ($14,000 - $11,500). As both of these amounts are in excess of $2,000, Mr. Gore would be required to pay instalments.

Amounts The amount of the instalments could be based on the net tax owing for 2004 or 2005. In addition, the first two 2005 instalments could be based on the net tax owing for 2003. However, since net tax owing for 2004 is nil, the best solution for Mr. Gore is to use that year. This means that, even though Mr. Gore meets the requirements for making instalment payments, the minimum amount of the required instalments would be nil.

If Mr. Gore did have to pay instalments, the due dates would have been March 15, June 15, September 15 and December 15.

Solution to Self Study Problem Two - 2

There are three possible payment schedules that could be used by Amalmor Inc. in this situation. The amounts involved are calculated as follows:

Current Year Base The payments could be 1/12th of the estimated taxes payable for the current year. This amount would be $7,917 ($95,000/12).

Previous Year Base The payments could be 1/12th of the taxes that were paid in the immediately preceding year. This amount would be $6,667 ($80,000/12).

Previous And Second Previous Years A final alternative would be to base the first two payments on 1/12th of the taxes paid in the second previous year, with the remaining ten payments based on the previous year total, less the amounts paid in the first two instalments. The first two amounts would be $5,208 ($62,500/12), or a total of $10,416. In the remaining 10 months of the year, the payments would be $6,958 [($80,000 - $10,416)/10].

The last alternative involves the same total as using the previous year as a base. However, this alternative is preferable to using the previous year as a base as it provides for lower payments in the first two months. Note that any remaining taxes payable must be paid within two months of the Company's year end (three months for companies that qualify for the small business deduction).

Solution to Self Study Problem Two - 3

Case One

A. The net tax owing in the current year is nil and, as a consequence, no instalments are required for 2005.

B. Given that instalments are not required, the minimum instalment would be nil.

Case Two

A. The net tax owing for the current year is $2,885. In addition, the net tax owing in 2004 was $5,216. As the net tax owing for the current year and one of the two preceding years exceeds $2,000, instalment payments are required.

B. The best alternative for instalment payments would be to use the current year estimate. This would result in required instalment payments of $721 ($2,885 ÷ 4) to be paid on March 15, June 15, September 15, and December 15. If the estimated taxes payable are below actual taxes payable for 2005, instalment interest may be charged.

The alternative that will be used by the CRA in its instalment notices will be based on the net tax owing for 2003 of $1,820 ($23,540 - $21,720) for the first two instalments. These instalment payments would be $455 per quarter, $266 lower than the $721 required using the current year as the instalment base. However, the third and fourth payments would be $2,153 {[$5,216 - (2)($455)] ÷ 2}. As this is $1,432 higher than the $721 required using the current year's net tax owing, the small savings in the first two quarters would quickly be wiped out and the taxpayer would wind up paying a much larger total ($5,216 vs. $2,885).

Case Three

A. Corporations are required to make instalment payments unless the taxes paid in the preceding taxation year or the estimated taxes payable for the current year are less than $1,000.

B. The best choice would be to use the previous year. This would result in instalment payments of $956 ($11,466 ÷ 12) to be paid at the end of each month beginning January 31.

Case Four

A. Corporations are required to make instalment payments unless the taxes paid in the preceding taxation year or the estimated taxes payable for the current year are less than $1,000.

B. The best choice is to use the current year as the base. This would result in instalment payments of $2,060 ($24,718 ÷ 12) to be paid at the end of each month beginning January 31. If 2003 is used as the base, the first two instalments would be $1,962 ($23,540 ÷ 12), somewhat less than the $2,060 amount required using the current year. However, the remaining 10 instalments would be a much higher $2,864 {[$32,560 - (2)($1,962)] ÷ 10}.

Solution to Self Study Problem Two - 4

The three taxable entities are individuals, corporations, and trusts. The required information for each is as follows:

Individuals For individuals without business income, the taxation year is the calendar year and the filing deadline is April 30 of the following year. Individuals with business income, and their spouse or common-law partner, have an extended filing deadline of June 15. Instalment payments for all individuals, if required, are to be made quarterly on March 15, June 15, September 15, and December 15.

Corporations Corporations can choose any fiscal year that does not exceed 53 weeks. The filing deadline is six months after the year end and instalments, when required, must be made on a monthly basis.

Trusts Testamentary trusts can choose any fiscal year not exceeding 12 months. Their filing deadline is 90 days after the year end and they are not required to pay instalments. Inter vivos trusts must use a calendar year. They are also required to file within 90 days of the year end and quarterly instalment payments are required under the same rules as those used by individuals. However, this requirement appears to be waived on an administrative basis.

Solution to Self Study Problem Two - 5

With respect to resolving the dispute, a first step may involve nothing more than a call to the CRA to discuss the matter. If Mr. Coffee feels that there has been a misunderstanding that can be resolved by providing a more detailed explanation of the relevant facts, this may be the only step required. However, in some cases more formal steps will be necessary and they can be outlined as follows:

Notice of Objection As the reassessment relates to the previous year's tax return, it is within the three year time limit and, therefore, a legitimate procedure for the Minister. This means that within 90 days of the mailing date on the notice of reassessment or (as Mr. Coffee is an individual) one year from the due date for the return under reassessment, a notice of objection can be filed. This objection, or Form T400A, should be sent by registered mail and should explain the facts and reasons why Mr. Coffee does not agree with the reassessment.

Tax Court of Canada If there is an adverse decision on the notice of objection, Mr. Coffee has up to 90 days after the mailing date of the response to the notice of objection to appeal to the Tax Court of Canada. Alternatively, if he does not receive a response to his notice of objection within 90 days, he will then be able to appeal to the Tax Court of Canada. As the amount involved is only $5,000, it would probably be advisable for Mr. Coffee to choose the informal procedures.

Federal Courts If Mr. Coffee has elected the informal Tax Court of Canada procedures, no appeal of an adverse decision is possible. An appeal to the Federal Court - Appeals Division would, however, be possible if an adverse decision was rendered under the general procedures. In theory, an adverse decision by the Federal Court could be appealed to the Supreme Court of Canada. However, this can only happen if the Federal Court recommends it or the Supreme Court authorizes such action. This would be extremely unlikely given the amount involved.

If you are to become involved in representing Mr. Coffee's interest in this matter, a signed Consent Form, T1013, which would give you authorization to discuss the case with the CRA would have to be on file with the CRA.

Chapter Two Learning Objectives

After completing Chapter 2, you should be able to:

1. Explain the nature of and need for source deductions (paragraphs 2-8 through 2-24).

2. Demonstrate a basic understanding of the situations in which an individual is required to file an income tax return (paragraphs 2-25 through 2-30).

3. List the dates on which income tax returns must be filed by individuals (paragraphs 2-31 through 2-36).

4. Explain the circumstances which result in an individual having to make income tax instalment payments (paragraphs 2-37 through 2-41).

5. Calculate the amount of any income tax instalment payments required for individual taxpayers (paragraphs 2-42 through 2-48).

6. Explain how the prescribed interest rate is used to calculate interest on late or insufficient income tax instalments for individuals (paragraphs 2-49 through 2-54).

7. Calculate the penalties that will be assessed for the late filing of individual income tax returns (paragraphs 2-55 through 2-57).

8. Identify the dates on which balances owing by individuals are due (paragraphs 2-58 and 2-59).

9. Identify the dates on which income tax returns must be filed by corporations (paragraph 2-60).

10. Calculate the amount of income tax instalment payments required for corporations (paragraphs 2-61 through 2-63).

11. Identify the dates on which balances owing by corporations are due (paragraph 2-64).

12. Explain how the prescribed interest rate is used to calculate interest on late or insufficient income tax instalments for corporations (paragraph 2-65).

13. Calculate the penalties that will be assessed for the late filing of corporate income tax returns (paragraph 2-66).

14. Demonstrate a basic understanding of the provisions regarding returns and payments for trusts (paragraphs 2-67 through 2-70).

15. Describe the assessment and reassessment rules for all taxpayers (paragraphs 2-84 through 2-87).

16. Explain the procedures for filing a notice of objection (paragraphs 2-94 through 2-104).

17. Describe further appeals procedures, including those made to the Tax Court of Canada, the Federal Court of Appeals, and the Supreme Court of Canada (paragraphs 2-105 through 2-112).

18. Explain the difference between tax avoidance and tax evasion, including the concepts involved in the General Anti-Avoidance Rule (paragraphs 2-113 through 2-129).

19. Demonstrate a basic understanding of the avenues of collection and enforcement available to the CRA (paragraphs 2-130 through 2-136).

20. Describe the penalties applicable to tax preparers and promoters (paragraphs 2-137 through 2-141).

21. Demonstrate a basic understanding of the provisions of the fairness package (paragraphs 2-142 through 2-148).

CHAPTER THREE

How To Work Through Chapter Three

We recommend the following approach in dealing with the material in this chapter:

Introduction To Liability For Income Tax

☐ Read pages 55 (from paragraph 3-1) through 57 (through paragraph 3-10) of the text.

☐ Complete Exercise Three-1. The Exercise is on page 57 of the text. The solution is on page S-15 of this Study Guide.

☐ Complete Self Study Problem Three-1. The Self Study Problem is on page 72 of the text. The solution is on page S-16 of this Study Guide.

Temporary Absences

☐ Read pages 57 (from paragraph 3-11) and 58 (through paragraph 3-14) of the text.

☐ Complete Exercise Three-2. The Exercise is on page 58 of the text. The solution is on page S-15 of this Study Guide.

Part Year Residence

☐ Read pages 58 (from paragraph 3-15) and 59 (through paragraph 3-16) of the text.

☐ Complete Exercise Three-3. The Exercise is on page 59 of the text. The solution is on page S-15 of this Study Guide.

Sojourners And Other Deemed Residents

☐ Read pages 59 (from paragraph 3-17) and 60 (through paragraph 3-23) of the text.

☐ Complete Exercises Three-4 and Three-5. The Exercises are on page 60 of the text. The solutions are on page S-15 of this Study Guide.

☐ Complete Self Study Problems Three-2, Three-3, and Three-4. The Self Study Problems are on pages 72 and 73 of the text. The solutions are on page S-17 of this Study Guide.

Residence Of Corporations

☐ Read page 61 (paragraphs 3-24 through 3-27) of the text.

☐ Complete Exercises Three-6 and Three-7. The Exercises are on page 61 of the text. The solutions are on page S-15 of this Study Guide.

Residence Of Trusts

☐ Read page 62 (paragraph 3-28) of the text.

Taxation Of Non-Residents

☐ Read pages 62 (from paragraph 3-29) and 63 (through paragraph 3-35) of the text.

☐ Complete Exercise Three-8. The Exercise is on page 63 of the text. The solution is on page S-15 of this Study Guide.

The Concept Of Income

☐ Read pages 63 (from paragraph 3-36) and 64 (through paragraph 3-46) of the text.

Computing Net Income For Tax Purposes

☐   Read pages 65 (from paragraph 3-47) through 67 (through paragraph 3-62) of the text.

☐   Complete Exercises Three-9 through Three-11. The Exercises are on page 68 of the text. The solutions are on pages S-15 and S-16 of this Study Guide.

☐   Complete Self Study Problems Three-5 and Three-6. The Self Study Problems are on pages 73 and 74 of the text. The solutions are on pages S-18 through S-20 of this Study Guide.

Principles Of Tax Planning

☐   Read pages 68 (from paragraph 3-63) through 70 (through paragraph 3-77) of the text.

☐   Complete Exercises Three-12 and Three-13. The Exercises are on pages 70 and 71 of the text. The solutions are on page S-16 of this Study Guide.

To Complete This Chapter

☐   Review the Key Terms Used In The Chapter on page 71 of the text. Consult the Glossary for the meaning of any key terms you do not know.

☐   Review the Learning Objectives of the Chapter found on page S-21 of this Study Guide.

☐   As a review, we recommend that you view the PowerPoint Slides for Chapter Three that are on your Companion CD-ROM. If you do not have access to the Microsoft PowerPoint program, the PowerPoint Viewer program can be installed from the Companion CD-ROM.

Solution to Chapter Three Exercises

Exercise Three - 1 Solution

In retaining his residence, he has maintained one of the primary residential ties. However, the fact that he was not able to sell the property, accompanied by the long-term lease to a third party, would probably be sufficient evidence that this is not a significant residential tie. The retention of his membership in the Ontario Institute Of Chartered Accountants would be viewed as a secondary residential tie. However, it is unlikely that this tie would be sufficient to cause Mr. Farr to be viewed as a Canadian resident.

Exercise Three - 2 Solution

Jane did, in fact, sever most of her residential ties with Canada. This would suggest that she would not be considered a Canadian resident during the 26 months that she worked in Florida. However, the fact that she returned frequently to visit her boyfriend might lead the CRA to assess her on the basis of being a Canadian resident during this period. However, it is not clear that such an assessment would be successful.

Exercise Three - 3 Solution

Mark would be taxed on his worldwide income for the part of the year that he was resident in Canada. This would be the period January 1 through June 15, the date that his wife and children fly to the U.S. June 15 would be latest of the dates that Mark leaves Canada (February 1), the date that Mark establishes U.S. residency (February 1), and the date that his wife and children depart Canada (June 15). It is unlikely that the fact that his house was not sold until a later date would influence his residence status.

Exercise Three - 4 Solution

Mr. Kirsh will be a part year resident and liable for Canadian taxes on his worldwide income, including any income on the U.S. bank accounts, for the period September 1 through December 31 of the current year.

Exercise Three - 5 Solution

While Ms. Blakey is the child of a Canadian High Commissioner, it appears that she is no longer a dependant of this individual. It would also appear that she has income in excess of the base for the basic personal tax credit for 2005 of $8,148. As a consequence, she would not be considered a deemed resident under ITA 250(1).

Exercise Three - 6 Solution

Roswell Ltd. would be considered to be a resident of Canada for tax purposes because the "mind and management" of the company appear to be located in Kemptville, Ontario.

Exercise Three - 7 Solution

As the Company was incorporated in Canada after April 26, 1965, it would be deemed to be a Canadian resident under ITA 250(4).

Exercise Three - 8 Solution

She is not correct. Under ITA 2(3) she would be subject to Canadian taxes on employment income earned in Canada.

Exercise Three - 9 Solution

His Net Income For Tax Purposes would be $38,000 ($42,000 + $24,000 - $13,000 - $15,000).

Exercise Three - 10 Solution

Her Net Income For Tax Purposes would be nil. She would have a non-capital loss carry over of $10,480 ($33,240 + $24,750 - $19,500 - $48,970).

Exercise Three - 11 Solution

Her Net Income For Tax Purposes would be $7,894 ($42,680 + Nil - $8,460 - $26,326). She would have an allowable capital loss carry over of $5,880 ($27,400 - $33,280).

Exercise Three - 12 Solution

Mr. Chung is involved in income splitting, tax deferral, and possibly tax avoidance. He is getting the deduction from taxable income now and his wife will be taxed on the income in the future. All RRSP contributions normally create a tax deferral. The contribution will be deductible and the earnings on the contribution will accumulate on a tax free basis. However, all of these amounts will be taxable when they are withdrawn from the plan. There may also be tax avoidance. This will happen if his spouse is taxed at a lower rate than is currently applicable to Mr. Chung when the funds become taxable to her.

Exercise Three - 13 Solution

As the dental plan is a benefit that can be received by Mr. Green without being taxed (private health care), tax avoidance is illustrated.

Solution to Self Study Problem Three - 1

A. Jane Smith would be deemed a Canadian resident because she is a dependent child of a Canadian ambassador [ITA 250(1)(f)].

B. Marvin Black would not be considered a resident of Canada as he does not live in Canada. However, he would be subject to Canadian taxation on the employment income earned in Canada [ITA 2(3)(a)]. Paragraph 21 of IT-221R3 makes it clear that time spent earning employment income in Canada does not count as sojourning in Canada.

C. John Leather would be considered a resident of Canada for the part of the year until September 12. As his presence in Canada during the first part of the year was not on a part time basis, he would not fall under the sojourning rules.

D. Members of the Canadian armed forces are deemed to be Canadian residents without regard to where they actually live. As Francine Donaire is exempt from French taxation due to her relationship to a deemed resident, she is a deemed resident of Canada [ITA 250(1)(g)].

E. More information would be required here. Robert would either be a part year resident of Canada or, alternatively, a non-resident earning employment income in Canada, depending on the nature of his stay in the country. If he, in fact, established residential ties in Canada, it is possible that he would be viewed as a resident during his short stay. The importance of this is that, under this interpretation of the facts, he would be subject to Canadian income tax on his worldwide income, not just his Canadian employment income.

F. The fact that Susan Allen is a Canadian citizen is irrelevant to the determination of residency. Since she appears to have no residential ties with Canada, she would not be considered a Canadian resident.

Solution to Self Study Problem Three - 2

A. As AMT Ltd. was incorporated prior to April 27, 1965, it is not automatically considered to be a resident of Canada under ITA 250(4)(a). However, based on the fact that the mind and management was in Canada subsequent to that date, it was a resident of Canada subsequent to April 26, 1965. As a consequence, it would still be deemed a Canadian resident under ITA 250(4)(c).

B. UIF Inc. was not incorporated in Canada and its mind and management are not currently within Canada. Therefore, UIF Inc. would not be considered a Canadian resident.

C. BDT Ltd. would be deemed a Canadian resident under ITA 250(4)(a). This is because it was incorporated in Canada subsequent to April 26, 1965.

D. While QRS Inc. was not incorporated in Canada, it would appear that its mind and management are located in Ontario. This would result in QRS Inc. being treated as a Canadian resident.

Solution to Self Study Problem Three - 3

A. Molly London would be considered a part year resident of Canada until October 31, the date of her departure. As her presence in Canada during the first part of the year was on a full time basis, she would not fall under the sojourning rules.

B. Daryl Bennett would not be considered a Canadian resident. He sojourned in Canada for less than 183 days. He would therefore not be considered a deemed resident by the sojourner rule. As his residential ties appear to be in the U.S., he would be a U.S. resident. His Canadian citizenship would not affect his residency status.

C. While Tweeks Inc. was not incorporated in Canada, it would appear that its mind and management are located in Quebec. This would result in Tweeks Inc. being treated as a Canadian resident.

D. Bordot Industries would be deemed a Canadian resident under ITA 250(4)(a). This is because it was incorporated in Canada subsequent to April 26, 1965.

Solution to Self Study Problem Three - 4

Mr. Aiken And Mr. Baker   Assuming that their respective moves were permanent in nature, both Mr. Aiken and Mr. Baker would be treated as part year residents. This means that they would be considered residents of Canada only for that portion of the year that they were actually in Canada. As a result, they will be liable for Canadian taxes only for a part of the current year. Deductions and credits are determined in accordance with ITA 114 and ITA 118.91.

Mr. Chase   While Mr. Chase was in Canada for the same number of days as the other individuals, the fact that he was present only on a temporary basis makes him subject to the sojourning rule. Under this rule [see ITA 250(1)(a)], he will be considered a resident for the full year if he sojourns in Canada for 183 days or more during any calendar year. As Mr. Chase was present for 192 days, he would be viewed as a Canadian resident throughout the year and would be subject to Canadian income taxes on his worldwide income. The Canada-U.S. tax agreement would have to be taken into consideration in this case.

Solution to Self Study Problem Three - 5

Case A The Case A solution would be calculated as follows:

Income Under ITA 3(a):		
Employment Income	$34,000	
Income From Property	21,000	$55,000
Income Under ITA 3(b):		
Taxable Capital Gains	$42,000	
Allowable Capital Losses	(57,000)	Nil
Balance From ITA 3(a) and (b)		$55,000
Subdivision e Deductions		(5,500)
Balance From ITA 3(c)		$49,500
Deduction Under ITA 3(d):		
Business Loss		(36,000)
Net Income For Tax Purposes (Division B Income)		$13,500

Miss Bain would have a carry over of unused allowable capital losses in the amount of $15,000 ($57,000 - $42,000).

Case B The Case B solution would be calculated as follows:

Income Under ITA 3(a):		
Employment Income	$18,500	
Income From Property	12,000	$30,500
Income Under ITA 3(b):		
Taxable Capital Gains	$ 9,000	
Allowable Capital Losses	(12,000)	Nil
Balance From ITA 3(a) and (b)		$30,500
Subdivision e Deductions		(10,500)
Balance From ITA 3(c)		$20,000
Deduction Under ITA 3(d):		
Business Loss		(28,200)
Net Income For Tax Purposes (Division B Income)		Nil

As Miss Bain's business loss exceeds the balance from ITA 3(c), her Net Income For Tax Purposes (Division B income) is nil. This means there would be a carry over of unused business losses in the amount of $8,200 ($28,200 - $20,000) and of unused allowable capital losses in the amount of $3,000 ($12,000 - $9,000).

Solution to Self Study Problem Three - 6

Case A   The Case A solution would be calculated as follows:

Income Under ITA 3(a):		
Employment Income	$45,000	
Income From Property	15,000	$60,000
Income Under ITA 3(b):		
Taxable Capital Gains	$25,000	
Allowable Capital Losses	(10,000)	15,000
Balance From ITA 3(a) And b)		$75,000
Subdivision e Deductions		(5,000)
Balance From ITA 3(c)		$70,000
Deduction Under ITA 3(d):		
Business Loss		(20,000)
Net Income For Tax Purposes (Division B Income)		$50,000

In this Case, there are no carry overs from the current year.

Case B   The Case B solution would be calculated as follows:

Income Under ITA 3(a):		
Employment Income	$17,000	
Income From Property	12,000	$29,000
Income Under ITA 3(b):		
Taxable Capital Gains	$22,000	
Allowable Capital Losses	(8,000)	14,000
Balance From ITA 3(a) And (b)		$43,000
Subdivision e Deductions		(6,000)
Balance From ITA 3(c)		$37,000
Deduction Under ITA 3(d):		
Business Loss		(42,000)
Net Income For Tax Purposes (Division B Income)		Nil

In this Case, Mr. Haynes' will have an unused business loss carry over from the current year of $5,000 ($42,000 - $37,000).

Case C The Case C solution would be calculated as follows:

Income Under ITA 3(a):		
Employment Income	$24,000	
Income From Property	47,000	$71,000
Income Under ITA 3(b):		
Taxable Capital Gains	$22,000	
Allowable Capital Losses	(73,000)	Nil
Balance From ITA 3(a) And (b)		$71,000
Subdivision e Deductions		(4,000)
Balance From ITA 3(c)		$67,000
Deduction Under ITA 3(d):		
Business Loss		(48,000)
Net Income For Tax Purposes (Division B Income)		$19,000

In this Case, Mr. Haynes will have a carry over from the current period of unused allowable capital losses in the amount of $51,000 $73,000 - $22,000).

Case D The Case D solution would be calculated as follows:

Income Under ITA 3(a):		
Employment Income	$18,000	
Income From Property	7,000	$25,000
Income Under ITA 3(b):		
Taxable Capital Gains	$13,000	
Allowable Capital Losses	(18,000)	Nil
Balance From ITA 3(a) And (b)		$25,000
Subdivision e Deductions		(12,000)
Balance From ITA 3(c)		$13,000
Deduction Under ITA 3(d):		
Business Loss		(20,000)
Net Income For Tax Purposes (Division B Income)		Nil

In this Case, Mr. Haynes has a carry over from the current year of unused business losses in the amount of $7,000 ($20,000 - $13,000) and of unused allowable capital losses in the amount of $5,000 ($18,000 - $13,000).

Chapter Three Learning Objectives

After completing Chapter 3, you should be able to:

1. Demonstrate a basic understanding of the charging provisions of the *Income Tax Act* (paragraphs 3-1 through 3-4).

2. Determine the residence of an individual based on an evaluation of primary and secondary residential ties (paragraphs 3-5 through 3-10).

3. Evaluate the residency status of an individual who is temporarily absent from Canada (paragraphs 3-11 through 3-14).

4. Explain the rules associated with the taxation of individuals in years in which they immigrate to Canada or emigrate from Canada (paragraphs 3-15 and 3-16).

5. Identify the types of individuals who will be deemed to be Canadian residents without regard to their actual physical location (paragraphs 3-17 through 3-23).

6. Determine the residence of corporations (paragraphs 3-24 through 3-27).

7. Determine the residence of trusts (paragraph 3-28).

8. List the three circumstances that will result in non-residents being subject to Canadian income taxes (paragraphs 3-29 through 3-34).

9. Describe, in general terms, the various views of income that are held by economists, accountants, and tax authorities (paragraphs 3-36 through 3-46).

10. Calculate Net Income For Tax Purposes by applying the rules found in Section 3 of the *Income Tax Act* (paragraphs 3-47 through 3-62).

11. Demonstrate a basic understanding of the concept of tax planning (paragraphs 3-63 through 3-65).

12. Explain and provide examples of tax avoidance or reduction (paragraphs 3-66 through 3-68).

13. Explain and provide examples of tax deferral (paragraphs 3-69 through 3-72).

14. Explain and provide examples of income splitting (paragraphs 3-73 through 3-77).

CHAPTER FOUR

How To Work Through Chapter Four

We recommend the following approach in dealing with the material in this chapter:

Introduction
☐ Read page 79 (paragraphs 4-1 through 4-3) of the text.

Transaction Tax Concepts
☐ Read pages 79 (from paragraph 4-4) through 83 (through paragraph 4-23) of the text.

☐ Complete Exercise Four-1. The Exercise is on page 83 of the text. The solution is on page S-25 of this Study Guide.

☐ Complete Self Study Problem Four-1. The Self Study Problem is on page 102 of the text. The solution is on page S-26 of this Study Guide.

Commercial Activity
☐ Read pages 83 (from paragraph 4-24) and 84 (through paragraph 4-31) of the text.

Accounting And The GST
☐ Read page 84 (paragraphs 4-32 through 4-36) of the text.

Concept Of Supply
☐ Read pages 85 (from paragraph 4-37) through 87 (through paragraph 4-48) of the text.

Liability For GST
☐ Read pages 87 (from paragraph 4-49) and 88 (through paragraph 4-58) of the text.

Small Suppliers Exemption
☐ Read pages 88 (from paragraph 4-59) and 89 (through paragraph 4-64) of the text.

☐ Complete Exercises Four-2 and Four-3. The Exercises are on pages 89 and 90 of the text. The solutions are on page S-25 of this Study Guide.

☐ Read page 90 (paragraph 4-65) of the text.

☐ Complete Self Study Problems Four-2 and Four-3. The Self Study Problems are on page 102 of the text. The solutions are on page S-27 of this Study Guide.

Input Tax Credits
☐ Read pages 90 (from paragraph 4-66) through 93 (through paragraph 4-79) of the text.

☐ Complete Exercises Four-4 through Four-6. The Exercises are on page 93 of the text. The solutions are on page S-25 of this Study Guide.

☐ Complete Self Study Problem Four-4. The Self Study Problem is on page 103 of the text. The solution is on page S-28 of this Study Guide.

Relief For Small Businesses
☐ Read pages 94 (from paragraph 4-80) and 95 (through paragraph 4-89) of the text.

☐ Complete Exercises Four-7 and Four-8. The Exercises are on page 95 of the text. The solutions are on pages S-25 and S-26 of this Study Guide.

Simplified Method For Input Tax Credits

☐ Read pages 95 (from paragraph 4-90) and 96 (through paragraph 4-93) of the text.

☐ Complete Exercise Four-9. The Exercise is on page 96 of the text. The solution is on page S-26 of this Study Guide.

Procedures And Administration

☐ Read pages 97 (from paragraph 4-94) through 100 (through paragraph 4-118) of the text.

Specific Applications

☐ Read page 100 (paragraphs 4-119 and 4-120) of the text.

Harmonized Sales Tax (HST)

☐ Read page 101 (paragraphs 4-121 through 4-125) of the text.

To Complete This Chapter

☐ Review the Key Terms Used In The Chapter on page 101 of the text. Consult the Glossary for the meaning of any key terms you do not know.

☐ Review the Learning Objectives of the Chapter found on page S-29 of this Study Guide.

☐ As a review, we recommend that you view the PowerPoint Slides for Chapter Four that are on your Companion CD-ROM. If you do not have access to the Microsoft PowerPoint program, the PowerPoint Viewer program can be installed from the Companion CD-ROM.

Solution to Chapter Four Exercises

Exercise Four - 1 Solution

Under a VAT system, the 5 percent would be applied to the value added, resulting in a tax of $7,600 [(5%)($416,000 - $264,000)]. Alternatively, under a GST system, $20,800 [(5%)($416,000)] would be owing on sales, but would be offset by an input tax credit of $11,650 [(5%)($233,000)] on purchases. The net tax owing in this case would be $9,150. The fact that the tax is larger under the GST system reflects the fact that the cost of goods sold exceeded the purchases of goods by $31,000.

Exercise Four - 2 Solution

As her sales exceed $30,000 in the third quarter, she will be required to begin collecting GST on the first sale in that quarter that exceeds the $30,000 threshold. This means she will have to begin collecting GST sometime between July 1 and September 30.

Exercise Four - 3 Solution

As Mr. Laughton's sales accumulate to more than $30,000 by the end of the second quarter, he will have to begin collecting GST on August 1, the first day of the second month of the third quarter.

Exercise Four - 4 Solution

The GST payable would be calculated as follows:

Sales [(7%)($1,223,000)]	$85,610
Input Tax Credits:	
Purchases [(7%)($843,000 + $126,000)]	(67,830)
Salaries, Interest, And Amortization	Nil
GST Payable For The Quarter	$17,780

Exercise Four - 5 Solution

The GST payable would be calculated as follows:

Sales [(7%)($124,000)]	$8,680
Input Tax Credits:	
Rent [(7%)($25,800)]	(1,806)
Assistant's Salary	Nil
Capital Expenditures [(7%)($36,000 + $20,000)]	(3,920)
GST Payable For The Year	$2,954

Exercise Four - 6 Solution

The pro rata input tax credit for the land and building acquisition would be $33,600 [(7%)(40%)($1,200,000)]. There would be no input tax credit for the office equipment as it is used less than 50 percent for taxable supplies.

Exercise Four - 7 Solution

The total GST included sales for the quarter would be $45,475 [(107%)($42,500)]. The purchases made do not affect the Quick Method calculation since they are non-capital. The GST payable under the Quick Method would be calculated as follows:

First $30,000 At 1.5%	$450
Remaining $15,475 At 2.5%	387
GST Payable For The Quarter	$837

Exercise Four - 8 Solution

If the Quick Method is not used, the GST payable (refund) would be calculated as follows:

Sales [(7%)($56,100)]	$3,927
Input Tax Credits:	
Current Costs [(7%)($23,400)]	(1,638)
Capital Expenditures [(7%)($42,000)]	(2,940)
GST Payable (Refund) For The Quarter	($ 651)

Alternatively, under the Quick Method, GST included sales would be $60,027 [(107%)($56,100)], and the calculation would be as follows:

First $30,000 At 1.5%	$ 450
Remaining $30,027 At 2.5%	751
Subtotal	$1,201
Input Tax Credit On Capital Expenditures	(2,940)
GST Payable (Refund) For The Quarter	($1,739)

As the Quick Method produces a larger refund, it would be the preferable method. Note that input tax credits on capital expenditures are available, even when the Quick Method is used.

Exercise Four - 9 Solution

Using the simplified method, the GST payable (refund) would be calculated as follows:

Sales [(7%)($321,000 ÷ 1.07)]	$21,000
Input Tax Credits On Purchases And Personal Capital Property	
[7/107][$192,600 + ($50,000)(107%)]	(16,100)
Input Tax Credits On Real Capital Property [(7%)($150,000)]	(10,500)
GST Payable (Refund) For The Year	($ 5,600)

Solution to Self Study Problem Four - 1

First, determine the selling price at each turnover.

Vendor	Cost	Value Added	Selling Price
Manufacturer	$100	$ 50	$150
Wholesaler	150	75	225
Distributor	225	112	337
Retailer	337	168	505

Under the normal GST system, a 7 percent tax is applied on the selling price at each stage and the business gets an input tax credit for the tax paid on purchased inputs. The net result is that all payments of GST by vendors are refunded as input tax credits, so there is no net out-of-pocket cost (other than administration) to vendors from the GST. The consumer bears the full cost of the tax by paying $35 [($505)(7%)] with no opportunity to get an input tax credit.

Turnover Tax Calculation

The turnover tax is similar to the GST, as it applies to revenue. However, the turnover tax is significantly different as there is no input tax credit for tax paid at each stage on purchased goods (inputs). The tax is passed on to the purchasers in the chain, resulting in pyramiding of the tax. Because of the multiple times goods get taxed, to raise the same amount of tax revenue, the turnover tax rate of 2.88 percent (as shown in the following calculation) is much lower than the 7 percent GST rate.

$$[(\$150)(X\%)] + [(\$225)(X\%)] + [(\$337)(X\%)] + [(\$505)(X\%)] = \$35$$
$$[(\$150 + \$225 + \$337 + \$505)(X\%)] = \$35$$
$$[(\$1,217)(X\%)] = \$35$$
$$X\% = \$35 \div \$1,217$$
$$X\% = 2.88\%$$

Solution to Self Study Problem Four - 2

Businesses are required to register for the GST if taxable revenues for the current calendar quarter or previous four quarters exceed $30,000. As revenues for the four quarters ending September 30, 2005 were under the $30,000 threshold, the business was not required to collect GST in the quarter ending December 31, or in the month of January, 2006.

However, the small supplier threshold was exceeded at the end of December, 2005, with revenues for the four quarters then ending totaling $36,500 ($29,000 - $4,000 + $11,500). Therefore, Chantelle Chance is required to start collecting GST on the first day of the second month following the quarter in which the $30,000 threshold is reached. This means that collections will begin on February 1, 2006. Application to register to collect GST, however, should be made within 30 days, or by March 2, 2006.

Solution to Self Study Problem Four - 3

The required GST remittance for Bombardeaux is based on Canadian GST included sales, and is calculated as follows:

First $30,000 at 4 Percent	$1,200
Remaining $44,900 ($74,900 - $30,000) At 5 Percent	2,245
Subtotal	$3,445
Input Tax Credit (GST Paid On Capital Expenditures) [(7%)($20,000)]	(1,400)
GST Remittance	$2,045

Solution to Self Study Problem Four - 4

The GST refund for Lassen Ltd. for the current year would be calculated as follows:

GST Collected [(7%)($5,700,000 - $1,200,000 - $2,400,000)]	$147,000
Input Tax Credits:	
Purchases [(7%)($2,600,000 - $200,000)]	(168,000)
Depreciation And Amortization	Nil
Salaries And Wages	Nil
Building [(7%)($3,000,000)(40%)]	(84,000)
Other Capital Expenditures	Nil
Other Operating Expenses [(7%)($370,000)]	(25,900)
Accrued Interest	Nil
GST Payable (Refund)	($130,900)

Notes:

- The fact that purchases on which GST was paid ($2,400,000) exceed fully taxable sales ($2,100,000) could be the result of zero-rated sales. Some zero-rated supplies involve selling items on which GST is paid. An example of this would be export sales.

- There is no need to depreciate or amortize capital expenditures for GST purposes.

- No GST is paid on salaries or wages and, therefore, no input tax credits are available.

- Input tax credits on real property are available based on a pro rata portion of their usage in providing taxable supplies.

- No input tax credits are available on capital expenditures other than real property if less than 50 percent of their usage is in providing taxable and zero-rated supplies.

- No GST is paid on accrued interest and, therefore, no input tax credits are available.

Chapter Four Learning Objectives

After completing Chapter 4, you should be able to:

1. Describe the different ways in which transaction taxes can be assessed (paragraphs 4-4 through 4-23).

2. Describe the meaning of commercial activity for GST purposes (paragraphs 4-24 through 4-31).

3. Describe the relationship between amounts determined for accounting purposes and amounts required for the filing of GST returns (paragraphs 4-32 through 4-36).

4. Outline the difference between fully taxable supplies, zero-rated supplies, and exempt supplies (paragraphs 4-37 through 4-45).

5. Identify a few examples of each type of supply (paragraphs 4-37 through 4-45).

6. Demonstrate an understanding of the concept of consideration for GST purposes (paragraphs 4-46 through 4-48).

7. Determine whether or not an entity is required to register for GST (paragraphs 4-49 through 4-65).

8. Apply the rules for calculating input tax credits on current expenditures (paragraphs 4-66 through 4-68).

9. Apply the rules for calculating input tax credits on real estate acquisitions (paragraphs 4-69 through 4-73).

10. Apply the rules for calculating input tax credits on acquisitions of capital property other than real estate (paragraphs 4-69 through 4-73).

11. Demonstrate an understanding of input tax credits as they relate to vendors of exempt and zero-rated supplies (paragraphs 4-74 through 4-79).

12. Apply the quick method of accounting for GST (paragraphs 4-81 through 4-89).

13. Apply the simplified method of accounting for input tax credits (paragraphs 4-90 through 4-93).

14. Outline the basic procedures and administration of the GST (paragraphs 4-94 through 4-118).

15. Briefly describe the listed specific applications of the GST (paragraphs 4-119 and 4-120).

16. Describe the general provisions of the harmonized sales tax (HST) that is applicable to some provinces (paragraphs 4-121 through 4-125).

CHAPTER FIVE

How To Work Through Chapter Five

We recommend the following approach in dealing with the material in this chapter:

General Rules And Bonus Arrangements

☐ Read pages 109 (from paragraph 5-1) and 110 (through paragraph 5-10) of the text.

☐ Complete Exercise Five-1. The Exercise is on page 110 of the text. The solution is on page S-34 of this Study Guide.

☐ Read page 111 (paragraphs 5-11 and 5-12) of the text.

Employee Versus Self-Employed

☐ Read pages 111 (from paragraph 5-13) through 114 (through paragraph 5-27) of the text.

Basic Inclusions

☐ Read pages 114 (from paragraph 5-28) through 116 (through paragraph 5-32) of the text.

☐ Complete Exercise Five-2. The Exercise is on page 117 of the text. The solution is on page S-34 of this Study Guide.

☐ Read page 117 (paragraph 5-33) of the text.

Tax Planning Considerations

☐ Read pages 117 (from paragraph 5-34) and 118 (through paragraph 5-38) of the text.

☐ Complete Exercise Five-3. The Exercise is on page 118 of the text. The solution is on page S-34 of this Study Guide.

☐ Read page 118 (paragraph 5-39) of the text.

Inclusions - Detailed Considerations

☐ Read page 119 (paragraphs 5-40 and 5-41) of the text.

☐ Complete Exercise Five-4. The Exercise is on page 119 of the text. The solution is on page S-34 of this Study Guide.

☐ Read page 119 (paragraphs 5-42 through 5-44) of the text.

Employer Supplied Automobiles

☐ Read pages 120 (from paragraph 5-45) through 124 (through paragraph 5-74) of the text.

☐ Complete Exercise Five-5. The Exercise is on page 124 of the text. The solution is on page S-34 of this Study Guide.

☐ Read pages 124 (from paragraph 5-75) and 125 (through paragraph 5-80) of the text.

☐ Complete Exercise Five-6. The Exercise is on page 125 of the text. The solution is on page S-34 of this Study Guide.

☐ Read pages 125 and 126 (paragraph 5-81) of the text.

☐ Complete Self Study Problems Five-1 and Five-2. The Self Study Problems are on pages 151 and 152 of the text. The solutions are on pages S-37 through S-39 of this Study Guide.

Allowances

☐ Read pages 126 (from paragraph 5-82) through 128 (through paragraph 5-88) of the text.

☐ Complete Exercises Five-7 and Five-8. The Exercises are on page 128 of the text. The solutions are on page S-35 of this Study Guide.

☐ Read pages 128 (from paragraph 5-89) and 129 (through paragraph 5-94) of the text.

☐ Complete Exercise Five-9. The Exercise is on page 129 of the text. The solution is on page S-35 of this Study Guide.

Employee Insurance Benefits

☐ Read pages 129 (from paragraph 5-95) and 130 (through paragraph 5-100) of the text.

☐ Complete Exercise Five-10. The Exercise is on page 130 of the text. The solution is on page S-35 of this Study Guide.

☐ Read pages 130 (from paragraph 5-101) and 131 (through paragraph 5-103) of the text.

Loans To Employees

☐ Read pages 131 (from paragraph 5-104) and 132 (through paragraph 5-105) of the text.

☐ Complete Exercise Five-11. The Exercise is on page 132 of the text. The solution is on page S-35 of this Study Guide.

☐ Read pages 132 (from paragraph 5-106) through 134 (through paragraph 5-115) of the text.

☐ Complete Exercise Five-12. The Exercise is on page 134 of the text. The solution is on pages S-35 and S-36 of this Study Guide.

☐ Complete Self Study Problem Five-3. The Self Study Problem is on page 152 of the text. The solution is on page S-40 of this Study Guide.

Stock Options - General Rules

☐ Read pages 134 (from paragraph 5-116) through 137 (through paragraph 5-130) of the text.

Stock Options - Public Companies

☐ Read pages 137 and 138 (paragraph 5-131) of the text.

☐ Complete Exercise Five-13. The Exercise is on page 138 of the text. The solution is on page S-36 of this Study Guide.

Stock Options - Canadian Controlled Private Corporations (CCPCs)

☐ Read pages 138 (from paragraph 5-132) and 139 (through paragraph 5-135) of the text.

☐ Complete Exercise Five-14. The Exercise is on page 139 of the text. The solution is on page S-36 of this Study Guide.

☐ Read pages 139 and 140 (paragraph 5-136) of the text.

Stock Options - Deferral On Publicly Traded Shares

☐ Read pages 140 (from paragraph 5-137) and 141 (through paragraph 5-142) of the text.

☐ Complete Exercises Five-15 and Five-16. The Exercises are on page 141 of the text. The solutions are on page S-36 of this Study Guide.

☐ Read pages 141 and 142 (paragraph 5-143) of the text.

☐ Complete Exercise Five-17. The Exercise is on page 142 of the text. The solution is on page S-37 of this Study Guide.

☐   Complete Self Study Problem Five-4. The Self Study Problem is on pages 152 and 153 of the text. The solution is on page S-41 of this Study Guide.

Other Inclusions
☐   Read pages 142 (from paragraph 5-144) and 143 (through paragraph 5-152) of the text.

Specific Deductions
☐   Read pages 143 (from paragraph 5-153) through 147 (through paragraph 5-168) of the text.

☐   Complete Exercise Five-18. The Exercise is on page 147 of the text. The solution is on page S-37 of this Study Guide.

☐   Read pages 147 (from paragraph 5-169) and 148 (through paragraph 5-177) of the text.

☐   Complete Self Study Problems Five-5 through Five-7. The Self Study Problems are on pages 153 through 156 of the text. The solutions are on pages S-42 through S-44 of this Study Guide.

Employee And Partner GST Rebate
☐   Read pages 148 (from paragraph 5-178) and 149 (through paragraph 5-184) of the text.

To Complete This Chapter
☐   Review the Key Terms Used In The Chapter on page 150 of the text. Consult the Glossary for the meaning of any key terms you do not know.

☐   Review the Learning Objectives of the Chapter found on page S-45 of this Study Guide.

☐   As a review, we recommend that you view the PowerPoint Slides for Chapter Five that are on your Companion CD-ROM. If you do not have access to the Microsoft PowerPoint program, the PowerPoint Viewer program can be installed from the Companion CD-ROM.

Solution to Chapter Five Exercises

Exercise Five - 1 Solution

The bonus will be taxed in Mr. Neelson's hands in the year of receipt. This means that it will be included in his 2006 tax return. With respect to Neelson Inc., the bonus is not payable until more that 180 days after the year end. As a consequence, the Company will not be able to deduct the bonus in the year ending September 30, 2005. It will be deducted in the year ending September 30, 2006.

Exercise Five - 2 Solution

The tax consequences of the various items would be as follows:

- IT-470R indicates that such benefits would not be taxable to John.
- It could be argued that this is "general employment-related training as described in IT-470R". If the argument is successful, the payment would not be taxable to John. If unsuccessful, the $2,000 would be a taxable benefit.
- While IT-470R indicates that uniforms or special clothing is not a taxable benefit, it is unlikely that business clothing would fall into this category. The $8,500 would probably be included in John's income as a taxable benefit.
- The $450 gift could be received tax free.
- ITA 6(1)(a) indicates that such benefits are not taxable.

Exercise Five - 3 Solution

From Jill's point of view, the best alternative is probably the dental plan. Its value is significantly enhanced by the fact that it can be received without tax consequences. The annual vacation trip is clearly a taxable benefit. Since the birthday gift has a value in excess of $500, Jill would have a taxable benefit for the fair market value of the season's tickets.

Exercise Five - 4 Solution

Ms. Correli's taxable benefit would be $4,815, the $4,500 cost of the trip, plus the additional $315 in GST.

Exercise Five - 5 Solution

The basic standby charge would be $6,900 [(2%)($28,750)(12)]. As her employment related driving is more than 50 percent of the total (16,000 out of 28,000), she can use the reduced standby charge calculation. Since her personal kilometers driven total 12,000 (28,000 - 16,000), the reduced amount would be $4,139 [(12,000 ÷ 20,004)($6,900)].

The operating cost benefit could be calculated as $2,400 [($0.20)(12,000)]. However, as her employment related use is greater than 50 percent, Mrs. Lee can use the alternative operating cost benefit calculation based on one-half the standby charge. This would produce a value of $2,070 [(1/2)($4,139)] and a minimum total benefit of $6,209 ($4,139 + $2,070).

Exercise Five - 6 Solution

The basic standby charge would be $4,428 [(2/3)($7,245)(11/12)]. The 11 is 325/30 rounded to the nearest whole number and represents the months available for use. As his employment related driving exceeds 50 percent of the total, this standby charge can be reduced. The reduced amount would be $724 [($4,428)(3,000/18,337)]. The 18,337 is based on multiplying 1,667 kilometers per month by the 11 months the car is available.

Mr. Forthwith's operating cost benefit could be calculated as $600 [($0.20)(3,000)], resulting in a total taxable benefit of $1,324 ($724 + $600). However, as his employment related use is greater than 50 percent, Mr. Forthwith can use the alternative operating cost benefit calculation based on one-half the standby charge. This gives an operating cost benefit of $362 [(1/2)($724)] and a minimum total benefit of $1,086 ($724 + $362).

Exercise Five - 7 Solution

She will have to include the $3,600 allowance that was received from her employer. She can deduct the employment related portion of her actual automobile costs against this amount. This would be $1,936 [($7,150)(6,500/24,000)]. The net inclusion would be $1,664 ($3,600 - $1,936).

Exercise Five - 8 Solution

Mr. Lorenz has two choices. As the milage allowance paid by the employer was based on the number of employment related kilometers driven, the $3,500 will not be included on his T4 Information Return and, as a consequence, it does not have to be included in his employment income. However, under this approach he will not be able to deduct his actual costs of owning and operating the automobile.

The alternative and, in this case, preferable solution would be to include the $3,500 allowance in his employment income and deduct his actual costs for employment related kilometers. This deduction would be $11,900 [($5,400 + $15,000)(35,000/60,000)]. The result would be a net reduction in his employment income of $8,400 ($11,900 - $3,500).

Exercise Five - 9 Solution

The hotel allowance would appear to be reasonable and would not be included in Ms. Ohm's T4. Given this, it will not be included in her net employment income. Even though her actual costs of $18,300 are in excess of the $16,400 allowance, it would be difficult for Ms. Ohm to argue that the $200 figure is not reasonable. Given this, she does not have the choice of including the $16,400 in income and deducting the actual amount of $18,300.

As the milage charge is based on kilometers it will not be included in her T4. In addition, since the amount appears to be reasonable in terms of actual costs, she does not have the choice of including it in income and deducting the actual costs. In fact, it would not be to Ms. Ohm's advantage to do so as her actual costs would be $2,880 [($7,200)(9,400/23,500)], which is less than the $3,666 reimbursement she received.

Exercise Five - 10 Solution

As his employer contributes to the plan, the $5,250 in benefits received during the year will be included in his employment income. This can be offset by the $600 in non-deductible contributions that he made during 2004 and 2005, leaving a net inclusion of $4,650.

Exercise Five - 11 Solution

The ITA 80.4(1) benefit would be $3,750 [($100,000)(4%)(1/4) + ($100,000)(5%)(1/4) + ($100,000)(3%)(2/4)]. As this is a home purchase loan, the annual benefit cannot exceed the benefit that would result from applying the 4 percent rate that was in effect when the loan was made. This benefit would be $4,000 [($100,000)(4%)]. Note that the 4 percent rate is not compared to the prescribed rate on a quarter-by-quarter basis, but on an annual basis. The lower figure of $3,750 would then be reduced by the $2,000 in interest paid [($100,000)(2%)], resulting in a net benefit of $1,750.

Exercise Five - 12 Solution

In the absence of the interest free loan, the employee would borrow $125,000 at 6 percent, requiring an annual interest payment of $7,500. The after tax cash outflow associated with the employer providing sufficient additional salary to carry this loan would be calculated as follows:

Required Salary [$7,500 ÷ (1.00 - .42)]	$12,931
Reduction In Corporate Taxes At 35 Percent	(4,526)
After Tax Cash Flow - Additional Salary	$ 8,405

Alternatively, if the loan is provided, the employee will have a taxable benefit of $2,500 [(2%)($125,000)], resulting in taxes payable of $1,050 [(42%)($2,500)]. To make this situation comparable to the straight salary alternative, the employer will have to provide the employee with both the loan amount and sufficient additional salary to pay the taxes on the imputed interest benefit. The amount of this additional salary would be $1,810 [$1,050 ÷ (1.00 - .42)]. The employer's after tax cash flow associated with providing the additional salary and the loan amount would be calculated as follows:

Required Salary [$1,050 ÷ (1.00 - .42)]	$1,810
Reduction In Corporate Taxes At 35 Percent	(634)
After Tax Cost Of Salary	$1,176
Employer's Lost Earnings [(7%)(1.00 - .35)($125,000)]	5,688
After Tax Cash Flow - Loan	$6,864

Given these results, providing the loan appears to be the better alternative.

Exercise Five - 13 Solution

At time of exercise, he will have an employment income benefit of $21,250 [($31.50 - $23.00)(2,500 Shares)]. As he sells the shares prior to the end of the year, deferral of the employment income is not possible. As the option price at issue exceeded the fair market value at issue, Mr. Guise will be able to deduct $10,625 [(1/2)($21,250)] in the determination of Taxable Income. The net effect on Taxable Income will be $10,625 ($21,250 - $10,625). In addition, there will be an allowable capital loss of $4,375 [($31.50 - $28.00)(2,500 Shares)(1/2)]. Mr. Guise will only be able to deduct this loss in 2005 to the extent that he has taxable capital gains on other dispositions. It cannot be deducted against the employment income inclusion.

Exercise Five - 14 Solution

At the time the shares are sold, there will be an employment income benefit of $58,500 [($75.00 - $42.50)(1,800 Shares)]. As she did not hold the shares for the required two years, there is no deduction under ITA 110(1)(d.1). Further, as the option price was below fair market value at the time the options were issued, there is no deduction under ITA 110(1)(d). The addition to Taxable Income is therefore $58,500. When she sells the shares, she will have an allowable capital loss of $23,400 [($49.00 - $75.00)(1,800 Shares)(1/2)]. Ms. Van will only be able to deduct this loss in 2005 to the extent that she has taxable capital gains on other dispositions. It cannot be deducted against the employment income inclusion.

Exercise Five - 15 Solution

The specified value of the shares involved with these options is $20,000 [(1,000)($20)]. As this is well below the $100,000 annual limit specified under ITA 7(8), she can defer all of the $22,000 [(1,000)($45 - $23)] employment benefit that is measured at the time of exercise. This means that the 2005 Taxable Income inclusion will be nil. As the shares are sold in 2006, the $22,000 employment income benefit will be recognized in that year. There will also be a 2006 deduction of $11,000 [(1/2)($22,000)] under ITA 110(1)(d). The 2006 net effect on Taxable Income is $11,000 ($22,000 - $11,000). She will also have a 2006 allowable capital loss of $1,500 [(1,000)($42 - $45)(1/2)]. Ms. Masterson will only be able to deduct this loss in 2006 to the extent that she has taxable capital gains on other dispositions. It cannot be deducted against the employment income inclusion.

Exercise Five - 16 Solution

The Taxable Income amounts for 2005 and 2006 would be identical to those in Exercise Five-15. The only difference is that no election is required to defer the 2005 employment income inclusion.

Exercise Five - 17 Solution

The specified value of the shares that vested in 2005 is $120,000 [(10,000)($12)]. This means that the ITA 7(8) election can only be made on 8,333 of the shares [(10,000 Shares)($100,000 ÷ $120,000)]. This results in a deferral of $166,660 [(8,333)($32 - $12)] and an income inclusion of $33,340 [(1,667)($32 - $12)]. The specified value of the shares that vested in 2006 is $180,000 [(15,000)($12)]. As was the case in 2005, the ITA 7(8) election can only be made on 8,333 of the shares [(15,000 Shares)($100,000 ÷ $180,000)], resulting in a deferral of $166,660 [(8,333)($32 - $12)] and an income inclusion of $133,340 [(6,667)($32 - $12)]. This information will be reflected in Mr. Traverse's 2007 T4 as a special item of deferred income of $333,320 ($166,660 + $166,660) and an employment income inclusion of $166,680 ($33,340 + $133,340). These two amounts total $500,000 ($333,320 + $166,680), the employment income created by exercising the options [(25,000)($32 - $12)].

Exercise Five - 18 Solution

The potential deduction is $27,100 [$8,000 + (1/2)($12,000) + $13,100]. However, this total exceeds his commission income and cannot be deducted under ITA 8(1)(f). If he deducts under ITA 8(1)(h), there is no limit on the total. However, he cannot deduct the advertising or the entertainment. As the travel costs that are deductible under ITA 8(1)(h) exceed the $12,200 limited deduction under ITA 8(1)(f), his maximum deduction is the $13,100 in travel costs that can be deducted under ITA 8(1)(h).

Solution to Self Study Problem Five - 1

Acura TL   The taxable benefit on this vehicle would be calculated as follows:

Standby Charge [(2%)(5)($39,000 + $2,730 + $2,730)(3,400 ÷ 8,335)]	$1,814
Operating Cost Benefit - Lesser Of:	
• [(3,400)($0.20) = $680]	
• [(1/2)($1,814) = $907]	680
Total Benefit On Acura TL	$2,494

With employment related usage at more than 50 percent of the total, Ms. Vines is eligible for the reduced standby charge calculation. Ms. Vines could have calculated the operating cost benefit as one-half of the standby charge, or $907, as employment related usage was more than 50 percent of total usage. The use of the alternative $0.20 per kilometer results in a lower operating cost benefit.

Ford Crown Victoria   The taxable benefit on this vehicle is calculated as follows:

Standby Charge [(2/3)(6)($625 + $37 + $37 - $100)]	$2,396
Operating Cost Benefit - Lesser Of:	
• [(14,600)($0.20) = $2,920]	
• [(1/2)($2,396) = $1,198]	1,198
Total Benefit On Ford Crown Victoria	$3,594

As the car was driven more than 50 percent for employment related purposes, a reduction in the standby charge is available. However, her total personal use kilometers exceed 10,002 [(6)(1,667)] and as a result the reduction is nil [($2,396)(10,002/10,002)]. The $100 insurance included in the monthly lease payment is removed from the standby charge calculation as it is an operating cost.

Solution to Self Study Problem Five - 2

As the car was driven more than 50 percent for employment related purposes, Ms. Vines can calculate the operating cost benefit as either one-half of the standby charge or $0.20 per kilometer of personal use. As the $0.20 per kilometer calculation results in a benefit of $2,920, the one-half standby charge approach is preferable. To use this approach, Ms. Vines must notify her employer before the end of the year.

Total Benefit   The total taxable benefit would be calculated as follows:

Total Benefit - Acura	$2,494
Total Benefit - Ford	3,594
Reimbursement To Company [($0.10)(3,400 Km + 14,600 Km)]	(1,800)
Total Taxable Benefit	$4,288

Notes:

- The taxable benefit calculation is not influenced by restrictions on the amount that the Company can deduct with respect to the Acura.

- Calculation of the operating cost benefits is not influenced by the employer's actual operating costs.

Solution to Self Study Problem Five - 2

Mr. Sam Stern   The taxable benefit for the president of the Company would be calculated as follows:

Standby Charge [(2%)(8)($78,000)]	$12,480
Operating Cost Benefit [(32,000)($0.20)]	6,400
Taxable Benefit	$18,880

As Mr. Stern did not drive the car more than 50 percent for employment related purposes, no reduction in the standby charge is available. Since his employment related use was not more than than 50 percent, he cannot use the alternative calculation of the operating cost benefit.

Ms. Sarah Blue   The taxable benefit for the marketing vice president would be calculated as follows:

Standby Charge [(2/3)(12)($900)(5,000/20,004)]	$1,800
Operating Cost Benefit - Lesser Of:	
• [(5,000)($0.20) = $1,000]	
• [(1/2)($1,800) = $900]	900
Taxable Benefit	$2,700

As employment related driving was more than 50 percent, Ms. Blue can reduce the standby charge on the basis of actual personal usage.

Mr. John Stack   The taxable benefit for the finance vice president would be calculated as follows:

Standby Charge [(2%)(12)($48,000)(10,000/20,004]	$5,759
Operating Cost Benefit - Lesser Of:	
• [(10,000)($0.20) = $2,000]	
• [(1/2)($5,759) = $2,880]	2,000
Payment For Use Of Company Car	(7,000)
Taxable Benefit	$ 759

Mr. Stack's employment related driving was more than 50 percent of the total and, as a consequence, he can reduce his standby charge on the basis of actual personal milage.

Mr. Alex Decker   The taxable benefit for the industrial relations vice president would be calculated as follows:

Standby Charge [(2/3)(10)($500)(8,500/16,670)]	$1,700
Operating Cost Benefit - Lesser Of:	
• [(8,500)($0.20) = $1,700]	
• [(1/2)($1,700) = $850]	850
Taxable Benefit	$2,550

As Mr. Decker's employment related driving is more than 50 percent of the total, he can reduce his standby charge on the basis of actual personal milage. While the $10,000 deposit will affect the deductibility of the lease payments by the employer, it does not influence the calculation of the taxable benefit to Mr. Decker.

Tax Planning   With respect to the tax planning of management compensation, two points can be made. First, the question of providing company cars as a method of compensation should be examined on a case-by-case basis. In situations where a car is owned by the Company and provided to an executive for a fairly long period of time, the taxable benefit assessed may exceed the value of the benefit. For example, over five years, the taxable benefit without regard for operating costs on Mr. Stern's Mercedes could total $93,600 [(2%)(60)($78,000)]. This is more than $15,000 in excess of the cost of the car. With the limitations on the deductibility of CCA and leasing costs on cars, the after tax cost to the Company of owning and leasing luxury cars can be very high. While a complete analysis of this issue will depend on a number of variables, it is possible that some of these executives would be better off receiving additional amounts of salary and billing the Company for employment related mileage driven in their own cars.

The second point to be made here is that, except in situations where the car is kept for very short periods of time, the employee will be allocated a smaller taxable benefit if the Company were to lease the car rather than buy it. In general, monthly lease payments on a three year lease will tend to be between 2 percent and 2.5 percent of the capital cost of the car. As the leasing standby charge is based on two-thirds of the monthly lease payment, it is clear that the standby charge under this type of arrangement will be less than the 2 percent per month that is assessed when the Company owns the car. However, for shorter lease terms, the lease payment will be a greater percentage of the capital cost and this relationship may reverse.

Other tax planning techniques would involve any procedure that would reduce the capital cost of purchased cars or the lease payments on leased cars. Such procedures would include high residual values on leasing arrangements and low trade in values assigned to old cars when new ones are purchased. In addition, it might be possible to reduce a taxable benefit, such as the one being allocated to Mr. Stern, by selling his car to a leasing company with an immediate leaseback arrangement. Although large refundable deposits on leasing arrangements would reduce the lease payment and therefore the standby charge, there would be a tax cost to the employer (see Chapter 8).

Solution to Self Study Problem Five - 3

Approach The appropriate comparison in evaluating the interest free loan arrangement would be to determine the cost to the Company of providing the loan and then compare this amount with the cost of providing an equivalent benefit in the form of straight salary.

Cost Of Providing Interest Payments On Mortgage As the problem indicates, Mr. Malone can borrow on a regular mortgage at a rate of interest of 5 percent. This means that the annual interest payments on $200,000 would amount to $10,000. However, Mr. Malone is in the 45 percent tax bracket and, as a consequence, $18,182 ($10,000 ÷ .55) of before tax salary would be required to provide the necessary $10,000 in after tax funds. The annual cost to the Company of this alternative would be as follows:

Gross Salary Increase	$18,182
Reduction In Corporate Taxes (At 40 Percent)	(7,273)
Net Cost To Company	$10,909

Cost Of Providing Interest Free Loan Mr. Malone would be assessed a taxable benefit on the loan in the amount of imputed interest at the Regulation 4301 rate. The benefit would amount to $6,000 [(3%)($200,000)] for one year. In order to make the two alternatives comparable, it is necessary to recognize that Mr. Malone would pay an additional $2,700 [(45%)($6,000)] in taxes on this benefit and, as a consequence, the Company would have to pay him an additional $4,909 ($2,700 ÷ .55) in salary to provide for this outflow of funds. Given this, the annual cost to the Company of the loan alternative can be calculated as follows:

Gross Salary Increase	$ 4,909
Reduction In Corporate Taxes (At 40 Percent)	(1,964)
Lost Earnings On Funds Loaned (At 18 Percent)	36,000
Corporate Taxes On Imputed Earnings (At 40 Percent)	(14,400)
Net Cost To Company	$24,545

Conclusion On the basis of the preceding analysis, it can be concluded that the Company should provide an additional $18,182 in salary rather than providing Mr. Malone with an interest free loan of $200,000. This alternative results in a net annual cost to the Company which is $13,636 lower.

Alternative Calculation An alternative solution to the question involves calculating the cost to the Company using the value of the interest free loan to Mr. Malone. The annual cost of the mortgage to Mr. Malone is $10,000 [(5%)($200,000)] and the cost of the taxable benefit on the interest free loan is $2,700 [(45%)(3%)(200,000)]. This means the value of the interest free loan to Mr. Malone is $7,300 ($10,000 - $2,700). He would require $13,273 [$7,300 ÷ (1 - .45)] in before tax salary to make up this difference. To the Company, the after tax cost of the additional $13,273 is $7,964 [($13,273)(1 - .4)]. The cost of the interest free loan to the Company, after taxes, is $21,600 [(18%)($200,000)(1 - .4)]. The difference in cost is $13,636 ($21,600 - $7,964) in favour of the increased salary. This is the same result that we arrived at under the first calculation.

Solution to Self Study Problem Five - 4

Case A   In 2005, the year in which the options are issued, there would be no tax consequences for Ms. Wu. The tax consequences in 2006 would be as follows:

Fair Market Value [(12,000)($31)]	$372,000
Option Price [(12,000)($22)]	(264,000)
Employment Income Inclusion	$108,000
Deduction Under ITA 110(1)(d) (One-Half)	(54,000)
Increase In Taxable Income	$ 54,000

As Ms. Wu is a specified shareholder, none of this amount can be deferred until the shares are sold.

When the shares are sold in 2007, the tax consequences would be as follows:

Proceeds Of Disposition [(12,000)($28)]	$336,000
Adjusted Cost Base [(12,000)($31)]	(372,000)
Capital Loss	($ 36,000)
Inclusion Rate	1/2
Allowable Capital Loss	($ 18,000)

Case B   In this Case, we have a public company. However, the results are different than in Case A as we are assuming that Ms. Wu is not a specified shareholder. This means that a portion of the gain at the time of exercise can be deferred until the shares are sold. This is limited to the first $100,000 of fair market value of shares at the time the options are granted. As the fair market value of the shares at the time the options are granted is $20 per share, this applies to the gain on 5,000 of the 12,000 shares acquired by Ms. Wu.

As in the previous Case, there would be no tax consequence associated with the issuance of the options in 2005. The 2006 tax consequences would be calculated as follows:

Fair Market Value [(12,000)($31)]	$372,000
Option Price [(12,000)($22)]	(264,000)
Employment Income	$108,000
Available Deferral [(5,000/12,000)($108,000)]	(45,000)
Employment Income Inclusion	$ 63,000
Deduction Under ITA 110(1)(d) (One-Half)	(31,500)
Increase In Taxable Income	$ 31,500

When the shares are sold in 2007, there would be an increase in Taxable Income of $22,500. This is made up of the deferred employment income inclusion of $45,000, less the one-half deduction under ITA 110(1)(d). In addition, there would be an $18,000 allowable capital loss, calculated as in Case A.

Case C   In this Case, because Imports Ltd. is a Canadian controlled private corporation, there are no consequences either in 2005, when the options are issued, or in 2006, when they are exercised. When the shares are sold in 2007, there would be an increase in Taxable Income of $54,000 and an allowable capital loss of $18,000. The calculation of these amounts is as in Case A.

Note that in all three Cases, the increase in Taxable Income due to the stock options for 2006 and 2007 totals $54,000.

Solution to Self Study Problem Five - 5

Salary From Maritime Trust [(6/12)($65,000)]		$32,500
Salary From Bolten [(6/12)($50,000)]		25,000
Total Salaries		$57,500
Maritime Trust Stock Options: (Note 1)		
Market Price Of Shares [(5,000)($16)]	$80,000	
Option Price [(5,000)($15)]	(75,000)	5,000
Bolton Financial Services Stock Options (Note 2)		Nil
Taxable Benefit - Car:		
Standby Charge [(2%)(4)($25,000)(6,668/6,668)]	$2,000	
Operating Cost Benefit - Lesser Of:		
• [(10,000)($0.20) = $2,000]		
• [(1/2)($2,000) = $1,000]	1,000	3,000
Taxable Benefit - Loan [(3%)($200,000)(6/12)]		3,000
Net Employment Income		$68,500

Notes:

1. Although there is an election to defer the employment income inclusion on the exercise of publicly traded company stock until the acquired shares are sold, Mr. Jurgens did not make this election.

2. As Bolten Financial Services is a Canadian controlled private corporation, the exercise of the options to purchase its common stock does not result in a taxable benefit at the time of exercise. When the shares are sold, he will have to include the difference between the option price and the fair market value at the time of exercise in employment income.

3. As Mr. Jurgens' employment related milage is more than 50 percent of the total milage, he can make use of the reduced standby charge formula. In this case, however, his personal usage exceeded the 6,668 [(4)(1,667)] kilometer maximum usage allowed by the reduction, so the reduction is nil. His employment related milage is more than 50 percent of the total and, as a consequence, he can elect to calculate the operating cost benefit as 50 percent of the standby charge. Since this amount of $1,000 [(50%)($2,000)] is less than the $2,000 [(10,000)($0.20)] determined through the usual calculation, the $1,000 would be the operating cost benefit.

4. The imputed interest on the interest free loan must be included in employment income under the requirements of ITA 6(9), a benefit which is defined in ITA 80.4(1). Note, however, there is a deduction under ITA 110(1)(j) for the amount of this benefit which relates to an interest free home relocation loan of $25,000. However, this is a deduction in the calculation of Taxable Income and will not affect the amount of net employment income.

5. The interest and dividend income is not included in the calculation of net employment income.

Solution to Self Study Problem Five - 6

Mr. Barth's net employment income for the year would be calculated as follows:

Gross Salary	$ 82,500
Bonus (Note One)	20,000
Registered Pension Plan Contributions	(3,200)
Professional Dues	(1,800)
Stock Option Benefit (Note Two)	3,000
Automobile Benefit (Note Three)	3,100
Counseling Benefit (Note Four)	1,500
Imputed Interest Benefit (Note Five)	750
Net Employment Income	$105,850

Note One   As the bonus is not payable until more than three years after the end of the employer's taxation year, it is a salary deferral arrangement and must be included in income under ITA 6(11).

Note Two   As Mr. Barth's employer is a public company, the employment income inclusion for stock options would normally occur when the options were exercised in 2004. This amount would have been $3,000 [($18 - $15)(1,000)]. However, the specified value of the securities is $12,000 [(1,000)($12)], well below the $100,000 limit on amounts that can be deferred. As a consequence, the $3,000 income inclusion can be deferred until the shares are sold. As the shares are sold in 2005, the $3,000 must be taken into net employment income in that year. We would also note that Mr. Barth is eligible for the ITA 110(1)(d) deduction of one-half the stock option benefit. However, it is a deduction in calculating Taxable Income and will not affect the amount of net employment income.

Note Three   Since Mr. Barth's employment related usage is not more than 50 percent, there is no reduction of the full standby charge. The automobile benefit is calculated as follows:

Standby Charge [(2%)(10)($27,500)]	$5,500
Operating Cost Benefit [(6,000)($0.20)]	1,200
Total Before Payments	$6,700
Payments Withheld	(3,600)
Taxable Benefit	$3,100

Note Four   IT-470R indicates that counseling services, with the exception of those items specified under ITA 6(1), are considered taxable benefits. The items specified under ITA 6(1) are counseling with respect to mental or physical health or with respect to re-employment or retirement. As a consequence, the counseling on personal finances is a taxable benefit.

Note Five   The imputed interest benefit is calculated as follows:

Basic Benefit [($150,000)(3%)(3/12)]	$1,125
Interest Paid	(375)
Taxable Benefit	$ 750

Note Six   Other items and the reasons for their exclusion would be as follows:

- Any income tax withheld is not deductible.
- CPP contributions, EI premiums, and United Way donations create a credit against taxes payable, but are not deductible in the determination of employment income.
- The payments for personal use of the company car are used in the calculation of the taxable benefit associated with this automobile.

Solution to Self Study Problem Five - 7

Ms. Firth's net employment income for the year would be calculated as follows:

Gross Salary	$ 72,000
Commission Income	14,000
Registered Pension Plan Contributions (Note One)	(3,200)
Disability Insurance Receipts, Less Employee's Premium ($2,000 - $250)	1,750
Automobile Benefit (Note Two)	9,671
Automobile Expenses (Note Two)	(5,728)
Term Life Insurance Benefit [($1,350)(2/3)]	900
Low Interest Loan Benefit [($400,000)(3%) - $3,000]	9,000
Christmas Gift (Note Three)	Nil
Stock Option Benefit [(1,000)($7 - $5)]	2,000
Entertainment Expenses [(50%)($6,500)]	(3,250)
Travel Meals [(50%)($1,300)]	(650)
Lodging	(3,500)
Travel Allowance	3,600
Net Employment Income	**$96,593**

Note One Contributions made to a registered pension plan under the terms of the plan are deductible. The matching contributions made by the employer are not a taxable benefit.

Note Two The personal benefit on the company car, taking into consideration the month she was in the hospital and unable to make use of the car, would be calculated as follows:

Reduced Standby Charge [(2%)(11)($58,000)(7,000/18,337)]	$ 4,871
Car Allowance	7,200
Operating Costs Benefit	-0-
Total Benefit	$12,071
Less: Payments Withheld By Employer	(2,400)
Taxable Benefit	**$ 9,671**

The deductible car expenses would be $5,728 [($6,200)(85,000 km/92,000 km)].

Note Three The December 15, 2001 CRA News Release titled "Gifts And Awards Given By Employers To Their Employees" describes the policy that allows employers to give their employees up to two non-cash gifts per year on a tax free basis, for a variety of special occasions. As the cost of the Christmas gift, including taxes, is less than $500 and the gift is non-cash, it is not a taxable benefit.

Excluded Items Other items not included and the reason for their exclusion:

- Federal and provincial income taxes withheld are not deductible.

- The purchase of Canada Savings Bonds is a non-deductible capital expenditure. Any interest charged on the payroll deduction purchase is deductible from Net Income For Tax Purposes, but does not affect employment income.

- The $2,500 membership to the Mountain Tennis Club paid by the Company for Ms. Firth is not a taxable benefit since the primary beneficiary appears to be the Company.

Chapter Five Learning Objectives

After completing Chapter 5, you should be able to:

1. Explain the basic concept of employment income (paragraphs 5-1 through 5-6).

2. Explain the reasons for using, and rules associated with, bonus arrangements for employees (paragraphs 5-7 through 5-11).

3. Distinguish between an employee and a self-employed individual earning business income (paragraphs 5-13 through 5-27).

4. List the benefits that can be excluded from employment income under ITA 6(1)(a) (paragraph 5-29).

5. List the benefits that must be included in income under the other paragraphs contained in ITA 6(1) (paragraph 5-30).

6. Apply the content of IT-470R with respect to the tax status of the various employee benefits described in the Bulletin (paragraphs 5-31 through 5-39).

7. Explain the basic elements of tax planning for employee benefits (paragraphs 5-34 through 5-39).

8. Describe the effects of GST on taxable benefits (paragraphs 5-40 and 5-41).

9. Explain the treatment of board and lodging benefits (paragraphs 5-42 through 5-44).

10. Calculate the standby charge and operating cost benefits that apply to employees who are provided with an automobile that is leased or owned by their employer (paragraphs 5-45 through 5-80).

11. Explain the basic elements of tax planning for company cars (paragraph 5-81).

12. Explain the tax treatment of allowances that are provided by employers to their employees for travel costs (paragraphs 5-82 through 5-94).

13. Describe the tax status of various types of insurance benefits that are provided by employers to their employees (paragraphs 5-95 through 5-103).

14. Calculate the tax consequences of low-rate or interest free loans to employees (paragraphs 5-104 through 5-115).

15. Calculate the employment income benefits that result from employers granting stock options to their employees (including the exercising of the options and the subsequent sale of the acquired shares) (paragraphs 5-116 through 5-143).

16. Demonstrate a basic understanding of specific other inclusions (paragraphs 5-144 through 5-152).

17. Demonstrate an understanding of deductions against employment income (paragraphs 5-153 through 5-172).

18. Explain the conditions that must be met for employees to deduct home office costs (paragraphs 5-173 through 5-177).

CHAPTER SIX

How To Work Through Chapter Six

We recommend the following approach in dealing with the material in this chapter:

Taxable Income Of Individuals

☐ Read pages 165 (from paragraph 6-1) through 167 (through paragraph 6-13) of the text.

☐ Complete Exercise Six-1. The Exercise is on page 168 of the text. The solution is on page S-53 of this Study Guide.

☐ Read page 168 (paragraph 6-14) of the text.

Federal And Provincial Tax Payable Before Credits

☐ Read pages 168 (from paragraph 6-15) through 170 (through paragraph 6-27) of the text.

☐ Complete Exercise Six-2. The Exercise is on page 170 of the text. The solution is on page S-53 of this Study Guide.

☐ Read page 170 (paragraph 6-28) of the text.

Credits Against Tax Payable - Calculating The Amount

☐ Read page 171 (paragraphs 6-29 through 6-32) of the text.

Personal Tax Credits - ITA 118(1)

☐ Read pages 171 (from paragraph 6-33) and 172 (through paragraph 6-36) of the text.

☐ Complete Exercise Six-3. The Exercise is on page 172 of the text. The solution is on page S-53 of this Study Guide.

Tax Credits - Eligible Dependant, Caregiver, And Infirm Dependant Over 17

☐ Read pages 172 (from paragraph 6-37) through 174 (through paragraph 6-52) of the text.

☐ Complete Exercises Six-4 and Six-5. The Exercises are on page 175 of the text. The solutions are on pages S-53 and S-54 of this Study Guide.

Age Tax Credit

☐ Read page 175 (paragraphs 6-53 and 6-54) of the text.

☐ Complete Exercise Six-6. The Exercise is on page 175 of the text. The solution is on page S-54 of this Study Guide.

Tax Credits - Pension Income And Charitable Donations

☐ Read pages 175 (from paragraph 6-55) through 177 (through paragraph 6-68) of the text.

☐ Complete Exercise Six-7. The Exercise is on page 177 of the text. The solution is on page S-54 of this Study Guide.

Medical Expense Tax Credit

☐ Read pages 177 (from Note On Legislation) through 179 (through paragraph 6-75) of the text.

☐ Complete Exercise Six-8. The Exercise is on page 180 of the text. The solution is on page S-55 of this Study Guide.

Refundable Medical Expense Supplement
☐ Read page 180 (paragraphs 6-76 through 6-78) of the text.

☐ Complete Exercise Six-9. The Exercise is on page 180 of the text. The solution is on page S-55 of this Study Guide.

Disability Tax Credit
☐ Read pages 181 (from paragraph 6-79) and 182 (through paragraph 6-86) of the text.

☐ Complete Exercise Six-10. The Exercise is on page 182 of the text. The solution is on page S-55 of this Study Guide.

Education Related Tax Credits
☐ Read pages 182 (from paragraph 6-87) and 183 (through paragraph 6-95) of the text.

☐ Complete Exercise Six-11. The Exercise is on page 184 of the text. The solution is on page S-55 of this Study Guide.

Transfer Of Tuition Fee And Education Tax Credits
☐ Read page 184 (paragraphs 6-96 through 6-98) of the text.

☐ Complete Exercise Six-12. The Exercise is on pages 184 and 185 of the text. The solution is on page S-56 of this Study Guide.

Employment Insurance And Canada Pension Plan Credits
☐ Read pages 185 (from paragraph 6-99) and 186 (through paragraph 6-107) of the text.

☐ Complete Exercise Six-13. The Exercise is on page 186 of the text. The solution is on page S-56 of this Study Guide.

Political Contributions Tax Credit
☐ Read pages 186 (from paragraph 6-110) and 187 (through paragraph 6-112) of the text.

☐ Complete Exercise Six-14. The Exercise is on page 187 of the text. The solution is on page S-56 of this Study Guide.

Labour Sponsored Funds Tax Credit
☐ Read page 187 (paragraphs 6-114 and 6-115) of the text.

☐ Complete Exercise Six-15. The Exercise is on page 187 of the text. The solution is on page S-56 of this Study Guide.

Refundable GST Credit, Child Tax Benefit, And Social Benefits Repayment
☐ Read pages 188 (from paragraph 6-116) through 190 (through paragraph 6-132) of the text.

☐ Complete Exercise Six-16. The Exercise is on page 190 of the text. The solution is on page S-56 of this Study Guide.

Comprehensive Example
☐ Read pages 190 (from paragraph 6-133) through 192 (through paragraph 6-133) of the text.

☐ Complete Self Study Problems Six-1 through Six-3. The Self Study Problems are on pages 202 through 205 of the text. The solutions are on pages S-57 through S-62 of this Study Guide.

Sample Personal Tax Return For Chapter 6

☐ Read the Sample Personal Tax Return For Chapter 6 on pages 194 and 195 of the text. The complete sample tax return is available on the Companion CD-ROM included with the text in two formats, a T1 ProFile return file and a .PDF file. The T1 ProFile version can be opened by going to the subdirectory "\Tax Return Files", and opening the file "Sample - Chapter 06.04T". The .PDF version, also located in the subdirectory "\Tax Return Problems", is called "PDF Sample - Chapter 06.pdf".

☐ Read the Suggestions For Working With Profile Software found on pages S-50 through S-52 of this Study Guide.

☐ When the updated Intuit ProFile software is available in January, 2006, a download site for the updated software program and updated sample tax returns and Cases using ProFile software will be available at:

www.pearsoned.ca/byrdchen/ctp2006

☐ Complete Self Study Case Six-1 using the ProFile T1 Software. The Self Study Case is on pages 205 through 207 of the text. The condensed solution is on pages S-62 through S-65 of this Study Guide. The complete sample tax return is available on the Companion CD-ROM included with the text in two formats, a T1 ProFile return file and a .PDF file. The T1 ProFile version can be opened by going to the subdirectory "\Tax Return Files", and opening the file "Self Study Case 06-1.04T". The .PDF version, also located in the subdirectory "\Tax Return Problems", is called "PDF Self Study Case 06-1.pdf". This Self Study Case is also extended in Self Study Problem Six-3, using 2005 rates.

To Complete This Chapter

☐ Review the Key Terms Used In The Chapter on page 192 of the text. Consult the Glossary for the meaning of any key terms you do not know.

☐ Review the Learning Objectives of the Chapter found on page S-66 of this Study Guide.

☐ As a review, we recommend that you view the PowerPoint Slides for Chapter Six that are on your Companion CD-ROM. If you do not have access to the Microsoft PowerPoint program, the PowerPoint Viewer program can be installed from the Companion CD-ROM.

Suggestions For Working With ProFile Software

Before You Start

To get the maximum benefit from using the ProFile tax preparation software program, we strongly advise that you do the tutorials "Getting Started" and "Using the Form Explorer" that are included with the program. The data in the sample tax return problems can be used in the tutorial.

A Quick Reference Card, as well as complete manuals, are available on the ProFile Tax Suite CD in .PDF format. To view .PDF files, you will need to have Adobe Acrobat installed on your system. This program is included on the Companion CD-ROM.

Sample Tax Returns

Included at the end of Chapters 6 and 14 are sample tax returns. The tax returns included in the 2005/6 edition of *Canadian Tax Principles* contain 2004 data as the 2005 version of the ProFile tax preparation software is not yet available. The ProFile software on the ProFile Tax Suite CD also contains the version for 2004 returns.

When viewing the ProFile (not .PDF) versions of the files (for example, Chapter 6 Sample Tax Return.04T), we offer the following suggestions:

- By pressing the F4 key you will open the Form Explorer. In the categories of forms appearing in the shaded box on the left, if you choose "A. Used" near the bottom of the column, all the forms that have calculations for the return will be shown. You can then double click on the form itself to view it. Note that if you cannot see a shaded box in the left column, choose any icon other than the "Key" mode icon in the top right corner of the Form Explorer menu.

- If you alternate click on a number in a field, a variety of options will become visible, including the form or schedule where the amount originated from.

- Clicking on "Show Auditor" under the "Audit" list will display any warnings or potential errors.

Creating New T1 Returns

To provide some guidance on how to use ProFile to create a simple new personal tax return, we suggest the following approach.

1. Start the ProFile software. Open a new file. Ensure you have chosen the a new file in the correct software and year.

2. By default, the software will open on the form "Info". Enter all relevant information here. At a minimum, you will need to enter the following information:

   - Taxpayer's Social Insurance Number (SIN)
   - Taxpayer's first and last name
   - Address, city, province, and postal code
   - Telephone number
   - Taxpayer's birth date

   If applicable, you will also need to enter any relevant information for the spouse on the "Info" form. At a minimum, the following information will be necessary:

   - Spouse's Social Insurance Number (SIN)
   - Spouse's first and last name
   - Address, city, province, and postal code
   - Telephone number
   - Spouse's birth date

3. Using the Form Explorer (F4), go to the Dependant form and enter all relevant information about any eligible dependants. At a minimum, the following information will be necessary:

    - Dependant's Social Insurance Number (SIN)
    - Dependant's first and last name
    - Dependant's relationship to the taxpayer
    - Dependant's birth date
    - Dependant's Net Income
    - Address, city, province, and postal code

    If the Dependant has tuition and education amounts and is not filing a tax return, the education related information should be entered on the Dependant form.

4. Using the Form Explorer (F4), open the relevant information slip form. Enter all relevant information in the appropriate forms. Some common information slip forms are:

    - T3 - Statement of Trust Income
    - T4 - Statement of Remuneration Paid
    - T5 - Statement of Investment Income
    - T2202 - Tuition and Education Amounts
    - T4AOAS - Statement of Old Age Security

5. Enter any other relevant income information on the appropriate forms. These forms may include, but are not limited to, the following:

    - T776 - Statement of Real Estate Rentals
    - T776Asset - T776 Asset Details
    - T776CCA - T776 CCA Details
    - T2032 - Statement of Professional Activities
    - T2032Asset - T2032 Asset Details
    - T2032CCA - T2032 CCA Details

6. Enter any relevant other deduction information on the appropriate forms. These forms may include, but are not limited to, the following:

    - RRSP - RRSP Deduction
    - T777 - Statement of Employment Expenses
    - T778 - Child Care Expense Deduction
    - Support - Support Payments
    - Auto - Motor Vehicle Expenses
    - LossNetCap - Net Capital Losses
    - LossNonCap - Non-Capital Losses

7. Enter any relevant tax credit information on the appropriate forms. These forms may include, but are not limited to, the following:

    - Donations - Charitable Donations
    - Medical - Medical Expenses

8. Enter any remaining relevant information in the appropriate schedule. These schedules may include, but are not limited to, the following:

    - S2 - Federal Amounts Transferred From Your Spouse or Common-Law Partner (primarily used if spouse or common-law partner is not filing a tax return)
    - S3Details - Capital Gains Entry (this form, not Schedule 3, must be used to input details on capital dispositions)

- S4 - Statement of Investment Income
(much of the information for this schedule will be carried forward from the T3, T5, and other information slips, but a few items such as carrying charges are entered directly on Schedule 4)

9. Use the function "Show Auditor" under the "Audit" list to check for warnings or potential errors.

Tips For Using ProFile Software

- Press the F5 key or choose Spouse from the Form menu to display the return of the spouse.

- Press the F4 key to view the Form Explorer. Choose the form "Summary" to see the tax data of both spouses on the same one page summary. (Second column will be blank for a single taxpayer.)

- Review marks can be used to flag information that should be reviewed. The cell with the review mark will be listed when the Show Auditor feature is turned on.

- A memo and/or a tape can be attached to a cell to provide backup information.

- If you cannot determine where a specific slip or other information should be input, one way to search for the correct form is to open the Form Explorer (F4) and choose the "Key" mode icon in the top right corner of the menu. If you type a key word into the line above the listing of key words, the appropriate form may be found.

- To see the effect of various changes such as province of residence or a change in an RRSP contribution, use the "Snapshot/Variance" feature. Information on this feature is available from the Help menu. Note you must press the "Enter" key for the change to take effect. The data monitor at the bottom of the screen should show the new balance/refund. The difference can also be seen on the "Summary" form. If you open the Auditor (F9) and select the Variance tab you will see a detailed analysis of the changes.

Solution to Chapter Six Exercises

Exercise Six - 1 Solution

The net effect of this home relocation loan on Taxable Income would be as follows:

Taxable Benefit Under ITA 80.4(1)(a) - [(4%)($82,000)]*	$3,280
Reduction For Payments Under ITA 80.4(1)(c) - [(2%)($82,000)]	(1,640)
Total ITA 80.4(1) Benefit	$1,640
ITA 110(1)(j) Deduction - Lesser Of:	
• ITA 80.4(1) Benefit = $1,640	
• [(4%)($25,000)(4/4)]* = $1,000	(1,000)
Net Addition To Taxable Income	$ 640

*Despite the fact that the prescribed rate has increased, the taxpayer can continue to use the rate in effect at the time the loan was made. This can continue for a period of five years. Note that the ITA 110(1)(j) deduction is also based on the rate in effect at the time the loan was made.

Exercise Six - 2 Solution

The required Tax Payable would be calculated as follows:

Federal Tax Payable:		
On First $35,595	$5,695	
On Next $11,105 ($46,700 - $35,595) At 22 Percent	2,443	$8,138
Provincial Tax Payable:		
On First $34,010 At 6.05 Percent	$2,058	
On Next $12,690 ($46,700 - $34,010) At 9.15 Percent	1,161	3,219
Total Tax Payable Before Credits		$11,357

Exercise Six - 3 Solution

The required amount would be calculated as follows:

Basic Personal Amount	$ 8,148
Spousal Amount [$6,919 - ($2,600 - $692)]	5,011
Credit Base	$13,159
Rate	16%
Personal Tax Credits	$ 2,105

Exercise Six - 4 Solution

The eligible dependant credit would be $322 {[16%][$6,919 - ($5,600 - $692)]}.

As her father's income is below the caregiver threshold of $13,141, if Melinda could claim the caregiver tax credit, the full credit of $616 would be available. However, the caregiver tax credit cannot be claimed as she is entitled to the eligible dependant credit. If her father's income was higher than $7,611 which would eliminate the eligible dependant credit, she would be eligible to claim the caregiver tax credit.

Note that she cannot use the ITA 118(1)(d) credit as her father does not appear to be dependent because of a mental or physical infirmity.

Exercise Six - 5 Solution

Her tax credits would be determined as follows:

Basic Personal Amount	$ 8,148
Eligible Dependant (Daughter) [$6,919 - ($1,800 - $692)]	5,811
Caregiver (Son)	3,848
Credit Base	$17,807
Rate	16%
Total Credits	$ 2,849

While the eligible dependant credit would have been larger had she claimed it for her son (he has no income above the threshold level), she could not have claimed the caregiver credit for her daughter. She is better off claiming the caregiver credit, plus the decreased eligible dependant credit. As a further alternative, Ms. Forest could have claimed the infirm dependant over 17 credit, instead of the caregiver credit, for her son. However, the credits are for the same amount. As a rule, the caregiver credit should be claimed as it has a higher income threshold.

Exercise Six - 6 Solution

Mr. Smythe's age credit for 2005 would be $111 {[16%][$3,979 - (15%)($51,500 - $29,619)]}.

Exercise Six - 7 Solution

The credit base for 2005 would be limited to $48,750 [(75%)($65,000)], leaving a carry forward of $51,250 ($100,000 - $48,750). The resulting credit would be:

$200 At 16 Percent	$ 32
$48,550 At 29 Percent	14,080
Total Credit	$14,112

As her income for 2006 is unchanged from 2005, the limit would be the same at $48,750 [(75%)($65,000)]. Since she still cannot claim all of the $51,250 unused amount, the credit for 2006 would be the same as the credit for 2005. The carry forward would be $2,500 [$100,000 - ($48,750)(2)].

For 2007, the remaining unused amount of $2,500 ($100,000 - $48,750 - $48,750) would result in a credit of:

$200 At 16 Percent	$ 32
$2,300 At 29 Percent	667
Total Credit	$699

Exercise Six - 8 Solution

Amount B Qualifying Expenses ($4,330 + $4,600)	$ 8,930
Amount C	
Lesser of:	
• [(3%)($150,000)] = $4,500	
• 2005 Threshold Amount = $1,844	(1,844)
Subtotal	$ 7,086
Amount D	
Max - Lesser Of:	
• [$8,425 - (3%)($8,250)] = $8,178	
• Absolute Limit = $10,000	8,178
Allowable Amount Of Medical Expenses	$15,264
Amount A The Appropriate Rate	16%
Medical Expense Tax Credit	$ 2,442

Exercise Six - 9 Solution

Ms. Brunt's allowable medical expenses for tax credit purposes would be $5,488 [$6,250 - (3%)($25,400)], resulting in a credit of $878 [(16%)($5,488)]. 25/16 of this amount would be $1,372. This means that the refundable supplement would be based on the maximum of $750, less a reduction of $187 [(5%)($25,400 - $21,663)], a balance of $563. Given this, her Tax Payable would be $212 [(16%)($25,400 - $8,148 - $6,919 - $5,488) - $563].

Exercise Six - 10 Solution

John has sufficient other medical expenses to exceed the 3 percent threshold. His income is too high to qualify for the refundable supplement. As Keith has no income, the regular disability credit can be transferred to John. However, as Keith is over 17, the disability supplement is not available. In addition to the disability credit, John will be able to take the credit for a physically infirm child over 17, as well as a credit for Keith's medical expenses. Keith's medical expense credit base is limited to the maximum of $10,000 . The total credits related to Keith would be as follows:

Disability - Regular Amount	$ 6,596
Infirm Dependant Over 17	3,848
Medical Expenses (Absolute Limit)	10,000
Total Credit Base	$20,444
Rate	16%
Total Credits Related To Keith	$ 3,271

Exercise Six - 11 Solution

Ms. Bright's education related tax credits would be calculated as follows:

Education Credit:		
Full Time [(4)($400)]		$1,600
Part Time [(2)($120)]		240
Tuition:		
Total (Including $1,000 Prepayment)	$3,200	
Ineligible Ancillary Fees ($400 - $250)	(150)	3,050
Interest On Student Loan		325
Total Credit Base		$5,215
Rate		16%
Total Available Credits		$ 834

Exercise Six - 12 Solution

Jerry's total available tuition and education amount would be $27,900 [(11)($400) + $23,500]. He must claim $1,102 ($9,250 - $8,148) of this amount. The remaining balance would be $26,798 ($27,900 - $1,102). Of this total, $3,898 ($5,000 - $1,102) could be transferred to a supporting parent. This would leave a carry forward of $22,900 ($27,900 - $1,102 - $3,898).

Exercise Six - 13 Solution

His tax credits would be calculated as follows:

Basic Personal Amount	$ 8,148
Spousal Amount	6,919
Age [$3,979 - (15%)($42,000 - $29,619)]	2,122
Pension Income	1,000
Spousal Age Transfer	3,979
Spousal Tuition Fee And Education Transfer [$2,200 + (4 Months)($400)]	3,800
Credit Base	$25,968
Rate	16%
Total Credits	$ 4,155

Exercise Six - 14 Solution

Ms. Unger's $487 credit would be calculated as follows:

	Contributions	Credit Rate	Tax Credit
First	$400	3/4	$300
Next	$350	1/2	175
Remaining	$ 35	1/3	12
Maximum Credit	$785		$487

Exercise Six - 15 Solution

The credit will be $450 [(15%)($3,000)]. As his acquisition is less than the $5,000 maximum, the full cost is eligible for the 15 percent credit.

Exercise Six - 16 Solution

Ms. Jacobi's income before deducting either the EI repayment or the tax on OAS benefits would be calculated as follows:

Net Employment Income	$50,000
EI Benefits	10,000
OAS Benefits	5,600
Income Before Deductions	$65,600

Dealing first with the EI repayment, Ms. Jacobi would have to repay $3,000 [(30%)($10,000)], which is the lesser of 30 percent of the EI benefits received and $5,055 [(30%)($65,600 - $48,750)].

Using this deduction, the tax on her OAS payments would be $269 [(15%)($65,600 - $3,000 - $60,806)]. As a result, her Net Income For Tax Purposes would be as follows:

Income Before Deductions	$65,600
ITA 60(v.1) Deduction (EI)	(3,000)
ITA 60(w) Deduction (OAS)	(269)
Net Income For Tax Purposes	$62,331

Solution to Self Study Problem Six - 1

Case A   The solution for this Case would be as follows:

Net Income For Tax Purposes And Taxable Income	$41,000

Gross Federal Tax [$5,695 + (22%)($41,000 - $35,595)]	$ 6,884
Basic Personal Credit [(16%)($8,148)]	(1,304)
Political Contributions Tax Credit	
[(3/4)($400) + (1/2)($350) + (1/3)($250)]	(558)
Federal Tax Payable	$ 5,022

Case B   The solution for this Case is as follows:

Net Income For Tax Purposes And Taxable Income		$41,000

Gross Federal Tax [$5,695 + (22%)($41,000 - $35,595)]		$ 6,884
Basic Personal Amount	($ 8,148)	
Spousal [$6,919 - ($4,650 - $692)]	(2,961)	
Medical Expenses [$3,150 - (3%)($41,000)]	(1,920)	
Credit Base	($13,029)	
Rate	16%	(2,085)
Federal Tax Payable		$ 4,799

As family Net Income For Tax Purposes is greater than $33,083, Stanley Murphy is not eligible for the $571 refundable medical expense supplement [($33,083 - $21,663)(5%) = $571].

Case C   The solution for this Case is as follows:

Net Income For Tax Purposes And Taxable Income		$41,000

Gross Federal Tax [$5,695 + (22%)($41,000 - $35,595)]		$ 6,884
Basic Personal Amount	($ 8,148)	
Spousal [$6,919 - ($5,050 - $692)]	(2,561)	
Albert's Education And Tuition: Lesser Of:		
• $5,000; and		
• $8,600 [($400)(8 Months) + $5,400]	(5,000)	
Credit Base	($15,709)	
Rate	16%	(2,513)
Federal Tax Payable		$ 4,371

The transfer of Albert's education and tuition credits is limited to $5,000. Alternatively, Albert can carry forward his tuition and education tax credits to be applied against his future income tax payable.

Solution to Self Study Problem Six - 1

Case D   The solution for this Case is as follows:

Net Income For Tax Purposes and Taxable Income		$41,450
Gross Federal Tax [$5,695 + (22%)($41,450 - $35,595)]		$ 6,983
Basic Personal Amount	($ 8,148)	
Spousal [$6,919 - ($6,300 - $692)]	(1,311)	
Age [$3,979 - (15%)($41,450 - $29,619)]	(2,204)	
Pension	(1,000)	
Spouse's Age	(3,979)	
Spouse's Disability	(6,596)	
Spouse's Pension	(450)	
Credit Base	($23,688)	
Rate	16%	(3,790)
Federal Tax Payable		$ 3,193

The Old Age Security and Canada Pension Plan receipts are not eligible for the pension income credit. As a result, Helen's pension income credit is limited to 16 percent of her Registered Pension Plan receipt. As Helen Murphy's income is below $29,619, there is no reduction in her age credit.

Case E   The solution for this Case can be completed as follows:

Net Income For Tax Purposes And Taxable Income		$41,000
Gross Federal Tax [$5,695 + (22%)($41,000 - $35,595)]		$ 6,884
Basic Personal Amount	($ 8,148)	
Caregiver	(3,848)	
Interest On Student Loans	(375)	
Credit Base	$ 12,371	
Rate	16%	(1,979)
Federal Tax Payable		$ 4,905

Since Mr. Murphy's father's Net Income For Tax Purposes is greater than $7,611, the amount for an eligible dependant is not available. If it had been available due to his father's infirmity, the infirm dependant over 17 credit would have been fully eroded as Stanley's father has Net Income For Tax Purposes greater than $9,308. Therefore, the use of the caregiver credit will minimize Tax Payable.

Solution to Self Study Problem Six - 2

Part A Marg has tuition and education amounts available totalling $9,500 [($400)(8 Months) + $6,300]. Her Tax Payable is nil, which can be calculated as follows:

Taxable Income		$12,400
Less:		
Basic Personal Amount	($8,148)	
CPP And EI ($242 + $441)	(683)	
Credit Base Before Tuition and Education Amounts	($8,831)	
Tuition And Education Amounts Claimed		
($12,400 - $8,831)	(3,569)	(12,400)
Subtotal		Nil
Rate		16%
Federal Tax Payable		Nil

Marg has an unused tuition and education amount of $5,931 ($9,500 - $3,569). She can transfer a maximum of $1,431 ($5,000 - $3,569) to her father. This leaves her with a carry forward amount of $4,500 ($9,500 - $3,569 - $1,431).

Note that her medical expenses were not claimed in this year as they can be transferred to her father. Since she cannot deduct a medical expense credit prior to deducting her tuition/education credit, she would not increase the tuition/education transfer to her father if she did.

Part B Mr. Barth's net employment income for the year would be calculated as follows:

Gross Salary	$ 82,500
Bonus (Note One)	20,000
Registered Pension Plan Contributions	(3,200)
Professional Dues	(1,800)
Stock Option Benefit [($18 - $15)(1,000)]	3,000
Automobile Benefit (Note Two)	3,100
Counselling Benefit (Note Three)	1,500
Imputed Interest Benefit (Note Four)	750
Net Employment Income	$105,850

Note One As the bonus is not payable until more than three years after the end of the employer's taxation year, it is a salary deferral arrangement and must be included in income under ITA 6(11).

Note Two Since Mr. Barth's employment related usage is not more than 50 percent, there is no reduction of the full standby charge. The automobile benefit is calculated as follows:

Standby Charge [(2%)(10)($27,500)]	$5,500
Operating Cost Benefit [(6,000)($0.20)]	1,200
Total Before Payments	$6,700
Payments Withheld	(3,600)
Taxable Benefit	$3,100

Solution to Self Study Problem Six - 2

Note Three   IT-470R indicates that counselling services, with the exception of those items specified under ITA 6(1), are considered taxable benefits. The items specified under ITA 6(1) are counselling with respect to mental or physical health or with respect to re-employment or retirement. As a consequence, the counselling on personal finances is a taxable benefit.

Note Four   The imputed interest benefit is calculated as follows:

Basic Benefit [($150,000)(3%)(3/12)]	$1,125
Interest Paid	(375)
Taxable Benefit	$ 750

Taxable Income   Mr. Barth's Taxable Income would be calculated as follows:

Net Income For Tax Purposes (Net Employment Income)	$105,850
Stock Option Deduction [(1/2)($3,000)]	(1,500)
Taxable Income	$104,350

Tax Payable   Mr. Barth's Tax Payable would be calculated as follows:

Tax On First $71,190		$ 13,526
Tax On Next $33,160 At 26 Percent		8,622
Federal Tax Before Adjustments		$ 22,148
Basic Personal Amount	($ 8,148)	
Spousal [$6,919 - ($1,250 - $692)]	(6,361)	
Spouse's Disability	(6,596)	
EI	(761)	
CPP	(1,861)	
Medical Expenses (Note Five)	(2,254)	
Marg's Education And Tuition (See Part A)	(1,431)	
Credit Base	($27,412)	
Rate	16%	(4,386)
Charitable Donations [(16%)($200) + (29%)($2,000 - $200)]		(554)
Net Federal Tax		$ 17,208
Amounts Withheld During Year		(16,000)
Federal Tax Payable		$ 1,208

Note Five Allowable medical expenses are as follows:

John And Spouse Medical Expenses ($200+ $3,550)	$3,750
Threshold (Limit Amount)	(1,844)
Subtotal	$1,906
Marg's Medical Expenses - Lesser Of:	
• [$720 - (3%)($12,400)] = $348	
• Absolute Limit = $10,000	348
Allowable Medical Expenses	$2,254

Solution to Self Study Problem Six - 3

This is an extension of Self Study Case Six-1 (tax return preparation case). It has been updated for 2005 rates.

The required calculations for Ms. Trubey's balance owing (refund) would be as follows:

Employment Income		$ 60,202
RPP Deduction		(2,406)
Union Dues		(749)
Net And Taxable Income		**$ 57,047**
Federal Tax On First $35,595		$5,695
Federal Tax On Next $21,452 At 22 Percent		4,719
Gross Federal Tax		$10,414
Basic Personal Amount	($ 8,148)	
Eligible Dependant - Amy	(6,919)	
CPP Contributions	(1,861)	
EI Premiums	(761)	
Caregiver - Marjorie	(3,848)	
Transfer Of Diane's Tuition And Education - Lesser Of:		
• $5,000		
• [$4,415 + (2)($120) + (8)($400)] = $7,855	(5,000)	
Medical Expenses (Note One)	(1,632)	
Credit Base	($28,169)	
Rate	16%	(4,507)
Charitable Donations [(16%)($200) +		
(29%)($175 + $375 + $50 - $200)]		(148)
Net Federal Tax		$ 5,759
Provincial Tax (Given)		2,390
Income Tax Deducted		(19,408)
Instalments Paid (Given)		(2,528)
Balance Owing (Refund)		**($13,787)**

Note One Allowable medical expenses are as follows:

Eleanor And Minor Child (Amy) Medical Expenses		
($392 + $1,350 + $450 + $1,120)	$3,312	
Threshold [(3%)($57,047)]	(1,711)	
Subtotal	$1,601	
Marjorie's Medical Expenses - Lesser Of:		
• [($50 + $75) - (3%($5,600)] = Nil		
• Absolute Limit = $10,000	Nil	
Diane's Medical Expense - Lesser Of:		
• [$100 - (3%)($2,300)] = $31		
• Absolute Limit = $10,000	31	
Allowable Medical Expenses	**$1,632**	

Notes To Eleanor's Tax Return

- Diane transfers the $5,000 maximum tuition and education credit to Eleanor and carries forward the remaining $2,855 [$4,415 + (2)($120) + (8)($400) - $5,000].

- Eleanor cannot claim the charitable donation made by Diane, but Diane can carry it forward for up to five years.

- Her daughter, Diane, should file a tax return to make her tuition and education tax credits and charitable donation tax credit available for carry forward. If she does not file, she will not be eligible for the GST credit and she will not benefit from the RRSP deduction room created during the year.

- Her mother, Marjorie, should file a tax return in order to receive the GST credit.

- Eleanor is eligible for the caregiver tax credit for her mother as her income is well below the threshold.

- Since Diane and Marjorie are over 17 years of age, their medical expenses are reduced by 3 percent of their Net Income For Tax Purposes. This means that none of Marjorie's medical expenses can be claimed by Eleanor.

- Eleanor paid too much in instalments. It should be determined why this happened, to try and prevent overpaying instalments again.

Solution to Self Study Case Six - 1

This solution includes selected schedules and worksheets from the ProFile T1 return. Note that the program can only be used to calculate 2004 (not 2005) tax returns, and the problem and solution reflect this fact. The complete tax return is available on the Companion CD-ROM in the subdirectory "\Tax Return Files" in two forms. The T1 ProFile return file is named "Self Study Case 06-1.04T" and the .PDF file is named "PDF Self Study Case 06-1.pdf. Please see the sample tax return in the text for suggestions on using the ProFile tax program.

Notes to tax return

- Her daughter, Diane, transfers the $5,000 maximum tuition and education credit to Eleanor and carries forward the remaining $2,855 [$4,415 + (2)($120) + (8)($400) - $5,000]

- Eleanor cannot claim the charitable donation made by Diane, but Diane can carry it forward for up to five years.

- Diane should file a tax return to make her tuition and education tax credits and charitable donation tax credit available for carry forward. If she does not file, she will not be eligible for the GST credit and she will not benefit from the RRSP deduction room created during the year.

- Her mother, Marjorie, should file a tax return in order to receive the GST credit. However, she will need to obtain a Social Insurance Number to do so.

- Eleanor is eligible for the caregiver tax credit for her mother as her income is well below the threshold.

- Since Diane and Marjorie are over 17 years of age, their medical expenses are reduced by 3 percent of their Net Income For Tax Purposes. This means that none of Marjorie's medical expenses can be claimed by Eleanor.

- Eleanor paid too much in instalments. It should be determined why this happened, to try and prevent overpaying instalments again.

Trubey, Eleanor Chap 6 Prob   SIN: 527 000 087

Summary

2004 Tax Summary

Total income	Eleanor Chap 6 Prob		Non-refundable tax credits	Eleanor Chap 6 Prob		
Employment	60,201	80	Basic personal amount	8,012	00	
Old Age Security			Age amount			
CPP/QPP benefits			Spouse / eligible dependant	6,803	00	
Other pensions			Infirm dependants			
Employment Insurance			CPP/QPP	1,831	50	
Taxable dividends			Employment Insurance	772	20	
Interest			Pension income amount			
Limited partnership			Caregiver amount	3,784	00	
Rental			Disability amount			
Taxable capital gains			Interest on student loans			
Support payments			Tuition / education			
RRSP			Transfers	5,000	00	
Other			Medical expenses	1,631	59	
Self-employment			**Subtotal**	27,834	29	
Workers' compensation and social assistance			Credit at 16%	4,453	49	
Total income	60,201	80	Donations and gifts	148	00	
			Non-refundable tax credits	4,601	49	
Net income			**Total payable**			
RPP	2,406	16	Federal tax	10,450	35	
RRSP			Non-refundable tax credits	4,601	49	
Union and professional dues	748	59	Dividend tax credit			
Child care expenses			Minimum tax carry-over/other			
Disability supports deduction			**Basic federal tax**	5,848	86	
Business investment loss			Non resident surtax			
Moving expenses			Foreign tax credits / other			
Support payments			**Federal tax**	5,848	86	
Carrying charges and interest			Political/investment tax credit			
CPP/QPP on self-employment			Labour-sponsored tax credit			
Exploration and development			Alternative minimum tax			
Employment expenses			Additional tax on RESP			
Social benefits repayment			**Net federal tax**	5,848	86	
Other deductions			CPP contributions payable			
Net income	57,047	05	Social benefits repayment			
Taxable income			Provincial/territorial tax	2,400	78	
Canadian Forces personnel			**Total payable**	8,249	64	
Home relocation loan			**Total credits**			
Security options deductions			Income tax deducted	19,408	00	
Other payments deduction			QC or YT abatement			
Losses of other years			CPP overpayment			
Capital gains deduction			EI overpayment			
Northern residents deductions			Medical expense supplement			
Additional deductions			GST/HST rebate			
Taxable income	57,047	05	Instalments	2,528	00	
2005 Estimated	Eleanor Chap 6 Prob		Provincial tax credits			
GST/HST credit			Other credits			
Child Tax Benefit	767	06	**Total credits**	21,936	00	
RRSP contribution limit	2,872	00	**Balance owing (refund)**	(13,686	36)	
			Combined balance (refund)	(13,686	36)	

Complete tax return available on the CD-ROM

Trubey, Eleanor Chap 6 Prob SIN: 527 000 087

T1-2004	**Federal Tax**	Schedule 1

Complete this schedule to claim your federal non-refundable tax credits and to calculate your net federal tax.

You must attach a copy of this schedule to your return.

Enter your **taxable income** from line 260 of your return _____ 57,047 05 **1**

Use the amount on line 1 to determine which **ONE** of the following columns you have to complete.

If the amount on line 1 is:	$35,000 or less	more than $35,000 but not more than $70,000	more than $70,000 but not more than $113,804	more than $113,804
Enter the amount from line 1 above	**2**	57,047 05 **2**	**2**	**2**
Base amount	**3**	35,000 00 **3**	70,000 00 **3**	113,804 00 **3**
Line 2 minus line 3 (this amount cannot be negative)	0 00 **4**	22,047 05 **4**	**4**	**4**
Rate	x 16.00 % **5**	x 22.00 % **5**	x 26.00 % **5**	x 29.00 % **5**
Multiply the amount on line 4 by the rate on line 5	**6**	4,850 35 **6**	**6**	**6**
Tax on base amount	0 00 **7**	5,600 00 **7**	13,300 00 **7**	24,689 00 **7**
Add lines 6 and 7	**8**	10,450 35 **8**	**8**	**8**

Federal non-refundable tax credits

Basic personal amount		**claim $8,012**	**300**	8,012 00
Age amount (if you were born in 1939 or earlier)		**(maximum $3,912)**	**301**	
Spouse or common-law partner amount:				
Base amount	7,484 00			
Minus: His or her net income (from page 1 of your return)	0 00			
Result: (if negative, enter "0")		**(maximum $6,803)** ▶	**303**	
Amount for an eligible dependant (**attach** Schedule 5)		**(maximum $6,803)**	**305**	6,803 00
Amount for infirm dependants age 18 or older (**attach** Schedule 5)			**306**	
CPP or QPP contributions:				
through employment from box 16 and box 17 on all T4 slips		**(maximum $1,831.50)**	**308**	1,831 50 •
on self-employment and other earnings (**attach** Schedule 8)			**310**	•
Employment Insurance premiums from box 18 on all T4 slips		**(maximum $772.20)**	**312**	772 20 •
Pension income amount		**(maximum $1,000)**	**314**	
Caregiver amount (**attach** Schedule 5)			**315**	3,784 00
Disability amount			**316**	
Disability amount transferred from a dependant			**318**	
Interest paid on your student loans			**319**	
Tuition and education amounts (**attach** Schedule 11)			**323**	
Tuition and education amounts transferred from a child			**324**	5,000 00
Amounts transferred from your spouse or common-law partner (**attach** Schedule 2)			**326**	

Medical expenses for **self, spouse or common-law partner, and your dependent children born in 1987 or later** (see the guide) **330** 3,312 00

Minus: $1,813, or 3% of line 236, whichever is **less** 1,711 41

Subtotal (if negative, enter "0") 1,600 59 (A)

Allowable amount of medical expenses for **other dependants** (see the calculation at line 331 in the guide and **attach** Schedule 5) **331** 31 00 (B)

Add lines (A) and (B). 1,631 59 ▶ **332** 1,631 59

Add lines 300 to 326, and 332. **335** 27,834 29

Multiply the amount on line 335 by 16% = **338** 4,453 49

Donations and gifts (**attach** Schedule 9) **349** 148 00

Total federal non-refundable tax credits: Add lines 338 and 349. **350** 4,601 49

Page 1 of 2

Trubey, Eleanor Chap 6 Prob SIN: 527 000 087

Net federal tax

Enter the amount from line 8		10,450 35	**9**
Federal tax on split income (from line 4 of Form T1206)	**424**	•	**10**
Add lines 9 and 10		10,450 35 ▶ 10,450 35	**11**

Enter the amount from line 350	350	4,601 49	
Federal dividend tax credit (13.3333% of the amount on line 120 of your return)	**425**	•	
Overseas employment tax credit (**attach** Form T626)	426		
Minimum tax carry-over (**attach** Form T691)	**427**	•	
Add lines 350, 425, 426, and 427		4,601 49 ▶ 4,601 49	**12**
Basic federal tax: Line 11 minus line 12 (if negative, enter "0") 429		5,848 86	**13**

Federal foreign tax credit:
Complete the federal foreign tax credit calculation below and enter the amount
from line (i) or line (ii), whichever is **less**   **14**

Federal logging tax credit

Federal tax: Line 13 minus line 14 (if negative, enter "0") 406	5,848 86	**15**

Total federal political contributions (**attach** receipts)	**409**		
Federal political contribution tax credit (see the guide)	**410**	•	
Investment tax credit (**attach** Form T2038(IND))	**412**	•	
Labour-sponsored funds tax credit			
Net cost **413** Allowable credit **414**		•	
Add lines 410, 412, and 414. 416	▶		**16**
Line 15 minus line 16 (if negative, enter "0")			
(if you have an amount on line 424 above, see Form T1206) 417		5,848 86	**17**
Additional tax on RESP accumulated income payments (**attach** Form T1172) 418			**18**
Net federal tax: Add lines 17 and 18			
Enter this amount on line 420 of your return. 420		5,848 86	**19**

Federal foreign tax credit: (see lines 431 and 433 in the guide)

Make a separate calculation for each foreign country. Enter the result on line 14 above.

Non-business income tax paid to a foreign country   **431**   • **(i)**

$$\frac{\text{Net foreign non-business income * } \boxed{433}}{\text{Net income **}} \quad X \quad \text{Basic federal tax ***} \underline{\qquad\qquad} = \underline{\qquad} \text{(ii)}$$

* Reduce this amount by any income from that foreign country for which you claimed a capital gains deduction, and by any income from that country that was, under a tax treaty, either exempt from tax in that country or deductible as exempt income in Canada (included on line 256). Also reduce this amount by the lesser of lines E and F on Form T626.

** Line 236 plus the amount on line 3 of Form T1206, minus the total of the amounts on lines 244, 248, 249, 250, 253, 254, and minus any amount included on line 256 for foreign income deductible as exempt income under a tax treaty, income deductible as net employment income from a prescribed international organization, or non-taxable tuition assistance from box 21 of the T4E slip. If the result is less than the amount on line 433, enter your **Basic federal tax***** on line (ii).

*** Line 429 plus the amount on lines 425 and 426, and minus any refundable Québec abatement (line 440) and any federal refundable First Nations abatement (line 441 on the return for residents of Yukon).

Chapter Six Learning Objectives

After completing Chapter 6, you should be able to:

1. Calculate federal Tax Payable before the consideration of any tax credits using a supplied schedule of rates and other data (paragraphs 6-1 through 6-28).

2. Calculate the personal tax credits using a supplied schedule of rates and other data (paragraphs 6-29 through 6-52).

3. Calculate the age tax credit using a supplied schedule of rates and other data (paragraphs 6-53 and 6-54).

4. Calculate the pension income tax credit using a supplied schedule of rates and other data (paragraphs 6-55 through 6-58).

5. Calculate the charitable donations tax credit using a supplied schedule of rates and other data (paragraphs 6-59 through 6-68).

6. Calculate the medical expenses tax credit using a supplied schedule of rates and other data (paragraphs 6-69 through 6-75).

7. Calculate the refundable medical expense supplement using a supplied schedule of rates and other data (paragraphs 6-76 through 6-78).

8. Calculate the disability tax credit using a supplied schedule of rates and other data (paragraphs 6-79 through 6-86).

9. Calculate the education related tax credits using a supplied schedule of rates and other data (paragraphs 6-87 through 6-95).

10. Calculate the amount of education related tax credits that can be transferred to a supporting parent or grandparent (paragraphs 6-96 through 6-98).

11. Calculate the Employment Insurance and Canada Pension Plan credits using a supplied schedule of rates and other data (paragraphs 6-99 through 6-105).

12. Recall the types and amounts of tax credits that can be transferred to a spouse or common-law partner (paragraphs 6-106 and 6-107).

13. Calculate the political contributions tax credit using a supplied schedule of rates and other data (paragraphs 6-110 through 6-112).

14. Calculate the labour sponsored funds tax credit using a supplied schedule of rates and other data (paragraphs 6-114 and 6-115).

15. Explain the basic provisions of the refundable GST credit and the child tax benefit system (paragraphs 6-116 through 6-123);

16. Calculate the OAS and EI clawbacks using a supplied schedule of rates and other data (paragraphs 6-124 through 6-132).

17. Create a simple tax return using tax preparation software.

CHAPTER SEVEN

How To Work Through Chapter Seven

We recommend the following approach in dealing with the material in this chapter:

Tax And Accounting Procedures Compared And General Rules
☐ Read pages 219 (from paragraph 7-1) through 224 (through paragraph 7-26) of the text.

☐ Complete Exercise Seven-1. The Exercise is on page 224 of the text. The solution is on page S-69 of this Study Guide.

Capital Cost Allowances - General Overview
☐ Read pages 224 (from paragraph 7-27) through 227 (through paragraph 7-29) of the text.

Half-Year (a.k.a First Year) Rules
☐ Read page 227 (paragraphs 7-30 through 7-34) of the text.

☐ Complete Exercises Seven-2 through Seven-4. The Exercises are on page 228 of the text. The solutions are on page S-69 of this Study Guide.

Short Fiscal Periods
☐ Read pages 228 (from paragraph 7-35) and 229 (through paragraph 7-38) of the text.

☐ Complete Exercise Seven-5. The Exercise is on page 229 of the text. The solution is on page S-69 of this Study Guide.

Tax Planning Considerations
☐ Read page 229 (paragraphs 7-39 through 7-43) of the text.

☐ Complete Exercise Seven-6. The Exercise is on page 230 of the text. The solution is on pages S-69 and S-70 of this Study Guide.

Dispositions Of Depreciable Assets
☐ Read pages 230 (from paragraph 7-44) and 231 (through paragraph 7-52) of the text.

☐ Complete Exercise Seven-7. The Exercise is on page 231 of the text. The solution is on page S-70 of this Study Guide.

Recapture Of Capital Cost Allowance
☐ Read pages 231 (from paragraph 7-53) and 232 (through paragraph 7-56) of the text.

☐ Complete Exercise Seven-8. The Exercise is on page 232 of the text. The solution is on page S-70 of this Study Guide.

Terminal Losses
☐ Read page 232 (paragraphs 7-57 through 7-60) of the text.

☐ Complete Exercise Seven-9. The Exercise is on page 233 of the text. The solution is on page S-70 of this Study Guide.

CCA Schedule - Example
☐ Read page 233 (paragraph 7-61) of the text.

Separate Class Election

☐ Read pages 233 (from paragraph 7-62) and 234 (through paragraph 7-69) of the text.

☐ Complete Exercise Seven-10. The Exercise is on page 235 of your text. The solution is on page S-70 of this Study Guide.

Special Rules For Buildings

☐ Read pages 235 (from paragraph 7-70) and 236 (through paragraph 7-73) of the text.

☐ Complete Exercise Seven-11. The Exercise is on page 236 of the text. The solution is on page S-70 of this Study Guide.

☐ Complete Self Study Problems Seven-1, Seven-2, and Seven-3. The Self Study Problems are on pages 250 and 251 of the text. The solutions are on pages S-71 through S-75 of this Study Guide.

Deferral Provision On Replacement Property

☐ Read pages 236 (from paragraph 7-74) through 238 (through paragraph 7-84) of the text.

☐ Complete Exercise Seven-12. The Exercise is on page 238 of the text. The solution is on page S-71 of this Study Guide.

☐ Read page 238 (paragraph 7-85) of the text.

Change In Use

☐ Read pages 238 (from paragraph 7-86) through 240 (through paragraph 7-94) of the text.

☐ Complete Exercise Seven-13. The Exercise is found on page 240 of the text. The solution is on page S-71 of this Study Guide.

☐ Read page 241 (paragraph 7-95) of the text.

Cumulative Eligible Capital

☐ Read pages 241 (from paragraph 7-96) through 244 (through paragraph 7-112) of the text.

☐ Complete Exercise Seven-14. The Exercise is on page 244 of the text. The solution is on page S-71 of this Study Guide.

CEC Disposal Election

☐ Read pages 244 (from paragraph 7-113) and 245 (through paragraph 7-115) of the text.

☐ Complete Exercise Seven-15. The Exercise is on page 245 of the text. The solution is on page S-71 of this Study Guide.

☐ Complete Self Study Problems Seven-4 and Seven-5. The Self Study Problems are on pages 252 and 253 of the text. The solutions are on pages S-75 through S-78 of this Study Guide.

Special Situations

☐ Read pages 245 (from paragraph 7-116) and 246 (through paragraph 7-119) of the text.

To Complete This Chapter

☐ Review the Key Terms Used In The Chapter on page 246 of the text. Consult the Glossary for the meaning of any key terms you do not know.

☐ Review the Learning Objectives of the Chapter found on page S-79 of this Study Guide.

☐ As a review, we recommend that you view the PowerPoint Slides for Chapter Seven that are on your Companion CD-ROM. If you do not have access to the Microsoft PowerPoint program, the PowerPoint Viewer program can be installed from the Companion CD-ROM.

Solution to Chapter Seven Exercises

Exercise Seven - 1 Solution

The correct classes for each of the assets would be as follows:

Asset	Class
Taxicab	16
Manufacturing and processing equipment	43
Franchise with a limited life	14
Passenger vehicle with a cost of $120,000*	10.1
Water storage tank	6
Photocopy machine	8
Leasehold improvements	13
Rental building*	1

*These two assets would have to be allocated to separate classes.

Exercise Seven - 2 Solution

CCA should have been $48,900 [($326,000)(1/2)(30%)]. The amount recorded was $6,520 [($326,000)(1/2)(4%)]. This error understated deductions and overstated income by $42,380 ($48,900 - $6,520).

Exercise Seven - 3 Solution

The CCA for 2005 on the 2000 capital costs would be $3,467 [($52,000 ÷ 15)]. The CCA on the 2005 capital costs, after taking into consideration the half-year rules, would be $1,550 [($31,000 ÷ 10)(1/2)]. The total for the year would be $5,017 ($3,467 + $1,550).

Exercise Seven - 4 Solution

The required information would be calculated as follows:

January 1, 2005 UCC Balance	$212,000
Additions	37,400
Dispositions	(18,300)
One-Half Net Additions [(50%)($37,400 - $18,300)]	(9,550)
CCA Base	$221,550
2005 CCA At 20 Percent	(44,310)
One-Half Net Additions	9,550
January 1, 2006 UCC Balance	$186,790

Exercise Seven - 5 Solution

The maximum CCA for the year is $4,821 [(20%)($115,000)(1/2)(153/365)].

Exercise Seven - 6 Solution

Following the rule that, when less than the maximum CCA is to be deducted, the amounts deducted should be taken from the class(es) with the lowest rates, the required calculations would be as follows:

Required Total		$45,000
Maximum CCA - Class 1 [(4%)($426,000)]	($17,040)	
Maximum CCA - Class 8 [(20%)($126,000)]	(25,200)	(42,240)
Required Balance		$ 2,760

Solution to Chapter Seven Exercises

As they are both 30 percent declining balance classes, the remaining $2,760 could be taken from either Class 10 or Class 10.1. It would be advisable to use Class 10.1, as recapture is not recorded for this class. In addition, if the Class 10.1 vehicle is going to be disposed of in the near future, it could be better tax planning to take the maximum CCA for Class 10.1 of $6,300 [(30%)($21,000)] and reduce the Class 8 CCA to $21,660 ($45,000 - $6,300 - $17,040). Since there is no recapture for Class 10.1, this could increase future deductions of the other classes. Whether this would be advantageous would depend on the anticipated proceeds of disposition.

Exercise Seven - 7 Solution
For accounting purposes, there would be a gain of $82,500, the full amount of which would be included in accounting Net Income. For tax purposes, there would be a capital gain of $29,000 ($126,000 - $97,000), of which one-half, or $14,500, would be included in income. The capital cost of $97,000 would be subtracted from the UCC, leaving a balance of $2,365,000. While this disposition would reduce the maximum CCA for the current and subsequent years, there would be no recapture (the balance in Class 8 is still positive) or terminal loss (there are still assets in Class 8).

Exercise Seven - 8 Solution
The effect would be an addition of $2,117 ($24,883 - $27,000) in recaptured CCA. While there would also be a taxable capital gain of $750 [($28,500 - $27,000)(1/2)], this would not be included in Subdivision b's net business income.

Exercise Seven - 9 Solution
As there is a positive balance in Class 8 at the end of the year, but no remaining assets, there would be a terminal loss of $6,883 ($24,883 - $18,000). This loss is fully deductible against other income.

Exercise Seven - 10 Solution
Photocopiers would be included in Class 8, a 20 percent declining balance class. If no election is made, there will be a deduction for CCA of $23,800 [($200,000 - $6,000 + $44,000)(1/2)(20%)]. Alternatively, if each machine is allocated to a separate class, there will be a deduction for CCA of $20,400 {[(8)($20,000) + (2)($22,000)][1/2][20%]}. In addition, there will be a terminal loss of $34,000 [($20,000 - $3,000)(2)]. The use of the election increases the total deductible amount by $30,600.

Exercise Seven - 11 Solution
In the absence of the special rules, there would be a capital gain of $325,000 ($750,000 - $425,000) on the land. The $162,500 [(1/2)($325,000)] taxable amount would be reduced by the $115,000 ($615,000 - $500,000) terminal loss on the building, resulting in a net income inclusion of $47,500 ($162,500 - $115,000). ITA 13(21.1)(a) modifies the results in such situations by deeming the proceeds of disposition for the building to be the lesser of:

FMV Of Land And Building	$1,250,000	
Reduced By The Lesser Of:		
The ACB And The FMV Of The Land	(425,000)	$825,000
The Greater Of:		
The FMV Of Building ($500,000)		
The Lesser Of Its Cost And UCC ($615,000)		$615,000

With the building proceeds at $615,000, the terminal loss is eliminated. The deemed proceeds for the land are $635,000 ($1,250,000 - $615,000), resulting in a capital gain of $210,000 ($635,000 - $425,000). In effect, this eliminates the terminal loss of $115,000 by reducing the capital gain by the same amount, from $325,000 to $210,000. The net income inclusion would be $105,000 [(1/2)($210,000)], an increase of $57,500 ($105,000 - $47,500) from the unadjusted result.

Exercise Seven - 12 Solution

The Company would have to record recapture of $750,000 ($650,000 - $1,400,000) for 2004. This is reversed during 2005 by electing under ITA 13(4). The result is that the UCC of the new building would be limited to $1,600,000 ($2,350,000 - $750,000).

Exercise Seven - 13 Solution

The amount that will be added to the UCC balance is $147,000 [$111,000 + (1/2)($183,000 - $111,000)]. The maximum CCA of $7,400 [(15%)($147,000)(1/2)(245/365)] involves both the half-year rule and the short fiscal period procedures.

Exercise Seven - 14 Solution

The required income inclusion can be calculated as follows:

	CEC Balance	CEC Deductions
2003 CEC Addition [(3/4)($85,600)]	$64,200	
2003 CEC Amount At 7 Percent	(4,494)	$4,494
Balance January 1, 2004	$59,706	
2004 CEC Amount At 7 Percent	(4,179)	4,179
Balance January 1, 2005	$55,527	
Proceeds From Sale [(3/4)($93,400)]	(70,050)	
Balance After Sale	($14,523)	$8,673

The negative balance in the CEC account after the sale is more than the total of the CEC deductions in the past two years ($8,673). Given this, the income inclusion will be as follows:

- $8,673 (the CEC deducted), plus
- $3,900 [(2/3)($14,523 - $8,673)].

As a result, $12,573 ($8,673 + $3,900) will be included in income in 2005. Note that the $3,900 income inclusion could also be calculated by taking one-half of the gain (similar to capital gains treatment) on the disposition [$3,900 = (1/2)($93,400 - $85,600)].

Exercise Seven - 15 Solution

The following table compares the balance in the CEC account assuming the election is not made with the balance assuming the election is made:

	No Election	With Election
2005 Addition [(3/4)($514,000)]	$385,500	$385,500
2005 CEC Amount [($385,500)(7%)]	(26,985)	(26,985)
January 1, 2006 CEC Balance	$358,515	$358,515
Proceeds Of Sale [(3/4)($296,000)]	(222,000)	Nil
Deemed Proceeds Of Sale [(3/4)($223,000)]	Nil	(167,250)
Balance After Sale	$136,515	$191,265

If no election is made, there will be no income inclusion and the only tax consequence of the disposition is a reduction in the current and future CEC amounts.

If an election is made, there would be a capital gain of $73,000 ($296,000 - $223,000), resulting in an income inclusion of $36,500 [(1/2)($73,000)].

Solution to Self Study Problem Seven - 1

The maximum 2005 deduction for CCA and the January 1, 2006 UCC can be calculated as follows:

	Class 8	Class 10	Class 1
Opening Balance	$ 96,000	$ 6,700	$115,000
Additions	52,000	8,000	-0-
Dispositions	(35,000)	(20,000)	(110,000)
One-Half Net Additions	(8,500)	N/A	N/A
CCA Base	$104,500	($ 5,300)	$ 5,000
CCA	(20,900)		
One-Half Net Additions	8,500		
Recapture		5,300	
Terminal Loss			(5,000)
January 1, 2006 UCC Balance	$ 92,100	Nil	Nil

Class 8 The CCA for Class 8 is $20,900 [(20%)($104,500)].

Class 10 As the cost of the used car is less than $30,000, its cost is added to Class 10. With respect to the retirement, only the capital cost of the truck sold is deducted from Class 10. The excess of the $25,000 proceeds over the capital cost of $20,000 is a $5,000 capital gain, one-half of which would be taxable. The $12,000 net deduction creates a negative balance in the class and, as a consequence, no CCA will be taken for 2005. However, the negative balance of $5,300 will have to be taken into income as recapture.

Class 1 In Class 1, since the building sold is the last asset in the class, there is a terminal loss of $5,000. Since the land that the building was situated on was leased, the special rules on dispositions of buildings at a loss do not apply.

Summary Results The preceding results can be summarized as follows:

CCA - Class 8	($20,900)
Recapture - Class 10	5,300
Terminal Loss - Class 1	(5,000)
Subtotal	($20,600)
Taxable Capital Gain - Class 10 [(1/2)($25,000 - $20,000)]	2,500
Decrease In Net Income For Tax Purposes	($18,100)

Solution to Self Study Problem Seven - 2

2000 Solution The required calculations are as follows:

Additions To Class [(20 Cars)($12,000)]	$240,000
One-Half Net Additions [(1/2)($240,000)]	(120,000)
CCA Base	$120,000
CCA [($120,000)(30%)(122/365)]	(12,033)
One-Half Net Additions	120,000
January 1, 2001 UCC Balance	$227,967

Note that one-half of the net additions for the year is deducted to provide the basis for calculating the 2000 CCA, and then added back to establish the opening UCC base for the next period. The other point that is illustrated in this first year is application of the short fiscal period rules. As the business was established on September 1, 2000, its operations were carried out for only 122 of the 365 days in that year. This means that only a proportionate share of the annual CCA charge may be taken. Note that it is the length of the taxation year, not the period of ownership of the assets, that establishes the fraction of the year for which CCA is to be recorded.

2001 Solution   The required calculations are as follows:

Opening Balance For The Class	$227,967
Additions [(5 Cars)($12,500)]	62,500
Dispositions (Proceeds)	(27,500)
One-Half Net Additions [(1/2)($62,500 - $27,500)]	(17,500)
CCA Base	$245,467
CCA At 30 Percent	(73,640)
One-Half Net Additions	17,500
January 1, 2002 UCC Balance	$189,327

Here again, one-half of the net additions for the year are deducted in establishing the base for calculating CCA, with the same amount being added back to determine the opening UCC for the next period.

2002 Solution   The required calculations are as follows:

Opening Balance For The Class	$189,327
Dispositions (Proceeds)	(38,000)
CCA Base	$151,327
CCA At 30 Percent	(45,398)
January 1, 2003 UCC Balance	$105,929

The calculations are simplified by the absence of additions to the delivery car fleet. To establish the CCA base, it is only necessary to deduct the proceeds of the dispositions. The new UCC is the CCA base, less the CCA for the period.

2003 Solution   The required calculations are as follows:

Opening Balance For The Class	$105,929
Dispositions (Proceeds)	(128,000)
Negative Balance	($ 22,071)
Recapture	22,071
January 1, 2004 UCC Balance	$ -0-

The inability to replace the fleet cars in a timely fashion was a costly mistake in that the $22,071 in recapture will be included in the 2003 Net Income. In a more realistic situation, it is likely that actions would have been taken to delay the retirement of the older cars and, thereby, avoid the tax implications of recapture. There is no election available to defer the recapture as the election would only apply if the voluntarily replaced property was real property. Note also that when recapture occurs, the balance in the class for the next period is reduced to zero.

2004 Solution   The required calculations are as follows:

Opening Balance For The Class	$ -0-
Acquisitions [(25 Cars)($16,000)]	400,000
One-Half Net Additions [(1/2)($400,000)]	(200,000)
CCA Base	$200,000
CCA At 30 Percent	(60,000)
One-Half Net Additions	200,000
January 1, 2005 UCC Balance	$340,000

As was the case in 2000 and 2001, one-half of the net additions must be deducted in establishing the base for CCA and then added back to determine the opening UCC balance for the next period.

2005 Solution   The required calculations are as follows:

Opening Balance For The Class	$340,000
Dispositions (Proceeds)	(268,000)
Terminal Loss	$ 72,000

At this point, all of the assets in Class 10 have been retired and there is still a $72,000 UCC balance. This results in a terminal loss that will be deducted in full from the Net Income of Golden Dragon Ltd.

Solution to Self Study Problem Seven - 3

Part A   The required calculation of the maximum CCA is as follows:

	Class 1	Class 8	Class 10
Opening Balance	$876,000	$220,000	$163,000
Additions	-0-	-0-	122,000
Proceeds Of Disposition	-0-	-0-	(87,000)
One-Half Net Additions	-0-	-0-	(17,500)
CCA Base	$876,000	$220,000	$180,500
CCA Rate	4%	20%	30%
Maximum CCA	$ 35,040	$ 44,000	$ 54,150

This gives a maximum amount for CCA of $133,190 for the taxation year.

Part B   Since Marion Enterprises only has 2005 Net and Taxable Income before CCA of $53,000, the business may wish to deduct less than the maximum CCA that is available to them. However, there is no question that the business will wish to deduct the $53,000 that is required to reduce the current year's Taxable Income to nil.

Assuming the 2005 CCA deduction is limited to $53,000, it would normally be deducted in the class or classes with the lowest rates. This would leave the unused amounts in classes with higher rates which, in turn, would maximize the amount that could be deducted in the first profitable years. Taking this approach, the $53,000 would be deducted as follows:

Class 1 (Maximum Available)	$35,040
Class 8 (Required Balance)	17,960
Total CCA	$53,000

This CCA deduction would reduce 2005 Taxable Income to nil.

Part C   It would be advisable to deduct an additional $46,000. This would create a business loss in 2005 of $46,000, which could then be carried back to claim refunds of taxes paid in the three preceding years.

Beyond the deduction of $99,000 ($53,000 + $46,000), the solution to the problem becomes less clear cut. If additional CCA is taken, it will serve to create a business loss that can only be deducted as a carry forward over the next 10 years. If there is not sufficient Taxable Income in the next 10 years to absorb this carry over, the benefit of the loss will not be realized. Given the uncertainty expressed about profits for the next 11 to 13 years, the prudent course of action may be to only deduct 2005 CCA of $99,000. However, the alternatives here should be explained and discussed with management.

Assuming the 2005 CCA deduction is limited to $99,000, it would normally be deducted in the class or classes with the lowest rates. This would leave the unused amounts in classes with higher rates which, in turn, would maximize the amount that could be deducted in the first profitable years. Taking this approach, the $99,000 would be deducted as follows:

Class 1 (Maximum Available)	$35,040
Class 8 (Maximum Available)	44,000
Class 10 (Required Balance)	19,960
Total CCA	$99,000

This CCA deduction would reduce 2005 Taxable Income to nil and would create an unused business loss carry back of $46,000.

Solution to Self Study Problem Seven - 4

Class 1 - Building   There were no additions or dispositions in this class. As a consequence, the maximum CCA would be $25,000 [(4%)($625,000)]. The January 1, 2006 UCC of Class 1 would be $600,000.

Class 8 - Office Furniture And Equipment   The required calculations for this class would be as follows:

Opening Balance	$155,000
Additions During Fiscal Year	27,000
Dispositions During Fiscal Year	(22,000)
One-Half Net Additions	(2,500)
CCA Base	$157,500
Capital Cost Allowance (20%)	(31,500)
One-Half Net Additions	2,500
January 1, 2006 UCC Balance	$128,500

With respect to the disposition during the year, there would be a capital gain of $13,000 ($35,000 - $22,000), one-half of which is taxable. Only the capital cost of $22,000 is deducted from the UCC of the class.

Class 10 - Vehicles   The required calculations for this class would be as follows:

Opening Balance	$118,000
Additions During Fiscal Year	33,000
Dispositions During Fiscal Year ($8,500 + $8,000)	(16,500)
One-Half Net Additions	(8,250)
CCA Base	$126,250
Capital Cost Allowance (30%)	(37,875)
One-Half Net Additions	8,250
January 1, 2006 UCC Balance	$ 96,625

Note that the amount received from the insurance company on the destroyed vehicle is treated as proceeds from a disposition.

Class 12 - Tools   The tools are eligible for a write-off rate of 100 percent, and they are not subject to the half-year rules on net additions. As a consequence, the entire $34,000 can be deducted as CCA for the current year, leaving no January 1, 2006 balance in the account.

Class 13 - Leasehold Improvements   In general, leasehold improvements will be written off over the term of the lease on a straight line basis. For purposes of applying this calculation, the term of the lease would include the first renewal option, beginning in a period after the improvements were made. In the case of the original improvements, the period to be used is 12 years. With respect to the improvements during the current year, the write-off period will be 9 years. Also note that Class 13 assets are subject to the half-year rules on net additions. The required calculations are as follows:

Opening Balance	$ 61,750
Additions	45,000
CCA Base	$106,750
Capital Cost Allowance:	
First Improvements ($78,000 ÷ 12)	(6,500)
Current Improvements [($45,000 ÷ 9)(1/2)]	(2,500)
January 1, 2006 UCC Balance	$ 97,750

Class 43 - Manufacturing Equipment   The required calculations are as follows:

Opening Balance	$217,000
Dispositions (Proceeds)	(188,000)
Terminal Loss	$ 29,000

At this point, all of the assets in Class 43 have been retired and there is still a $29,000 UCC balance. This results in a terminal loss that will be deducted in full from the Net Income of Atlantic Manufacturing Company.

Class 45 - Computers   The rate for Class 45 is 45 percent and the class is subject to the first year rules. The required calculations for this class would be as follows:

Opening Balance	Nil
Additions During Fiscal Year	$28,000
One-Half Net Additions	(14,000)
CCA Base	$14,000
Capital Cost Allowance (45%)	(6,300)
One-Half Net Additions	14,000
January 1, 2006 UCC Balance	$ 21,700

Cumulative Eligible Capital   The required calculations for the sale of the licence would be as follows:

Opening Balance	$ -0-
Proceeds Of Disposition [($87,000)(3/4)]	(65,250)
Balance	($65,250)
Addition To Balance	65,250
January 1, 2006 Balance	$ - 0 -

The proceeds are based on 75 percent of the amount received. Therefore, 75 percent of the proceeds of $87,000 would be deducted, thereby creating a negative balance for cumulative eligible capital in the amount of $65,250. As no CEC has been deducted in previous years, the entire negative balance in the cumulative eligible capital account would be multiplied by two-thirds (1/2 ÷ 3/4), resulting in an income inclusion of $43,500. In effect, the entire $87,000 proceeds is being given capital gains treatment, with only one-half of this amount being included in income. The $65,250 will also be added back to the CEC balance, restoring the balance to nil.

Summary Of The Results   The maximum CCA for the year and the January 1, 2006 UCC balances can be summarized as follows:

	Maximum CCA	January 1, 2006 UCC
Class 1	$ 25,000	$600,000
Class 8	31,500	128,500
Class 10	37,875	96,625
Class 12	34,000	-0-
Class 13	9,000	97,750
Class 43	Nil	Nil
Class 45	6,300	21,700

In addition, the following income effects resulted from the information provided in the problem:

Taxable Capital Gain On Class 8 Assets [(1/2)($13,000)]	$ 6,500
Terminal Loss On Class 43 Assets	(29,000)
Income From License Sale [(2/3)($65,250)]	43,500
Total Inclusion	$210,000

Solution to Self Study Problem Seven - 5

The required schedule showing the relevant balances in the cumulative eligible capital account would be as follows:

	CEC Balance	CEC Deductions
2002 Addition [(3/4)($500,000)]	$375,000	
2002 CEC Amount At 7 Percent	(26,250)	$26,250
CEC Balance, January 1, 2003	$348,750	
2003 CEC Amount At 7 Percent	(24,413)	24,413
CEC Balance, January 1, 2004	$324,337	
2004 CEC Amount At 7 Percent	(22,704)	22,704
CEC Balance, January 1, 2005	$301,633	
Proceeds From Sale [(3/4)($780,000)]	(585,000)	
Balance After Sale	($283,367)	$73,367

As can be seen in the preceding table, $73,367 of the negative balance reflects CEC deductions that have been made in previous years. This full amount will have to be included in 2005 income. The remaining $210,000 ($283,367 - $73,367) reflects three-quarters of the $280,000 ($780,000 - $500,000) gain on the disposition. This will have to be converted to the one-half capital gains inclusion rate by multiplying by two-thirds, which will result in a further income inclusion in 2005 of $140,000 [(2/3)($210,000)]. This gives a total 2005 income inclusion of $213,367 ($73,367 + $140,000).

Chapter Seven Learning Objectives

After completing Chapter 7, you should be able to:

1. Describe the differences between the accounting procedures used for depreciable assets and the tax procedures used for these assets (paragraphs 7-1 through 7-10).

2. Determine the types of costs that are included in the amounts that are added to depreciable asset classes (paragraphs 7-11 through 7-19).

3. Demonstrate an understanding of the available for use rules (paragraphs 7-20 through 7-22).

4. Recall the general rules for segregating depreciable assets into classes (paragraphs 7-23 through 7-25).

5. Recall the types of assets that must be allocated to separate classes (paragraph 7-26).

6. Demonstrate an understanding of the basic elements of the CCA system (paragraphs 7-27 and 7-28).

7. Recall the rates and methods that are applicable to common CCA classes in order to determine the maximum CCA for the period (paragraph 7-29).

8. Apply the first year rules in the determination of maximum CCA for the period (paragraphs 7-30 through 7-34).

9. Apply the short fiscal period rules in the determination of maximum CCA for the period (paragraphs 7-35 through 7-38).

10. Explain the tax planning considerations that are involved when a business takes less than maximum CCA (paragraphs 7-39 through 7-43).

11. Determine the tax consequences associated with dispositions of depreciable assets, including recapture, terminal losses, and capital gains (paragraphs 7-44 through 7-61).

12. Apply the provisions relating to separate class elections (paragraphs 7-62 through 7-69).

13. Apply the replacement property rules associated with voluntary and involuntary dispositions of depreciable assets (paragraphs 7-70 through 7-85).

14. Determine the tax consequences of changing the use of a depreciable asset (paragraphs 7-86 through 7-95).

15. Apply the provisions relating to eligible capital expenditures (paragraphs 7-96 through 7-115).

16. Apply the provisions relating to the listed special situations (paragraphs 7-116 through 7-119).

CHAPTER EIGHT

How To Work Through Chapter Eight

We recommend the following approach in dealing with the material in this chapter:

Defining Business Income
☐ Read pages 259 (from paragraph 8-1) and 260 (through paragraph 8-4) of the text.

Business Income Vs. Capital Gains
☐ Read pages 260 (from paragraph 8-5) and 261 (through paragraph 8-10) of the text.

☐ Complete Exercise Eight-1. The Exercise is on page 261 of the text. The solution is on page S-84 of this Study Guide.

Business Income And GAAP
☐ Read pages 262 (from paragraph 8-11) and 263 (through paragraph 8-13) of the text.

Inclusions - Amounts Received And Receivable
☐ Read page 263 (paragraphs 8-14 and 8-15) of the text.

Reserves - The General System
☐ Read pages 263 (from paragraph 8-16) and 264 (through paragraph 8-19) of the text.

Reserves For Bad Debts
☐ Read page 264 (paragraphs 8-20 through 8-23) of the text.

☐ Complete Exercise Eight-2. The Exercise is on pages 264 and 265 of the text. The solution is on page S-84 of this Study Guide.

Reserves For Undelivered Goods And Services
☐ Read page 265 (paragraph 8-24) of the text.

☐ Complete Exercise Eight-3. The Exercise is on page 265 of the text. The solution is on page S-84 of this Study Guide.

Reserves For Unpaid Amounts
☐ Read page 265 (paragraph 8-25) of the text.

☐ Complete Exercise Eight-4. The Exercise is on page 266 of the text. The solution is on page S-84 of this Study Guide.

Other Inclusions
☐ Read page 266 (paragraphs 8-26 and 8-27) of the text.

Restrictions On Deductions From Business And Property Income
☐ Read pages 266 (from paragraph 8-28) through 270 (through paragraph 8-53) of the text.

☐ Complete Exercise Eight-5. The Exercise is on page 270 of the text. The solution is on page S-84 of this Study Guide.

☐ Read pages 270 (from paragraph 8-54) through 272 (through paragraph 8-66) of the text.

Restrictions On Deductions From Business, Property, And Employment Income

☐ Read pages 273 (from paragraph 8-67) and 274 (through paragraph 8-79) of the text.

☐ Complete Exercise Eight-6. The Exercise is on page 275 of the text. The solution is on page S-84 of this Study Guide.

☐ Read pages 275 (from paragraph 8-80) and 276 (through paragraph 8-84) of the text.

☐ Complete Exercise Eight-7. The Exercise is on page 277 of the text. The solution is on page S-85 of this Study Guide.

Leasing Property

☐ Read page 277 (paragraphs 8-85 through 8-88) of the text.

☐ Complete Exercise Eight-8. The Exercise is on page 277 of the text. The solution is on page S-85 of this Study Guide.

Restrictions On Claiming Input Tax Credits

☐ Read page 278 (paragraph 8-89) of the text.

Specific Deductions From Business Income

☐ Read pages 278 (from paragraph 8-90) and 279 (through paragraph 8-96) of the text.

☐ Complete Exercise Eight-9. The Exercise is on page 279 of the text. The solution is on page S-85 of this Study Guide.

☐ Read pages 279 and 280 (paragraph 8-97) of the text.

Reconciliation Of Accounting Net Income And Net Income For Tax Purposes

☐ Read pages 281 (from paragraph 8-98) through 283 (through paragraph 8-103) of the text.

Taxation Year

☐ Read pages 283 (from paragraph 8-104) and 284 (through paragraph 8-110) of the text.

Income For Farmers

☐ Read pages 284 (from paragraph 8-111) and 285 (through paragraph 8-116) of the text.

☐ Complete Exercise Eight-10. The Exercise is on page 285 of the text. The solution is on page S-85 of this Study Guide.

☐ Read pages 285 (from paragraph 8-117) and 286 (through paragraph 8-120) of the text.

Income For Professionals

☐ Read pages 286 (from paragraph 8-121) and 287 (through paragraph 8-122) of the text.

☐ Complete Exercise Eight-11. The Exercise is on page 287 of the text. The solution is on page S-85 of this Study Guide.

Scientific Research And Experimental Development

☐ Read page 287 (paragraphs 8-123 through 8-126) of the text.

Ceasing To Carry On A Business

☐ Read pages 287 (from paragraph 8-127) and 288 (through paragraph 8-132) of the text.

☐ Complete Exercise Eight-12. The Exercise is on page 289 of the text. The solution is on page S-85 of this Study Guide.

☐ Complete Self Study Problems Eight-1 through Eight-5. The problems are on pages 297 through 302 of the text. The solutions are on pages S-85 through S-91 of this Study Guide.

If The Appendix To Chapter 8 (Overview Of Corporate Tax) Has Been Assigned

☐ Read the Appendix To Chapter 8 on pages 291 (from paragraph 8A-1) through 296 (through paragraph 8A-37) of the text.

To Complete This Chapter

☐ Review the Key Terms Used In The Chapter on page 289 of the text. Consult the Glossary for the meaning of any key terms you do not know.

☐ Review the Learning Objectives of the Chapter found on page S-92 of this Study Guide.

☐ As a review, we recommend that you view the PowerPoint Slides for Chapter Eight that are on your Companion CD-ROM. If you do not have access to the Microsoft PowerPoint program, the PowerPoint Viewer program can be installed from the Companion CD-ROM.

Solution to Chapter Eight Exercises

Exercise Eight - 1 Solution
Provided that she can demonstrate that her intent was to operate the building as a rental property, the gain should qualify as a capital gain.

Exercise Eight - 2 Solution
The net decrease for the year will be $19,600 ($16,000 - $17,200 - $18,400).

Exercise Eight - 3 Solution
The amount to be included in net business income would be calculated as follows:

Cash Sales	$53,400
Accounts Receivable	26,300
Reserve For Undelivered Services	(5,600)
Reserve For Bad Debts	(425)
Net Business Income	$73,675

Exercise Eight - 4 Solution
As some of the proceeds are not receivable for more than two years, a reserve can be deducted under ITA 20(1)(n). The maximum reserve, based on the gross profit of $65,000, for each of the five years would be as follows:

2005 [(100%)($65,000)]	$65,000
2006 [(75%)($65,000)]	48,750
2007 [(50%)($65,000)]	32,500
2008	Nil
2009	Nil

As December 31, 2008 is more than 36 months after the sale was made, no reserve can be deducted for 2008 or 2009.

Exercise Eight - 5 Solution
As Ms. Johnson owns 30 percent of the common shares, she is clearly a specified shareholder. Her relevant equity balance would be $1,620,000 [(30%)($2,400,000) + (100%)($900,000)]. Given this, the disallowed interest would be calculated as follows:

Total Interest Paid To Ms. Johnson [(9%)($4,500,000)]	$405,000
Maximum Deductible Interest [(9%)(2)($1,620,000)]	(291,600)
Disallowed Interest	$113,400

Exercise Eight - 6 Solution
With respect to the amount of CCA, since the business commenced operations on September 15, 2005, the CCA is limited to the proportion of the year the business was in operation (108/365) and the first year rules would apply. The base amount for the CCA calculation is limited to the Class 10.1 maximum of $30,000. With respect to the interest, the car was financed for a total of 108 days with a limit of $10 per day. As a result, the amounts that can be deducted are as follows:

CCA [(1/2)(108/365)(30%)($30,000)]	$1,332
Interest Costs [($10)(108 Days)]	1,080
Total Deduction	$2,412

Exercise Eight - 7 Solution

The amount he can deduct is limited to $2,229, the least of:

- $4,925 [($985)(5)];
- $4,080 [($800)(153/30)]; and
- $2,229 {[$4,925][$30,000 ÷ (85%)($78,000)]}.

Exercise Eight - 8 Solution

For tax purposes, the lease would be treated as an operating lease, with the deduction being based only on the lease payments. Under GAAP, the lease would have to be treated as a purchase (capitalized). This is because the lease term is more than 75 percent of the asset's expected useful life. This means that the accounting deductions would be for amortization on the capitalized asset and interest costs on the associated liability.

Exercise Eight - 9 Solution

The required adjustment will be an addition of $2,300 ($13,500 - $11,200) to cost of sales, with a corresponding reduction in net business income.

Exercise Eight - 10 Solution

Ms. Morph appears to be a part-time farmer and, as a consequence, her farm losses will be restricted. Since her loss is greater than $15,000, the amount she can deduct for 2005 will be limited to $8,750 [$2,500 + (1/2)($15,000 maximum - $2,500)]. The remaining $9,950 ($18,700 - $8,750) restricted farm loss is available for carry over.

Exercise Eight - 11 Solution

Mr. Winters' income for the current year under the three alternatives would be as follows:

Cash Basis The cash basis income would be $252,000 ($35,000 + $57,000 + $160,000).

Billed Basis The billed basis income would be $220,000 ($35,000 + $185,000).

Accrual Basis The accrual basis income would be $245,000.

Exercise Eight - 12 Solution

The tax effect for Mr. Donato would be a net deduction in the determination of business income of $1,450 [$3,800 - ($53,450 - $48,200)]. Mr. Labelle would have to include the $5,250 ($53,450 - $48,200) difference between the face value and the price paid in income. Subsequent to the sale, any difference between the $53,450 face value of the receivables and amounts actually collected will be fully deductible in the calculation of net business income.

Solution to Self Study Problem Eight - 1

Part A   In Part A(i), Ms. Wise is an employee and, because her income includes commissions, she can deduct expenses related to the production of employment income under ITA 8(1)(f), provided no deduction is made for traveling expenses (including automobile costs other than capital costs) under ITA 8(1)(h) or ITA 8(1)(h.1). Deductions under ITA 8(1)(f) are limited to the amount of commissions earned. Alternatively, traveling costs can be deducted under ITA 8(1)(h) and ITA 8(1)(h.1) without being limited to commission income. A further limitation, which is not illustrated in this problem, prevents the deduction of home office costs from creating an employment loss. The deduction of dues and other expenses under ITA 8(1)(i) and automobile capital costs under ITA 8(1)(j) is permitted without regard to other provisions used.

Solution to Self Study Problem Eight - 1

The first column of the solution that follows calculates the available deduction using ITA 8(1)(h), (h.1), (i), and (j). Note that when this approach is used, home office costs are limited to utilities and maintenance. Further, there is no deduction for entertainment costs. This provides for a total deduction of $32,925.

The second and third columns calculate the available deductions under ITA 8(1)(i) and (j), as well as separately under ITA 8(1)(f). The deduction for home office costs has been split between ITA 8(1)(i) and (f). Since the maintenance portion can be deducted under ITA 8(1)(i), it is not limited by the commission income. The insurance and property tax components are limited as they are deducted under ITA 8(1)(f).

As the ITA 8(1)(f) amount is limited to the $15,000 in commission income, the total deduction is $22,975 ($7,975 + $15,000), $9,950 less than the amount available using ITA 8(1)(h), (h.1), (i), and (j). Of the non-deductible costs arising under this approach, the $2,260 ($380 + $1,880) in home office costs can be carried forward to be deducted under ITA 8(1)(f) in a subsequent year.

| | Part A(i) | Part A(i) | | Part A(ii) |
	ITA 8(1)(h), (h.1), (i), and (j)	ITA 8(1) (i) and (j)	ITA 8(1)(f)	
Professional Dues	$ 600	$ 600		$ 600
Automobile Costs:				
Operating Costs [(35,000/50,000)($8,500)]	5,950		$5,950	5,950
CCA (Note One)	5,355	5,355		5,355
Home Office Costs:				
Utilities [(40%)($3,550)]	1,420	1,420		1,420
Maintenance [(40%)($1,500)]	600	600		600
Insurance [(40%)($950)]			380	380
Property Taxes [(40%)($4,700)]			1,880	1,880
Interest [(40%)($13,500)]				5,400
CCA [($120,000)(4%)(40%)]				1,920
Travel Costs	23,000		23,000	23,000
Non-Deductible Meals [(50%)($8,000)]	(4,000)		(4,000)	(4,000)
Entertainment Expenses			12,000	12,000
Non-Deductible (Note Two)			(7,250)	(7,250)
Total	$32,925	$7,975	$31,960	$47,255

Note One The car will be allocated to Class 10.1 at a value of $30,000, the 2004 limit. The excess of $3,000 will not be deductible. Maximum CCA for 2004 would have been $4,500 [(30%)(1/2)($30,000)]. The January 1, 2005 UCC would be $25,500 ($30,000 - $4,500) and 2005 CCA equals $5,355 [(30%)($25,500)(70%)]. Her 2004 business usage would not be relevant as the maximum CCA would be deducted from the UCC, but only the portion of CCA related to her business use of the car would be deducted from employment or business income.

Note Two The non-deductible costs charged by the local country club are as follows:

Membership Dues	$2,500
Entertainment Costs [(50%)($9,500)]	4,750
Total Non-Deductible	$7,250

Comparing Parts A (i) and A (ii), there is a difference of $14,330 ($47,255 - $32,925) between the maximum employee and self-employed calculations, illustrating the importance of the difference between being an employee and being self-employed. This problem is, of course, somewhat unrealistic in that, if Ms. Wise was an employee, it is likely that she would be compensated or reimbursed for at least part of her employment related expenses.

Part B The deduction of CCA would be virtually certain to trigger recapture and capital gains on a proportionate part of her personal residence when it is eventually sold. While taxation on capital gains might occur even if no CCA is taken, the deduction of CCA makes taxes on a proportionate part of recapture and capital gains virtually certain.

Solution to Self Study Problem Eight - 2

The required calculations would be as follows:

Accounting Net Income		$298,000
Additions:		
LIFO Excess ($296,000 - $271,000) (Item 1)	$ 25,000	
Increase In Warranty Reserve (Item 2)	14,500	
Income Tax Expense (Item 3)	158,000	
Depreciation Expense (Item 5)	53,750	
Contributions To Registered Charity (Item 7)	4,300	
Life Insurance Premium (Item 10)	3,100	
Golf Club Membership (Item 12)	1,400	
50% Of Business Meals (50% of $3,400) (Item 12)	1,700	
Cost Of Amending Articles (Note One) (Item 13)	14,300	
Appraisal Costs (Note Two) (Item 14)	7,400	
Stock Issue Costs (Note Three) (Item 15)	12,480	295,930
Subtotal		$593,930
Deduction:		
Bond Premium Amortization (Item 11)		(5,900)
Net Income For Tax Purposes		$588,030

Note One The cost of amending the Company's articles would be considered an eligible capital expenditure, three-quarters of which would be added to cumulative eligible capital.

Note Two The fees paid to appraise certain Company assets for sale would be added to the adjusted cost base of these assets.

Note Three ITA 20(1)(e) requires the deduction of stock issue costs over a five year period at a rate of 20 percent per year. For the current year, 80% of the total stock issue costs of $15,600 are non-deductible and added to accounting Net Income.

Other Items Further explanation related to the items not included in the preceding calculation of Net Income For Tax Purposes are as follows:

Item 4 As the landscaping costs have already been deducted in accounting Net Income, they do not require adjustment for tax purposes.

Item 6 While interest on late income tax instalments is clearly not deductible, there does not appear to be a similar prohibition against interest on late property taxes. We would note here that the 2004 budget proposals proposes the elimination of deductibility for all fines and penalties. This would not appear to include interest for late payment of municipal taxes.

Item 8 The tax treatment of such payments would be the same as the accounting treatment.

Item 9 The tax treatment of volume discounts would be the same as the accounting treatment.

Solution to Self Study Problem Eight - 3

The required calculations would be as follows:

Accounting Income Before Taxes		$426,000
Additions:		
Contributions To Charities (Item 2)	$ 2,500	
Contributions To Political Parties (Item 2)	1,000	
LIFO/FIFO Adjustment (Item 3 - Note One)	4,000	
Amortization Expense (Item 4)	241,000	
Amount Paid To Cousin (Item 5 - Note Two)	10,000	
Warranty Reserve (Item 8 - Note Three)	9,000	
Non-Deductible Meals And Entertainment		
(50% Of $13,500) (Item 12)	6,750	
Amortization Of Bond Discount (Item 13)	1,800	
Non-Deductible Lease Payments		
(Item 14 - Note Four)	13,037	289,087
Deductions:		
Capital Cost Allowance (Item 6)	($389,000)	
Issue Costs (Item 10 - Note Five)	(1,600)	
Landscaping Costs (Item 11)	(11,000)	(401,600)
Net Income For Tax Purposes		$313,487

Note One   As LIFO cannot be used for tax purposes, the tax figures will have to be adjusted to a FIFO basis. This will require a $20,000 ($366,000 - $346,000) increase in the opening inventory and a $24,000 ($447,000 -$423,000) increase in the closing inventory. This will reduce cost of goods sold by $4,000 and increase Taxable Income by a corresponding amount.

Note Two   Under ITA 67, this amount would be disallowed as not being reasonable in the circumstances.

Note Three   For tax purposes, warranty costs can only be deducted as incurred. Therefore, the $9,000 ($27,000 - $18,000) increase in the warranty reserve must be added back to accounting income.

Note Four   Under ITA 67.3, the deductible amount of the lease payments is limited to the least of:

- $18,000
- [($800)(365/30)] = $9,733
- {[$18,000][$30,000 ÷ (85%)($128,000)]} = $4,963

The non-deductible portion of the lease payments is $13,037 ($18,000 - $4,963).

Note Five   Under ITA 20(1)(e), issue costs must be amortized at the rate of 20 percent per year. As the full amount was treated as an asset in the accounting records, the required adjustment is a deduction of $1,600 [(20%)($8,000)].

Several of the items described in the problem did not require any adjustment. The explanations for these omissions are as follows:

Item 1   As the accounting income figure is before taxes, no adjustment is required for the estimate of income tax expense.

Item 7   As the advertising was not directed at the Canadian market, it can be deducted for tax purposes and no adjustment is required.

Item 9   As the same bad debt estimates were used for tax purposes and accounting purposes, no adjustment is required with respect to bad debts.

Solution to Self Study Problem Eight - 4

The required calculations would be as follows:

Accounting Income (Loss) Before Taxes	($113,000)
Additions:	
Item 2 - Property Taxes On Recreational Facility	1,100
Item 3 - Donations (Note One)	13,700
Item 6 - Lease Cancellation Payment (Note Two)	17,000
Item 8 - Insurance Premium (Note Three)	9,500
Item 9 - Excess Of FIFO Inventory Value Over LIFO Value	37,200
Item 13 - Renovation Costs (Note Four)	153,000
Item 14 - Wife's Convention Expenses	1,900
Item 15 - Bond Discount Amortization	950
Item 16 - Cost Of Amending Articles (Note Five)	3,600
Item 17 - Non-Deductible Portion Of Meals And Entertainment [(50%)($12,500)]	6,250
Net Income For Tax Purposes	$131,200

Note One   The contributions to registered charities will be deductible in the computation of Taxable Income, but not in the computation of income from a business. Charitable contributions are still a deduction for corporations, although they are eligible for tax credit treatment for individuals. The political contributions are not deductible at any stage, but will generate a credit in determining the amount of Tax Payable.

Note Two   ITA 20(1)(z) requires that lease cancellation payments be amortized over the term of the lease remaining immediately before cancellation. The amount to be deducted is a pro rata calculation based on the number of days remaining subsequent to the cancellation. As the cancellation occurred on December 31, 2005, none of the amount would be deductible during the current year. The $17,000 would be deducted over the seven years that would have remained of the lease term, at the rate of $2,429 per year.

Note Three   Life insurance premiums where the employer is the beneficiary are not considered to be incurred for the purpose of earning income and are therefore not deductible except where they are required by a creditor in relation to financing.

Note Four   These amounts serve to extend the life of the relevant asset and should be treated as capital expenditures.

Note Five   The payment to amend the articles of incorporation would be an eligible capital expenditure and three-quarters of the $3,600 would be added to the cumulative eligible capital amount. The Company would be able to deduct amortization of this amount. However, you have been instructed to ignore such deductions in this problem.

Other Items   Further explanation related to the items not included in the preceding calculation of Net Income For Tax Purposes are as follows:

Item 1   If the damages relate to a transaction that produces business income, they are considered a business expense.

Item 4   Landscaping costs are fully deductible under ITA 20(1)(aa).

Item 5   Losses of this type, unless they result from the activity of senior officers or shareholders, are considered to be deductible as a normal cost of doing business.

Item 7   The bonus to the president would be deductible in 2005.

Item 10   Such appraisal costs are considered to be deductible as a normal cost of doing business.

Item 11 The $51,000 in management bonuses would be deductible in 2005. The forfeited bonuses would be given the same treatment for tax purposes as they were in the accounting records. The $34,000 of unpaid bonuses that were forfeited would result in a denial of the expenses in 2004. As a result, 2004 Taxable Income would increase by $34,000 since the unpaid bonuses were not paid within the 6 month ITA 78(4) deadline.

Item 12 The bad debts would be fully deductible.

Item 14 The $3,300 in costs associated with the president attending the convention would be deductible.

Item 16 Both the costs of defending against the breach of contract action, as well as the costs related to the income tax reassessment, would be fully deductible.

Solution to Self Study Problem Eight - 5

The current year Net Income For Tax Purposes of Darlington Inc. would be calculated as follows:

Accounting Income		$ 596,000
Additions:		
Income Tax Expense	$ 55,000	
LIFO Inventory Adjustment	5,000	
Depreciation Expense	623,000	
Taxable Capital Gain On Class 8 Disposition [($550,000 - $400,000)(1/2)]	75,000	
Non-Deductible Meals And Entertainment [(50%)($41,400)]	20,700	
Club Fees	2,500	
Property Taxes On Vacant Land	15,000	796,200
		$1,392,200
Deductions:		
Landscaping Costs	($ 95,000)	
CCA	(930,500)	
Terminal Loss	(113,000)	
Gain On Class 8 Disposition	(225,000)	(1,363,500)
Net Income For Tax Purposes		$ 28,700

CCA Calculations

Class 1 - Building The new building acquired is a Class 1 property. The half-year rule applies and this gives a maximum CCA amount of $10,500 [($650,000 - $125,000)(1/2)(4%)]. This leaves a January 1, 2006 UCC balance of $514,500 ($650,000 - $125,000 - $10,500).

Class 3 - Building There were no additions or dispositions in this class. As a consequence, the maximum CCA would be $50,000 [(5%)($1,000,000)]. The January 1, 2006 UCC balance is $950,000 ($1,000,000 - $50,000).

Class 8 - Office Furniture And Equipment   The required calculations for this class would be as follows:

January 1, 2005 UCC Balance	$4,200,000
Additions	700,000
Dispositions (Cost)	(400,000)
One-Half Net Additions	(150,000)
CCA Base	$4,350,000
CCA At 20 Percent	(870,000)
One-Half Net Additions	150,000
January 1, 2006 UCC Balance	$3,630,000

With respect to the sale that occurred during the year, there would be a capital gain of $150,000 ($550,000 - $400,000). One-half, or $75,000, is included in the Company's Net Income For Tax Purposes, and the accounting gain of $225,000 is deducted.

Class 10 - Vehicles   All of the cars were sold during the year for proceeds that totalled less than their capital cost and the UCC of the class. The remaining balance in the class of $113,000 ($800,000 - $687,000) is a terminal loss that is fully deductible.

Summary Of The Results   The maximum CCA and January 1, 2006 UCC balances can be summarized as follows:

	Maximum CCA	UCC
Class 1	$ 10,500	$ 514,500
Class 3	50,000	950,000
Class 8	870,000	3,630,000

In addition, there was a taxable capital gain on the sale of the Class 8 assets of $75,000 and a terminal loss in Class 10 of $113,000.

Other Notes

- The cost of goods sold for the year under the LIFO inventory valuation assumption was $5,000 ($20,000 - $15,000) higher than it would have been using FIFO. As a result, this difference must be added to Net Income For Tax Purposes.

- ITA 19.01 provides for the full deduction of advertising costs in foreign periodicals directed at the Canadian market, provided 80 percent or more of their non-advertising content is original editorial content. If the original editorial content is less than 80 percent, the deduction is equal to 50 percent of the costs. Note that this applies only to periodicals and not other print or broadcast media.

- Landscaping costs are fully deductible.

- The property taxes on the vacant land are not deductible. They can be added to the cost of the land if the land was acquired for the purpose of earning either business or property income and may be deducted to the extent of any net income earned on the land.

Chapter Eight Learning Objectives

After completing Chapter 8, you should be able to:

1. Distinguish between business income and capital gains, including the criteria used by the courts in making this distinction (paragraphs 8-1 through 8-10).

2. Describe the major differences between net business income and Net Income as determined under GAAP (paragraphs 8-11 through 8-13).

3. Recall the various items that are included in net business income (paragraphs 8-14 through 8-27).

4. Apply the system of reserves that can be used in determining net business income (paragraphs 8-16 through 8-25).

5. Apply the restrictions on deductions that apply to business or property income only (paragraphs 8-28 through 8-66).

6. Apply the restrictions on deductions that apply to business, property, or employment income (paragraphs 8-67 through 8-88).

7. Recall the restrictions on claiming input tax credits (paragraph 8-89).

8. Apply the inventory valuation procedures that are used for determining net business income (paragraphs 8-90 through 8-96).

9. Recall the deductions that are specified in the *Income Tax Act* for calculating net business income (paragraph 8-97).

10. Be able to reconcile accounting Net Income with net business income (paragraphs 8-98 through 8-103).

11. Recall the rules for determining taxation years (paragraphs 8-104 through 8-110).

12. Apply the special provisions related to farming activities (paragraphs 8-111 through 8-120).

13. Apply the special rules for the income of professionals (paragraphs 8-121 and 8-122).

14. Apply the special rules that apply to scientific research and experimental development expenditures (paragraphs 8-123 through 8-126).

15. Apply the provisions related to the disposition of inventories and accounts receivable in situations where a business is being sold (paragraphs 8-127 through 8-132).

If The Appendix To Chapter 8 (Overview Of Corporate Tax) Has Been Assigned

16. Demonstrate a basic understanding of Taxable Income and Tax Payable for corporations (paragraphs 8A-1 through 8A-37).

CHAPTER NINE

How To Work Through Chapter Nine

We recommend the following approach in dealing with the material in this chapter:

Property Income - General Concept
☐ Read pages 315 (from paragraph 9-1) and 316 (through paragraph 9-4) of the text.

Interest As A Deduction
☐ Read pages 316 (from paragraph 9-5) through 320 (through paragraph 9-33) of the text.

Discount And Premium On Long-Term Issued Debt
☐ Read page 321 (paragraphs 9-34 through 9-37) of the text.

☐ Complete Exercise Nine-1. The Exercise is on page 321 of the text. The solution is on page S-95 of this Study Guide.

☐ Read page 322 (paragraphs 9-38 and 9-39) of the text.

☐ Complete Exercise Nine-2. The Exercise is on page 322 of the text. The solution is on page S-95 of this Study Guide.

Interest Income - General Provisions
☐ Read pages 323 (from paragraph 9-40) and 324 (through paragraph 9-46) of the text.

☐ Complete Exercise Nine-3. The Exercise is on page 324 of the text. The solution is on page S-95 of this Study Guide.

Discount And Premium On Long-Term Debt Holdings
☐ Read page 324 (paragraphs 9-47 and 9-48) of the text.

Prescribed Debt Obligations
☐ Read pages 324 (from paragraph 9-49) and 325 (through paragraph 9-51) of the text.

☐ Complete Exercise Nine-4. The Exercise is on page 325 of the text. The solution is on page S-96 of this Study Guide.

Indexed Debt Obligations
☐ Read page 326 (paragraphs 9-52 and 9-53) of the text.

Accrued Interest At Transfer
☐ Read page 326 (paragraphs 9-54 and 9-55) of the text.

☐ Complete Exercise Nine-5. The Exercise is on page 327 of the text. The solution is on page S-96 of this Study Guide.

Royalties And Payments Based On Production Or Use
☐ Read page 327 (paragraphs 9-56 through 9-59) of the text.

Rental Income
☐ Read pages 327 (from paragraph 9-60) through 329 (through paragraph 9-69) of the text.

☐ Complete Exercise Nine-6. The Exercise is on pages 329 and 330 of the text. The solution is on page S-96 of this Study Guide.

☐ Complete Self Study Problem Nine-1. The Self Study Problem is on page 343 of the text. The solution is on pages S-98 and S-99 of this Study Guide.

Dividends From Canadian Corporations

☐ Read pages 330 (from paragraph 9-70) through 332 (through paragraph 9-81) of the text.

☐ Complete Exercise Nine-7. The Exercise is on page 332 of the text. The solution is on page S-96 of this Study Guide.

Comparison Of Investment Returns

☐ Read pages 332 (from paragraph 9-82) and 333 (through paragraph 9-85) of the text.

☐ Complete Self Study Problems Nine-2 and Nine-3. The Self Study Problems are on pages 343 and 344 of the text. The solutions are on pages S-99 and S-100 of this Study Guide.

Stock Dividends And Capital Dividends

☐ Read page 333 (paragraphs 9-86 through 9-88) of the text.

Mutual Funds

☐ Read pages 333 (from paragraph 9-89) through 335 (through paragraph 9-99) of the text.

☐ Complete Exercise Nine-8. The Exercise is on page 335 of the text. The solution is on page S-96 of this Study Guide.

Income Trusts

☐ Read pages 335 (from paragraph 9-100) and 336 (through paragraph 9-107) of the text.

Foreign Source Income

☐ Read pages 336 (from paragraph 9-108) and 337 (through paragraph 9-111) of the text.

☐ Complete Exercise Nine-9. The Exercise is on page 337 of the text. The solution is on page S-97 of this Study Guide.

Shareholder Benefits

☐ Read pages 338 (from paragraph 9-112) through 340 (through paragraph 9-125) of the text.

☐ Complete Exercises Nine-10 through Nine-12. The Exercises are on pages 340 and 341 of the text. The solutions are on page S-97 of this Study Guide

☐ Complete Self Study Problem Nine-4. The Self Study Problem is on page 344 of the text. The solution is on page S-101 of this Study Guide.

Tax Credits Revisited

☐ Read page 341 (paragraphs 9-126 through 9-128) of the text.

To Complete This Chapter

☐ Review the Key Terms Used In The Chapter on page 342 of the text. Consult the Glossary for the meaning of any key terms you do not know.

☐ Review the Learning Objectives of the Chapter found on page S-102 of this Study Guide.

☐ As a review, we recommend that you view the PowerPoint Slides for Chapter Nine that are on your Companion CD-ROM. If you do not have access to the Microsoft PowerPoint program, the PowerPoint Viewer program can be installed from the Companion CD-ROM.

Solution to Chapter Nine Exercises

Exercise Nine - 1 Solution

In each of the years 2005, 2006, and 2007, Moreau would have a deduction for interest of $40,000 [(4%)($1,000,000)]. When the bonds are retired in 2007, there would be a loss of $15,000 ($1,000,000 - $985,000). As the bonds are sold for more than 97 percent of their maturity amount and the four-thirds test is met since the effective rate of 4.6 percent is less than four-thirds of the coupon rate [(4%)(4/3) = 5.3%], it would appear that this loss would be fully deductible. This gives a total deduction of $135,000 over the three year period [(3)($40,000) + $15,000].

For accounting purposes, interest expense would be $45,000 in each of the three years. This is made up of the annual payment of $40,000, plus amortization of the discount of $5,000 [(1/3)($1,000,000 - $985,000)]. Note that the total for the three year period would be the same $135,000 [(3)($45,000)] that was deducted for tax purposes.

Exercise Nine - 2 Solution

The tax consequences under each of the three assumptions would be as follows:

Money Lender In this case, there would be an income inclusion of $400,000 ($1,400,000 - $1,000,000) in the current year. The interest deduction for the year would be $180,000 [(18%)($1,000,000)].

No Deliberate Premium In this case, the premium would have no immediate tax consequences and there would be no tax consequences when the bonds mature. The interest deduction for the year would be $180,000 [(18%)($1,000,000)]. Given that the bonds are paid off for less than the proceeds from their issuance, this result provides the issuer of the bonds with an untaxed gain of $400,000.

Deliberate Premium In this case, the premium would be amortized at the rate of $40,000 per year ($400,000 ÷ 10). This means the interest deduction for the year would be $140,000 ($180,000 - $40,000).

Exercise Nine - 3 Solution

The total interest to be recorded on the investment is $28,800 [($60,000)(8%)(6 years)]. It will be allocated as follows: 2005 - nil, 2006 - $4,800, 2007 - $4,800, 2008 - $6,000, 2009 - $3,600, 2010 - $4,800, and 2011 - $4,800.

As no anniversary date occurred and no interest was received during 2005, no interest will have to be included in Ms. Dumont's 2005 tax return.

In 2006, the first anniversary date occurs on September 30 and this requires the recognition of $4,800 [(8%)($60,000)] of interest.

In 2007, the second anniversary date occurs and this requires the recognition of an additional $4,800 of interest.

In 2008, the third anniversary date requires the recognition of $4,800 and, in addition, a $15,600 [(8%)($60,000)(3.25 Years)] payment is received. As $14,400 [(3)($4,800)] of this amount has been accrued on the three anniversary dates, only $1,200 of this amount will be added to income. This gives a total for the year 2008 of $6,000 ($4,800 + $1,200).

In 2009, the anniversary date will require recognition of $4,800. However, only $3,600 of this amount will be included as $1,200 was recognized in 2008.

In 2010, $4,800 will be recognized on the anniversary date.

In 2011, a payment of $13,200 [(2.75)($4,800)] will be received. As $8,400 ($3,600 + $4,800) of the amount received has been recorded on the 2009 and 2010 anniversary dates, the total for 2011 will be $4,800 ($13,200 - $8,400).

Solution to Chapter Nine Exercises

Exercise Nine - 4 Solution

With respect to the maturity amount, the interest to be included in the purchaser's tax return would be calculated as follows:

Year	Initial Balance	Interest At 7%	Closing Balance
2005	$204,075	$14,285	$218,360
2006	218,360	15,285	233,645
2007	233,645	16,355	250,000

Calculations with respect to the coupon payments are as follows:

Year	Initial Balance	Interest At 7%	Interest Received	Closing Balance
2005	$45,925	$3,215	($17,500)	$31,640
2006	31,640	2,215	(17,500)	16,355
2007	16,355	1,145	(17,500)	Nil

Exercise Nine - 5 Solution

Mr. Lay will have to include the full $6,000 received. However, under ITA 20(14) he is eligible for a deduction of $2,000 [($3,000)(4/6)], reflecting the interest that was accrued on the bonds at the time of his purchase. The net amount that will be included in his tax return is $4,000.

Exercise Nine - 6 Solution

As the improvements will have to be added to her CCA base, her maximum available CCA on the rental property is $3,560 [(4%)(1/2)($185,000 - $42,000 + $35,000)]. However, the maximum CCA that she can deduct will be limited by her net rental income before CCA. This amount is $2,100 ($7,200 - $5,100).

Exercise Nine - 7 Solution

The Tax Payable by Mr. Johns would be calculated as follows:

Dividends Received	$17,000.00
Gross Up At 25%	4,250.00
Taxable Dividends [(1.25)($17,000)]	$21,250.00
Taxes At 41% (29% + 12%)	$8,712.50
Dividend Tax Credit [(2/3 + 30%)($4,250)]	(4,108.33)
Federal And Provincial Tax Payable	$ 4,604.17

The after tax retention is $12,395.83 ($17,000.00 - $4,604.17). Note that to calculate this amount, the taxes are deducted from the dividends received and not the grossed up taxable dividends.

Exercise Nine - 8 Solution

Given the purchase price per unit is $13, the reinvestment will result in Ms. Tiompkins receiving 80.77 ($1,050 ÷ $13) additional units. This will leave her holding 3,580.77 units with an adjusted cost base of $40,425 ($39,375 + $1,050). Her adjusted cost base per unit after the reinvestment is $11.29 ($40,425 ÷ 3,580.77).

Exercise Nine - 9 Solution

Part A If the foreign source income is non-business income, the withholding in excess of 15 percent is a deduction rather than a tax credit. This means that the total withholding of $7,500 will be divided into a credit of $4,500 [($30,000)(15%)] and a deduction of $3,000 [($30,000)(25% - 15%)]. Norah's incremental Taxable Income will be $27,000 ($30,000 - $3,000) and her incremental Tax Payable will be $3,330 [($27,000)(29%) - $4,500].

Part B If the foreign source income is business income, all of the $7,500 withholding will be treated as a tax credit. This means that Norah's incremental Taxable Income will be $30,000 and her incremental Tax Payable will be $1,200 [($30,000)(29%) - $7,500]. Note the significant reduction in Tax Payable when the full amount of withholding is treated as a credit, as opposed to part of it being treated as a deduction.

Exercise Nine - 10 Solution

It is likely that Ms. Rourke will have to include the $50,000 principal amount of the loan in her Net Income For Tax Purposes for the current year. She owns more than 10 percent of the shares, making her a specified employee. While she is an employee, it is unlikely that this type of loan would be generally available to all employees and, as a consequence, it is likely that she received the loan because of her shareholder status as opposed to her employee status. In the unlikely event that the loan is not included in income, she will have to include imputed interest at the prescribed rate for the period of the loan. For the current year, the rate is 3 percent and her shareholder benefit for the year is $750 [(3%)($50,000)(6/12)]. The imputed interest rate and benefit will vary as the prescribed rate changes. Note, however, if imputed interest is assessed, some portion of the amount may be deductible as it relates to the acquisition of an automobile to be used in employment duties.

Exercise Nine - 11 Solution

Part A If the loan is repaid on January 1, 2006, it will not be included in two consecutive Generic Inc. Balance Sheets. As a consequence, the principal amount will not have to be included in Ms. Fisk's income. However, as it is a low interest loan, she will be assessed with a taxable benefit on the loan. The amount would be $2,835 [($162,000)(5% - 2%)(7/12)].

Part B If the loan is not repaid until December 31, 2006, it will appear in two consecutive Generic Inc. Balance Sheets. This means the $162,000 in principal will have to be included in Ms. Fisk's income for the taxation year ending December 31, 2005. However, there will be no imputed interest benefit based on the loan's low rate of interest. In addition, when the loan is repaid, the payment can be deducted from Net Income For Tax Purposes.

Exercise Nine - 12 Solution

It was assumed that this loan did not qualify as a home relocation loan.

Provided Mr. Hasid receives the loan in his capacity as an employee of Hasid Ltd., the loan is one of the exceptions listed under ITA 15(2). This means that the principal amount will not have to be included in income. However, as the loan is interest free, a taxable benefit will arise. It will be calculated by applying the prescribed rate of 5 percent to the principal of the loan for all periods that it is outstanding. The amounts would be $1,025 [($123,000)(5%)(2/12)] for 2005 and $6,150 [($123,000)(5%)] for 2006.

If Mr. Hasid cannot claim that he received the loan in his capacity as an employee of Hasid Ltd., the $123,000 principal amount will have to be included in income in 2005. However, no taxable benefit will be assessed for the fact that it is an interest free loan. When the loan is repaid in 2007, Mr. Hasid will be able to deduct $123,000 from his Net Income For Tax Purposes.

Solution to Self Study Problem Nine - 1

CCA On Properties A And B   Properties A and B cost less than $50,000 and, as a consequence, can be included in a single Class 1 account. Maximum CCA on these properties would be calculated as follows:

Balance, January 1 ($21,500 + $43,000)	$64,500
Disposition (At Capital Cost)	(36,000)
Balance At End Of Year	$28,500
CCA Rate	4%
Maximum CCA For The Year	$ 1,140

Note the proceeds of disposition for CCA purposes are not the actual proceeds of $72,000, but only the capital cost of $36,000. The extra $36,000 would be a capital gain, resulting in a taxable capital gain of $18,000 [(1/2)($36,000)].

CCA On Other Class 1 Properties   The other properties will be allocated to separate Class 1 balances. The recapture and maximum CCA for the year on these properties will be calculated as follows:

	Property C	Property D	Property E
Balance, January 1	$46,000	$64,000	Nil
Additions (Dispositions)	(61,000)	-0-	$192,000
Recapture	($15,000)		
Transfer To Income	15,000		
Balance Before Adjustments	$ -0-	$64,000	$192,000
One-Half Net Additions		-0-	(96,000)
CCA Base		$64,000	$ 96,000
Maximum CCA At 4 Percent		(2,560)	(3,840)
One-Half Net Additions		-0-	96,000
Balance, December 31 (If Maximum Is Taken)		$61,440	$188,160

Total Maximum CCA   This gives a total maximum CCA for Class 1 of $7,540 ($1,140 + $2,560 + $3,840).

Property Income   In calculating the net property income (loss) for Mr. Drake, the rules that restrict CCA deductions on rental properties must be taken into consideration. These rules are discussed in IT-195R4, "Rental Property - Capital Cost Restrictions". This Interpretation Bulletin makes it clear that in determining the maximum CCA deduction, net rental income, before CCA for all classes of rental properties, must first be determined. The maximum CCA deduction that can then be taken is limited to the amount that will reduce this balance to nil. Using this approach, net property income is calculated as follows:

	Rental Revenues	Cash Expenses
Property A	$ 5,200	$ 3,450
Property B	6,700	3,350
Property C	12,200	12,250
Property D	15,300	21,150
Property E	2,000	2,900
Totals	$41,400	$43,100

Income (Loss) Before CCA And Recapture ($41,400 - $43,100)	($ 1,700)
Recapture From Sale Of Property C	15,000
Rental Income Before CCA	$13,300)
Maximum CCA	(7,540)
Net Property Income	$ 5,760

In addition to the net property income calculated above, there is also the taxable capital gain of $18,000 resulting from the sale of Property A.

Solution to Self Study Problem Nine - 2

After Tax Return On The Bonds   This amount would be calculated as follows:

Interest Received [(7.75%)($20,000)]	$1,550.00
Taxes At 38% (26% + 12%)	(589.00)
After Tax Return	$ 961.00

After Tax Return On Preferred Shares   This amount would be calculated as follows:

Dividends Received [(5%)($20,000)]	$1,000.00
Gross Up Of 25 Percent	250.00
Taxable Dividends	$1,250.00

Taxes At 38% (26% + 12%)	$475.00
Dividend Tax Credit [(2/3 + 30%)($250)]	(241.67)
Tax Payable	$233.33

Dividends Received	$1,000.00
Tax Payable	(233.33)
After Tax Return	$ 766.67

Conclusion   Based on after tax returns, the investment in bonds is the better alternative.

Solution to Self Study Problem Nine - 3

The after tax cash flows associated with the alternative investments would be as follows:

Guaranteed Investment Certificate   The before tax return here would be $5,500 and this would result in an after tax return calculated as follows:

Interest [($100,000)(5.5%)]	$5,500
Federal/Provincial Tax Payable [($5,500)(29% + 15%)]	(2,420)
After Tax Cash Flow	$3,080

Solution to Self Study Problem Nine - 3

Rental Property The net rental income from the property would be calculated as follows:

Gross Rents	$13,200
Expenses	(9,600)
CCA (Property Sold Prior To Year End)	Nil
Net Rental Income	$ 3,600

In addition to this net rental income, Ms. Holmes anticipates a capital gain of $10,000 ($175,000 - $165,000), of which one-half, or $5,000, would be included in her income. The total after tax cash flow would be as follows:

Net Rental Income	$ 3,600
Capital Gain	10,000
Tax Payable [($3,600 + $5,000)(29% + 15%)]	(3,784)
After Tax Cash Flow	$ 9,816

Norton Ltd. Shares The calculations here would be as follows:

Dividends Received	$5,000	
Gross Up (25 Percent)	1,250	
Taxable Dividends		$6,250
Capital Gain	$6,000	
Inclusion Rate	1/2	
Taxable Capital Gain		3,000
Net Income For Tax Purposes		$9,250

Tax At 44% (29% + $15%)	$4,070
Dividend Tax Credit [($1,250)(2/3 + 35%)]	(1,271)
Tax Payable	$2,799

Before Tax Cash Flow ($5,000 + $6,000)	$11,000
Tax Payable	(2,799)
After Tax Cash Flow	$ 8,201

Based on cash flow considerations only, it would appear that Ms. Holmes should acquire the rental property. However, this alternative probably involves the highest degree of risk and can require significant personal involvement if there are problems with the tenant or repairs become necessary. In addition, the real estate investment is the least liquid of the three alternatives and Ms. Holmes might encounter difficulties in the disposition of this investment. While you were not asked to consider transaction costs, we would also point out that they would be much higher on this investment than on either of the other two.

In choosing between the guaranteed investment certificate and the shares of Norton Ltd., the after tax cash flows from the shares are considerably higher. However, the return on the shares is made up of dividends and a potential capital gain, both of which are more uncertain than the interest on the guaranteed investment certificate. Given this, the possibility of greater than anticipated dividends and/or capital gains must be weighed against the additional risk of lower than anticipated returns.

You might also wish to note that the interest and principal on guaranteed investment certificates are only covered by government insurance to a maximum of $60,000 with any one issuer. This would suggest the use of two different certificates with different financial institutions.

Solution to Self Study Problem Nine - 4

Mr. Blaine is an employee and shareholder of Blaine Enterprises. As a result, if the loan is outstanding on two successive Balance Sheet dates for the corporation, the entire principal amount will have to be included in Mr. Blaine's personal income for tax purposes in the year the loan was granted. Note, however, if the principal amount of the loan is included in Mr. Blaine's income, no taxable benefit will be assessed with respect to imputed interest.

It does not appear that Blaine Enterprises is offering other employees loans to acquire houses. If this was the case, and Mr. Blaine was granted the loan in his capacity as an employee, he would not have to include the loan in income. However, he would be assessed a taxable benefit in the amount of imputed interest on the outstanding loan balance. The interest rate to be used is established on a quarterly basis in ITR 4301. This loan would not qualify for a home relocation loan deduction as the property that he is acquiring is not 40 kilometers closer to his work.

Given the fact that Mr. Blaine is a shareholder as well as an employee, the proposal does not offer any fundamental advantage over paying himself additional salary and, as a consequence, Mr. Blaine should be advised that his interest free loan plan will not work as smoothly as he has anticipated. The one advantage would be that, unlike salary that cannot be removed from income at a later point in time, repayment of the loan will allow Mr. Blaine to deduct the amount repaid under ITA 20(1)(j).

Chapter Nine Learning Objectives

After completing Chapter 9, you should be able to:

1. Explain the nature of property income (paragraphs 9-1 through 9-4).

2. Describe the rules applicable to the deductibility of interest payments and be able to apply these rules to various types of borrowing (paragraphs 9-5 through 9-33).

3. Apply the provisions relating to the treatment of discount and premium on long-term issued debt (paragraphs 9-34 through 9-39).

4. Calculate the taxable amount of interest income for both individuals and corporations (paragraphs 9-40 through 9-46).

5. Explain the tax treatment of discounts and premiums on long-term debt holdings (paragraphs 9-47 and 9-48).

6. Explain the tax treatment of prescribed debt obligations and indexed debt obligations (paragraphs 9-49 through 9-53).

7. Apply the provisions related to accrued interest at the time of transfer of debt obligations (paragraphs 9-54 and 9-55).

8. Demonstrate a basic understanding of the tax procedures for royalties and payments based on production or use (paragraphs 9-56 through 9-59).

9. Calculate net rental income (paragraphs 9-60 through 9-69).

10. Apply the dividend gross up and tax credit mechanism to determine the tax consequences of receiving dividend income (paragraphs 9-70 through 9-81).

11. Compare the after-tax returns from various types of investments (paragraphs 9-82 through 9-85).

12. Explain the general treatment of stock dividends and capital dividends (paragraphs 9-86 through 9-88).

13. Demonstrate an understanding of the provisions relating to mutual funds (paragraphs 9-89 through 9-99).

14. Demonstrate an understanding of the provisions relating to income trusts (paragraphs 9-100 through 9-107).

15. Calculate the tax consequences of receiving foreign source income (paragraphs 9-108 through 9-111).

16. Determine the tax consequences of various shareholder benefits (paragraphs 9-112 through 9-125).

17. Recall the dividend tax credit and the credit for foreign taxes paid on foreign source income (paragraphs 9-126 through 9-128).

CHAPTER TEN

How To Work Through Chapter Ten

We recommend the following approach in dealing with the material in this chapter:

Economic Background And General Rules
☐ Read pages 353 (from paragraph 10-1) through 357 (through paragraph 10-25) of the text.

☐ Complete Exercises Ten-1 and Ten-2. The Exercises are on page 357 of the text. The solutions are on page S-106 of this Study Guide.

☐ Read pages 357 (from paragraph 10-26) and 358 (through paragraph 10-30) of the text.

Assets Acquired Before 1972
☐ Read pages 358 (from paragraph 10-31) and 359 (through paragraph 10-35) of the text.

Identical Properties
☐ Read pages 359 (from paragraph 10-36) and 360 (through paragraph 10-37) of the text.

☐ Complete Exercise Ten-3. The Exercise is on page 360 of the text. The solution is on page S-106 of this Study Guide.

☐ Complete Self Study Problem Ten-1. The Self Study Problem is on page 388 of the text. The solution is on pages S-109 and S-110 of this Study Guide.

☐ Read page 360 (paragraphs 10-38 through 10-41) of the text.

Partial Dispositions
☐ Read pages 360 and 361 (paragraph 10-42) of the text.

Warranties
☐ Read page 361 (paragraph 10-43) of the text.

☐ Complete Exercise Ten-4. The Exercise is on page 361 of the text. The solution is on page S-106 of this Study Guide.

Bad Debts On Sales Of Capital Property
☐ Read page 361 (paragraphs 10-44 and 10-45) of the text.

☐ Complete Exercise Ten-5. The Exercise is on page 361 of the text. The solution is on page S-106 of this Study Guide.

Capital Gains Reserves
☐ Read pages 362 (from paragraph 10-46) and 363 (through paragraph 10-60) of the text.

☐ Complete Exercise Ten-6. The Exercise is on page 363 of the text. The solution is on page S-107 of this Study Guide.

☐ Complete Self Study Problem Ten-2. The Self Study Problem is on page 388 of the text. The solution is on pages S-110 and S-111 of this Study Guide.

Deferral Provisions On Replacement Property

☐ Read pages 363 (from paragraph 10-61) through 366 (through paragraph 10-75) of the text.

☐ Complete Exercise Ten-7. The Exercise is on page 366 of the text. The solution is on page S-107 of this Study Guide.

☐ Complete Self Study Problems Ten-3 and Ten-4. The Self Study Problems are on pages 388 through 390 of the text. The solutions are on pages S-111 through S-115 of this Study Guide.

Deferral Provisions On Small Business Investments

☐ Read pages 366 (from paragraph 10-76) through 368 (through paragraph 10-78) of the text.

☐ Complete Exercise Ten-8. The Exercise is on page 368 of the text. The solution is on page S-107 of this Study Guide.

Changes In Use

☐ Read pages 368 (from paragraph 10-79) and 369 (through paragraph 10-82) of the text.

☐ Complete Exercise Ten-9. The Exercise is on page 369 of the text. The solution is on page S-107 of this Study Guide.

Principal Residence

☐ Read pages 369 (from paragraph 10-83) and 370 (through paragraph 10-89) of the text.

☐ Complete Exercises Ten-10 and Ten-11. The Exercises are on pages 370 and 371 of the text. The solutions are on pages S-107 and S-108 of this Study Guide.

☐ Read pages 371 (from paragraph 10-90) through 373 (through paragraph 10-102) of the text.

☐ Complete Self Study Problem Ten-5. The Self Study Problem is on page 390 of the text. The solution is on pages S-116 and S-117 of this Study Guide.

☐ Read pages 373 (from paragraph 10-103) and 374 (through paragraph 10-104) of the text.

Personal Use Property

☐ Read pages 374 (from paragraph 10-105) and 375 (through paragraph 10-112) of the text.

☐ Complete Exercise Ten-12. The Exercise is on page 375 of the text. The solution is on page S-108 of this Study Guide.

Gains And Losses On Foreign Currency

☐ Read pages 375 (from paragraph 10-113) and 376 (through paragraph 10-114) of the text.

☐ Complete Exercise Ten-13. The Exercise is on page 376 of the text. The solution is on page S-108 of this Study Guide.

☐ Read pages 376 (from paragraph 10-115) and 377 (through paragraph 10-121) of the text.

Options

☐ Read pages 377 (from paragraph 10-122) and 378 (through paragraph 10-125) of the text.

Capital Gains And Tax Planning

☐ Read page 378 (paragraphs 10-126 and 10-127) of the text.

Capital Property And The GST

☐ Read pages 378 (from paragraph 10-128) through 382 (through paragraph 10-156) of the text.

☐ Complete Self Study Problems Ten-6 and Ten-7. The Self Study Problems are on pages 390 and 391 of the text. The solutions are on pages S-117 and S-118 of this Study Guide.

If The Appendix To Chapter 10
(Disposition Of Shares Acquired With Stock Options) Has Been Assigned

☐ Read the Appendix To Chapter 10 on pages 384 (from paragraph 10A-1) through 386 (through paragraph 10A-5) of the text.

☐ Complete Exercise Ten-14. The Exercise is on page 386 of the text. The solution is on pages S-108 and S-109 of this Study Guide.

To Complete This Chapter

☐ Review the Key Terms Used In The Chapter on page 382 of the text. Consult the Glossary for the meaning of any key terms you do not know.

☐ Review the Learning Objectives of the Chapter found on pages S-119 and S-120 of this Study Guide.

☐ As a review, we recommend that you view the PowerPoint Slides for Chapter Ten that are on your Companion CD-ROM. If you do not have access to the Microsoft PowerPoint program, the PowerPoint Viewer program can be installed from the Companion CD-ROM.

Solution to Chapter Ten Exercises

Exercise Ten - 1 Solution

The capital cost of this Class 1 asset would be $3,500,000 ($5,600,000 - $600,000 - $1,500,000). Given this, the maximum CCA in this first year would $70,000 [(1/2)($3,500,000)(4%)].

Exercise Ten - 2 Solution

The total loss on the sale of 1,000 shares would be $8,500 [(1,000)($14.50 - $23.00)]. As she acquires 600 shares of identical property within 30 days of the sale, 60 percent (600/1,000) of the loss would be disallowed. This $5,100 [(60%)($8,500)] disallowed loss would be added to the adjusted cost base of the new shares. This gives a total adjusted cost base for the new shares of $13,350 [(600)($13.75) + $5,100], or $22.25 per share. The remaining capital loss of $3,400 will create an allowable capital loss of $1,700 [(1/2)($3,400)].

Exercise Ten - 3 Solution

The average cost of the shares purchased in 2004 is $23.76 {[(650)($23.50) + (345)($24.25)] ÷ 995}. Given this, Ms. Montrose's taxable capital gain for 2004 is calculated as follows:

Proceeds Of Disposition [($25.50)(210)]	$5,355.00
Adjusted Cost Base [($23.76)(210)]	(4,989.60)
Capital Gain	$ 365.40
Inclusion Rate	1/2
Taxable Capital Gain	$ 182.70

When her 2005 purchase is added to this balance, her average cost becomes $25.34 {[(785)($23.76) + (875)($26.75)] ÷ 1,660}. Given this, Ms. Montrose's taxable capital gain for 2005 is calculated as follows:

Proceeds Of Disposition [($29.50)(340)]	$10,030.00
Adjusted Cost Base [($25.34)(340)]	(8,615.60)
Capital Gain	$ 1,414.40
Inclusion Rate	1/2
Taxable Capital Gain	$ 707.20

Exercise Ten - 4 Solution

For 2004, there will be a taxable capital gain of $27,500 [(1/2)($292,000 - $237,000)]. During 2005, there will be an allowable capital loss of $2,400 [(1/2)($4,800)]. This allowable capital loss will only be deductible in 2005 against 2005 taxable capital gains. However, it can be carried back and deducted against the 2004 capital gain in the determination of 2004 Taxable Income.

Exercise Ten - 5 Solution

For 2005, there will be an allowable capital loss of $7,500 [(1/2)($110,000 - $125,000)]. For 2006, there will be an allowable capital loss of $17,500 [(1/2)(Nil - $35,000)]. These allowable capital losses will only be deductible against taxable capital gains. However, they can be carried over to other years in which the taxpayer has taxable capital gains and deducted in the determination of Taxable Income.

Exercise Ten - 6 Solution

Mr. Goodson's capital gain on this transaction is $71,800 ($382,000 - $293,000 - $17,200). The maximum reserve for 2005 is $56,387, the lesser of:

- $56,387 [($71,800)($300,000 ÷ $382,000)]
- $57,440 [($71,800)(20%)(4 - 0)]

For 2006, the maximum reserve is $43,080, the lesser of :

- $45,110 [($71,800)($240,000 ÷ $382,000)]
- $43,080 [($71,800)(20%)(4 - 1)]

Exercise Ten - 7 Solution

As the replacement did not occur until 2006, Hadfeld's 2005 tax return will include a taxable capital gain of $112,500 [(1/2)($950,000 - $725,000)], and recapture of $101,850 ($725,000 - $623,150). In 2006, these amounts can be removed from income and asset values through an amended return. The capital cost of the new building will be $755,000 [$980,000 - ($950,000 - $725,000)]. Its UCC will be $653,150 ($755,000 - $101,850).

Each of these amounts are $30,000 more than the old capital cost and UCC. This reflects the $30,000 ($980,000 - $950,000) over and above the insurance proceeds that the Company spent on replacing the building.

Exercise Ten - 8 Solution

The capital gain is $600,000 ($1,350,000 - $750,000) and the lesser of the proceeds of disposition and the cost of the replacement shares is the $1,200,000 cost of the replacement shares. Given this, the permitted deferral would be $533,333 [($600,000)($1,200,000 ÷ $1,350,000)]. This means that the adjusted cost base of the JH Inc. shares is $666,667 ($1,200,000 - $533,333).

Exercise Ten - 9 Solution

This change in use will be a deemed disposition and re-acquisition of the property. For capital gains purposes, the transaction will take place at the fair market value of $111,000, resulting in a taxable capital gain for Ms. Larson of $44,000 [(1/2)($111,000 - $23,000)]. The new adjusted cost base for the property will be $111,000. As the change is from personal to business use and the fair market value is greater than the cost, the new UCC for the property will be its cost, plus one-half of the difference between the fair market value and the cost. This amount is $67,000 [$23,000 + (1/2)($111,000 - $23,000)]. Maximum CCA on this amount would be $1,340 [($67,000)(4%)(1/2)].

Exercise Ten - 10 Solution

There would be no tax consequences due to the sales. There would be a capital gain on the first sale of $20,500 ($109,500 - $89,000). This gain could be eliminated by designating the first property as his principal residence for the six years 1996 through 2001. The gain reduction would be calculated as follows:

$$\left(\$20,500 \times \frac{6}{6} \right) = \$20,500$$

The $26,000 ($178,000 - $152,000) capital gain on the second home could be eliminated by designating the second property as his principal residence for the years 2002 through 2005 and adding the plus one in the numerator. The gain reduction would be calculated as follows:

$$\left(\$26,000 \times \frac{(4+1)}{5} \right) = \$26,000$$

Exercise Ten - 11 Solution

The annual gain on the house is $6,000 [($198,000 - $126,000) ÷ 12 Years], while the annual gain on the cottage is $6,500 [($143,500 - $85,000) ÷ 9 Years]. Given this, the years 1998 through 2005 should be allocated to the cottage. When these eight years are combined with the plus one in the numerator of the reduction formula, the $58,500 gain on the cottage will be completely eliminated. This leaves the years 1994 through 1997 for the Ottawa house, resulting in the following gain reduction:

$$\left(\$72,000 \times \frac{(4+1)}{12} \right) = \$30,000$$

This will leave a total capital gain on the sale of the two properties of $42,000 ($72,000 + $58,500 - $58,500 - $30,000).

Exercise Ten - 12 Solution

The results would be as follows:

	Personal Use Property	Listed Personal Property
Gain On Sailboat ($68,000 - $43,000)	$25,000	
Gain On Oil Painting ($25,000 - $1,000)		$24,000
Loss On Personal Automobile	Nil	
Loss On Necklace ($23,000 - $46,000)		(23,000)
Capital Gain	$25,000	$ 1,000
Inclusion Rate	1/2	1/2
Net Taxable Capital Gain	$12,500	$ 500

The total taxable capital gain on the dispositions is equal to $13,000 ($12,500 + $500). While the loss on the automobile is not deductible as it is personal use property, the loss on the diamond necklace can be deducted against the gain on the oil painting because it is listed personal property. The adjusted cost base of the oil painting is deemed to be $1,000 using the $1,000 floor rule.

Exercise Ten - 13 Solution

In 2004, as a result of his share purchase, Mr. Pratt will have an exchange gain of $612 [(450)(TT$68)(C$0.20 - C$0.18)]]. As this qualifies as an ITA 39(2) transaction, he will only include $206 [(1/2)($612 - $200)] of this in his Net Income For Tax Purposes.

In 2005, there will be a capital gain of $2,952 {[(C$0.21)(450)(TT$96)] - [(C$0.20)(450)(TT$68)]} on the sale. None of this gain qualifies under ITA 39(2), so there would be no $200 exclusion. Mr. Pratt's 2005 Net Income For Tax Purposes will include $1,476, or one-half, of this gain.

Exercise Ten - 14 Solution

The total specified value of the shares acquired through options during 2005 is $10,000 [(500 Shares)($20)]. This means he can defer all of the employment income, a total of $11,250 [(250)($35 - $20) + (250)($50 - $20)]. There is no effect on 2005 income.

The 700 shares sold during 2006 would be made up of his original holding of 500 non-deferral shares, plus 200 of the option shares acquired on January 15. The tax consequences would be as follows:

Taxable Capital Gains:	
[(500 Shares)($55.00 - $23.50)(1/2)]	$ 7,875
[(200 Shares)($55.00 - $35.00)(1/2)]	2,000
Employment Income [(200 Shares)($35.00 - $20.00)]	3,000
ITA 110(1)(d) Deduction [(1/2)($3,000)]	(1,500)
2006 Increase In Taxable Income	$11,375

The 300 shares sold during 2007 would be made up of the 50 remaining shares acquired on January 15, 2005, along with the 250 acquired on October 3, 2005. The tax consequences would be as follows:

Employment Income:	
[(50)($35.00 - $20.00)]	$ 750
[(250)($50.00 - $20.00)]	7,500
ITA 110(1)(d) Deduction [(1/2)($7,500 + $750)]	(4,125)
2007 Increase In Taxable Income	$4,125

Taxable Capital Gains (Losses):	
[(50)($30.00 - $35.00)(1/2)]	($ 125)
[(250)($30.00 - $50.00)(1/2)]	(2,500)
2007 Allowable Capital Loss	($2,625)

Note that these two amounts cannot be netted, as allowable capital losses are not deductible against employment income. Unless Jean has taxable capital gains on other 2007 dispositions, he will not be able to deduct the $2,625 allowable capital loss in the current year.

Solution to Self Study Problem Ten - 1

Acquisition Or Sale Date	Purchased (Sold)	Per Share	Total Cost	Cost/Share
October 15, 1999	5,500	$40.00	$220,000	
November 8, 1999	(1,500)	(40.00)	(60,000)	
December 12, 2001	3,200	79.00	252,800	
Subtotal	7,200		$412,800	$ 57.33
February 3, 2002	(2,600)	(57.33)	(149,058)	
Subtotal	4,600		$263,742	
January 15, 2003 Stock Dividend	460	99.00	45,540	
June 15, 2003	3,800	104.00	395,200	
Subtotal	8,860		$704,482	
December 23, 2004 Stock Dividend	886	125.00	110,750	
March 15, 2005 Balances	9,746		$815,232	

The taxable capital gain resulting from the November 8, 1999 sale of shares would be calculated as follows:

Proceeds Of Disposition [(1,500)($52)]	$78,000
Adjusted Cost Base [(1,500)($40)]	(60,000)
Capital Gain	$18,000
1999 Inclusion Rate	3/4
Taxable Capital Gain	$13,500

The taxable capital gain resulting from the February 3, 2002 sale of shares would be calculated as follows:

Proceeds Of Disposition [(2,600)($94)]	$244,400
Adjusted Cost Base [(2,600)($57.33)]	
(See preceding table for per share adjusted cost base)	(149,058)
Capital Gain	$ 95,342
Inclusion Rate	1/2
Taxable Capital Gain	$ 47,671

The taxable capital gain resulting from the March15, 2005 sale of shares would be calculated as follows:

Proceeds Of Disposition [(9,746)($174)]	$1,695,804
Adjusted Cost Base (Remainder)	(815,232)
Capital Gain	$ 880,572
Inclusion Rate	1/2
Taxable Capital Gain	$ 440,286

Solution to Self Study Problem Ten - 2

Total Gain   The total amount of the taxable capital gain can be calculated as follows:

Proceeds Of Disposition		$500,000
Less:		
Adjusted Cost Base	$230,000	
Disposition Costs	20,000	250,000
Total Capital Gain		$250,000
Inclusion Rate		1/2
Total Taxable Capital Gain		$125,000

Reserve Limits   As Miss Stevens has not received the entire proceeds in the year of sale, she is entitled under ITA 40(1) to establish a reserve. The reserve that would be available at the end of each year would be the lesser of:

- [(Capital Gain)(Proceeds Not Yet Due ÷ Total Proceeds)]
- [(20%)(Capital Gain)(4 - Number Of Preceding Years Ending After Disposition)]

2005 Gain   As the cash proceeds during 2005 are well in excess of 20 percent of the total proceeds, the maximum reserve at the end of 2005 would be calculated as follows:

[($250,000)($300,000 ÷ $500,000)] = $150,000

With a reserve of $150,000, the capital gain to be recognized for 2005 would be $100,000 ($250,000 - $150,000). This would result in a taxable capital gain of $50,000.

2006 Gain   At the end of 2006, the two calculations provide equal results as follows:

- [($250,000)($300,000 ÷ $500,000)] = $150,000
- [(20%)($250,000)(Four Years - One Year)] = $150,000

This means the 2006 taxable capital gain would be calculated as follows:

Addition Of The 2005 Reserve	$ 150,000
Deduction Of The 2006 Reserve	(150,000)
2006 Capital Gain	$ -0-

2007, 2008, And 2009 Gains   In these three years no further proceeds are receivable and, as a consequence, the reserve calculation based on proceeds not receivable until after December 31 would remain unchanged at $150,000. However, the alternative calculations would decline to:

- $100,000 at the end of 2007 [(20%)($250,000)(Four Years - Two Years)],
- $50,000 at the end of 2008 [(20%)($250,000)(Four Years - Three Years)],
- nil at the end of 2009 [(20%)($250,000)(Four Years - Four Years)].

This means that a gain of $50,000 would be recognized in each of the three years and would require the inclusion of a taxable capital gain of $25,000 in each year's Net Income For Tax Purposes. At this point, the entire taxable capital gain of $125,000 would have been taken into income as per the following schedule:

Year	Capital Gain	Taxable Capital Gain
2005	$100,000	$50,000
2006	-0-	-0-
2007	50,000	25,000
2008	50,000	25,000
2009	50,000	25,000
Total	$250,000	$125,000

2010 And 2011 Gains   As the entire taxable capital gain was taken into Net Income For Tax Purposes by the end of 2009, no further gains will be recognized in either 2010 or 2011.

Solution to Self Study Problem Ten - 3

Part A - With respect to Net Income For Tax Purposes, the 2005 tax effects related to the involuntary dispositions would be as follows:

Land   In the absence of the ITA 44(1) election, the taxable capital gain on the land would be as follows:

Proceeds Of Disposition	$723,000
Adjusted Cost Base	(256,000)
Capital Gain	$467,000
Inclusion Rate	1/2
Taxable Capital Gain	$233,500

Building   In the absence of the ITA 44(1) election, the taxable capital gain on the building would be as follows:

Proceeds Of Disposition	$4,800,000
Adjusted Cost Base	(3,700,000)
Capital Gain	$1,100,000
Inclusion Rate	1/2
Taxable Capital Gain	$ 550,000

If the ITA 13(4) election is not used, the disposition of the building would result in recapture as per the following calculation:

Capital Cost	$3,700,000
UCC	(1,856,000)
Recaptured CCA	$1,844,000

Building Contents   In the absence of the ITA 44(1) election, the taxable capital gain on the building contents would be as follows:

Proceeds Of Disposition	$1,256,000
Adjusted Cost Base	(972,000)
Capital Gain	$ 284,000
Inclusion Rate	1/2
Taxable Capital Gain	$ 142,000

If the ITA 13(4) election is not used, the disposition of the building contents would result in recapture as per the following calculation:

Capital Cost	$972,000
UCC	(72,000)
Recaptured CCA	$900,000

Part B   The effects of using the ITA 13(4) and ITA 44(1) elections can be calculated as follows:

Land   The taxable capital gain can be reduced to the following under the ITA 44(1) election:

Proceeds Of Disposition	$723,000
Cost Of Replacement Property	(500,000)
Capital Gain	$223,000
Inclusion Rate	1/2
Taxable Capital Gain	$111,500

If the election is used, the adjusted cost base of the replacement property (which is equal to the adjusted cost base of the expropriated land) would be calculated as follows:

Actual Cost	$500,000
Capital Gain Deferred By Election ($467,000 - $223,000)	(244,000)
Deemed Cost	$256,000

Building   The taxable capital gain can be reduced to the following under the ITA 44(1) election:

Proceeds Of Disposition	$4,800,000
Cost Of Replacement Property	(5,700,000)
Capital Gain	$ -0-

The adjusted cost base of the replacement property (which is equal to the adjusted cost base of the old building plus the $900,000 excess of the cost of the new building over the insurance proceeds) would be calculated as follows:

Actual Cost	$5,700,000
Capital Gain Deferred By Election ($1,100,000 - Nil)	(1,100,000)
Deemed Cost	$4,600,000

Use of the ITA 13(4) election would eliminate the recapture and leave the following UCC for the new property:

Capital Cost	$4,600,000
Recapture Deferred By Election ($1,844,000 - Nil)	(1,844,000)
UCC	$2,756,000

Building Contents   If this were a voluntary disposition, the building contents would not be "former business property" and would not qualify for either the ITA 13(4) election or the ITA 44(1) election. However, as this is an involuntary disposition, both elections are available. Use of the ITA 44(1) election would reduce the capital gain on the building contents to the amount shown in the following calculation:

Proceeds Of Disposition	$1,256,000
Cost Of Replacement Property	(1,233,000)
Capital Gain	$ 23,000
Inclusion Rate	1/2
Taxable Capital Gain	$ 11,500

The capital cost of the new building contents would be as follows:

Actual Cost	$1,233,000
Capital Gain Deferred By Election ($284,000 - $23,000)	(261,000)
Deemed Cost	$ 972,000

Use of the ITA 13(4) election would eliminate the recapture and leave the following UCC for the new property:

Capital Cost	$972,000
Recapture Deferred By Election ($900,000 - Nil)	(900,000)
UCC	$ 72,000

Part C   As there was a $223,000 capital gain remaining on the land and no gain remaining on the building, a reduction of Net Income For Tax Purposes can be achieved under the ITA 44(6) election. In fact, the excess of replacement cost over the old cost for the building is sufficient that all of the gain can be eliminated on the land without creating a gain on the building. This is accomplished by electing under ITA 44(6) to transfer $223,000 of the land proceeds to the building proceeds. This will completely eliminate the $223,000 capital gain on the land and will increase the capital gain removed by elections on the building by $223,000. In turn, the deemed cost of the building will now be $4,377,000 ($4,600,000 - $223,000) and the UCC will be $2,533,000 ($4,600,000 - $223,000 - $1,844,000). The adjusted cost base of the land will remain at $256,000.

Note that this election is not made without a cost. Had the $223,000 been left as a capital gain, tax would have applied on only one-half of the total. While we have eliminated this $111,500 in income, we have given up future CCA for the full amount of the $223,000. In other words, we have given up $223,000 in future deductions in return for eliminating $111,500 of income in 2005. This makes the use of this election somewhat questionable. Factors that should be considered include whether capital gains are taxed at different rates than business income (corporations) and the anticipated future tax rates and timing of Taxable Income.

Solution to Self Study Problem Ten - 4

Part A   With respect to Net Income For Tax Purposes, the sale of the Toronto property would have the following tax effects:

Land   In the absence of the ITA 44(1) election, the capital gain on the land would be as follows:

Proceeds Of Disposition	$772,000
Adjusted Cost Base	(137,000)
Capital Gain - No ITA 44(1) Election	$635,000

However, this can be reduced under the ITA 44(1) election as follows:

Proceeds Of Disposition	$772,000
Cost Of Replacement Property	(253,000)
Capital Gain Using ITA 44(1) Election	$519,000

This will result in a $259,500 [(1/2)($519,000)] taxable capital gain being included in 2005 Net Income For Tax Purposes. The adjusted cost base of the replacement property, which is equal to the adjusted cost base of the land sold, would be calculated as follows:

Actual Cost	$253,000
Capital Gain Deferred By Election ($635,000 - $519,000)	(116,000)
Deemed Cost	$137,000

Building   In the absence of the ITA 44(1) election, the capital gain on the building would be as follows:

Proceeds Of Disposition	$989,000
Adjusted Cost Base	(605,000)
Capital Gain - No ITA 44(1) Election	$384,000

This gain can be eliminated by using the ITA 44(1) election as follows:

Proceeds Of Disposition	$ 989,000
Cost Of Replacement Property	(1,042,000)
Capital Gain Using ITA 44(1) Election	$ -0-

No capital gain would be included in 2005 Net Income For Tax Purposes and the adjusted cost base of the new building, which is equal to the adjusted cost base of the building that was sold, plus the $53,000 excess of the cost of the new building over the proceeds from the old building, would be calculated as follows:

Actual Cost	$1,042,000
Capital Gain Deferred By Election	(384,000)
Deemed Cost	$ 658,000

If the ITA 13(4) election is not used, the disposition of the building results in recapture as follows:

Capital Cost	$605,000
UCC	(342,000)
Recapture - No ITA 13(4) Election	$263,000

Use of the ITA 13(4) election would eliminate the recapture and leave the following UCC for the new property:

Capital Cost	$658,000
Recapture Deferred By Election	(263,000)
UCC	$395,000

Note that the UCC for the new building is equal to the UCC of the old building ($342,000), plus the additional $53,000 in funds required for its acquisition.

Equipment   As this is a voluntary disposition, the equipment does not qualify as "former business property" and, as a consequence, neither the ITA 44(1) nor the ITA 13(4) election can be used. However, as there were no other assets in the class at the end of 2005, there will be a terminal loss of $13,000 ($127,000 - $114,000). The new equipment has a capital cost equal to its actual cost of $205,000. This is also equal to the UCC.

Part B   As calculated in Part A, there was a $519,000 capital gain on the land and no gain on the building. Some reduction of Net Income For Tax Purposes can be achieved under the ITA 44(6) election. However, the reduction is limited to the $53,000 difference between the $989,000 fair market value of the old building and the $1,042,000 cost of the replacement building. This would reduce the capital gain on the land by $53,000. The adjusted cost base of the replacement land would remain at $137,000. This would still leave the capital gain on the building at nil. This can be shown as follows:

Deemed Proceeds Of Disposition ($989,000 + $53,000)	$1,042,000
Less: Cost Of Replacement Property	1,042,000
Capital Gain	$ -0-

Using this election, Net Income For Tax Purposes would be reduced by $26,500 [(1/2)($53,000)]. It would be possible to further reduce the gain on the land by transferring more of the proceeds to the building. The result, however, would be a new gain on the building that would be equal to the gain reduction on the land.

Also note that there is a cost involved with this election. While the Company has reduced its 2005 Net Income For Tax Purposes by one-half of the $53,000 capital gain, it has forgone future CCA for the full amount of $53,000.

With the use of this election, the deemed cost of the new building would be $605,000 [$1,042,000 - ($989,000 + $53,000 - $605,000)] and the UCC would be reduced to $342,000 ($605,000 - $263,000).

Solution to Self Study Problem Ten - 5

Part A - Use Of ITA 40(2)(b)   The calculations here begin with the calculation of the gain per year of ownership for the entire period 1972 through 2005. The amounts would be as follows:

English Bay = [($515,000 - $125,000) ÷ 34] = $11,471

Cottage = [($320,000 - $40,000) ÷ 29] = $9,655

As the annual gain is greater on the English Bay property, this should be the designated principal residence for most of the years. The gain on this property can be completely eliminated by designating 33 years to the property, and adding the one additional year that is available in the exemption formula. This will leave one year to be used on the cottage, and the exemption here would be calculated as follows:

{[(1 + 1) ÷ 29]($280,000)} = $19,310

Under this approach, the total capital gain to be recognized in 2005 would be as follows:

Gain On English Bay	$390,000
Exemption On English Bay	(390,000)
Gain On Cottage	280,000
Exemption On Cottage	(19,310)
Total Capital Gain Using ITA 40(2)(b)	$260,690

Part B - Use Of ITA 40(6)   Under this approach, there would be separate calculations of the annual gains on the two properties for both the pre-1982 period and the post-1981 period. These calculations are as follows:

Annual Gains, 1972 Through 1981

English Bay = [($335,000 - $125,000) ÷ 10] = $21,000

Cottage = [($205,000 - $40,000) ÷ 5] = $33,000

Total Gains, 1982 Through 2005

English Bay = ($515,000 - $335,000) = $180,000

Cottage = ($320,000 - $205,000) = $115,000

Under this alternative approach, it would be appropriate to maximize the exemption for the cottage during the ten year period 1972 through 1981, as the per year amount for the cottage is $33,000, vs. $21,000 for the English Bay property. As this property was only owned for five years during this period, the complete elimination of the gain on the cottage would require the use of four designated years, plus the one additional year. This would leave six years for the English Bay property, and the exemption would be calculated as follows:

[(6 + 1) ÷ 10][$335,000 - $125,000] = $147,000

For the period 1982 through 2005, the larger gain would be on the English Bay property and, as a consequence, the exemption on this property should be maximized. As the plus one rule does not apply in this period, the entire 24 years will be required to eliminate the gain on this property, and no years can be allocated to the cottage. Summarizing the results under this dual approach, we would use the following calculations:

Cottage Gain - 1972-1981	$165,000
Exemption	(165,000)
English Bay Gain - 1972-1981	210,000
Exemption	(147,000)
English Bay Gain - 1982-2005	180,000
Exemption	(180,000)
Cottage Gain - 1982-2005	115,000
Exemption	(-0-)
Total Capital Gain Using ITA 40(6) Election	$178,000

Note that the use of ITA 40(6) results in a significantly lower gain than was the case using ITA 40(2)(b). The difference is $82,690 ($260,690 - $178,000).

Solution to Self Study Problem Ten - 6

A. The purchase of the commercial property will be taxable at 7 percent. Therefore, GST of $700,000 [($10,000,000)(7%)] will be payable by Tiffany.

B. As Tiffany is a GST registrant, the Company is responsible for remitting the GST on the purchase. No election is required. When Tiffany's GST return is filed for the period including the purchase date, the required remittance of $700,000 should be reported. At the same time, Tiffany can also claim any available input tax credit. The input tax credit is $476,000 {[($700,000)(60%)] + [($700,000)(40%)(20%)]}.

Therefore, the required GST remittance will be $700,000, for the GST on the purchase, from which a $476,000 input tax credit can be deducted, for a net cash outlay of $224,000. In the calculation of the input tax credit, we assume that the 20 percent general administrative expense allocation is also a reasonable allocation for Tiffany's commercial use of the space.

C. The lease to commercial tenants is a commercial activity, so Tiffany will have to charge GST on the lease.

Solution to Self Study Problem Ten - 7

The GST and total cost of each purchase would be:

Shuswap Cedar A-Frame

GST = Nil
Total Cost = $120,000

Millcreek Bi-Level

GST = [($90,000+$14,000)(7%)] - [($90,000+$14,000)(2.52%)] + [($10,000)(7%)]
= $7,280 - $2,621 + $700
= $5,359

Total Cost = $90,000 + $24,000 + $5,359 = $119,359

Sunset Beach Cottage

The renovations are considered substantial. If the renovations were carried out by the vendor prior to the sale, the purchase would be deemed to be that of a "new" home. Therefore, the purchase price would be subject to the full GST and a new housing rebate could be claimed on the total, as follows:

GST = [($116,000)(7%)] - [($116,000)(2.52%)]
= $8,120 - $2,923
= $5,197

Total Cost = $116,000 + $5,197 = $121,197

Chapter Ten Learning Objectives

After completing Chapter 10, you should be able to:

1. Explain the economic basis for treating capital gains more favourably than other types of income (paragraphs 10-1 through 10-12).

2. Apply the general rules for the determination of gains and losses on the disposition of capital assets (paragraphs 10-13 through 10-30).

3. Demonstrate an understanding of why capital gains and losses on assets acquired prior to December 31, 1971 are determined using alternative rules (paragraphs 10-31 through 10-35).

4. Calculate capital gains and losses on dispositions of identical properties (paragraphs 10-36 through 10-41).

5. Calculate capital gains and losses on partial dispositions of capital property and on properties that are sold with warranties (paragraphs 10-42 and 10-43).

6. Determine the tax consequence of a bad debt arising on debts acquired through the sale of capital assets (paragraphs 10-44 and 10-45).

7. Apply the rules related to capital gains reserves (paragraphs 10-46 through 10-60).

8. Apply the deferral provisions for capital gains arising on voluntary and involuntary dispositions of property that is subsequently replaced (paragraphs 10-61 through 10-75).

9. Apply the deferral provisions available on the disposition of small business investments (paragraphs 10-76 through 10-78).

10. Determine the amount of capital gain or loss resulting from a change in the use of a capital asset (paragraphs 10-79 through 10-82).

11. Apply the basic rules related to the reduction of taxation of capital gains arising from the disposition of a principal residence (paragraphs 10-83 through 10-89).

12. Describe the principal residence elections that are available under ITA 45(1), 45(3), and 40(6) (paragraphs 10-90 through 10-102).

13. Demonstrate a basic understanding of the procedures associated with the disposition of farm property that is also a principal residence (paragraphs 10-103 and 10-104).

14. Determine the tax consequences that result from dispositions of personal use property (paragraphs 10-105 through 10-109)

15. Determine the tax consequences that result from dispositions of listed personal property (paragraphs 10-110 through 10-112).

16. Determine the tax consequences that result from foreign currency transactions (paragraphs 10-113 through 10-121).

17. Determine the tax consequences that result from dispositions of options (paragraphs 10-122 through 10-125).

18. Explain the role of capital gains and losses in tax planning (paragraphs 10-126 and 10-127).

19. Calculate the effects of GST on the acquisition and disposition of capital property (paragraphs 10-128 through 10-156).

If The Appendix To Chapter 10
(Disposition Of Shares Acquired With Stock Options) Has Been Assigned

20. Demonstrate an understanding of the provisions associated with the dispositions of shares acquired with stock options (paragraphs 10-A1 through 10-A5).

CHAPTER ELEVEN

How To Work Through Chapter Eleven

We recommend the following approach in dealing with the material in this Chapter:

Other Income And Deductions - Introduction

☐ Read page 401 (paragraphs 11-1 through 11-4) of the text.

Other Sources Of Income - Subdivision d

☐ Read pages 402 (from paragraph 11-5) and 403 (through paragraph 11-14) of the text.

Spousal Support And Child Support Received

☐ Read pages 403 (from paragraph 11-15) through 405 (through paragraph 11-31) of the text.

☐ Complete Exercise Eleven-1. The Exercise is on page 405 of the text. The solution is on page S-123 of this Study Guide.

☐ Complete Self Study Problem Eleven-1. The Self Study Problem is on page 423 of the text. The solution is on page S-124 of this Study Guide.

Income Inclusions From Deferred Income Plans And Annuities

☐ Read pages 405 (from paragraph 11-32) through 407 (through paragraph 11-39) of the text.

☐ Complete Exercise Eleven-2. The Exercise is on page 407 of the text. The solution is on page S-123 of this Study Guide.

Assistance Payments

☐ Read pages 407 (from paragraph 11-40) and 408 (through paragraph 11-42) of the text.

Lump-Sum Payments

☐ Read pages 408 (from paragraph 11-43) and 409 (through paragraph 11-48) of the text.

Registered Education Savings Plans (RESPs) And Canada Learning Bonds

☐ Read pages 409 (from paragraph 11-49) and 410 (through paragraph 11-54) of the text.

☐ Complete Exercise Eleven-3. The Exercise is on page 410 of the text. The solution is on page S-123 of this Study Guide.

☐ Read pages 410 (from paragraph 11-55) through 413 (through paragraph 11-72) of the text.

Other Deductions - Subdivision e

☐ Read pages 413 (from paragraph 11-73) and 414 (through paragraph 11-77) of the text.

Moving Expenses

☐ Read pages 414 (from paragraph 11-78) through 416 (through paragraph 11-87) of the text.

☐ Complete Exercise Eleven-4. The Exercise is on page 416 of the text. The solution is on page S-123 of this Study Guide.

☐ Complete Self Study Problem Eleven-2. The Self Study Problem is on pages 423 and 424 of the text. The solution is on pages S-124 and S-125 of this Study Guide.

Child Care Expenses

☐   Read pages 416 (from paragraph 11-88) through 419 (through paragraph 11-98) of the text.

☐   Complete Exercise Eleven-5. The Exercise is on page 419 of the text. The solution is on page S-123 of this Study Guide.

☐   Complete Self Study Problem Eleven-3. The Self Study Problem is on page 424 of the text. The solution is on page S-125 of this Study Guide.

Disability Supports Deduction

☐   Read pages 419 (from paragraph 11-99) through 421 (through paragraph 11-102) of the text.

☐   Complete Exercise Eleven-6. The Exercise is on page 421 of the text. The solution is on page S-123 of this Study Guide.

To Complete This Chapter

☐   Review the Key Terms Used In The Chapter on page 422 of the text. Consult the Glossary for the meaning of any key terms you do not know.

☐   Review the Learning Objectives of the Chapter found on page S-118 of this Study Guide.

☐   As a review, we recommend that you view the PowerPoint Slides for Chapter Eleven that are on your Companion CD-ROM. If you do not have access to the Microsoft PowerPoint program, the PowerPoint Viewer program can be installed from the Companion CD-ROM.

Solution to Chapter Eleven Exercises

Exercise Eleven - 1 Solution

The total required child support is $9,000 [(6 Months)($1,500)] and Sandra's payments will be allocated to this requirement first. This means that $9,000 of her payment will not be deductible to her or taxable to Jerry. The remaining $2,000 ($11,000 - $9,000) will be considered a payment towards spousal support and will be deductible to Sandra and taxable to Jerry.

Exercise Eleven - 2 Solution

A total of $63,492 [(4)($15,873)] in payments will be received from this annuity. The $15,873 will be included in his annual tax return. However, the net taxable amount is $2,123 ($15,873 - $13,750) because the annuity was purchased with after tax funds and he is eligible for a deduction equal to:

$$\left(\frac{\$55,000}{\$63,492} \right)(\$15,873) = \underline{\$13,750}$$

Exercise Eleven - 3 Solution

For 2005, the contributions to Jeanine's RESP total $1,700. This is within the annual limit of $4,000, as well as the $2,000 limit for contributions eligible for CESGs. This means that the 2005 CESG would be $440 {[(40%)($500)] + [(20%)($1,700 - $500)]}.

For 2006, the contributions to Jeanine's RESP total $3,900. This is within the annual limit of $4,000 and, as a consequence, there will be no tax on excess contributions. However, Jeanine's plan has accumulated only $4,000 in room for contributions eligible for CESGs. As $1,700 of this was used in 2005, only $2,300 remains for use in 2006. This means that the 2006 CESG would be $560 {[(40%)($500)] + [(20%)($2,300 - $500)]} and $1,600 ($1,700 + $3,900 - $4,000) of the total contributions will not be eligible for CESGs. This would suggest that Jeanine's grandfather should limit his 2006 contribution to $800 and defer the extra $1,600 to the following year. In that year, it would eligible for a grant.

Exercise Eleven - 4 Solution

Her potentially deductible costs are $7,600 ($6,400 + $1,200). While she cannot personally deduct the $1,300 related to the visit to Regina her employer can pay for these costs without creating a taxable benefit. This leaves $4,700 ($6,000 - $1,300) of her employer's contribution that must be applied to her deductible costs. In turn, this leaves $2,900 ($7,600 - $4,700) that she can potentially deduct in 2005. However, the 2005 deduction is limited to the $2,000 that she earned at the new work location, leaving $900 to be carried forward and deducted in 2006.

Exercise Eleven - 5 Solution

The deduction will have to be made by the lower income spouse, Mr. Sampras. The deduction will be the least of the following amounts:

- The actual costs of $10,500.
- Annual Expense Amount of $15,000 [(1)($7,000) + (2)($4,000)].
- 2/3 of Mr. Sampras' earned income, an amount of $24,000 [(2/3)($36,000)].

The least of these three amounts is $10,500.

Exercise Eleven - 6 Solution

As Jos is not eligible for the ITA 118.3 disability tax credit, he will deduct the cost of full time attendant care under ITA 64. When combined with the other disability support costs, the qualifying costs total $36,000 ($23,000 + $18,000 - $5,000). As this is less than his income from employment, he will be able to deduct the full amount of these costs.

Solution to Self Study Problem Eleven - 1

The minimum Net Income For Tax Purposes for the Madison brothers would be calculated as follows:

	Arthur	Jules	Stanley
Net Employment Income	$ 6,000	$18,000	$23,000
Net Business Income	-0-	5,000	-0-
Net Property Income	8,000	-0-	11,000
Employment Insurance Received	3,000	-0-	-0-
Pension Benefits Received	-0-	3,000	-0-
Income Under ITA 3(a)	$17,000	$26,000	$34,000
Net Taxable Capital Gains - ITA 3(b)	2,813	-0-	-0-
Total Under ITA 3(a) And 3(b)	$19,813	$26,000	$34,000
Spousal Support Payments - ITA 3(c)	-0-	-0-	(4,800)
Total Under ITA 3(a), 3(b), 3(c)	$19,813	$26,000	$29,200
Business And Property Loss - ITA 3(d)	-0-	(4,000)	(12,000)
Net Income For Tax Purposes	$19,813	$22,000	$17,200

One-half of Arthur's capital gain is included in income. Jules Madison has an unused capital loss of $3,000 ($17,000 - $14,000) and Stanley Madison has an unused capital loss of $10,000 that can be carried over to other years.

While the charitable donations and tuition fees will generate credits against Tax Payable, they are not deductible in the computation of Net Income For Tax Purposes.

Solution to Self Study Problem Eleven - 2

The allowable moving expenses can be calculated as follows:

First Trip Hotel And Food After Acquiring New Residence (4 Days At $150)		$ 600
Selling Costs Of Old Residence ($9,500 + $1,400)		10,900
Acquisition Cost Of New Residence ($1,850 + $600)		2,450
Halifax Hotel And Food (3 days At $140)		420
Expenses Of Travel To Regina:		
Gasoline	$350	
Hotels (7 Days At $95)	665	
Food (7 Days At $45)	315	1,330
Moving Company Fees		3,800
Hotel And Food In Regina (8 Days At $140)		1,120
Total Allowable Expenses		$20,620
Employment Income In New Location		(10,500)
Carry Over To Next Year		$10,120

Notes:

1. With respect to the first trip, only the cost of meals and lodging that occurred after the acquisition of the new residence would be allowed. The airfare, the cost of car rentals, and the cost of meals and lodging prior to the acquisition of the new residence would not be deductible.

2. The taxes on the old home to the date of sale would not be an allowable moving expense.

3. Food and lodging costs near the old or new residences are limited to 15 days in total. For Ms. Fox, this would include 4 days on her first trip to Regina, the 3 days in Halifax, but only 8 of the 16 days during which she lived in a hotel on arriving in Regina. Note that the 7 days spent travelling to Regina are not included in the 15 day total.

4. The storage costs are deductible.

5. The unused moving cost balance of $10,120 can be carried over and applied against employment income in the following year only.

To use the simplified method to calculate milage, Ms. Fox would need to know how many kilometers she drove related to the move, as well as the appropriate rate for Nova Scotia.

Solution to Self Study Problem Eleven - 3

Generally, the spouse with the lower income must claim the deduction for child care expenses. However, under certain circumstances, for example if this spouse is hospitalized, the spouse with the higher income can claim the deduction for the period of hospitalization. Thus, Mr. Pleasant can claim the least of the following:

Actual Payments (48 weeks at $100)	$ 4,800
Annual Amount [(3)($4,000)]	12,000
2/3 Of Earned Income [(2/3)($33,000)]	22,000
Periodic Amount [($100)(3)(6 weeks)]	1,800

There does not appear to be any requirement that actual child care costs claimed by the higher income spouse need to be limited to the specific amounts paid during the six week period of eligibility. This means that the lowest of the preceding figures would be $100 per child for six weeks, which would result in a deduction of $1,800 for Mr. Pleasant.

Mrs. Pleasant's deduction will be based on the least of:

Actual Payments	$ 4,800
Annual Amount	12,000
2/3 Of Earned Income [(2/3)($18,000)]	12,000

Here the lowest figure is the actual costs of $4,800. This amount will be reduced by the $1,800 that was deducted by Mr. Pleasant. This results in a $3,000 deduction for Mrs. Pleasant.

Chapter Eleven Learning Objectives

1. Identify the major other sources of income that are listed under Subdivision d of the *Income Tax Act* (paragraphs 11-1 through 11-14).

2. Demonstrate an understanding of the tax treatment of child support and spousal support payments (paragraphs 11-15 through 11-31).

3. Identify the income inclusions from deferred income plans (paragraphs 11-32 and 11-33).

4. Apply the rules related to annuity payments, education assistance payments, social assistance, and workers' compensation payments (paragraphs 11-34 through 11-42).

5. Apply the rules related to lump-sum payments (paragraphs 11-43 through 11-48).

6. Demonstrate an understanding of the provisions associated with Registered Education Savings Plans (RESPs) and Canada Learning Bonds (paragraphs 11-49 through 11-72).

7. Identify the deductions under ITA 60(a), 60(b), and 60(e) (paragraphs 11-73 through 11-77).

8. Determine the deductible amount of moving expenses for an individual (paragraphs 11-78 through 11-87).

9. Determine the deductible amount of child care expenses for an individual (paragraphs 11-88 through 11-98).

10. Apply the provisions related to the disability supports deduction (paragraphs 11-99 through 11-102).

CHAPTER TWELVE

How To Work Through Chapter Twelve

We recommend the following approach in dealing with the material in this Chapter:

Non-Arm's Length Transfers Of Property

☐ Read pages 431 (from paragraph 12-1) through 433 (through paragraph 12-8) of the text.

☐ Complete Exercises Twelve-1 and Twelve-2. The Exercises are on page 433 of the text. The solutions are on page S-130 of this Study Guide.

☐ Complete Self Study Problem Twelve-1. The Self Study Problem is on page 458 of the text. The solution is on page S-132 of this Study Guide.

Applicability Of ITA 69

☐ Read pages 433 (from paragraph 12-9) and 434 (through paragraph 12-12) of the text.

☐ Complete Exercise Twelve-3. The Exercise is on page 434 of the text. The solution is on page S-130 of this Study Guide.

Inter Vivos Transfers To A Spouse And Others

☐ Read pages 434 (from paragraph 12-13) through 436 (through paragraph 12-22) of the text.

☐ Complete Exercise Twelve-4. The Exercise is on page 436 of the text. The solution is on page S-130 of this Study Guide.

Transfer Of Farm Property To A Child

☐ Read pages 436 (from paragraph 12-23) and 437 (through paragraph 12-24) of the text.

☐ Complete Exercise Twelve-5. The Exercise is on page 437 of the text. The solution is on page S-130 of this Study Guide.

Income Attribution

☐ Read pages 437 (from paragraph 12-25) through 440 (through paragraph 12-39) of the text.

☐ Complete Exercises Twelve-6 through Twelve-8. The Exercises are on pages 440 and 441 of the text. The solutions are on page S-131 of this Study Guide.

☐ Complete Self Study Problems Twelve-2 through Twelve-4. The Self Study Problems are on pages 458 though 460 of the text. The solutions are on pages S-133 through S-137 of this Study Guide.

Anti-Avoidance Provisions And Tax Planning

☐ Read pages 441 (from paragraph 12-40) and 442 (through paragraph 12-45) of the text.

Leaving Or Entering Canada

☐ Read pages 443 (from paragraph 12-46) and 444 (through paragraph 12-52) of the text.

☐ Complete Exercises Twelve-9 and Twelve-10. The Exercises are on page 444 of the text. The solutions are on page S-131 of this Study Guide.

☐ Read pages 444 (from paragraph 12-53) and 445 (through paragraph 12-55) of the text.

Elective Dispositions

☐ Read page 445 (paragraphs 12-56 and 12-57) of the text.

☐ Complete Exercise Twelve-11. The Exercise is on page 445 of the text. The solution is on page S-131 of this Study Guide.

Emigration - Security For Departure Tax

☐ Read pages 445 (from paragraph 12-58) and 446 (through paragraph 12-62) of the text.

Emigration - Unwinding A Deemed Disposition

☐ Read pages 446 (from paragraph 12-63) and 447 (through paragraph 12-67) of the text.

Emigration - Short-Term Residents

☐ Read page 447 (paragraphs 12-68 and 12-69) of the text.

Emigration And Stock Options

☐ Read pages 447 (from paragraph 12-70) and 448 (through paragraph 12-75) of the text.

Death Of A Taxpayer - Representation And Deemed Dispositions

☐ Read pages 448 (from paragraph 12-76) and 449 (through paragraph 12-81) of the text.

Rollover To A Spouse, A Common-Law Partner, Or A Spousal Trust

☐ Read page 449 (paragraphs 12-82 through 12-85) of the text.

☐ Complete Exercise Twelve-12. The Exercise is on page 450 of the text. The solution is on page S-132 of this Study Guide.

Tax Free Transfers Other Than To A Spouse Or Common-Law Partner

☐ Read page 450 (paragraph 12-86) of the text.

☐ Complete Self Study Problem Twelve-5. The Self Study Problem is on page 460 of the text. The solution is on pages S-137 through S-139 of this Study Guide.

Filing Returns And Payment Of Taxes

☐ Read pages 450 (from paragraph 12-87) through 453 (through paragraph 12-102) of the text.

Allowable Capital Losses

☐ Read pages 453 (from paragraph 12-103) and 454 (through paragraph 12-106) of the text.

☐ Complete Exercise Twelve-13. The Exercise is on page 454 of the text. The solution is on page S-132 of this Study Guide.

Deferred Income Plans At Death

☐ Read pages 454 (from paragraph 12-107) and 455 (through paragraph 12-109) of the text.

Charitable Donations And Medical Expenses

☐ Read page 456 (paragraphs 12-110 and 12-111) of the text.

To Complete This Chapter

☐ Review the Key Terms Used In The Chapter on page 456 of the text. Consult the Glossary for the meaning of any key terms you do not know.

☐ Review the Learning Objectives of the Chapter found on pages S-140 and S-141 of this Study Guide.

☐ As a review, we recommend that you view the PowerPoint Slides for Chapter Twelve that are on your Companion CD-ROM. If you do not have access to the Microsoft PowerPoint program, the PowerPoint Viewer program can be installed from the Companion CD-ROM.

Solution to Chapter Twelve Exercises

Exercise Twelve - 1 Solution

Mr. Lipky's proceeds of disposition will be the amount received of $95,000, resulting in a capital loss of $5,000 ($95,000 - $100,000). His brother's adjusted cost base will be the fair market value of the land, or $75,000. There will be double taxation on a subsequent sale by his brother on the difference between $95,000 and $75,000.

Exercise Twelve - 2 Solution

As the transfer was to a related party for an amount less than the fair market value of the asset, Ms. Lee will be deemed to have received the fair market value of $56,600. This will result in a taxable capital gain of $1,800 [(1/2)($56,600 - $53,000)] and recapture of CCA of $15,800 ($53,000 - $37,200). The capital cost of the property to her father will be $37,200, the amount paid for the asset. There will be double taxation on a subsequent sale by her father on the difference between $56,600 and $37,200.

Exercise Twelve - 3 Solution

Under ITA 69(1.2), the proceeds of disposition in this case will be the greater of the $33,000 actual proceeds and the $211,000 fair market value of the property without considering the lease. The greater amount would be $211,000, resulting in a taxable capital gain for Mr. Bates of $89,000 [(1/2)($211,000 - $33,000)]. The adjusted cost base to the corporation would be the actual transfer price of $33,000. This would lead to double taxation on a subsequent sale of the property on the difference between $211,000 and $33,000.

Exercise Twelve - 4 Solution

If Ms. Sharp does not elect out of ITA 73(1), the property will be transferred at the UCC of $110,000. There would be no tax consequences at the time of transfer. While the spouse would receive the property with a UCC of $110,000, the capital cost of $175,000 would be retained, with the difference being considered deemed CCA. The $300,000 proceeds of disposition do not affect these results.

If she elects out of ITA 73(1), the transfer will be made at $300,000, resulting in a capital gain of $125,000 ($300,000 - $175,000). In addition, she will have recapture of $65,000 ($175,000 - $110,000). With Ms. Sharp electing out of ITA 73(1), ITA 69 becomes applicable. Because the transfer was made for consideration in excess of the fair market value of the property, the capital cost to her spouse will be limited to the fair market value of $225,000, raising the possibility of double taxation on any subsequent sale.

Exercise Twelve - 5 Solution

With respect to the land, the $280,000 paid is between the $250,000 adjusted cost base floor and the $325,000 fair market value ceiling. Therefore, the proceeds of disposition would be $280,000, resulting in a capital gain for Mr. Nobel of $30,000 ($280,000 - $250,000). The $280,000 would also be the adjusted cost base for his daughter.

With respect to the barn, as there was no consideration given, the transfer would take place at the UCC floor of $85,000. There would be no tax consequences for Mr. Nobel. With respect to his daughter, she would assume a UCC value of $85,000. However, the old capital cost of $115,000 would be retained, with the $30,000 difference being treated as deemed CCA.

Exercise Twelve - 6 Solution

As ITA 73(1) provides for a tax free rollover of capital property to a spouse, there would be no tax consequences for either Mr. or Mrs. Moreau in 2004. For 2005, both the dividends and the capital gain would be attributed to Mrs. Moreau. There would be no tax consequences for Mr. Moreau in 2005. The taxable amount of the dividends would be $3,125 [(1.25)($2,500)] and the taxable capital gain would be $9,500 [(1/2)($42,000 - $23,000)].

Exercise Twelve - 7 Solution

As there is no provision for a tax free transfer of shares to a child, Mrs. Moreau will have a taxable capital gain in 2004 of $7,000 [(1/2)($37,000 - $23,000)]. For 2005, the taxable amount of the dividends of $3,125 [(1.25)($2,500)] would be attributed to Mrs. Moreau. However, the 2005 taxable capital gain of $2,500 [(1/2)($42,000 - $37,000)] would be taxed in Nicki's hands.

Exercise Twelve - 8 Solution

Unless Mr. Bronski elects out of ITA 73(1) by including a gain in his 2004 tax return, there will be no tax consequences to either Mr. or Mrs. Bronski in 2004. In addition, because the transfer is a tax free rollover, the adjusted cost base of the bonds to Mrs. Bronski will be $115,000.

If Mr. Bronski does not elect out of ITA 73(1), the income attribution rules will apply. Even if he did elect out of ITA 73(1), the rules would still apply as the loan does not bear interest at the prescribed rate.

All of the 2005 interest income on the bonds will be attributed to Mr. Bronski. In addition to the interest of $6,100, there would be a taxable capital gain of $7,000 [(1/2)($129,000 - $115,000)], which would also be attributed to Mr. Bronski. The total addition to Mr. Bronski's income for 2005 is $13,100 ($6,100 + $7,000).

Exercise Twelve - 9 Solution

There would be a deemed disposition on her departure, leaving her liable for the taxes on a $10,500 [(1/2)($49,000 - $28,000)] taxable capital gain.

Exercise Twelve - 10 Solution

As real property is exempt from the deemed disposition provision contained in ITA 128.1(4)(b), there would be no tax consequences with respect to the rental property at the time of Mr. Chrysler's departure. However, real property is Taxable Canadian Property and, as a consequence, he would be liable for Canadian taxes on both recapture and capital gains resulting from a subsequent sale of the property, even after he becomes a non-resident.

Exercise Twelve - 11 Solution

With respect to the shares of the Canadian private company, there would be a required deemed disposition, resulting in a taxable capital gain of $57,500 [(1/2)($235,000 - $120,000)]. In the absence of an election on the rental property, this would be the only tax consequence resulting from her departure. However, if Ms. Lopez elects under ITA 128.1(4)(d) to have a deemed disposition on her rental property, the result will be a terminal loss on the building of $42,000 ($142,000 - $100,000) and an allowable capital loss on the land of $15,000 [(1/2)($60,000 - $30,000)]. These amounts can be used to eliminate income tax on all but $500 of the $57,500 taxable capital gain on the securities.

Exercise Twelve - 12 Solution

With respect to truck A, it would be transferred to her husband at its UCC value of $25,500 [($51,000)($33,000/$66,000)]. No income would be included in Ms. Lardner's final tax return and, while the UCC value for the truck in Michel's hands would be the $25,500 transfer value, it would retain its original capital cost of $42,000. Truck B would be transferred to Melinda at its fair market value of $33,000. This would result in $7,500 ($33,000 - $25,500) in recapture being included in Ms. Lardner's final tax return. The $33,000 transfer price would be the UCC value to Melinda. Since Ms. Lardner's original capital cost exceeds the $33,000 fair market value, Melinda would retain Ms. Lardner's $42,000 capital cost with the difference between the two values being treated as deemed CCA.

Exercise Twelve - 13 Solution

The carry forward must be applied on an adjusted basis to eliminate the 2005 taxable capital gain. To implement this, the $7,500 amount (three-quarter basis) must be adjusted to $5,000 (one-half basis). The $2,000 taxable capital gain will use $2,000 of the adjusted 1990 carry forward, leaving $3,000. This amount must be adjusted back to the 3/4 inclusion rate. The resulting $4,500 [(3/2)($3,000)] can be applied against any other type of income in 2005 or, if there is not sufficient other income in that year, against any other type of income in 2004 (amended return).

Solution to Self Study Problem Twelve - 1

Case A   In this Case, the shares were transferred at a price that was below market value. However, John Bolton will have deemed proceeds under ITA 69(1)(b) equal to the fair market value of $525,000 [(5,000)($105)]. With his cost base at $225,000 [(5,000)($45)], this will result in a capital gain of $300,000, one-half of which would be included in John's Net Income For Tax Purposes. From the point of view of Alex Bolton, his cost base for the shares will be the actual price paid of $375,000 [(5,000)($75)]. This means that, if Alex Bolton sells these shares at some later point in time for a price in excess of $75, the difference between his proceeds of disposition and the price per share he paid of $75 would be taxed in his hands. In effect, any gain arising from a sales price of up to $105 will be subject to double taxation.

Case B   In this situation, the gain to be recorded by John Bolton would be based on $625,000 [(5,000)($125)], the actual amount received. This would result in a capital gain of $400,000 ($625,000 - $225,000), one-half of which would be included in John's Net Income For Tax Purposes. From the point of view of Alex Bolton, ITA 69(1)(a) would limit his adjusted cost base to $525,000, the fair market value of the shares at the time of purchase. In a manner similar to Case A, there is the likelihood of double taxation being assessed on the difference between the $625,000 price paid and the $525,000 fair market value at the time of the sale.

Case C   In this Case, both the proceeds to John Bolton and the adjusted cost base to Alex Bolton will be equal to the amount paid for the shares. This will result in John recording a capital gain of $300,000 as calculated in Case A, one-half of which would be included in John's Net Income For Tax Purposes. However, in this Case, the adjusted cost base to Alex Bolton will be $525,000 and no double taxation will arise.

Case D   In this Case, Mr. John Bolton will be deemed to have received proceeds equal to the fair market value of $525,000. This will result in the same $300,000 capital gain that was calculated in Cases A and C, one-half of which will be included in John's Net Income For Tax Purposes. As in Case C, the adjusted cost base to Alex Bolton will be $525,000 and no double taxation will arise.

Solution to Self Study Problem Twelve - 2

Mr. Langdon would be assessed for income attribution of $10,500 ($5,000 + $5,500). As Heather did not use the funds to produce income, there would be no tax consequences of making the loan to her.

Solution to Self Study Problem Twelve - 3

Case A With ITA 73(1) in effect, the December 31, 2005 transfer would be a deemed disposition at the adjusted cost base of $185,000. This means that Dr. Bolt would not record a capital gain at the time of the transfer and the adjusted cost base of the securities to Mr. Bolt would be $185,000. In 2006, the $23,125 in taxable dividends would be attributed back to Dr. Bolt and included in her Net Income For Tax Purposes for that year. When Mr. Bolt sells the securities, the 2007 taxable capital gain of $37,500 [(1/2)($260,000 - $185,000)] would also be attributed back to Dr. Bolt. This transfer would not affect Mr. Bolt's Net Income For Tax Purposes in any of the three years under consideration.

Case B With ITA 73(1) in effect, the December 31, 2005 transfer would still take place at the adjusted cost base of $185,000, and the resulting 2005, 2006, and 2007 results for both Dr. Bolt and Mr. Bolt would be identical to Case A.

Case C With the decision to elect out of ITA 73(1) and payment of consideration equal to fair market value, the transfer will be recorded as a disposition at fair market value. This will result in a 2005 taxable capital gain for Dr. Bolt of $20,000 [(1/2)($225,000 - $185,000)] and an adjusted cost base to Mr. Bolt of $225,000. Given that the transfer was at fair market value and Dr. Bolt chose to elect out of ITA 73(1), there would be no attribution of either income or capital gains. The taxable dividends of $23,125 will be included in Mr. Bolt's 2006 Net Income For Tax Purposes, and the 2007 taxable capital gain of $17,500 [(1/2)($260,000 - $225,000)] will be included in his 2007 Net Income For Tax Purposes. The transfer would not affect Dr. Bolt's Net Income For Tax Purposes in either 2006 or 2007.

Case D As ITA 73(1) continues to be applicable in this Case, the transfer would take place at the adjusted cost base of $185,000, and both dividends and capital gains would be attributed back to Dr. Bolt. For both Dr. and Mr. Bolt, the results for all three years would be identical to those described in Case A.

Case E When a taxpayer elects out of ITA 73(1) and a transfer is made for consideration that is less than fair market value, the provisions of ITA 69(1) are applicable to the transferor. Under these provisions, if a taxpayer disposes of a property for less than its fair market value, the proceeds of disposition are deemed to be the fair market value amount. This will result in Dr. Bolt recording a 2005 taxable capital gain of $20,000 [(1/2)($225,000 - $185,000)]. As the transfer is for consideration that is less than the fair market value of the securities, the income attribution rules will be applicable, resulting in the 2006 taxable dividends of $23,125 being included in Dr. Bolt's 2006 Net Income For Tax Purposes. In addition, the 2007 taxable capital gain of $60,000 [(1/2)($260,000 - $140,000)] would also be attributed back to her and included in her 2007 Net Income For Tax Purposes.

Note that the adjusted cost base for the securities is based on the actual price paid by Mr. Bolt, subjecting the $40,000 ($225,000 - $185,000) difference between the transfer price and Dr. Bolt's adjusted cost base to double taxation if the shares are sold at a price between $185,000 and $225,000. In addition, Dr. Bolt's $45,000 ($185,000 - $140,000) loss on the sale would not be deductible. Since Mr. Bolt's adjusted cost base is $140,000, if the shares are sold at a price between $140,000 and $185,000, he will be taxed on the capital gain, despite the fact that Dr. Bolt's loss was disallowed.

Dr. Bolt's total taxable capital gain on these shares is $80,000 ($20,000 + $60,000). This is $42,500 more than the taxable capital gain in Case A and represents [(1/2)($225,000 - $140,000)]. The transfer would not affect Mr. Bolt's Net Income For Tax Purposes in any of the three years under consideration.

Case F Under ITA 69, a non-arm's length gift is deemed to be a disposition and acquisition to be recorded by both parties at fair market value. This means that Dr. Bolt would have to record a 2005 taxable capital gain of $20,000 [(1/2)($225,000 - $185,000)]. As a gift to a minor was involved, income attribution rules will apply and the 2006 taxable dividends of $23,125 will have to be included in the 2006 Net Income For Tax Purposes of Dr. Bolt. However, the attribution rules do not apply to capital gains when the attribution results from a transfer to someone under 18 years of age. As a consequence, Dolly Bolt will include a taxable capital gain of $17,500 [(1/2)($260,000 - $225,000)] in her 2007 Net Income For Tax Purposes. The transfer will have no effect on the 2005 and 2006 Net Income For Tax Purposes of Dolly Bolt, nor on the 2007 Net Income For Tax Purposes of Dr. Bolt.

Case G The transfer at fair market value will result in Dr. Bolt recording a taxable capital gain of $20,000 [(1/2)($225,000 - $185,000)] in 2005. As the transfer is at fair market and the related loan requires interest at commercial rates, the income attribution rules are not applicable. This means that Dolly will include taxable dividends of $23,125 in her 2006 Net Income For Tax Purposes and a taxable capital gain of $17,500 [(1/2)($260,000 - $225,000)] in her 2007 Net Income For Tax Purposes. The transaction will have no effect on the 2006 and 2007 Net Income For Tax Purposes of Dr. Bolt, nor on the 2005 Net Income For Tax Purposes of Dolly Bolt.

Case H As the transfer is at fair market value, Dr. Bolt will have a taxable capital gain of $20,000 [(1/2)($225,000 - $185,000)] included in her 2005 Net Income For Tax Purposes. Dirk's adjusted cost base for the securities will be $225,000, and the transfer will not affect his 2005 Net Income For Tax Purposes. As Dirk is not under 18 years of age, the attribution rules found in ITA 74.1(2) do not apply. However, ITA 56(4.1) indicates that income attribution applies in situations where an interest free or low interest loan has been given to a non-arm's length individual, and one of the main purposes of the loan is to reduce or avoid taxes. As Dirk has only limited income and would be in a lower tax bracket than Dr. Bolt, it is likely that this condition would apply in this Case. As a result, the 2006 taxable dividends of $23,125 would be included in the 2006 Net Income For Tax Purposes of Dr. Bolt, rather than in the Net Income For Tax Purposes of her son. However, the 2007 taxable capital gain of $17,500 [(1/2)($260,000 - $225,000)] would not be attributed back to Dr. Bolt. Rather, it would be included in the 2007 Net Income For Tax Purposes of Dirk Bolt.

Solution to Self Study Problem Twelve - 4

Note As the farm would be considered qualified farm property, any capital gains arising from a transfer would be eligible for the $500,000 lifetime capital gains deduction. If Long Consulting Ltd. is a qualified small business corporation, capital gains on the disposition of these shares would also be eligible for the $500,000 deduction.

Long Consulting Ltd. - Gift To Spouse ITA 73(1) permits transfers of a capital property to a spouse at its tax value (adjusted cost base or UCC). This means that the shares in Long Consulting Ltd. could be gifted to Mr. Long with no immediate tax consequences. However, the tax basis for these shares would remain at the adjusted cost base of $210,000 and income attribution would apply.

Any dividends paid on the shares would be attributed to Mrs. Long. In addition, should Mr. Long subsequently sell these shares for $475,000, the resulting taxable capital gain of $132,500, as calculated below, would also be attributed to Mrs. Long.

Proceeds (Fair Market Value)	$475,000
Adjusted Cost Base	(210,000)
Capital Gain	$265,000
Inclusion Rate	1/2
Taxable Capital Gain	$132,500

As an alternative, Mrs. Long could elect out of the provisions of ITA 73(1). Under ITA 69, the gift would be recorded as a disposition at the $475,000 fair market value. Mrs. Long would have an immediate taxable capital gain of $132,500 (as calculated in the preceding paragraph) and Mr. Long's adjusted cost base would be $475,000. However, if the transfer is a gift, and Mr. Long does not use his own funds to purchase the shares, income attribution would apply to any dividends received by Mr. Long and to any capital gain arising from a later sale at an amount in excess of $475,000.

Long Consulting Ltd. - Gift To Children   Under ITA 69, a gift to a related party is deemed to be a transfer at fair market value. Given this, a taxable capital gain of $132,500 (as calculated for Mr. Long) would result from a transfer to either child.

The adjusted cost base to the children would be the fair market value of $475,000. The effect of the gift on Mrs. Long's immediate tax situation would be the same, regardless of which child receives the gift.

As Mary is under 18 years of age, a transfer to her would result in all dividend income received by Mary prior to her reaching age 18 being attributed back to Mrs. Long. However, if Mary sells the shares for more or less than her adjusted cost base of $475,000, the resulting capital gain or loss would not be attributed back to Mrs. Long. This would be the case whether or not Mary was 18 or older at the time of the sale. As Barry is over 18, the gift would not result in attribution of either dividends or capital gains.

Rental Property - Gift To Spouse   Here again, ITA 73(1) would permit a transfer to Mr. Long at tax values with no immediate tax consequences. The tax basis of the property would not be changed. However, as the transfer is a gift, income attribution rules would apply. This means that any net rental income would be attributed to Mrs. Long. In addition, if Mr. Long were to later sell the property for its current fair market value of $275,000, the following amounts would be attributed to Mrs. Long:

Capital Cost	$190,000
UCC	(125,000)
Recaptured CCA	$ 65,000
Proceeds Of Disposition	$275,000
Adjusted Cost Base	(190,000)
Capital Gain	$ 85,000
Inclusion Rate	1/2
Taxable Capital Gain	$ 42,500

Mrs. Long could also elect out of the provisions of ITA 73(1) and transfer the rental property at its fair market value. However, if she does, she would immediately be taxed on the recapture as well as the taxable capital gain. Electing out of ITA 73(1) would not change the fact that the transfer is a gift to a spouse and, as a consequence, future rental income, capital gains, and recapture would be attributed to Mrs. Long.

Rental Property - Gift To Children   There is no exemption from the general rules of ITA 69 for transfers of depreciable property to children. As a consequence, Mrs. Long would be subject to taxation based on a disposition of the property at its fair market value of $275,000. This would result in immediate taxation on a $42,500 taxable capital gain and recapture in the amount of $65,000 (see preceding calculations).

The tax base to either of the children would be $275,000 and a sale at this price would have no tax consequences for either Mrs. Long or the children. Here again, however, if this property were given to Mary, the income attribution rules of ITA 74.1 would apply to any amount of property income subsequently earned. This would mean that until Mary reached 18 years of age, all property income would be attributed to Mrs. Long. Alternatively, if the property were gifted to her son, Barry, all subsequent income would be taxed in his hands. There would be no attribution of further capital gains on a gift to either child.

Dynamics Inc. - Gift To Spouse   As with the other properties, these shares could be given to Mr. Long and, under the provisions of ITA 73(1), no immediate tax consequences would arise. However, any dividend income on the shares would be attributed to Mrs. Long and, if Mr. Long were to sell them for their fair market value of $384,000, the income attribution rules of ITA 74.1 would require that the following taxable capital gain be attributed to the income of Mrs. Long:

Proceeds Of Disposition	$384,000
Adjusted Cost Base	(212,000)
Capital Gain	$172,000
Inclusion Rate	1/2
Taxable Capital Gain	$ 86,000

Mrs. Long could elect out of ITA 73(1) by recording the $86,000 taxable capital gain at the time of the transfer to her spouse. However, as long as the property was transferred as a gift, attribution would apply to both dividend income received by Mr. Long and to any further capital gains realized on a subsequent sale.

Dynamics Inc. - Gift To Children   In the case of a transfer to either of her children, ITA 69 would require that the gift be treated as a deemed disposition with the proceeds at the fair market value of $384,000. This would result in an immediate taxable capital gain of $86,000, as was calculated in the preceding paragraph. However, the tax base to the children would be the fair market value of $384,000 and there would be no tax consequences for any of the parties if a sale took place at that price.

As was the case with the other properties considered, a transfer to Mary would result in the application of the income attribution rules of ITA 74.1. This would mean that subsequent dividend income on these shares would be allocated to Mrs. Long until Mary reaches 18 years of age. If Mary were to sell the property for more than $384,000, there would be no attribution of the capital gain. If the shares were transferred to Barry, there would be no attribution of either dividends or capital gains.

Farm Land - Gift To Spouse   As with all of the other properties, Mrs. Long could make a tax free transfer of the farm land to her husband under ITA 73(1). The transfer would take place at the adjusted cost base of $80,000 and, in the event of a subsequent sale, the following taxable capital gain would be attributed to Mrs. Long under ITA 74.1:

Proceeds Of Disposition	$175,000
Adjusted Cost Base	(80,000)
Capital Gain	$ 95,000
Inclusion Rate	1/2
Taxable Capital Gain	$ 47,500

Alternatively, Mrs. Long could elect out of ITA 73(1) and transfer the property at its fair market value of $175,000, resulting in the taxable capital gain of $47,500 being recognized at the time of transfer.

As farm income is considered to be business income rather than property income, there would be no attribution of any farm income that arises while Mr. Long is holding the property.

Farm Land - Gift To Children   ITA 73(3) permits the inter vivos transfer of farm property used by the taxpayer or her family to a child on a tax free basis. The deemed proceeds would be Mrs. Long's adjusted cost base, which means that Mrs. Long would incur no taxation at the time of the gift to either child. The adjusted cost base to either child would be the same $80,000 that was deemed to be the proceeds of the disposition.

As noted in our discussion of the transfer of this property to Mr. Long, because farm income is business income rather than property income, there will be no attribution of farm income in the case of a transfer to either child.

On most transfers to related minors, there is no attribution of capital gains. This is a reflection of the fact that, unlike the rules for transfers to a spouse, there is no general rollover provision for transfers to related minors on a tax free basis. However, when a transfer is made to a related minor under the provisions of ITA 73(3) and the transfer value is below fair market value, ITA 75.1 requires that any subsequent gain resulting from a disposition by the transferee before they reach age 18 be attributed back to the transferor.

This means that, if the farm property is transferred to Mary and she sells the property for $175,000 before she reaches age 18, a taxable capital gain of $47,500 (see preceding calculations for Mr. Long) will be attributed to Mrs. Long.

Solution to Self Study Problem Twelve - 5

Note   As the farm would be considered qualified farm property, any capital gains would be eligible for the $500,000 lifetime capital gains deduction. Further, if Caswell Enterprises is a qualified small business corporation, capital gains on the disposition of these shares would also be eligible for the $500,000 deduction.

Case A   Whenever a taxpayer dies, there is a deemed disposition of all of his property. If the transfer is to a spouse, the disposition is deemed to have taken place at the adjusted cost base of capital property other than depreciable property, or at the UCC of depreciable property. This would mean that there would be no immediate tax consequences associated with Mr. Caswell's death in this Case, where all of the property is transferred to his spouse. Note, however, that on a subsequent disposition by Mr. Caswell's spouse, her tax base would be the same as Mr. Caswell's. These values would be as follows:

Rental Property - UCC	$ 67,000
Rental Property - Capital Cost	95,000
General Industries Ltd. - Adjusted Cost Base	200,000
Farm Land - Adjusted Cost Base	325,000
Caswell Enterprises - Adjusted Cost Base	275,000

It is possible, after Mr. Caswell's death, for his legal representative to elect to have assets transferred to his spouse at fair market values. This would result in taxable capital gains and other income being included in his final tax return. However, this would not be a reasonable alternative unless Mr. Caswell has unused loss carry forwards at the time of his death, or the lifetime capital gains deduction can be utilized on his final return.

Case B This Case is more complex and would follow the general rules applicable to transfers made at death to anyone other than a spouse. For both depreciable and non-depreciable property, other than farm property, the transfer will be deemed to have taken place at fair market value.

In the case of the rental property, the deemed proceeds would be $133,000, resulting in Taxable Income of $47,000 for Mr. Caswell's estate. This would be calculated as follows:

Deemed Proceeds Of Disposition	$133,000
Adjusted Cost Base	(95,000)
Capital Gain	$ 38,000
Inclusion Rate	1/2
Taxable Capital Gain	$ 19,000

Capital Cost	$ 95,000
UCC	(67,000)
Recaptured CCA	$ 28,000

The capital cost and UCC for his son, John, is the fair market value of $133,000.

In the case of the General Industries shares, the deemed proceeds would be $350,000 and the tax consequences to Mr. Caswell's estate would be as follows:

Deemed Proceeds Of Disposition	$350,000
Adjusted Cost Base	(200,000)
Capital Gain	$150,000
Inclusion Rate	1/2
Taxable Capital Gain	$ 75,000

In the case of farm land that is being used by the taxpayer or a member of his family, ITA 70(9) permits a tax free transfer of such property to a child, at the time of death. The deemed proceeds would be Mr. Caswell's adjusted cost base, resulting in no tax consequences for his estate. As you would expect, the adjusted cost base to Mr. Caswell's son, John, would be the same $325,000 that was deemed to be the proceeds of the disposition on Mr. Caswell's death.

With respect to the shares of a Canadian controlled private corporation, the tax consequences to Mr. Caswell's estate would be as follows:

Deemed Proceeds Of Disposition	$426,000
Adjusted Cost Base	(275,000)
Capital Gain	$151,000
Inclusion Rate	1/2
Taxable Capital Gain	$ 75,500

This gives a total increase in Net Income of $197,500.

Case C With respect to the departure from Canada, ITA 128.1(4)(b) requires a deemed disposition of all property except real property, property used in a Canadian business, and excluded personal property [i.e., a variety of items specified under ITA 128.1(9)]. This means there would be a deemed disposition for Mr. Caswell of both the General Industries Ltd. shares and the Caswell Enterprises shares. The tax consequences of the two dispositions would be as follows:

Deemed Proceeds (General Industries)	$350,000
Adjusted Cost Base	(200,000)
Capital Gain	$150,000
Inclusion Rate	1/2
Taxable Capital Gain	$ 75,000
Deemed Proceeds (Caswell Enterprises)	$426,000
Adjusted Cost Base	(275,000)
Capital Gain	$151,000
Inclusion Rate	1/2
Taxable Capital Gain	$ 75,500

This gives a total increase in Net Income of $150,500.

Two additional facts might be noted here. First, Mr. Caswell could elect under ITA 128.1(4)(d) to have a deemed disposition of the other properties at the time of his departure. Given the amounts already added to his income, this would not appear to be a desirable alternative unless he can utilize the lifetime capital gains deduction on the farm land. Also of importance is the fact that Mr. Caswell can defer the taxation on these amounts. Provided adequate security is provided, ITA 220(4.5) allows an emigrant to defer the taxation on deemed dispositions created by ITA 128.1(4)(b) until such time as the assets are sold. This would likely be an attractive alternative to Mr. Caswell.

Chapter Twelve Learning Objectives

After completing Chapter 12, you should be able to:

1. Determine the tax consequences of non-arm's length transfers of property to related individuals at values other than fair market value (paragraphs 12-1 through 12-12).

2. Describe the special rollover provisions applicable to inter vivos transfers of property to a spouse and inter vivos transfers of farm property to a child (paragraphs 12-13 through 12-24).

3. Apply the income attribution rules to inter vivos transfers of property to a spouse and to related individuals who are under the age of 18 (paragraphs 12-25 through 12-39).

4. Describe some of the anti-avoidance provisions that relate to the income attribution rules (paragraphs 12-40 and 12-41).

5. Be able to describe some of the tax planning techniques that are available to mitigate the income attribution rules (paragraph 12-42).

6. Describe the income attribution rules applicable to transfers to other related parties (paragraphs 12-43 through 12-45).

7. List the types of assets that are subject to the deemed disposition rules on entering or leaving Canada (paragraphs 12-46 through 12-48).

8. Demonstrate an understanding of the tax provisions related to immigration to Canada (paragraphs 12-49 and 12-50).

9. Demonstrate an understanding of the tax provisions related to emigration from Canada (paragraphs 12-51 through 12-55).

10. Describe the availability and use of elective dispositions on departures from Canada (paragraphs 12-56 and 12-57).

11. Explain the security for departure tax and its application (paragraphs 12-58 through 12-62).

12. Describe the provisions available for unwinding a deemed disposition on departure from Canada (paragraphs 12-63 through 12-67).

13. Explain the rules applicable to short-term residents of Canada (paragraphs 12-68 and 12-69).

14. Calculate the tax consequences of the deemed disposition on departure from Canada of shares acquired through the exercise of stock options (paragraphs 12-70 through 12-75).

15. Calculate the tax consequences resulting from the deemed disposition of all capital property at the time of an individual's death (paragraphs 12-76 through 12-81).

16. Apply the rollover provisions that are available at the time of an individual's death (paragraphs 12-82 through 12-86).

17. List the different tax returns that can be filed by the representatives of a deceased person (paragraph 12-87).

18. Explain the reasons for filing multiple tax returns for a deceased person in the year of death (paragraphs 12-88 through 12-96).

19. Explain the concept of a rights or things return (paragraphs 12-97 through 12-99).

20. Demonstrate an understanding of the procedures for the payment of taxes arising on the death of a taxpayer (paragraphs 12-101 and 12-102).

21. Demonstrate an understanding of the treatment of allowable capital losses in relation to a deceased taxpayer (paragraphs 12-103 through 12-106).

22. Demonstrate an understanding of the provisions related to the treatment of deferred income plans at death (paragraphs 12-107 through 12-109).

23. Demonstrate a basic understanding of the treatment of charitable donations and medical expenses in the year of death (paragraphs 12-110 and 12-111).

CHAPTER THIRTEEN

How To Work Through Chapter Thirteen

We recommend the following approach in dealing with the material in this Chapter:

Planning For Retirement
☐ Read pages 467 (from paragraph 13-1) through 470 (through paragraph 13-14) of the text.

Registered Retirement Savings Plans (RRSPs)
☐ Read pages 470 (from paragraph 13-15) through 473 (through paragraph 13-33) of the text.

☐ Complete Exercise Thirteen-1. The Exercise is on page 474 of the text. The solution is on page S-146 of this Study Guide.

Earned Income
☐ Read page 474 (paragraphs 13-34 and 13-35) of the text.

☐ Complete Exercises Thirteen-2 and Thirteen-3. The Exercises are on pages 474 and 475 of the text. The solutions are on page S-146 of this Study Guide.

Pension Adjustments (PAs)
☐ Read page 475 (paragraphs 13-36 through 13-38) of the text.

☐ Complete Exercise Thirteen-4 The Exercise is on page 475 of the text. The solution is on page S-146 of this Study Guide.

Money Purchase RPPs And DPSPs
☐ Read pages 475 (from paragraph 13-39) and 476 (through paragraph 13-44) of the text.

☐ Complete Exercise Thirteen-5. The Exercise is on page 477 of the text. The solution is on page S-146 of this Study Guide.

☐ Read page 477 (paragraph 13-45) of the text.

☐ Complete Self Study Problem Thirteen-1. The Self Study Problem is on page 500 of the text. The solution is on pages S-147 and S-148 of this Study Guide.

Past Service Pension Adjustments (PSPAs)
☐ Read pages 477 (from paragraphs 13-46) and 478 (through paragraph 13-50) of the text.

Pension Adjustment Reversals (PARs)
☐ Read page 478 (paragraphs 13-51 through paragraph 13-53) of the text.

Examples Of RRSP Deduction Calculations
☐ Read pages 478 (from paragraph 13-54) and 479 (through paragraph 13-54) of the text.

☐ Complete Exercise Thirteen-6. The Exercise is on page 480 of the text. The solution is on page S-146 of this Study Guide.

Undeducted And Excess RRSP Contributions

☐ Read pages 480 (from paragraph 13-55) and 481 (through paragraph 13-57) of the text.

☐ Complete Exercise Thirteen-7. The Exercise is on page 481 of the text. The solution is on page S-146 of this Study Guide.

Tax Planning - Excess RRSP Contributions

☐ Read pages 481 (from paragraph 13-58) and 482 (through paragraph 13-61) of the text.

☐ Complete Self Study Problems Thirteen-2 and Thirteen-3. The Self Study Problems are on pages 500 and 501 of the text. The solutions are on pages S-148 and S-149 of this Study Guide.

RRSP And RRIF Administration Fees

☐ Read page 482 (paragraph 13-62) of the text.

RRSP Withdrawals And Voluntary Conversions

☐ Read pages 482 (from paragraph 13-63) and 483 (through paragraph 13-67) of the text.

Involuntary Termination Due To Age Limitation

☐ Read page 483 (paragraphs 13-68 through 13-70) of the text.

Other Plan Terminations

☐ Read pages 483 (from paragraph 13-71) and 484 (through paragraph 13-76) of the text.

Spousal RRSP

☐ Read pages 484 (from paragraph 13-77) and 485 (through paragraph 13-84) of the text.

☐ Complete Exercise Thirteen-8. The Exercise is on page 485 of the text. The solution is on page S-147 of this Study Guide.

Home Buyers' Plan (HBP)

☐ Read pages 485 (from paragraph 13-85) through 487 (through paragraph 13-93) of the text.

☐ Complete Exercise Thirteen-9. The Exercise is on page 488 of the text. The solution is on page S-147 of this Study Guide.

Lifelong Learning Plan (LLP)

☐ Read pages 488 (from paragraph 13-94) and 489 (through paragraph 13-104) of the text.

☐ Complete Exercise Thirteen-10. The Exercise is on page 489 of the text. The solution is on page S-147 of this Study Guide.

Registered Pension Plans (RPPs)

☐ Read pages 489 (from paragraph 13-105) through 491 (through paragraph 13-116) of the text.

Registered Retirement Income Funds (RRIFs)

☐ Read pages 491 (from paragraph 13-117) through 493 (through paragraph 13-128) of the text.

☐ Complete Exercise Thirteen-11. The Exercise is on page 493 of the text. The solution is on page S-147 of this Study Guide.

Deferred Profit Sharing Plans (DPSPs) And Profit Sharing Plans (PSPs)

❑ Read pages 493 (from paragraph 13-129) and 494 (through paragraph 13-136) of the text.

Retirement Compensation Arrangements

❑ Read pages 494 (from paragraph 13-137) and 495 (through paragraph 13-145) of the text.

Salary Deferral Arrangements

❑ Read pages 495 (from paragraph 13-146) and 496 (through paragraph 13-149) of the text.

Individual Pension Plans (IPPs) And Tax Pre-Paid Savings Plans (TPSPs)

❑ Read page 496 (paragraphs 13-150 through 13-152) of the text.

Transfers Between Plans

❑ Read pages 496 (from paragraph 13-153) and 497 (through paragraph 13-154) of the text.

Retiring Allowances

❑ Read page 497 (paragraphs 13-155 and 13-156) of the text.

❑ Complete Exercise Thirteen-12. The Exercise is on page 497 of the text. The solution is on page S-147 of this Study Guide.

❑ Complete Self Study Problems Thirteen-4 and Thirteen-5. The Self Study Problems are on page 502 of the text. The solutions are on pages S-150 through S-152 of this Study Guide.

To Complete This Chapter

❑ Review the Key Terms Used In The Chapter on page 498 of the text. Consult the Glossary for the meaning of any key terms you do not know.

❑ Review the Learning Objectives of the Chapter found on pages S-153 and S-154 of this Study Guide.

❑ As a review, we recommend that you view the PowerPoint Slides for Chapter Thirteen that are on your Companion CD-ROM. If you do not have access to the Microsoft PowerPoint program, the PowerPoint Viewer program can be installed from the Companion CD-ROM.

Solution to Chapter Thirteen Exercises

Exercise Thirteen - 1 Solution

The addition to the RRSP deduction room for 2005 is $6,840 [(18%)($38,000)]. At the end of the year, his Unused RRSP Deduction Room would be $7,140 ($4,800 + $6,840 - $4,500).

Exercise Thirteen - 2 Solution

His Earned Income for RRSP purposes would be $70,500 ($56,000 + $2,500 + $12,000).

Exercise Thirteen - 3 Solution

Her Earned Income for RRSP purposes would be $54,500 ($82,000 + $3,000 - $12,500 - $18,000).

Exercise Thirteen - 4 Solution

The basic mechanism here is the Pension Adjustment (PA). Individuals who belong to an RPP or a DPSP have their RRSP Deduction Limit reduced by the amount of their PA for the previous year. PAs are designed to reflect the amount of contributions or benefits that have been accumulated in employer sponsored RPPs and DPSPs.

Exercise Thirteen - 5 Solution

The Pension Adjustment will be $6,400 ($2,300 + $1,800 + $2,300).

Exercise Thirteen - 6 Solution

The required calculations would be as follows:

Unused Deduction Room - End Of 2004	$10,750
Lesser Of:	
• 2005 RRSP Dollar Limit = $16,500	
• 18% Of 2004 Earned Income Of $66,530* = $11,975	11,975
Less 2004 PA	(4,800)
2005 RRSP Deduction Limit	$17,925
Lesser Of:	
• RRSP Deduction Limit = $17,925	
• Available Contributions = $19,760 ($6,560 + $13,200)	(17,925)
Unused Deduction Room - End Of 2005	$ Nil

*Earned Income = $6,530 - $18,000 + $75,600 + $2,400

While he has no Unused RRSP Deduction Room, he has $1,835 ($19,760 - $17,925) in undeducted contributions.

Exercise Thirteen - 7 Solution

Ms. Brownell will have a $15,500 addition to her deduction room in 2004, and a $16,500 addition in 2005. These are the RRSP Dollar Limits for these years, as both of these figures are less than 18 percent of her Earned Income for 2003 and 2004 (Earned Income effect has a one year lag). Her 2005 Earned Income will affect her 2006 RRSP deduction room and is not relevant to this Exercise. As her 2004 contribution is $16,500, she will only be in excess of her deduction room by $1,000 and no penalty will be assessed. However, when she makes the May 1, 2005 contribution, she will be over her deduction room by $3,000 [$16,500 + $18,500 - ($15,500 + $16,500)]. A 1 percent per month penalty is applicable to amounts above $2,000. As a consequence, there will be a 2004 penalty of $80 [(1%)($3,000 - $2,000)(8)].

Exercise Thirteen - 8 Solution

As the withdrawal occurs before January 1, 2006, Mrs. Garveau will be responsible for the taxes on $5,000 of the withdrawal, the amount of her contribution. The remaining $4,000 will be taxed in the hands of her husband.

Exercise Thirteen - 9 Solution

Ms. DeBoo will have to repay $867 [(1/15)($18,000 - $5,000)] during 2005. Note that the voluntary payment that was made during 2004 did not reduce the fraction of the remaining balance that must be paid in 2005.

Exercise Thirteen - 10 Solution

There are no tax consequences associated with the withdrawal of $5,000. As he will have no education tax credit in either 2006 or 2007, his repayment period begins in 2007. As he makes the required payments of $500 within 60 days of the end of each of the years 2007 through 2016, there are no tax consequences associated with his repayments.

Exercise Thirteen - 11 Solution

He has no required minimum withdrawal for 2005, the year the RRIF is established. His minimum withdrawal for 2006 will be $26,042 [$625,000 ÷ (90 - 66)].

Exercise Thirteen - 12 Solution

It would appear that Mr. Bartoli began working for his employer in 1976. Given this, he can rollover a total of $59,500 [($2,000)(20 Years Before 1996) + ($1,500)(13 Years Before 1989)] to his RRSP. The remainder of the retiring allowance will be taxed in 2005.

Solution to Self Study Problem Thirteen - 1

Mr. Barnes' 2004 Earned Income for RRSP purposes would be calculated as follows:

Salary	$55,000
Taxable Benefits	1,150
Union Dues	(175)
Net Employment Income	$55,975
Business Income	4,150
Rental Loss	(11,875)
Spousal Support Received	2,400
Earned Income	$50,650

Part A - Not A Member Of RPP Or DPSP   Under the assumption that Mr. Barnes is not a member of a Registered Pension Plan or a Deferred Profit Sharing Plan, the increase in his RRSP Deduction Limit for 2005 is the lesser of $16,500 and $9,117 (18 percent of 2004 Earned Income). In this case, $9,117 would be the smaller amount.

Also note that Canada Pension Plan contributions do not reduce Earned Income for RRSP purposes.

Based on the preceding, Mr. Barnes' maximum deductible RRSP contribution for 2005 is calculated as follows:

2004 Unused RRSP Deduction Room	$ 700
2005 Earned Income Limit (18% Of $50,650)	9,117
RRSP Deduction Limit	$9,817

Part B - Member Of RPP   In this case, the maximum 2005 deduction would be the amount calculated in Part A, reduced by his 2004 Pension Adjustment of $4,200. This would leave a maximum deductible RRSP contribution of only $5,617 ($9,817 - $4,200). Note that while Mr. Barnes' actual net employment income for 2004 would be reduced by any RPP contributions made for that year, the employment income amount used in the calculation of Earned Income for RRSP purposes does not reflect this reduction.

Solution to Self Study Problem Thirteen - 2

Part A   Mr. Beasley's net employment income for 2004 would be $22,700, his gross salary of $24,000, reduced by his RPP contributions of $1,300.

Part B   Mr. Beasley's maximum deductible 2005 RRSP contribution would be equal to the lesser of $16,500 and 18 percent of his 2004 Earned Income, reduced by his 2004 Pension Adjustment. His Earned Income would be calculated as follows:

Net Employment Income	$22,700
RPP Contributions	1,300
Spousal Support	9,000
Net Rental Loss	(5,000)
Earned Income	$28,000

Eighteen percent of this amount is $5,040, which is less than the limit of $16,500. Therefore, his maximum deductible 2005 RRSP contribution would be $2,440, $5,040 less the 2004 Pension Adjustment of $2,600. Note that the damage award, royalties, interest, dividends, and gift are not included in Earned Income.

Part C   As Mr. Beasley has made no contributions prior to 2005, he has no undeducted contributions. In addition, he has interest income and dividends that are subject to current Tax Payable. This would suggest that Mr. Beasley should contribute the maximum deductible amount of $2,440 in 2005. In addition, he should make a further 2005 contribution of $2,000, the maximum over contribution that would not subject him to the 1 percent per month penalty on such amounts. While he could not currently deduct this over contribution, it will enjoy the benefit of having any income earned while in the plan compounded on a tax free basis. Further, this amount can be deducted in any future year, subject to the usual RRSP deduction limits.

Note that this $4,440 contribution should be made, whether or not Mr. Beasley decides to make the maximum deduction of $2,440 in 2005. Since he will not be in the maximum federal tax bracket until 2006, it could be advantageous to defer taking the $2,440 available deduction until 2006.

Solution to Self Study Problem Thirteen - 3

Part A Ms. Stratton's net employment income would be calculated as follows:

Gross Salary	$120,000
Additions:	
Employer's Contribution To Provincial Health Insurance Plan	482
Employer's Contributions For Life Insurance	96
Trip To Bermuda	4,500
Deductions:	
RPP Contributions	(2,390)
Professional Dues	(225)
Net Employment Income	$122,463

The reasons for not including the other items given in the problem in the preceding calculation are as follows:

1. Income taxes withheld cannot be deducted in the calculation of Net Income For Tax Purposes or Taxable Income.

2. Contributions to registered charities create a credit against Tax Payable, but cannot be deducted in the calculation of net employment income.

3. Employer payments to employee dental plans and private health care plans are not a taxable benefit.

4. Employer payments to employee group income protection plans are not a taxable benefit.

5. The EI and CPP contributions are eligible for tax credit treatment.

6. Employer payments for membership fees in social or recreational clubs are generally not a taxable benefit to the employee, provided the facilities are used for business purposes.

7. As the travel allowance is based on actual milage and costs, it does not have to be included in the employee's income.

8. Contributions to the Registered Retirement Savings Plan can be deducted under Subdivision e, but not in the calculation of net employment income.

Part B Ms. Stratton's maximum deductible 2005 RRSP contribution is calculated as follows:

The Lesser Of:	
• $16,500	
• [(18%)($122,463 + $2,390)] = $22,474	$16,500
Reduced by the 2004 PA	(5,560)
Maximum Deductible RRSP Contribution	$10,940

This means that $1,560 ($12,500 - $10,940) of the contribution will not be deductible in 2005.

However, the $12,500 contribution is still a good idea. Funds invested in an RRSP accumulate earnings on a tax free basis and, unless non-deductible contributions accumulate to $2,000 or more, no penalty is applied. Further, contributions that are not deducted can be carried forward and are available for deduction in any subsequent year. This means that Ms. Stratton will enjoy the benefits of tax free compounding without experiencing any unfavourable tax consequences.

Solution to Self Study Problem Thirteen - 4

Part A With respect to the retiring allowance, ITA 56(1)(a)(ii) requires that the entire $125,000 must be included in income. Then, to the extent that such amounts are transferred or contributed to an RRSP for which the taxpayer is the annuitant, the taxpayer is entitled to a deduction under ITA 60(j.1), equal to $2,000 for each year of service prior to 1996 with the employer, plus an additional $1,500 for each year of service before 1989, for which the employee was not a member of an RPP or a DPSP. This provides for the following maximum deduction under ITA 60(j.1):

19 Years At $2,000 Per Year	$38,000
12 Years At $1,500 Per Year	18,000
Allowable Rollover	$56,000

Given this calculation, the maximum RRSP deduction that Mr. Colt would be allowed for 2005 would be calculated as follows:

Retiring Allowance Rollover (See Preceding)	$56,000
Opening RRSP Deduction Room	32,000
Addition For Year [(18%)($46,000)]	8,280
Pension Adjustment	(8,000)
Maximum Deduction	$88,280

Part B Mr. Colt will be able to deduct the full $50,000 of the retiring allowance that was transferred to his own RRSP. While another $38,280 could have been deducted under ITA 60(j.1), the amounts transferred to a spousal RRSP are not eligible for this deduction. However, contributions to the spousal RRSP can be deducted under ITA 60(i). Using the assumed maximum ITA 60(i) deduction calculated in the preceding paragraph, we can calculate the following amount of non-deductible contributions:

Total Contributions	$125,000
Maximum Deduction Under ITA 60(j.1)	(50,000)
Maximum Regular Deduction ($88,280 - $56,000)	(32,280)
Non-Deductible Contributions	$ 42,720

To the extent that non-deductible contributions exceed $2,000, they are subject to a heavy penalty of 1 percent per month. As a consequence, Mr. Colt should immediately withdraw $40,720 ($42,720 - $2,000) from the spousal RRSP. If this occurs before March 2, 2006, he can contribute and deduct an additional $6,000 ($56,000 - $50,000) to his own RRSP.

Unless he is in need of the funds, he should leave the $2,000 non-deductible contribution in the spousal plan and contribute $2,000 more to his own RRSP, in order to enjoy the advantages of tax free accumulation of earnings on the $2,000 cushion that is available.

Solution to Self Study Problem Thirteen - 5

The most desirable solution would be to find benefits that would be fully deductible to the Company and free of taxation for Mr. Jones. The only items that fall into this category would be payments for private health care plans and discounts on company merchandise. Discounts on industrial engines are not likely to be of any value to Mr. Jones. However, Mr. Jones should arrange to have the Company provide private health care coverage, including a dental plan. The Company could also pay the premiums on a disability insurance plan without it becoming a taxable benefit to Mr. Jones at the time of payment. Any benefits received under such a plan would have to be taken into income when received.

In terms of tax deferral, Mr. Jones should be included in the Company's Registered Pension Plan (RPP). Once he is admitted to the plan, both he and the Company should make the maximum contributions that are permitted under the terms of the plan. The limiting factor here is that these contributions cannot result in a Pension Adjustment that is in excess of the lesser of 18 percent of Mr. Jones' compensation for the year or the money purchase limit for the year under consideration ($18,000 for 2005).

While there is no indication that the Company has such an arrangement, a Deferred Profit Sharing Plan (DPSP) might also be useful. Whether or not Mr. Jones would be able to use such an arrangement would depend on the total employee/employer contributions to the Company's RPP. Contributions to a DPSP are included in the calculation of Mr. Jones' Pension Adjustment and, when combined with the RPP contributions, the total is subject to the limitation described in the preceding paragraph.

It would also be advisable for Mr. Jones to arrange for some of the compensation to be received in the form of a retiring allowance to be paid to a Registered Retirement Savings Plan (RRSP) at the end of the three years. As he will have been employed a total of 14 years by Martin, 11 of them prior to 1996, a total of $22,000 ($2,000 per year of pre-1996 service) could be rolled over in this form. In addition, an amount of $1,500 per year of pre-1989 service while not a member of the RPP could also be rolled over on a tax free basis to this RRSP.

The Company could provide a loan to Mr. Jones to purchase his new residence. As Mr. Jones is moving, he is eligible for a deduction of the benefit associated with a $25,000 interest free "home relocation" loan. Any additional low interest or interest free loan will result in imputed interest being added to Mr. Jones' Taxable Income without an offsetting deduction. Whether or not this will be beneficial will depend on a number of factors including whether he is able to raise the funds at a rate lower than that specified under Regulation 4301 for assessing imputed interest. As the Regulation 4301 rate changes on a quarterly basis, some attention would also have to be given to expected future movements of this rate. However, Mr. Jones can use the rate in effect at the time the loan is made for the first five years.

The Company could provide Mr. Jones with an automobile. In this case, Mr. Jones will be assessed for a personal benefit of a standby charge (24 percent per year of the capital cost or two-thirds of the lease payments, if he is not eligible for a reduction) and for operating costs (one-half of the standby charge or $0.20 per kilometer of personal use). Whether or not this will be desirable depends on an analysis of how Mr. Jones would actually use the car. In some cases, especially if the car has a list price of more than $30,000, the taxable benefit may exceed the actual benefit, making this an undesirable form of compensation.

The Company could pay the dues for any recreational facilities that Mr. Jones might wish to use. While these amounts will not be treated as a taxable benefit to Mr. Jones, the payments will not be deductible to the Company. Given that both the Company and Mr. Jones will be subject to similar marginal tax rates, there would appear to be no significant advantage to this type of arrangement.

The Company could provide assistance with the costs that will be incurred by Mr. Jones in moving to Hamilton. With respect to costs that Mr. Jones would be permitted to deduct, it makes little difference whether the Company pays the costs, or simply pays an equivalent amount in salary and lets Mr. Jones pay the costs and deduct them. However, certain types of moving costs that would not be deductible by Mr. Jones can be paid by the Company without creating a taxable benefit. An example of this would be compensation for a loss on a personal residence owned by Mr. Jones in Vancouver. (See Chapter 11)

If Martin Manufacturing has a year end after July 6, it can declare a bonus in the third year, but not pay it until the following calendar year. This will defer Mr. Jones' taxation of the bonus by one year without deferring Martin's deduction.

Since Mr. Jones has been operating as a consultant for the last 11 years, it may be possible to structure the project so that he will be considered an independent contractor rather than an employee. This would considerably increase the amount and type of expenditures that would be deductible by him and also create an opportunity to income split with his wife, if she could assist him in the project in some way. In considering this alternative it should be kept in mind that, if Mr. Jones is not an employee, some of the possibilities that have been previously discussed would no longer be feasible. For example, unless Mr. Jones is an employee, it would not be possible for him to be a member of the Company's RPP.

Another possibility would be for Mr. Jones to provide his services through a corporation. However, this would probably not be helpful. Given his relationship with Martin Manufacturing Company, any corporation would likely be viewed as a personal services business and taxed at full corporate rates.

As an incentive, the Company could grant Mr. Jones options to purchase its stock. This would have no cost to the Company. The timing of the tax cost of the options for Mr. Jones could be delayed until after retirement.

Chapter Thirteen Learning Objectives

After completing Chapter 13, you should be able to:

1. Explain the general procedures used to provide tax deferral on retirement saving (paragraphs 13-1 through 13-12).

2. Describe the difference between a defined benefit pension plan and a defined contribution (a.k.a. money purchase) pension plan (paragraphs 13-13 and 13-14).

3. Describe the basic operation of RRSPs (paragraphs 13-15 through 13-25).

4. Calculate the RRSP Deduction Limit for an individual (paragraphs 13-26 through 13-35).

5. Calculate an individual's Unused RRSP Deduction Room (paragraphs 13-30 and 13-31).

6. Calculate Earned Income for RRSP purposes (paragraphs 13-34 and 13-35).

7. Demonstrate an understanding of the concepts underlying Pension Adjustments (PAs) (paragraphs 13-36 through 13-45).

8. Demonstrate an understanding of the concepts underlying Past Service Pension Adjustments (PSPAs) (paragraphs 13-46 through 13-50).

9. Demonstrate an understanding of the concepts underlying Pension Adjustment Reversals (PARs) (paragraphs 13-51 through 13-54).

10. Apply the tax treatment of undeducted RRSP contributions (paragraph 13-55).

11. Determine whether an individual has made "excess" contributions to an RRSP and identify associated tax planning issues (paragraphs 13-56 through 13-61).

12. Recall the tax treatment of RRSP and RRIF administration fees (paragraph 13-62).

13. Apply the provision relating to voluntary withdrawals and conversions of RRSPs (paragraphs 13-63 through 13-67).

14. Apply the provisions relating to RRSP terminations due to age limitation (paragraphs 13-68 through 13-70).

15. Apply the provisions relating to other plan terminations (paragraphs 13-71 through 13-76).

16. Apply the provisions associated with spousal RRSPs and identify associated tax planning issues (paragraphs 13-77 through 13-84).

17. Describe and apply the provisions of the Home Buyers' Plan (paragraphs 13-85 through 13-93).

18. Describe and apply the provisions of the Lifelong Learning Plan (paragraphs 13-94 through 13-104).

19. Demonstrate an understanding of the provisions associated with Registered Pension Plans (RPPs) (paragraphs 13-105 through 13-116).

20. Describe the role that RRIFs play in tax planning related to retirement, as well as the basic operation of these plans (paragraphs 13-117 through 13-128).

21. Demonstrate an understanding of the provisions related to Deferred Profit Sharing Plans (DPSPs) (paragraphs 13-129 through 13-134).

22. Demonstrate a basic understanding of Profit Sharing Plans (PSPs) (paragraphs 13-135 and 13-136).

23. Demonstrate a basic understanding of the provisions related to Retirement Compensation Arrangements (paragraphs 13-137 through 13-145).

24. Demonstrate a basic understanding of Salary Deferral Arrangements (paragraphs 13-146 through 13-149).

25. Recall the basic nature of Individual Pension Plans (IPPs) and Tax Pre-Paid Savings Plans (TPSPs) (paragraphs 13-150 through 13-152).

26. Recall the tax free transfers that can be made between various types of plans (paragraphs 13-153 and 13-154).

27. Apply the special rules associated with retiring allowances (paragraphs 13-155 and 13-156).

CHAPTER FOURTEEN

How To Work Through Chapter Fourteen

On-Line Survey

We would appreciate your feedback on this text. Your comments will help us to improve it. In addition, students who complete the survey will have their name entered in a draw for a $100 cash prize.

To complete a brief, on-line survey, visit the "Student And General Resources" web page on our web site at:

www.pearsoned.ca/byrdchen/ctp2006/

We recommend the following approach in dealing with the material in this Chapter:

Taxable Income Introduction And Overview

☐ Read pages 511 (from paragraph 14-1) and 512 (through paragraph 14-6) of the text.

Revoked Stock Option Election

☐ Read pages 512 (from paragraph 14-7) and 513 (through paragraph 14-9) of the text.

☐ Complete Exercise Fourteen-1. The Exercise is on page 513 of the text. The solution is on page S-159 of this Study Guide.

Treatment Of Losses

☐ Read pages 514 (from paragraph 14-10) through 516 (through paragraph 14-25) of the text.

☐ Complete Exercise Fourteen-2. The Exercise is on page 516 of the text. The solution is on page S-159 of this Study Guide.

Non-Capital Losses

☐ Read pages 516 (from paragraph 14-26) and 517 (through paragraph 14-28) of the text.

☐ Complete Exercise Fourteen-3. The Exercise is on page 517 of the text. The solution is on page S-159 of this Study Guide.

☐ Read pages 517 (from paragraph 14-29) and 518 (through paragraph 14-30) of the text.

Net Capital Losses

☐ Read pages 518 (from paragraph 14-31) through 520 (through paragraph 14-39) of the text.

☐ Complete Exercise Fourteen-4. The Exercise is on page 520 of the text. The solution is on page S-159 of this Study Guide.

Allowable Business Investment Losses (ABILs)

☐ Read pages 520 (from paragraph 14-40) and 521 (through paragraph 14-48) of the text.

☐ Complete Exercise Fourteen-5. The Exercise is on page 521 of the text. The solution is on page S-160 of this Study Guide.

Farm Losses

☐ Read page 522 (paragraphs 14-49 through 14-52) of the text.

☐ Complete Exercise Fourteen-6. The Exercise is on page 522 of the text. The solution is on page S-160 of this Study Guide.

☐ Complete Self Study Problem Fourteen-1. The Self Study Problem is on page 552 of the text. The solution is on pages S-164 through S-166 of this Study Guide.

Lifetime Capital Gains Deduction

☐ Read pages 522 (from paragraph 14-53) through 526 (through paragraph 14-74) of the text.

☐ Complete Exercise Fourteen-7. The Exercise is on page 526 of the text. The solution is on page S-160 of this Study Guide.

☐ Read pages 526 (from paragraph 14-75) through 528 (through paragraph 14-82) of the text.

☐ Complete Exercise Fourteen-8. The Exercise is on page 528 of the text. The solution is on pages S-160 and S-161 of this Study Guide.

Ordering Of Deductions And Losses

☐ Read pages 528 (from paragraph 14-83) through 530 (through paragraph 14-91) of the text.

☐ Complete Exercise Fourteen-9. The Exercise is on page 530 of the text. The solution is on page S-161 of this Study Guide.

☐ Complete Self Study Problem Fourteen-2. The Self Study Problem is on page 552 of the text. The solution is on page S-166 of this Study Guide.

Tax Payable Overview

☐ Read page 531 (paragraphs 14-92 through 14-96) of the text.

Tax On Split Income

☐ Read pages 531 (from paragraph 14-97) through 533 (through paragraph 14-103) of the text.

☐ Complete Exercise Fourteen-10. The Exercise is on page 533 of the text. The solution is on page S-161 of this Study Guide.

Transfer Of Dividends To A Spouse Or Common-Law Partner

☐ Read page 533 (paragraph 14-104) of the text.

☐ Complete Exercise Fourteen-11. The Exercise is on page 534 of the text. The solution is on page S-162 of this Study Guide.

☐ Complete Self Study Problem Fourteen-3. The Self Study Problem is on pages 552 and 553 of the text. The solution is on page S-167 of this Study Guide.

Charitable Donations Credit Revisited

☐ Read pages 534 (from paragraph 14-105) through 537 (through paragraph 14-124) of the text.

☐ Complete Exercise Fourteen-12. The Exercise is on page 537 of the text. The solution is on page S-162 of this Study Guide.

☐ Complete Self Study Problem Fourteen-4. The Self Study Problem is on pages 553 and 554 of the text. The solution is on pages S-168 and S-169 of this Study Guide.

☐ Read pages 537 (from paragraph 14-125) and 538 (through paragraph 14-130) of the text.

☐ Complete Exercise Fourteen-13. The Exercise is on page 538 of the text. The solution is on page S-162 of this Study Guide.

Foreign Tax Credits Revisited

☐ Read pages 539 (from paragraph 14-131) and 540 (through paragraph 14-140) of the text.

☐ Complete Exercise Fourteen-14. The Exercise is on page 540 of the text. The solution is on page S-163 of this Study Guide.

☐ Complete Self Study Problem Fourteen-5. The Self Study Problem is on pages 554 and 555 of the text. The solution is on pages S-170 through S-172 of this Study Guide.

Alternative Minimum Tax (AMT)

☐ Read pages 541 (from paragraph 14-141) through 543 (through paragraph 14-152) of the text.

☐ Complete Exercise Fourteen-15. The Exercise is on page 543 of the text. The solution is on page S-163 of this Study Guide.

☐ Complete Self Study Problem Fourteen-6. The Self Study Problem is on pages 555 and 556 of the text. The solution is on pages S-172 and S-173 of this Study Guide.

Comprehensive Example

☐ Read the Sample Personal Tax Return For Chapter 14 on pages 544 through 551 of the text. For comparison purposes, you may wish to refer to the Sample Personal Tax Return For Chapter 6 (pages 194 through 200 of the text). The complete sample tax return is available on the CD-ROM included with the text in two formats, a T1 ProFile return file and a .PDF file. The T1 ProFile version can be opened by going to the subdirectory "\Tax Return Files", and opening the file "Sample - Chapter 14.04T". The .PDF version, also located in the subdirectory "\Tax Return Problems", is called "PDF Sample - Chapter 14.pdf".

Comprehensive Tax Payable

☐ Complete Self Study Problem Fourteen-7. The Self Study Problem is on pages 556 through 558 of the text. The solution is on pages S-173 through S-176 of this Study Guide.

Tax Return Software

☐ You may wish to review the Suggestions For Working With Profile Software found on pages S-50 through S-52 of this Study Guide.

☐ When the updated ProFile software is available in January, 2006, a download site for the updated software program and updated sample tax returns and Cases using ProFile software will be available at:

www.pearsoned.ca/byrdchen/ctp2006/

☐ Complete Self Study Case Fourteen-1 using the ProFile T1 Software. The Self Study Case is on pages 558 through 561 of the text. The condensed solution is on pages S-176 through S-180 of this Study Guide. The complete sample tax return is available on the CD-ROM included with the text in two formats, a T1 ProFile return file and a .PDF file. The T1 ProFile version can be opened by going to the subdirectory "\Tax Return Files", and opening the file "Self Study Case 14-1.04T". The .PDF version, also located in the subdirectory "\Tax Return Problems", is called "PDF Self Study Case 14-1.pdf". Additionally, as this Self Study Case is a continuation of Self Study Case 6-1, referring to the Chapter 6 version may be of assistance. This Self Study Case is also extended in Self Study Problem Fourteen-7, using 2005 rates.

To Complete This Chapter

☐ Review the Key Terms Used In The Chapter on page 543 of the text. Consult the Glossary for the meaning of any key terms you do not know.

☐ Review the Learning Objectives of the Chapter found on page S-181 of this Study Guide.

☐ As a review, we recommend that you view the PowerPoint Slides for Chapter Fourteen that are on your Companion CD-ROM. If you do not have access to the Microsoft PowerPoint program, the PowerPoint Viewer program can be installed from the Companion CD-ROM.

Solution to Chapter Fourteen Exercises

Exercise Fourteen - 1 Solution

The specified value of the $20 options is $80,000 [(4,000)($20)]. Her election on these options defers employment income of $30 ($50 - $20) per option, or a total of $120,000 [(4,000)($30)].

The specified value of the $25 options is $200,000 [(8,000)($25)]. As a result, her maximum deferral would be on $100,000, or one-half, of the $25 options. The maximum potential deferral here is $115 ($140 - $25) per share, or a total of $460,000 [(1/2)(8,000)($115)]. If Ms. Flux does not revoke her election on the $20 options, she will only be able to elect on a specified value of $20,000 on these $25 options. This would result in an additional deferral of $92,000 [(10%)(8,000)($115)], resulting in a total 2005 deferral of $212,000 ($120,000 + $92,000).

Alternatively, if she revokes the election on the $20 options, she will be able to elect on the maximum $100,000 specified value of the $25 options, resulting in a deferral of $460,000. This is clearly the better alternative.

Exercise Fourteen - 2 Solution

Mr. Smothers will have a net capital loss carry forward on listed personal property from 2004 of $5,500 [(1/2)($89,000 - $100,000)]. This can only be applied against the 2005 taxable gain of $2,000 [(1/2)($5,000 - $1,000)]. As this is a listed personal property loss carry forward, it will be deducted in the calculation of Net Income For Tax Purposes, leaving this balance at the amount of his employment income, $62,000. This will also be his 2005 Taxable Income. In addition, he will have a net capital loss carry forward on listed personal property of $3,500 ($5,500 - $2,000).

Exercise Fourteen - 3 Solution

In this Exercise, the E in the ITA 111(8) formula would be equal to $60,200 ($58,000 + $2,200), F [income under ITA 3(c)] would be equal to $48,000 ($35,000 + $13,000), and D would be equal to $2,200. This leaves a non-capital loss balance of $10,000 ($60,200 - $48,000 - $2,200). Note that this is the excess of the business loss of $58,000, over the positive sources of income for the year. The additional farm loss of $2,200 would be allocated to a separate loss balance. It is included in the E component and then deducted in the D component. Since it is less than $2,500, the farm loss is fully deductible, whether restricted or not.

Exercise Fourteen - 4 Solution

Her Net Income For Tax Purposes for 2005 will be $10,000 ($40,000 - $30,000). Since she does not anticipate future capital gains, she will want to use as much of her net capital loss carry forward as she can. As the amount of this net capital loss carry forward is less than the current year's taxable capital gain, she can apply all of it in 2005. To do so, she will convert $5,000 of her non-capital loss to a non-capital loss carry over. This is calculated as follows:

Amount E ($30,000 + $15,000)	$45,000
Amount F [ITA 3(c) Income]	(40,000)
Non-Capital Loss Carry Over	$ 5,000

Her minimum Taxable Income will be nil after deducting the $15,000 net capital loss carry forward. The only loss carry over available at the end of the year is a $5,000 non-capital loss carry over.

Exercise Fourteen - 5 Solution

The Allowable Business Investment Loss for the year would be calculated as follows:

Loss On Disposition	$50,000
Disallowed Portion [(2/1)($13,000)]	(26,000)
Business Investment Loss	$24,000
Inclusion Rate	1/2
Allowable Business Investment Loss	$12,000

All of the $12,000 can be deducted against Mr. Latvik's employment income. With respect to the disallowed $26,000, it becomes an ordinary capital loss, of which $18,000 can be deducted against the current year's capital gains on the publicly traded securities. This leaves a net capital loss carry over of $4,000 [(1/2)($26,000 - $18,000)].

Exercise Fourteen - 6 Solution

During 2004, her farm loss was limited to $8,750 [$2,500 + (1/2)($12,500)]. The remaining restricted farm loss of $7,250 ($16,000 - $8,750) can be carried forward to 2005. In 2005, $3,500 of this carry forward can be deducted against the 2005 farm income. The remaining restricted farm loss of $3,750 ($7,250 - $3,500) will be carried forward to future years. Ms. Bodkin's 2005 Net Income For Tax Purposes is $88,500 ($85,000 + $3,500) and her 2005 Taxable Income is $85,000 ($85,000 + $3,500 - $3,500).

Exercise Fourteen - 7 Solution

The A components of the annual gains limit formula would be equal to $42,000, the lesser of:

- $74,000 ($114,000 - $82,000 + $42,000); and
- $42,000.

The B component would be $16,000 , the sum of:

- $13,000 (the amount by which $45,000, exceeds $32,000 ($74,000 - $42,000); and
- $3,000.

This gives an annual gains limit of $26,000 ($42,000 - $16,000). Note that the net taxable capital gain on non-qualifying property was $32,000 ($114,000 - $82,000). The mechanics of the annual gains limit formula are such that the first $32,000 of the $45,000 net capital loss deduction was charged against these gains and did not erode the annual gains limit. Only the remaining $13,000 ($45,000 - $32,000) served to reduce the annual gains limit.

It would be advisable for Ms. Slovena to deduct only $32,000 of the net capital loss carry forward. If she did this, her annual gains limit would increase to $39,000 ($42,000 - Nil - $3,000). Although she would have used $13,000 ($39,000 - $26,000) more of her lifetime capital gains deduction, her tax liability for 2005 would not change and she would have a net capital loss carry forward of $13,000 ($45,000 - $32,000) that could be applied against any type of capital gain for an unlimited period of time.

Exercise Fourteen - 8 Solution

For 2005, his maximum lifetime capital gains deduction is $223,500, the least of the following three items:

Available Deduction His remaining deduction would be $232,000 [$250,000 - $5,000 - (1/2)($26,000)].

Annual Gains Limit In the absence of capital gains on non-qualifying property in any of the years under consideration, the simplified version of this calculation can be used. The annual gains limit for 2005 would be the qualifying taxable capital gain of $255,000 [(1/2)($510,000)], reduced by the net capital loss carry forward deducted of $31,500 [(1/2)($63,000)]. This leaves a net amount of $223,500 ($255,000 - $31,500).

Cumulative Gains Limit   In the absence of capital gains on non-qualifying property in 1986 and 1989, the annual gains limits for 1986 and 1989 would simply be the amount of the taxable capital gains on qualifying property in those years.   Given this, the required calculation would be as follows:

Sum Of Annual Gains Limits	
($5,000 + $17,333 + $255,000)	$277,333
Previous Years' Capital Gains Deduction ($5,000 + $17,333)	(22,333)
Net Capital Loss Carry Forward Deducted	(31,500)
Cumulative Gains Limit	$223,500

Note that if he had deducted only $23,000 of his net capital loss carry forward, he would have been able to totally utilize his remaining lifetime capital gains deduction of $232,000.

Exercise Fourteen - 9 Solution

Alan's Net Income For Tax Purposes would be calculated as follows:

Income Under ITA 3(a):		
Business Income	$12,000	
Employment Income	56,000	
Farming Income	3,500	$71,500
Income Under ITA 3(b):		
Taxable Capital Gains		9,000
Net Income For Tax Purposes		$80,500

Alan's Taxable Income is as follows:

Net Income For Tax Purposes	$80,500
Loss Carry Forwards:	
Restricted Farm Losses (Limited to farming income)	(3,500)
Net Capital Losses (Limited to taxable capital gains)	(9,000)
Non-Capital Losses (All)	(36,000)
Taxable Income	$32,000

The restricted farm loss carry forward would be $4,500 ($8,000 - $3,500). The capital loss carry forward on a 100 percent basis would be $22,000 ($40,000 - $18,000). The 1990 net capital loss balance would be $16,500 [(3/4)($22,000)]. There would be no non-capital loss carry forward.

Exercise Fourteen - 10 Solution

Norton's Taxable Income is calculated as follows:

Taxable Dividends [(125%)($15,000)]	$18,750
Employment Income	12,200
Subtotal	$30,950
Split Income Deduction - ITA 20(1)(ww)	(18,750)
Net And Taxable Income	$12,200

His federal Tax Payable before credits would be calculated as follows:

Tax On Split Income [(29%)($18,750)]	$5,438
Regular Tax [(16%)($12,200)]	1,952
Federal Tax Payable Before Credits	$7,390

Exercise Fourteen - 11 Solution

Without the transfer, Mr. Ho's wife would have income of $7,750 [(125%)($6,200)] and, as her income is greater than $7,611, he would have no spousal tax credit. With the transfer, he would be eligible for the full $1,107. Given this, the analysis of his position at the federal level is as follows:

Additional Taxes On Dividends [(125%)($6,200)(29%)]	$2,248
Spousal Tax Credit	(1,107)
Dividend Tax Credit [(2/3)(25%)($6,200)]	(1,033)
Tax Increase (Decrease)	$ 108

As there is an increase in federal Tax Payable, the election would not be desirable.

Exercise Fourteen - 12 Solution

With the gift being made at $85,000, Ms. Felder will have a taxable capital gain of $11,500 [(1/2)($85,000 - $62,000)], plus recapture of $34,000 ($62,000 - $28,000), for a total Net Income For Tax Purposes of $45,500. Given this, her maximum credit base would be calculated as follows:

75 Percent Of Net Income For Tax Purposes [(75%)($45,500)]	$34,125
25 Percent Of Taxable Capital Gain [(25%)($11,500)]	2,875
25 Percent Of Recaptured CCA [(25%)($34,000)]	8,500
Total Limit And Net Income For Tax Purposes	$45,500

Using this base, the maximum credit would be $13,169 [(16%)($200) + (29%)($45,500 - $200)]. However, she does not need all of this credit to reduce her Tax Payable to nil:

Tax On First $35,595	$5,695
Tax At 22 Percent On Remaining $9,905	2,179
Tax Before Credits	$7,874
Basic Personal Credit	(1,304)
Tax Payable Before Donations Credit	$6,570

Given this amount of Tax Payable, the use of $22,745 of her donation will produce the $6,570 [(16%)($200) + (29%)($22,745 - $200)] credit that will reduce her federal Tax Payable to nil. This leaves a carry forward of $62,255 ($85,000 - $22,745).

Exercise Fourteen - 13 Solution

With the inclusion of the taxable capital gain resulting from the donation, Mr. Radeem's Taxable Income for 2005 would be $90,000 [$70,000 + (1/4)($110,000 - $30,000)]. In determining his charitable donations tax credit, the maximum base for this credit would be $72,500 {[(75%)($90,000)] + [(25%)(1/4)($110,000 - $30,000)]}. However, he does not need all of this credit to reduce his Tax Payable to nil:

Tax On First $71,190	$13,526
Tax At 26 Percent On Remaining $18,810	4,891
Tax Before Credits	$18,417
Tax Credits (Given)	(4,000)
Tax Payable Before Donations Credit	$14,417

Given this amount of Tax Payable, the use of $49,803 of his donation will produce the $14,417 [(16%)($200) + (29%)($49,803 - $200)] credit that will reduce his federal Tax Payable to nil. This leaves a carry over of $60,197 ($110,000 - $49,803).

Exercise Fourteen - 14 Solution

Ms. Cheung's credit for foreign tax paid would be the lesser of $420 [(12%)($3,500)] and an amount determined by the following formula:

$$\left[\frac{\text{Foreign Non-Business Income}}{\text{Adjusted Division B Income}}\right][\text{Tax Otherwise Payable}]$$

In this formula, the Adjusted Division B Income would be $47,500 ($50,000 - $2,500). Tax Otherwise Payable would be $6,130 [$5,695 + (22%)($43,500 - $35,595) - $1,304]. Using these figures, the calculation would be as follows:

$$\left[\frac{\$3,500}{\$47,500}\right][\$6,130]=\$452$$

As the foreign tax paid would be the lesser of the two figures, her tax credit for 2005 would be $420.

Exercise Fourteen - 15 Solution

Mr. Blouson's regular Tax Payable would be calculated as follows:

Tax On First $71,190	$13,526
Tax At 26 Percent On Next $13,810	3,591
Total	$17,117
Basic Personal Credit	(1,304)
Dividend Tax Credit [(2/3)($5,000)]	(3,333)
Regular Federal Tax Payable	$12,480

For alternative minimum tax purposes, his adjusted taxable income would be calculated as follows:

Regular Taxable Income	$85,000
30 Percent Of Capital Gains [(30%)($45,000)]	13,500
Dividend Gross Up	(5,000)
Adjusted Taxable Income	$93,500

Calculation of the alternative minimum tax would be as follows:

Adjusted Taxable Income	$93,500
Basic Exemption	(40,000)
Amount Subject To Tax	$53,500
Rate	16%
Minimum Tax Before Credit	$ 8,560
Basic Personal Credit	(1,304)
Alternative Minimum Tax	$ 7,256

Mr. Blouson would not pay the alternative minimum tax as $7,256 is less than the regular Tax Payable of $12,480. Note that the $50,000 RRSP deduction does not affect the alternative minimum tax calculation.

Solution to Self Study Problem Fourteen - 1

2002 Analysis   Mr. Fox's Net Income For Tax Purposes and Taxable Income would be calculated as follows:

ITA 3(a)		
Employment Income	$18,000	
Business Income	14,500	
Grossed Up Dividends [($5,000)(125%)]	6,250	$38,750
ITA 3(b)		
Taxable Capital Gains	$ Nil	
Allowable Capital Losses [(1/2)($3,600)]	(1,800)	Nil
ITA 3(c)		$38,750
ITA 3(d)		
Farming Income (Loss)*		(4,250)
Net Income For Tax Purposes And Taxable Income		$34,500

*Given that Mr. Fox is only a part time farmer, his deductible farm loss would be restricted as follows:

Total Farm Loss		$6,000
Deductible Amount:		
First $2,500	($2,500)	
One-Half Of $3,500	(1,750)	(4,250)
Farm Loss Carry Over		$1,750

In addition to the preceding farm loss carry over, Mr. Fox would have a net capital loss carry forward of $1,800 [(1/2)($3,600)].

2003 Analysis   Mr. Fox's Net Income For Tax Purposes and Taxable Income would be calculated as follows:

ITA 3(a)		
Employment Income	$15,000	
Farming Income	1,000	
Grossed Up Dividends [($6,525)(125%)]	8,156	$24,156
ITA 3(b)		
Taxable Capital Gains [(1/2)($7,400)]	$ 3,700	
Allowable Capital Losses	Nil	3,700
ITA 3(c)		$27,856
ITA 3(d)		
Business Income (Loss)		(39,000)
Net Income For Tax Purposes		$ Nil
2002 Net Capital Loss Carry Forward		(1,800)
Taxable Income		$ Nil

Since there are taxable capital gains this year, the net capital loss carry forward of $1,800 is added to the balance of the non-capital loss. The non-capital loss for the year would be calculated as follows:

Business Loss	$39,000
2002 Net Capital Loss Deducted	1,800
ITA 3(c) Income	(27,856)
Non-Capital Loss Carry Over For 2003	$12,944

This non-capital loss will be carried back to 2002, resulting in the following amended Taxable Income for that year:

2002 Taxable Income (As Reported)	$34,500
Non-Capital Loss Carry Back From 2003	(12,944)
2002 Amended Taxable Income	$21,556

Given this carry back, the only remaining loss carry forward at the end of 2003 would be the $1,750 restricted farm loss from 2002.

2004 Analysis Mr. Fox's Net Income For Tax Purposes and Taxable Income would be calculated as follows:

ITA 3(a)		
Employment Income	$19,000	
Business Income	34,000	
Farming Income	8,000	
Grossed Up Dividends [($8,000)(125%)]	10,000	$71,000
ITA 3(b)		
Taxable Capital Gains [(1/2)($6,300)]	$ 3,150	
Allowable Capital Losses	Nil	3,150
ITA 3(c)		$74,150
ITA 3(d)		Nil
Net Income For Tax Purposes		$74,150
Farm Loss Carry Forward (Less Than $8,000)		(1,750)
Taxable Income		$72,400

Given the deduction of the farm loss carry forward, there are no loss carry overs remaining at the end of 2004.

2005 Analysis Mr. Fox's Net Income For Tax Purposes and Taxable Income would be calculated as follows:

ITA 3(a)		
Employment Income	$12,000	
Grossed Up Dividends [($10,125)(125%)]	12,656	$24,656
ITA 3(b)		
Taxable Capital Gains	$ Nil	
Allowable Capital Losses [(1/2)($6,000)]	(3,000)	Nil
ITA 3(c)		$24,656
ITA 3(d)		
Business Income (Loss)	($52,000)	
Farm Income (Loss)	(2,000)	(54,000)
Net Income For Tax Purposes And Taxable Income		$ Nil

The non-capital loss carry over for the year would be calculated as follows:

Business Loss	$52,000
Farm Loss	2,000
ITA 3(c) Income	(24,656)
Non-Capital Loss Carry Over For 2005	$29,344

In addition to the non-capital loss carry over, there would be a $3,000 net capital loss carry over for the year. The entire non-capital loss carry over can be carried back to 2004. It includes a $2,000 farm loss that can only be deducted against farm income. After the deduction of the farm loss carry forward in 2004, there is still $6,250 ($8,000 - $1,750) of farm income which allows for the deduction of the $2,000 farm loss.

The entire net capital loss carry over can also be carried back to 2004, since the carry back is less than the $3,150 taxable capital gains recorded in 2004. This will result in the following amended Taxable Income for that year:

2004 Taxable Income (As Reported)	$72,400
Non-Capital Loss Carry Back From 2005	(29,344)
Net Capital Loss Carry Back From 2005	(3,000)
2004 Amended Taxable Income	$40,056

Solution to Self Study Problem Fourteen - 2

Mr. Borgen's minimum Taxable Income would be calculated as follows:

Net Employment Income	$36,000
Net Taxable Capital Gains ($37,500 - $9,000)	28,500
Interest Expense	(17,000)
Net Income For Tax Purposes	$47,500
Lifetime Capital Gains Deduction (See Note)	(11,500)
Taxable Income	$36,000

Note The lifetime capital gains deduction is the least of:

Capital Gains Deduction Available	$250,000
Annual Gains Limit	$ 28,500
Cumulative Net Taxable Capital Gains	$ 28,500
Cumulative Net Investment Loss	(17,000)
Cumulative Gains Limit	$ 11,500

It would have been possible for Mr. Borgen to deduct the $9,900 net capital loss carry forward instead of $9,900 of the lifetime capital gains deduction. In view of the uncertainty associated with the continuing availability of this deduction on the sale of shares of a qualified small business corporation, and the fact that there is an unlimited carry forward period on net capital losses, use of the lifetime capital gains deduction is probably the better alternative.

Solution to Self Study Problem Fourteen - 3

Mr. and Mrs. Bahry's Taxable Income would be calculated as follows:

	Mr. Bahry	Mrs. Bahry
Old Age Security Pension	$ 5,600	$ 5,600
Registered Pension Plan Receipts	12,340	820
Registered Retirement Income Fund Receipts	N/A	700
Canada Pension Plan Receipts	3,690	830
Taxable Dividends (125%)	2,000	420
Interest On Savings Accounts	1,239	443
Net Taxable Capital Gain:		
Mr. Bahry	Nil	
Mrs. Bahry		Nil
Taxable Income	$24,869	$ 8,813

Mr. Bahry's maximum tax credits would be as follows:

Base Amount	$ 8,148
Age (No Reduction Required)	3,979
Pension	1,000
Transfers From Mrs. Bahry (See Note)	4,314
Credit Base	$17,441
Rate	16%
Total	$ 2,791
Charitable Donations [(16%)($200) + (29%)($1,510 - $200)]	412
Dividend Tax Credit [(2/3)(25%)($1,600)]	267
Total Credits	$ 3,470

Note   Mr. Bahry cannot take the spousal credit because Mrs. Bahry's income is too high. Mrs. Bahry's age credit and pension income credit are eligible for transfer under ITA 118.8.   Mrs. Bahry's Tax Payable before any credits would be $1,410 [(16%)($8,813)], of which $1,304 would be eliminated by her basic personal credit. Mr. Bahry is not eligible for the ITA 82(3) election to include his wife's dividends in his income, as the transfer would not increase or create a spousal credit.

Mrs. Bahry must include the $84 gross up on her dividends in her Taxable Income, which decreases the amount of tax credits she can transfer. She must decrease the amount of the age and pension credits she can transfer by the excess of her Taxable Income (including the dividends) over the basic personal amount. As a result, she will not need to claim the dividend tax credit. Since Mr. Bahry is not eligible for the ITA 82(3) election, her dividend tax credit will be lost. The total credit base (the credits will be 16 percent of this amount) that can be transferred is calculated as follows:

Age	$3,979
Pension	1,000
Less Excess Of Taxable Income Over Basic Personal Amount ($8,813 - $8,148)	(665)
Credit Base Transferred To Spouse	$4,314

Neither Mr. Bahry's allowable capital loss of $1,988 [(50%)($3,975)] nor Mrs. Bahry's unused allowable capital loss of $160 [(50%)($820 - $500)] can be deducted in 2005. They can be carried back three years and carried forward indefinitely to be applied against taxable capital gains.

Solution to Self Study Problem Fourteen - 4

Taxable Income   Ms. Worthmore's minimum Taxable Income is calculated as follows:

Employment Income		
Gross Salary - Intra Graphics	$72,476	
Gross Salary - Lindworth Inc.	2,500	
RPP Contributions	(1,233)	
Premium For Provincial Health Care	413	$74,156
Income From Property		
Dividend Attribution (Note One)	$ 228	
Dividends From Lindworth (Note Two)	5,406	
Loan Principal (Note Two)	5,000	10,634
Taxable Capital Gains		
Attribution From Husband (Note Three)	$ 1,144	
Transfer To Jayne (Note Four)	122	
Lackmere Shares (Note Five)	394	
Agricultural Land (Note Six)	9,000	10,660
Other Income And Deductions		
RRSP Deduction (Note Seven)	($ 6,923)	
Spousal Support Payments	(2,700)	(9,623)
Net Income For Tax Purposes And Taxable Income		$85,827

Note One   There would be income attribution for the dividends received by Mr. Dalton on the shares received as a gift. The amount would be $228 [($3.50)(52)(125%)].

Note Two   The dividends from Lindworth Inc. would be included in the amount of $5,406 [($4,325)(125%)]. With respect to the loan principal, it will be outstanding on more than two consecutive corporate year ends and, as a consequence, it must be included in Ms. Worthmore's Net Income For Tax Purposes. However, there will be no imputed interest on the loan and, when it is repaid, it can be deducted by Ms. Worthmore.

Note Three   In the case of transfers to a spouse, unless an election is made not to have Section 73 apply, the property is transferred at the adjusted cost base of the transferor. There is no recognition of capital gains at the time of transfer. However, when Mr. Dalton sells the shares on August 31, 2005, there would be attribution of taxable capital gains in the amount of $1,144 [($56 - $12)(52)(1/2)].

Note Four   In the case of a gift to a minor child, it is treated as a deemed disposition at fair market value. This results in a taxable capital gain at the time of transfer in the amount of $122 [($27 - $18)(27)(1/2)].

Note Five   The taxable capital gain on the Lackmere Ltd. shares would be computed using the average value for the shares. The average value would be calculated as follows:

122 Shares At $92	$11,224
178 Shares At $71	12,638
Total Cost	$23,862
Average Cost ($23,862 ÷ 300 Shares)	$ 79.54

This results in a taxable capital gain of $394 [($86 - $79.54)(122)(1/2)].

Note Six   When there is a non-arms' length transfer of property for consideration of less than fair market value, ITA 69 deems that, for the transferor, the transfer takes place at fair market value.   This will result in a taxable capital gain of $9,000 [($28,000 - $10,000)(1/2)].   Note that for the transferee, the adjusted cost base will only be the transfer price of $10,000.   This could result in double taxation of some, or all, of the $18,000 capital gain if the transferee subsequently sells the land for more than $10,000.

Note Seven   Ms. Worthmore's 2004 Earned Income (assumed to be equal to the 2005 figure) is as follows:

Gross Salary - Intra	$72,476
Gross Salary - Lindworth	2,500
Employment Benefit - Provincial Health Care	413
Spousal Support Paid And Deducted	(2,700)
Earned Income	$72,689

Eighteen percent of this is $13,084, which is less than the 2005 RRSP Dollar Limit of $16,500. Therefore, Ms. Worthmore's deduction limit is $6,923 ($13,084, less the 2004 pension adjustment of $6,161). The excess contribution of $577 ($7,500 - $6,923) can be carried forward and deducted in future years.

Tax Payable   Ms. Worthmore's Tax Payable can be calculated as follows:

Tax On First $71,190		$13,526
Tax On Next $14,637 ($85,827 - $71,190) At 26 Percent		3,806
Gross Federal Tax Payable		$17,332
Basic Personal Amount	$ 8,148	
Spousal [$6,919 - ($750 + $2,475 - $692)]	4,386	
CPP	1,861	
EI	761	
Transfer Of Spouse's Tuition	2,300	
Transfer Of Spouse's Education [(4 Months)($400)]	1,600	
Medical Expenses (Note Eight)	10,619	
Credit Base	$29,675	
Rate	16%	(4,748)
Dividend Tax Credit [(2/3)(25%)($182 + $4,325)]		(751)
Charitable Donations [(16%)($200) + (29%)($342 - $200)]		(73)
Political Contributions [(75%)($100)]		(75)
Federal Tax Payable		$11,685

Note Eight   Ms. Worthmore can use all of the medical expenses of her daughters, Joyce and June, as they are both under 18 years of age. The eligible medical expenses of $10,619 ($2,200 + $9,850 + $413 - $1,844) include her provincial health care premiums.   We have deducted the $1,844 because it is less than 3 percent of Ms. Worthmore's Net Income For Tax Purposes.

Solution to Self Study Problem Fourteen - 5

Taxable Income   Mr. Slater's Net Income For Tax Purposes And Taxable Income would be calculated as follows:

Employment Income - Salary (Note One)		$ 35,000
Proprietorship Income (Note Two)		26,000
Income From Investments:		
Interest On Savings Account	$ 4,600	
Interest On Loans To Friends	12,000	
Taxable Canadian Dividends [($44,000)(125%)]	55,000	
Dividends From U.S Corporations		
(Before Withholding, No Gross Up)	10,000	
	$81,600	
Safety Deposit Box Rental	(150)	81,450
Taxable Capital Gain [(1/2)($111,500 - $23,000)]		44,250
Restricted Farm Loss (Note Three):		
Revenues	$36,000	
Expenses	(45,000)	
Total Loss	($ 9,000)	
Non-Deductible Portion [(1/2)($9,000 - $2,500)]	3,250	(5,750)
CPP Benefits		5,100
Old Age Security		5,600
Net Income Before OAS Repayment		$191,650
OAS Repayment - Lesser Of:		
• $5,600		
• $19,627 [(15%)($191,650 - $60,806)]		(5,600)
Net Income For Tax Purposes And Taxable Income		$186,050

Note One   Since Mr. Slater is over 70 years old, he does not have deductions from salary for EI or CPP.

Note Two   The drawings from the proprietorship have no effect on the Net Income For Tax Purposes of Mr. Slater. The proprietorship income of $28,300 is reduced by the interest of $2,300 on the proprietorship bank loan.

Note Three   Since Mr. Slater is not a full time farmer, his farm loss would be restricted to $2,500, plus 50 percent of the next $6,500 ($9,000 - $2,500), a total of $5,750. The $3,250 balance could be carried back to the preceding three years and forward for ten years, to be deducted against farming income.

Tax Payable   Mr. Slater's Tax Payable would be calculated as follows:

Tax On First $115,739		$25,109
Tax On Next $70,311 ($186,050 - $115,739) At 29 Percent		20,390
Gross Federal Tax		$45,499
Tax Credits:		
Basic Personal Amount	$ 8,148	
Mr. Slater's Age ($3,979 - $3,979)	Nil	
Spousal	6,919	
Spouse's Disability	6,596	
Credit Base	$21,663	
Rate	16%	(3,466)
Charitable Donations		
[(16%)($200) + (29%)($2,700 - $200)]		(757)
Dividend Tax Credit [(2/3)(25%)($44,000)]		(7,333)
Basic Federal Tax Payable		$33,943
Foreign Tax Credit (Note One)		(1,500)
Federal Political Contributions Tax Credit (Note Two)		(350)
Federal Tax Payable		$32,093
Credits:		
Employer Withholding	($9,000)	
Instalments	(2,500)	(11,500)
Balance Before Interest And Penalties		$20,593
Late Filing Penalty (Note Three)		1,236
Interest (Note Four)		296
Amount Owing On June 30		$22,125

Note One   The federal foreign tax credit will be the lesser of the foreign tax actually paid of $1,500 and an amount determined by the following formula:

[(Foreign Non-Business Income ÷ Adjusted Net Income)(Taxes Otherwise Payable*)]

*Basic Federal Tax before the dividend tax credit is deducted.

This amount would be ($10,000 ÷ $186,050) multiplied by ($33,943 + $7,333). This equals $2,219, leaving the actual taxes of $1,500 as the lesser amount.

Note Two   The political contributions tax credit can be calculated as follows:

3/4 Of First $400	$300
1/2 Of The Next $100	50
Total Credit	$350

Note Three   The due date for Mr. Slater's return is June 15, as he has business income. The penalty for the late filing of a return is 5 percent plus 1 percent per month for each complete month after the filing deadline. By filing on July 15, 2006, Mr. Slater's penalty will be 6 percent of $20,593, or $1,236.

Note Four   Although interest calculations are based on daily compounding, this is difficult to compute. As such, the use of simple interest is commonly used in problems. Simple interest on late taxes at a rate of 7 percent from May 1, 2006 is calculated as follows:

$$[(\$20,593)(7\%)(75/365)] = \$296$$

Other Notes   Other points that should be noted are as follows:

- The gambling income would not be taxable unless Mr. Slater's activity was extensive enough to be considered a business.

- Inheritances are capital receipts and do not constitute Taxable Income.

- Drawings from the proprietorship are not Taxable Income and funds invested are capital and not deductible.

- The life insurance premiums are not deductible.

- The mortgage payments on his personal residence are not deductible.

Solution to Self Study Problem Fourteen - 6

Regular Tax Payable   The minimum regular Taxable Income and Tax Payable calculations would be as follows:

	Cheryl	Alma	Irene
Employment And Business Income	$ 60,800	$36,000	$ 22,900
Dividends Received	26,300	Nil	29,400
Dividend Gross Up (25%)	6,575	Nil	7,350
Taxable Capital Gains	9,100	Nil	300,000
Retiring Allowance	Nil	58,000	Nil
RRSP Deductions (Note 1)	(2,344)	(58,000)	Nil
Net Income For Tax Purposes	$100,431	$36,000	$359,650
Lifetime Capital Gains Deduction	(9,100)	Nil	(250,000)
Taxable Income	$ 91,331	$36,000	$109,650
Federal Tax (Note 2)	$ 18,763	$ 5,784	$ 23,526
Basic Personal Credit	(1,304)	(1,304)	(1,304)
Dividend Tax Credit (2/3 of Gross Up)	(4,383)	Nil	(4,900)
Regular Federal Tax Payable	$ 13,076	$ 4,480	$ 17,322

Note 1   Cheryl's maximum 2005 RRSP deduction of $2,344 is the least of:

- $3,500, her actual contribution.
- $7,900, the 2005 RRSP Dollar Limit of $16,500, reduced by her 2004 Pension Adjustment of $8,600.
- $2,344, 18% of 2004 Earned Income of $60,800 (assumed to be equal to her 2005 Earned Income), reduced by her 2004 Pension Adjustment of $8,600.

Note 2   The federal Tax Payable, before the dividend tax credit, was calculated as follows:

	Taxable Income	Federal Tax Calculations	Federal Tax
Cheryl	$ 91,331	$13,526 + (26%)($20,141)	$18,763
Alma	$ 36,000	$ 5,695 + (22%)($ 405)	$ 5,784
Irene	$109,650	$13,526 + (26%)($38,460)	$23,526

Alternative Minimum Tax Payable   The alternative minimum tax (AMT) calculations would be as follows:

	Cheryl	Alma	Irene
Regular Taxable Income	$91,331	$36,000	$109,650
30% Of Capital Gains (Note)	5,460	Nil	180,000
Dividend Gross Up	(6,575)	Nil	(7,350)
Adjusted Taxable Income	$90,216	$36,000	$282,300
AMT Exemption	(40,000)	(40,000)	(40,000)
AMT Base	$50,216	$ Nil	$242,300
Rate	16%		16%
Federal AMT Before Credit	$ 8,035		$ 38,768
Basic Personal Credit	(1,304)		(1,304)
Federal AMT	$ 6,731		$ 37,464
Regular Federal Tax Payable	(13,076)		(17,322)
Additional Tax Required	$ Nil		$ 20,142

Note The 30 percent capital gain inclusion can be calculated by taking 30 percent of double the taxable capital gain.

The excess of AMT over regular tax payable for Irene can be carried forward for seven years and applied against any future excess of regular Tax Payable over the alternative minimum tax.

Solution to Self Study Problem Fourteen - 7

Note To Students This is an extension of Self Study Case 14-1 (tax return preparation case). It has been updated for 2005 rates.

The required calculations for Ms. Trubey's balance owing (refund) would be as follows:

Employment Income	$ 60,202	
RPP Deduction	(2,406)	
Union Dues	(749)	$57,047
CPP Benefits		4,823
Pension Income		22,249
Taxable Amount Of Dividends		2,324
Interest Income ($509 + $311)		820
Rental Income (See Note)		5,553
Taxable Capital Gains [(1/2)($982)]		491
RRSP Deduction - Lesser Of:		
• [(18%)($38,873) - $4,376] = $2,621		
• ($1,665 + $2,620) = $4,285		(2,621)
Child Care Expenses [(2)($100) + $400]		(600)
Net And Taxable Income		$90,086

Solution to Self Study Problem Fourteen - 7

Federal Tax On First $71,190		$13,526
Federal Tax On Next $18,896 At 26 Percent		4,913
Gross Federal Tax		**$18,439**
Basic Personal Amount	($ 8,148)	
Eligible Dependant - Amy	(6,919)	
CPP Contributions	(1,861)	
EI Premiums	(761)	
Caregiver - Marjorie	(3,848)	
Pension	(1,000)	
Transfer Of Diane's Tuition And Education - Lesser Of:		
• $5,000		
• [$4,415 + (2)($120) + (8)($400)] = $7,855	(5,000)	
Medical Expenses (Note One)	(1,499)	
Credit Base	**($29,036)**	
Rate	16%	(4,646)
Charitable Donations [(16%)($200) +		
(29%)($175 + $375 + $50 - $200)]		(148)
Dividend Tax Credit [(13.333%)($2,324)]		(310)
Net Federal Tax		**$13,335**
Provincial Tax (Given)		6,105
Income Tax Deducted ($19,408 + $3,511)		(22,919)
Instalments Paid (Given)		(2,528)
Balance Owing (Refund)		**($ 6,007)**

Note One Allowable medical expenses are as follows:

Eleanor And Minor Child (Amy) Medical Expenses		
($392 + $1,350 + $450 + $1,120)		$3,312
Threshold - Lesser Of: [(3%)($90,086)] And $1,844		(1,844)
Subtotal		**$1,468**
Marjorie's Medical Expenses - Lesser Of:		
• [($50 + $75) - (3%)($5,600)] = Nil		
• Absolute Limit = $10,000		Nil
Diane's Medical Expense - Lesser Of:		
• [$100 - (3%)($2,300)] = $31		
• Absolute Limit = $10,000		31
Qualifying Medical Expenses		**$1,499**

Notes To Eleanor's Tax Return

• Diane transfers the $5,000 maximum tuition and education credit to Eleanor and carries forward the remaining $2,855 [$4,415 + (2)($120) + (8)($400) - $5,000].

• Eleanor cannot claim the charitable donation made by Diane, but Diane can carry it forward for up to five years.

• Her daughter, Diane, should file a tax return to make her tuition and education tax credits and charitable donation tax credit available for carry forward. If she does not file, she will not be eligible for the GST credit and she will not benefit from the RRSP deduction room created during the year.

• Her mother, Marjorie, should file a tax return in order to receive the GST credit.

• Eleanor is eligible for the caregiver tax credit for her mother as her income is well below the threshold.

- Since Diane and Marjorie are over 17 years of age, their medical expenses are reduced by 3 percent of their Net Income For Tax Purposes. This means that none of Marjorie's medical expenses can be claimed by Eleanor.

- Eleanor paid too much in instalments. It should be determined why this happened, to try and prevent overpaying instalments again.

- The child care costs for overnight camps are limited to $100 per week, but the Y Day Camp cost is not limited as it is not an overnight camp.

- Since Eleanor is currently renting out her house, but plans to move back into it, no CCA is taken on the Class 1 building to preserve her principal residence status. Since the cost is equal to the UCC, no CCA has been taken on the building in the previous year. Her CCA on the appliances would not affect her principal residence election and should be taken. The payments on principal are not deductible. If she chose to take CCA on the building, the maximum potential CCA for the year would be $6,756 [(4%)($168,900)] since the first year one-half rule does not apply to her second year of rental. The maximum deductible CCA on the building would be limited to the net rental income after the CCA on the appliances of $5,553 ($5,887 - $334). This would reduce her Tax Payable for 2005, but she would no longer be eligible for the principal residence gain reduction on the property. In addition, the CCA would be recaptured on a subsequent sale if the proceeds were greater than the UCC.

Note   Ms. Trubey's net rental income can be calculated as follows:

Gross Rental Income		$15,600
Less Expenses:		
Property Taxes	$2,190	
Insurance	1,093	
Interest	5,378	
Maintenance And Repairs ($291 + $300)	591	
Legal Fees	173	
Utilities	288	(9,713)
Rental Income Before CCA		$ 5,887
CCA On Class 8 Assets [(20%)($921 + $1,500 - $750)]		(334)
Net Rental Income		$ 5,553

Part B

Eleanor 2005 Earned Income is calculated as follows:

Employment Income	$ 60,202	
Union Dues	(749)	$59,453
Rental Income (See Part A)		5,553
Earned Income		$65,006

The maximum deductible RRSP contribution that Eleanor can make for 2006 is calculated as follows:

The Lesser Of:	
• $16,500	
• [(18%)($65,006)] = $11,701	$11,701
Less Her 2005 PA	(7,829)
Maximum 2006 RRSP Deduction	$ 3,872
Undeducted RRSP Contributions From 2005 ($4,285 - $2,621)	(1,664)
Maximum Deductible RRSP Contribution For 2006	$ 2,208

Note that if Eleanor chooses to deduct CCA on her rental building and reduces her net rental income to nil, her maximum deductible RRSP contribution will be reduced by $1,000 [(18%)($5,553)].

Eleanor should contribute at least the maximum deductible contribution as early in 2005 as possible. She can overcontribute up to $2,000 without penalty. Since she is holding Bank of Montreal shares outside of her RRSP (her T5 shows dividends), if she does not have the funds available, she could consider transferring some of those shares into her RRSP. However, if there is a gain on the shares, she will create a tax liability for the capital gain. If there is a loss, it will be denied.

Solution to Self Study Case Fourteen - 1

This solution includes selected schedules and worksheets from the ProFile T1 return. Note that the program can only be used to calculate 2004 (not 2005) tax returns, and the problem and solution reflect this fact. The complete tax return is available on the Companion CD-ROM in the subdirectory "\Tax Return Files" in two forms. The T1 ProFile return file is named "Self Study Case 14-1.04T" and the .PDF file is named "PDF Self Study Case 14-1.pdf". Please see the sample tax return in the text for suggestions on using the ProFile tax program.

Notes to tax return

- Her daughter, Diane, transfers the $5,000 maximum tuition and education credit to Eleanor and carries forward the remaining $2,855 [$4,415 + (2)($120) + (8)($400) - $5,000].

- Eleanor cannot claim the charitable donation made by Diane, but Diane can carry it forward for up to five years.

- Diane should file a tax return to make her tuition and education tax credits and charitable donation tax credit available for carry forward. If she does not file, she will not be eligible for the GST credit and she will not benefit from the RRSP deduction room created during the year.

- Her mother, Marjorie, should file a tax return in order to receive the GST credit. However, she will need to obtain a Social Insurance Number to do so.

- Eleanor is eligible for the caregiver tax credit for her mother as her income is well below the threshold.

- Since Diane and Marjorie are over 17 years of age, their medical expenses are reduced by 3 percent of their Net Income For Tax Purposes. This means that none of Marjorie's medical expenses can be claimed by Eleanor.

- Eleanor paid too much in instalments. It should be determined why this happened, to try and prevent overpaying instalments again.

- The child care costs for overnight camps are limited to $100 per week, but the Y Day Camp cost is not limited as it is not an overnight camp.

- Since Eleanor is currently renting out her house, but plans to move back into it, no CCA is taken on the Class 1 building to preserve her principal residence status. Since the cost is equal to the UCC, no CCA has been taken on the building in the previous year. Her CCA on the appliances would not affect her principal residence election and should be taken. The payments on principal are not deductible. If she chose to take CCA on the building, the maximum potential CCA for the year would be $6,756 [(4%)($168,900)] since the first year one-half rule does not apply to the second year of rental. The maximum deductible

CCA on the building would be limited to the net rental income after the CCA on the appliances of $5,553 ($5,887 - $334). This would reduce her Tax Payable for 2004, but she would no longer be eligible for the principal residence gain reduction on the property. In addition, the CCA would be recaptured on a subsequent sale if the proceeds were greater than the UCC.

Part B

The maximum deductible RRSP contribution that Eleanor can make for 2005 is calculated as $2,208 by the program on the form "RRSPLimit". To access the form, press <F4> and type "RRSPlimit" in the form box.

Note that if Eleanor chooses to deduct CCA on her rental building and reduces her net rental income to nil, her maximum deductible RRSP contribution will be reduced by $1,000 [(18%)($5,553)].

Eleanor should contribute at least the maximum deductible contribution as early in 2005 as possible. She can overcontribute up to $2,000 without penalty. Since she is holding Bank of Montreal shares outside of her RRSP (her T5 shows dividends), if she does not have the funds available, she could consider transferring some of those shares into her RRSP. However, if there is a gain on the shares, she will create a tax liability for the capital gain. If there is a loss, it will be denied.

Solution to Self Study Case Fourteen - 1

Summary

2004 Tax Summary

Eleanor Chap 14 Prob				Eleanor Chap 14 Prob			
Total income				**Non-refundable tax credits**			
Employment	60,201	80		Basic personal amount	8,012	00	
Old Age Security				Age amount			
CPP/QPP benefits	4,823	28		Spouse / eligible dependant	6,803	00	
Other pensions	22,249	44		Infirm dependants			
Employment Insurance				CPP/QPP	1,831	50	
Taxable dividends	2,324	15		Employment Insurance	772	00	
Interest	820	39		Pension income amount	1,000	00	
Limited partnership				Caregiver amount	3,784	00	
Rental	5,552	40		Disability amount			
Taxable capital gains	491	11		Interest on student loans			
Support payments				Tuition / education			
RRSP				Transfers	5,000	00	
Other				Medical expenses	1,530	00	
Self-employment				**Subtotal**	28,732	50	
Workers' compensation and social assistance				Credit at 16%	4,597	20	
				Donations and gifts	148	00	
Total income	96,462	57		**Non-refundable tax credits**	4,745	20	
Net income				**Total payable**			
RPP	2,406	16		Federal tax	18,522	57	
RRSP	2,621	00		Non-refundable tax credits	4,745	20	
Union and professional dues	748	59		Dividend tax credit	309	89	
Child care expenses	600	00		Minimum tax carry-over/other			
Disability supports deduction				**Basic federal tax**	13,467	48	
Business investment loss				Non resident surtax			
Moving expenses				Foreign tax credits / other			
Support payments				**Federal tax**	13,467	48	
Carrying charges and interest				Political/investment tax credit			
CPP/QPP on self-employment				Labour-sponsored tax credit			
Exploration and development				Alternative minimum tax			
Employment expenses				Additional tax on RESP			
Social benefits repayment				**Net federal tax**	13,467	48	
Other deductions				CPP contributions payable			
Net income	90,086	82		Social benefits repayment			
Taxable income				Provincial/territorial tax	6,200	30	
Canadian Forces personnel				**Total payable**	19,667	78	
Home relocation loan				**Total credits**			
Security options deductions				Income tax deducted	22,918	78	
Other payments deduction				QC or YT abatement			
Losses of other years				CPP overpayment			
Capital gains deduction				EI overpayment			
Northern residents deductions				Medical expense supplement			
Additional deductions				GST/HST rebate			
Taxable income	90,086	82		Instalments	2,528	00	
2005 Estimated	Eleanor Chap 14 Prob			Provincial tax credits			
GST/HST credit				Other credits			
Child Tax Benefit	106	26		**Total credits**	25,446	78	
RRSP contribution limit	2,208	00		**Balance owing (refund)**	(5,779	00)	
				Combined balance (refund)	(5,779	00)	

Complete tax return available on the CD-ROM

Trubey, Eleanor Chap 14 Prob   SIN: 527 000 087

| **T1-2004** | | **Federal Tax** | | | | | **Schedule 1** | |

Complete this schedule to claim your federal non-refundable tax credits and to calculate your net federal tax.

You must attach a copy of this schedule to your return.

Enter your **taxable income** from line 260 of your return _____ 90,086|82 **1**

Use the amount on line 1 to determine which **ONE**
of the following columns you have to complete.

If the amount on line 1 is:	$35,000 or less	more than $35,000 but not more than $70,000	more than $70,000 but not more than $113,804	more than $113,804
Enter the amount from line 1 above	**2**	**2**	90,086|82 **2**	**2**
Base amount	**3**	35,000|00 **3**	70,000|00 **3**	113,804|00 **3**
Line 2 minus line 3 (this amount cannot be negative)	0|00 **4**	**4**	20,086|82 **4**	**4**
Rate	x 16.00 % **5**	x 22.00 % **5**	x 26.00 % **5**	x 29.00 % **5**
Multiply the amount on line 4 by the rate on line 5	**6**	**6**	5,222|57 **6**	**6**
Tax on base amount	0|00 **7**	5,600|00 **7**	13,300|00 **7**	24,689|00 **7**
Add lines 6 and 7	**8**	**8**	18,522|57 **8**	**8**

Federal non-refundable tax credits

Basic personal amount	claim $8,012 **300**	8,012|00	
Age amount (if you were born in 1939 or earlier)	(maximum $3,912) **301**		
Spouse or common-law partner amount:			
Base amount	7,484|00		
Minus: His or her net income (from page 1 of your return)	0|00		
Result: (if negative, enter "0")	(maximum $6,803) ▶ **303**		
Amount for an eligible dependant (**attach** Schedule 5)	(maximum $6,803) **305**	6,803|00	
Amount for infirm dependants age 18 or older (**attach** Schedule 5)	**306**		
CPP or QPP contributions:			
through employment from box 16 and box 17 on all T4 slips	(maximum $1,831.50) **308**	1,831|50 ●	
on self-employment and other earnings (**attach** Schedule 8)	**310**	●	
Employment Insurance premiums from box 18 on all T4 slips	(maximum $772.20) **312**	772|00 ●	
Pension income amount	(maximum $1,000) **314**	1,000|00	
Caregiver amount (**attach** Schedule 5)	**315**	3,784|00	
Disability amount	**316**		
Disability amount transferred from a dependant	**318**		
Interest paid on your student loans	**319**		
Tuition and education amounts (**attach** Schedule 11)	**323**		
Tuition and education amounts transferred from a child	**324**	5,000|00	
Amounts transferred from your spouse or common-law partner (**attach** Schedule 2)	**326**		

Medical expenses for **self, spouse or common-law partner, and your**
dependent children born in 1987 or later (see the guide)   **330**   3,312\|00

Minus: $1,813, or 3% of line 236, whichever is **less**   1,813\|00

Subtotal (if negative, enter "0")   1,499\|00 (A)

Allowable amount of medical expenses for **other dependants**
(see the calculation at line 331 in the guide and **attach** Schedule 5)   **331**   31\|00 (B)

Add lines (A) and (B).   1,530\|00 ▶ **332**   1,530\|00

Add lines 300 to 326, and 332.   **335**   28,732\|50

Multiply the amount on line 335 by 16% =   **338**   4,597\|20

Donations and gifts (**attach** Schedule 9)   **349**   148\|00

Total federal non-refundable tax credits: Add lines 338 and 349.   **350**   4,745\|20

Page 1 of 2

Trubey, Eleanor Chap 14 Prob   SIN: 527 000 087

Net federal tax

Enter the amount from line 8		18,522 57	**9**
Federal tax on split income (from line 4 of Form T1206)	**424**		• **10**
Add lines 9 and 10		18,522 57 ▶	18,522 57 **11**

Enter the amount from line 350	350	4,745 20		
Federal dividend tax credit (13.3333% of the amount on line 120 of your return)	**425**	309 89	•	
Overseas employment tax credit (**attach** Form T626)	426			
Minimum tax carry-over (**attach** Form T691)	**427**		•	
Add lines 350, 425, 426, and 427		5,055 09 ▶		5,055 09 **12**
Basic federal tax: Line 11 minus line 12 (if negative, enter "0")	429			13,467 48 **13**

Federal foreign tax credit:
Complete the federal foreign tax credit calculation below and enter the amount
from line (i) or line (ii), whichever is **less**   **14**
Federal logging tax credit

Federal tax: Line 13 minus line 14 (if negative, enter "0")	406	13,467 48	**15**

Total federal political contributions (**attach** receipts)	**409**		
Federal political contribution tax credit (see the guide)	**410**	•	
Investment tax credit (**attach** Form T2038(IND))	**412**	•	
Labour-sponsored funds tax credit Net cost **413** Allowable credit **414**		•	
Add lines 410, 412, and 414. 416		▶	**16**
Line 15 minus line 16 (if negative, enter "0") (if you have an amount on line 424 above, see Form T1206)	417	13,467 48	**17**
Additional tax on RESP accumulated income payments (**attach** Form T1172)	418		**18**
Net federal tax: Add lines 17 and 18 Enter this amount on line 420 of your return.	420	13,467 48	**19**

Federal foreign tax credit: (see lines 431 and 433 in the guide)

Make a separate calculation for each foreign country. Enter the result on line 14 above.

Non-business income tax paid to a foreign country				**431**		• **(i)**
Net foreign non-business income *	**433**	310 94	X Basic federal tax ***	13,777 37	=	47 55 **(ii)**
Net income **		90,086 82				

* Reduce this amount by any income from that foreign country for which you claimed a capital gains deduction, and by any income from that country that was, under a tax treaty, either exempt from tax in that country or deductible as exempt income in Canada (included on line 256). Also reduce this amount by the lesser of lines E and F on Form T626.
** Line 236 plus the amount on line 3 of Form T1206, minus the total of the amounts on lines 244, 248, 249, 250, 253, 254, and minus any amount included on line 256 for foreign income deductible as exempt income under a tax treaty, income deductible as net employment income from a prescribed international organization, or non-taxable tuition assistance from box 21 of the T4E slip. If the result is less than the amount on line 433, enter your **Basic federal tax*** on line (ii).
*** Line 429 plus the amount on lines 425 and 426, and minus any refundable Québec abatement (line 440) and any federal refundable First Nations abatement (line 441 on the return for residents of Yukon).

Chapter Fourteen Learning Objectives

After completing Chapter 14, you should be able to:

1. Recall the specified deductions from Net Income For Tax Purposes in the calculation of Taxable Income (paragraphs 14-1 through 14-6).

2. Apply the provision for revoking the election to defer the employment income benefit associated with stock options (paragraphs 14-7 through 14-9).

3. Recall the general rules for the treatment of losses (paragraphs 14-10 through 14-20).

4. Explain the treatment of losses on personal use property (paragraph 14-21).

5. Apply the loss carry over provisions applicable to losses on listed personal property (paragraphs 14-22 through 14-25).

6. Apply the loss carry over provisions applicable to non-capital losses (paragraphs 14-26 through 14-30).

7. Apply the loss carry over provisions applicable to net capital losses (paragraphs 14-31 through 14-35).

8. Apply the rules for the conversion of a net capital loss carry over to a non-capital loss carry over (paragraphs 14-36 through 14-39).

9. Explain the special features associated with Allowable Business Investment Losses (paragraphs 14-40 through 14-48).

10. Apply the loss carry over provisions applicable to regular and restricted farm losses (paragraphs 14-49 through 14-52).

11. Apply the provisions of the lifetime capital gains deduction (paragraphs 14-53 through 14-82).

12. Demonstrate an understanding of the importance of ordering of deductions and losses in computing Net Income For Tax Purposes and Taxable Income (paragraphs 14-83 through 14-91).

13. Recall the basic calculations involved in determining Tax Payable (paragraphs 14-92 through 14-96).

14. Calculate the amount of federal Tax Payable on split income (paragraphs 14-97 through 14-103).

15. Apply the provisions for the transfer of dividends to a spouse or common-law partner (paragraph 14-104).

16. Calculate the charitable donations tax credit for donations of various types of property (paragraphs 14-105 through 14-130).

17. Calculate foreign business and non-business income tax credits (paragraphs 14-131 through 14-140).

18. Apply the provisions associated with the alternative minimum tax (paragraphs 14-141 through 14-152).

19. Complete a personal tax return using the ProFile T1 tax preparation software program (pages 544 through 551).

CHAPTER FIFTEEN

How To Work Through Chapter Fifteen

Web Site
As a reminder, the web site for this book can be found at:

www.pearsoned.ca/byrdchen/ctp2006/

Here you will find

- Updates and corrections to the textbook
- Links to other web sites
- A "Guide to Using Your Companion CD-ROM"
- When the updated ProFile software is available in January, 2006, a download site for the updated software program and updated sample tax returns and Cases using ProFile software

We recommend the following approach in dealing with the material in this Chapter:

Computation Of Net Income For Corporations
❑ Read pages 577 (from paragraph 15-1) and 578 (through Figure 15-1) of the text.

❑ Complete Exercise Fifteen-1. The Exercise is on page 578 of the text. The solution is on page S-187 of this Study Guide.

Deductions Available For Corporations In The Computation Of Taxable Income
❑ Read pages 579 (from paragraph 15-4) and 580 (through Figure 15-2) of the text.

❑ Complete Self Study Problem Fifteen-1. The Self Study Problem is on page 631 of the text. The solution is on page S-193 of this Study Guide.

Dividends Received From Other Corporations
❑ Read page 580 (paragraphs 15-9 and 15-10) of the text.

❑ Complete Exercise Fifteen-2. The Exercise is on page 581 of the text. The solution is on page S-187 of this Study Guide.

Dividends - Other Situations
❑ Read pages 581 (from paragraph 15-11) and 582 (through paragraph 15-19) of the text.

❑ Complete Exercise Fifteen-3. The Exercise is on page 582 of the text. The solution is on page S-187 of this Study Guide.

❑ Complete Self Study Problem Fifteen-2. The Self Study Problem is on page 632 of the text. The solution is on page S-194 of this Study Guide.

Foreign Source Dividends Received
❑ Read pages 582 (from paragraph 15-20) and 583 (through paragraph 15-20) of the text.

Loss Carry Overs And Acquisition Of Control
❑ Read pages 583 (from paragraph 15-21) and 584 (through paragraph 15-30) of the text.

❑ Complete Exercise Fifteen-4. The Exercise is on pages 584 and 585 of the text. The solution is on page S-187 of this Study Guide.

❑ Read pages 585 (from paragraph 15-31) through 587 (through paragraph 15-39) of the text.

❑ Complete Exercise Fifteen-5. The Exercise is on page 587 of the text. The solution is on page S-188 of this Study Guide.

❑ Complete Self Study Problem Fifteen-3. The Self Study Problem is on page 633 of the text. The solution is on pages S-194 through S-197 of this Study Guide.

Non-Capital Loss Carry Over For A Corporation

❑ Read pages 587 (from paragraph 15-40) and 588 (through paragraph 15-47) of the text.

❑ Complete Exercises Fifteen-6 and Fifteen-7. The Exercises are on pages 588 and 589 of the text. The solutions are on page S-188 of this Study Guide.

Ordering Of Deductions

❑ Read page 589 (paragraphs 15-48 through 15-52) of the text.

❑ Complete Self Study Problem Fifteen-4. The Self Study Problem is on page 633 of the text. The solution is on pages S-197 and S-198 of this Study Guide.

Geographical Allocation Of Income

❑ Read pages 590 (from paragraph 15-53) and 591 (through paragraph 15-61) of the text.

❑ Complete Self Study Problem Fifteen-5. The Self Study Problem is on page 634 of the text. The solution is on pages S-198 and S-199 of this Study Guide.

Federal Tax Payable For Corporations

❑ Read pages 591 (from paragraph 15-62) and 592 (through paragraph 15-71) of the text.

❑ Complete Exercise Fifteen-8. The Exercise is on page 593 of the text. The solution is on pages S-188 and S-189 of this Study Guide.

Provincial Tax Payable For Corporations

❑ Read pages 593 (from paragraph 15-72) through 595 (through paragraph 15-80) of the text.

Other Goals Of The Corporate Tax System

❑ Read page 595 (paragraphs 15-81 and 15-82) of the text.

Large Corporations Tax

❑ Read pages 595 (from paragraph 15-83) through 598 (through paragraph 15-93) of the text.

❑ Complete Exercise Fifteen-9. The Exercise is on page 598 of the text. The solution is on page S-189 of this Study Guide.

❑ Complete Self Study Problem Fifteen-6. The Self Study Problem is on pages 634 and 635 of the text. The solution is on pages S-199 and S-200 of this Study Guide.

Introduction To The Small Business Deduction

❑ Read pages 598 (from paragraph 15-94) through 601 (through paragraph 15-114) of the text.

Associated Companies

❑ Read pages 602 (from paragraph 15-115) through 605 (through paragraph 15-130) of the text.

❑ Complete Exercise Fifteen-10. The Exercise is on page 606 of the text. The solution is on page S-189 of this Study Guide.

❑ Complete Self Study Problem Fifteen-7. The Self Study Problem is on page 635 of the text. The solution is on page S-200 of this Study Guide.

Calculating The Small Business Deduction

❑ Read pages 606 (from paragraph 15-131) through 608 (through paragraph 15-140) of the text.

❑ Complete Exercise Fifteen-11. The Exercise is on page 608 of the text. The solution is on page S-189 of this Study Guide.

Elimination Of The Small Business Deduction For Large CCPCs

❑ Read pages 608 (from paragraph 15-141) through 610 (through paragraph 15-152) of the text.

❑ Complete Exercise Fifteen-12. The Exercise is on page 610 of the text. The solution is on page S-190 of this Study Guide.

Personal Services Corporations

❑ Read pages 610 (from paragraph 15-153) and 611 (through paragraph 15-157) of the text.

Professional Corporations And Management Companies

❑ Read page 611 (paragraphs 15-158 and 15-159) of the text.

Manufacturing And Processing Profits Deduction

❑ Read pages 611 (from paragraph 15-160) through 613 (through paragraph 15-171) of the text.

❑ Complete Exercise Fifteen-13. The Exercise is on page 613 of the text. The solution is on page S-190 of this Study Guide.

❑ Read pages 614 (from paragraph 15-172) through 616 (through paragraph 15-189) of the text.

❑ Complete Exercise Fifteen-14. The Exercise is on pages 616 and 617 of the text. The solution is on page S-191 of this Study Guide.

❑ Complete Self Study Problem Fifteen-8. The Self Study Problem is on pages 635 and 636 of the text. The solution is on pages S-200 and S-201 of this Study Guide.

General Rate Reduction

❑ Read pages 617 (from paragraph 15-190) and 618 (through paragraph 15-194) of the text.

❑ Complete Exercise Fifteen-15. The Exercise is on page 618 of the text. The solution is on page S-191 of this Study Guide.

❑ Read pages 618 (from paragraph 15-195) and 619 (through paragraph 15-199) of the text.

❑ Complete Exercise Fifteen-16. The Exercise is on page 619 of the text. The solution is on pages S-191 and S-192 of this Study Guide.

❑ Complete Self Study Problems Fifteen-9, Fifteen-10, and Fifteen-11. The Self Study Problems are on pages 636 and 637 of the text. The solutions are on pages S-201 through S-203 of this Study Guide.

Accelerated Rate Reduction

❑ Read page 619 (paragraph 15-200) of the text.

Foreign Tax Credits For Corporations - Introduction
☐ Read page 620 (paragraph 15-201) of the text.

Foreign Non-Business (Property) Income Tax Credit
☐ Read pages 620 (from paragraph 15-202) and 621 (through paragraph 15-206) of the text.

Foreign Business Income Tax Credit
☐ Rad page 621 (paragraphs 15-207 through 15-210) of the text.

☐ Complete Exercise Fifteen-17. The Exercise is on page 621 of the text. The solution is on page S-192 of this Study Guide.

☐ Complete Self Study Problem Fifteen-12. The Self Study Problem is on pages 637 and 638 of the text. The solution is on pages S-204 through S-206 of this Study Guide.

Investment Tax Credits
☐ Read pages 622 (from paragraph 15-211) through 624 (through paragraph 15-227) of the text.

☐ Complete Exercise Fifteen-18. The Exercise is on page 624 of the text. The solution is on pages S-192 and S-193 of this Study Guide.

☐ Read pages 624 (from paragraph 15-228) and 625 (through paragraph 15-230) of the text.

Special Incentives For SR&ED Expenditures
☐ Read pages 625 (from paragraph 15-231) through 628 (through paragraph 15-254) of the text.

To Complete This Chapter
☐ Review the Key Terms Used In The Chapter on page 629 of the text. Consult the Glossary for the meaning of any key terms you do not know.

☐ Review the Learning Objectives of the Chapter found on pages S-207 and S-208 of this Study Guide.

☐ As a review, we recommend that you view the PowerPoint Slides for Chapter Fifteen that are available on the web site at:

www.pearsoned.ca/byrdchen/ctp2006/

If you do not have access to the Microsoft PowerPoint program, the PowerPoint Viewer program can be installed from the Companion CD-ROM.

Solution to Chapter Fifteen Exercises

Exercise Fifteen - 1 Solution

Item 1   You would add the accounting loss of $5,600 ($48,300 - $53,900). You would also add the recapture of CCA of $13,700 ($34,600 - $48,300), for a total addition of $19,300.

Item 2   As goodwill is not amortized for accounting purposes and there was no impairment during the year, no adjustment of the accounting figures is required. However, when the goodwill is added to the CEC balance, it would be subject to amortization at a rate of 7 percent per year. This means that you would subtract CEC amortization of $9,450 [($180,000)(3/4)(7%)].

Item 3   You would add the charitable donations of $15,000.

Item 4   You would deduct the premium amortization of $4,500.

Exercise Fifteen - 2 Solution

Net Income For Tax Purposes	$263,000
Dividends Received	(14,200)
Charitable Donations	(8,600)
Non-Capital Loss Carry Forward	(82,000)
Net Capital Loss Carry Forward*	(14,250)
Taxable Income	$143,950

*At the current year's inclusion rate, the potential deduction for the 1998 net capital loss is $18,000 [(1/2)($36,000)]. However, the actual deduction is limited to the current year's taxable capital gains of $14,250.

The political contributions are eligible for a tax credit, but do not affect Taxable Income.

Exercise Fifteen - 3 Solution

As Loren has not held the shares for 365 days, this transaction would be subject to the stop loss rules. The deductible loss would be calculated as follows:

Proceeds Of Disposition [($21.15)(1,000)]	$21,150
Adjusted Cost Base [($25.30)(1,000)]	(25,300)
Total Loss	($ 4,150)
Disallowed Portion [($2.16)(1,000)]	2,160
Capital Loss	($ 1,990)
Inclusion Rate	1/2
Allowable Capital Loss	($ 995)

Exercise Fifteen - 4 Solution

No Acquisition Of Control   Taxable Income for 2004 would be nil, with a non-capital loss carry over of $135,000 ($57,000 - $192,000). Net Income For Tax Purposes for 2005 would be $289,000 ($42,000 + $247,000) and, if there was no acquisition of control, the total $135,000 non-capital loss carry forward could be deducted, resulting in a 2005 Taxable Income of $154,000 ($289,000 - $135,000).

Acquisition Of Control   The results for 2004 would be the same — a Taxable Income of nil, with a non-capital loss carry over of $135,000. However, if there was an acquisition of control on January 1, 2005, the non-capital loss carry forward could only be used to the extent of the pen business income of $42,000. This means that Taxable Income would be $247,000 ($289,000 - $42,000), with a non-capital loss carry forward of $93,000 ($135,000 - $42,000).

Solution to Chapter Fifteen Exercises

Exercise Fifteen - 5 Solution

It would clearly be desirable to elect to have a deemed disposition of the non-depreciable assets. This could be achieved by electing to have a deemed disposition of the non-depreciable assets for $650,000. This would result in a $75,000 taxable capital gain [(1/2)($650,000 - $500,000)] on the deemed disposition. This will leave $35,000 ($110,000 - $75,000) of the net capital loss carry forward.

This $35,000 could be eliminated by electing to have a deemed disposition of the depreciable property at an elected value of $470,000. This election would produce the required taxable capital gain of $35,000 [(1/2)($470,000 - $400,000)].

The election would also produce recapture of $50,000 ($400,000 - $350,000). As this is $5,000 ($50,000 - $45,000) greater than the operating loss, this would result in Taxable Income and Tax Payable. However, the ability to use the remaining $35,000 net capital loss carry forward is probably worth the cost of the Tax Payable on the extra $5,000 of income.

Exercise Fifteen - 6 Solution

The non-capital loss balance at the end of the year would be calculated as follows:

Amount E	
ABIL	$ 5,250
Dividends Received	48,000
Business Loss	273,000
Net Capital Loss Carry Forward Deducted*	13,500
Total	$339,750
Amount F - ITA 3(c) Income	
[$48,000 + $27,200 + (1/2)($111,000 - $84,000)]	(88,700)
Non-Capital Loss At End Of Year	$251,050

*Limited to net taxable capital gains of $13,500 [(1/2)($111,000 - $84,000)]. There is a 1997 net capital loss carry forward of $8,250 [$28,500 - ($13,500)(3/4 ÷ 1/2)] at the end of the year.

Exercise Fifteen - 7 Solution

The net capital loss carry over balance at the end of the year would be $7,650 [(1/2)($23,100 - $38,400)]. The allowable portion of the Business Investment Loss would be $75,750 [(1/2)($151,500)]. As only $63,500 of this amount can be deducted against current income, the remainder would be a non-capital loss carry over of $12,250 ($75,750 - $63,500).

Exercise Fifteen - 8 Solution

The percentage of Taxable Income earned in each province would be calculated as follows:

	Gross Revenues		Wages And Salaries	
	Amount	Percent	Amount	Percent
Ontario	$1,303,000	44.6%	$ 52,000	31.5%
Manitoba	896,000	30.7%	94,000	57.0%
Not Related To A Province	724,000	24.7%	19,000	11.5%
Total	$2,923,000	100.0%	$165,000	100.0%

The average of the two percentages applicable for income not related to a province is 18.1%, leaving an average for income related to a province of 81.9%. Given this, federal Tax Payable can be calculated as follows:

Base Amount Of Part I Tax [(38%)($226,000)]	$85,880
Surtax [(4%)(28%)($226,000)]	2,531
Federal Tax Abatement [(10%)(81.9%)($226,000)]	(18,509)
General Rate Reduction [(7%)($226,000)]	(15,820)
Federal Tax Payable	$54,082

Exercise Fifteen - 9 Solution

Taxable Capital	$77,900,000
Percentage Employed In Canada	78%
Taxable Capital Employed In Canada	$60,762,000
Capital Deduction	(50,000,000)
Amount Subject To Part I.3 Tax	$10,762,000
Part I.3 Rate For 2005	.00175
Large Corporations Tax Before Surtax	$ 18,834
Canadian Surtax Paid*	(5,443)
Part I.3 Large Corporations Tax Payable	$ 13,391

*The Canadian surtax paid would be $5,443 [($623,000)(4%)(28%)(78%)]. Note that only the surtax related to income earned in a Canadian jurisdiction is available as a credit against the Part I.3 tax on large corporations.

Exercise Fifteen - 10 Solution

Top And Middle Top and Middle are associated under ITA 256(1)(a) as Top controls Middle.

Top And Bottom Top and Bottom are associated under ITA 256(1)(b) as they are both controlled by the same person, Mr. Top. He controls Top directly. In addition, he controls Bottom through a combination of indirect ownership (Middle's 22 percent) and direct ownership {his own 5 percent, his minor son's 15 percent [deemed his by ITA 256(1.3)], and a further 10 percent through options [deemed his by ITA 256(1.4)]}.

Middle And Bottom Middle and Bottom are associated under ITA 256(1)(b) as they are both controlled by the same person, Mr. Top. Mr. Top controls Middle indirectly through Top. He controls Bottom through a combination of direct and indirect control, as described in the discussion of Top and Bottom.

Exercise Fifteen - 11 Solution

As a CCPC throughout the year and with no associated companies, Kartoom is eligible for the full amount of the $300,000 annual business limit. Further, its active business income is greater than $300,000. However, the amount eligible for the small business deduction will be limited by the adjusted Taxable Income of $195,000. This amount is calculated as follows:

Net Income For Tax Purposes	$470,000
Dividends	(85,000)
Non-Capital Loss Carry Forward	(160,000)
Taxable Income	$225,000
10/3 Times Foreign Non-Business Tax Credit [(10/3)(15%)($60,000)]	(30,000)
Adjusted Taxable Income	$195,000

Solution to Chapter Fifteen Exercises

Exercise Fifteen - 12 Solution

The B component of the ITA 125(5.1) reduction formula is $2,275 [(.00175)($11,300,000 - $10,000,000)]. Given this, the required reduction would be calculated as follows:

$$[(\$300,000)(\$2,275 \div \$11,250)] = \underline{\$60,667}$$

This reduction leaves the annual business limit at $239,333 ($300,000 - $60,667).

The foreign non-business income tax credit is equal to $5,400 [(15%)($36,000)]. The small business deduction for Largely Small Inc. is equal to 16 percent of the least of:

• Active Business Income ($1,233,000 - $36,000)		$1,197,000
• Taxable Income ($1,233,000 - $914,000)	$319,000	
Less 10/3 Times Non-Business Income FTC		
Of $5,400	(18,000)	$ 301,000
• Annual Business Limit ($300,000 - $60,667)		$ 239,333

The small business deduction is equal to $38,293 [(16%)($239,333)].

Exercise Fifteen - 13 Solution

The small business deduction for Marion Manufacturing would be equal to 16 percent of the least of:

• Active Business Income		$311,000
• Taxable Income ($362,000 - $210,000)	$152,000	
Less 3 Times Business Income FTC Of $3,150	(9,450)	$142,550
• Annual Business Limit		$300,000

Based on this, the small business deduction would be $22,808 [(16%)($142,550)].

The M&P deduction would be equal to 7 percent of the lesser of:

• M&P Profits	$311,000	
Less Amount Eligible For Small Business Deduction	(142,550)	$168,450
• Taxable Income	$152,000	
Less:		
Amount Eligible For Small Business Deduction	(142,550)	
3 Times Business Income FTC Of $3,150	(9,450)	
Aggregate Investment Income	(30,000)	$ Nil

The M&P profits deduction would be equal to nil.

It would have been possible to increase the small business deduction to the annual maximum of $300,000 by increasing Taxable Income to $309,450. This could be done by deducting only $52,550 ($362,000 - $300,000 - $9,450) of the charitable donations. The remaining unclaimed donations of $157,450 ($210,000 - $52,550) could be carried forward for up to five years.

Although this increases Taxable Income and the total Tax Payable for the year, there could still be an ultimate tax savings with this approach, as the small business deduction cannot be carried over, while charitable donations can be.

Exercise Fifteen - 14 Solution

The components of the M&P formula would be as follows:

• Adjusted Active Business Income		$ 333,000
• Cost Of Capital:		
Owned Assets [(10%)($1,432,000)]	$143,200	
Leased Assets	26,000	$ 169,200
• Cost Of M&P Capital		
Total Capital	$169,200	
Non-Qualifying:		
Storing Finished Goods [(12%)($143,200)]	(17,184)	
Purchasing Operations [(10%)($143,200)]	(14,320)	
Employee Facilities [(10%)($143,200)]	(14,320)	$ 123,376
Fraction		100/85
Total		$ 145,148
• Cost Of Labour ($987,000 + $45,000)		$1,032,000
• Cost Of M&P Labour		
Cost Before Adjustment		$ 987,000
Fraction		100/75
Total		$1,316,000

As $1,316,000 is larger than the cost of labour figure, we will use the $1,032,000 cost of labour figure.

Using these numbers, the M&P formula provides the following M&P profits:

$$(\$333,000)\left(\frac{\$145,148 + \$1,032,000}{\$169,200 + \$1,032,000}\right) = \$326,332$$

Exercise Fifteen - 15 Solution

The federal Tax Payable for Marchand Inc. would be calculated as follows:

Base Amount Of Part I Tax [(38%)($320,000)]	$121,600
Corporate Surtax [(4%)(28%)($320,000)]	3,584
Federal Tax Abatement [(10%)($320,000)]	(32,000)
M&P Deduction [(7%)($180,000)]	(12,600)
General Rate Reduction [(7%)($320,000 - $180,000)]	(9,800)
Federal Tax Payable	$ 70,784

Exercise Fifteen - 16 Solution

The federal Tax Payable for Redux Ltd. would be calculated as follows:

Base Amount Of Part I Tax [(38%)($200,000)]	$76,000
Federal Surtax [(4%)(28%)($200,000)]	2,240
Federal Tax Abatement [(10%)($200,000)]	(20,000)
Small Business Deduction (Note One)	(16,800)
M&P Deduction (Note Two)	(2,800)
General Rate Reduction (Note Three)	(3,850)
Federal Tax Payable	$34,790

Note One   The small business deduction would be equal to 16 percent of the least of active business income ($200,000), Taxable Income ($200,000), and the Company's business limit ($105,000). The deduction is $16,800 [(16%)($105,000)].

Note Two   The M&P deduction would be equal to 7 percent of the lesser of $40,000 (M&P profits of $145,000, reduced by the $105,000 that is eligible for the small business deduction), and $95,000 (Taxable Income, reduced by the $105,000 that is eligible for the small business deduction). The M&P deduction would be $2,800 [(7%)($40,000)].

Note Three   The general rate reduction would be calculated as follows:

Taxable Income		$200,000
Less:		
Amount Eligible For The SBD	($105,000)	
Amount Eligible For The M&P Deduction	(40,000)	(145,000)
Base For General Rate Reduction		$ 55,000
Rate		7%
ITA 123.4(2) General Rate Reduction		$ 3,850

Exercise Fifteen - 17 Solution

The Taxable Income figure would be $16,000 ($146,000 - $30,000 - $75,000 - $25,000). Based on this figure, the required calculation of Part I Tax Payable would be as follows:

Base Amount Of Part I Tax [(38%)($16,000)]	$6,080
Corporate Surtax [(4%)(28%)($16,000)]	179
Subtotal	$6,259
Federal Tax Abatement [(85%)(10%)($16,000)]	(1,360)
General Rate Reduction [(7%)($16,000)]	(1,120)
Foreign Business Income Tax Credit (See Note)	(1,129)
Part I Tax Payable	$2,650

Note   The foreign business income tax credit would be the least of:

- The amount withheld $3,000

- $\left[\dfrac{\$20,000}{\$146,000 - \$30,000 - \$25,000} \right]$ [$6,259 − $1,120] $1,129

- $6,259 $6,259

The unused foreign tax amount of $1,871 ($3,000 - $1,129) can be carried back three years and forward for ten years.

Exercise Fifteen - 18 Solution

The total amount of investment tax credits available can be calculated as follows:

Qualified Property [(10%)($123,000)]		$ 12,300
SR&ED Current Expenditures [(35%)($1,200,000)]		420,000
SR&ED Capital Expenditures:		
1st $800,000 [(35%)($2,000,000 - $1,200,000)]	$280,000	
Remaining $700,000 [(20%)($1,500,000 - $800,000)]	140,000	420,000
Total Available Amount		$852,300

The refund available would be as follows:

Qualified Property [(40%)($12,300)]	$ 4,920
SR&ED Current Expenditures [(100%)($420,000)]	420,000
SR&ED Capital Expenditures [(40%)($420,000)]	168,000
Total Refund Available	$592,920

The non-refunded investment tax credit of $259,380 ($852,300 - $592,920) can be carried back three years and forward ten years to be applied against Tax Payable.

The deductible R&D expenditures for the following year will be reduced by the refundable investment tax credit of $588,000 ($420,000 + $168,000) and the cost of the qualified property will be similarly reduced in the following year by $4,920.

Solution to Self Study Problem Fifteen - 1

1. The required adjustments would be:

    • Add: Amortization expense of $254,000.
    • Deduct: CCA of $223,000.

2. The required adjustment would be:

    • Deduct: Premium amortization of $2,000.

3. The maximum capital gains reserve, based on the receipt of one-half of the proceeds, is equal to $10,000 [(1/2)(1/2)($120,000 - $80,000)]. The required adjustments would be:

    • Deduct: Accounting gain of $67,000 ($120,000 - $53,000).
    • Add: Taxable capital gain, net of the maximum capital gains reserve, of $10,000 [(1/2)($120,000 - $80,000) - $10,000].

    There is no recapture on this disposition as the Company still owns Class 43 assets, and there is a positive balance in the class at the end of the year.

4. The required adjustments would be:

    • Add: Membership fees of $8,000.
    • Add: Non-deductible entertainment expenses of $6,000 [(50%)($12,000)].

5. The required adjustment would be:

    • Add: Charitable donations of $11,000.

6. The required adjustments would be:

    • Add: Accounting loss of $16,000 ($23,000 - $39,000).
    • Add: Recapture of $23,000 (Nil - $23,000).

Solution to Self Study Problem Fifteen - 2

The minimum Net Income For Tax Purposes and Taxable Income of Margo Ltd. would be calculated as follows:

Pre-Tax Accounting Income		$ 31,940
Additions:		
Inventory Reserve	$15,000	
Property Taxes On Vacant Land	1,200	
Depreciation Expense	35,600	
Write-Down Of Goodwill (Impairment Loss)	1,700	
Charitable Donations	19,800	
Taxable Capital Gain [(1/2)($30,500 - $21,000)]	4,750	
Warranty Provision	5,500	
Social Club Membership Fees	7,210	
Interest On Late Income Tax Instalments	1,020	
Foreign Taxes Withheld	270	
Premium On Share Redemption	480	92,530
Deductions:		
CCA	($78,000)	
Amortization Of Cumulative Eligible Capital (Note)	(1,785)	
Accounting Gain On Sale Of Investments	(9,500)	(89,285)
Net Income For Tax Purposes		$ 35,185
Deductions:		
Charitable Donations	($19,800)	
Dividends	(3,000)	(22,800)
Taxable Income		$ 12,385

Note The cumulative eligible capital account has an addition of $25,500 [(3/4)($34,000)] for the goodwill acquired. Amortization for the year is $1,785 [(7%)($25,500)].

Solution to Self Study Problem Fifteen - 3

Deemed Year End As a result of the acquisition of control, LF will have a deemed taxation year end on April 30, 2005. This results in a short January 1, 2005 through April 30, 2005 taxation year for LF. The effects of this include:

- An additional year will be counted towards the expiry of the non-capital losses.
- If CCA is to be taken, it will have to be calculated for a portion of the year.
- Any net capital loss balance that can't be used will expire.
- All of the usual year end procedures (timing of bonuses, inclusion of reserves, etc.) will have to be carried out.

For the first year after the acquisition of control, LF can choose a new fiscal year end, on any date up to 53 weeks after the deemed year end.

Non-Capital Loss Balance   The non-capital loss balance at April 30, 2005 is calculated as follows:

2003 And 2004 Non-Capital Losses ($180,000 + $140,000)		$320,000
Short Fiscal Period Loss:		
Operating Loss To April 30, 2005	$55,000	
Class 43 - Excess Of UCC Over FMV		
[Required Write-Down To FMV Under ITA 111(5.1)]	90,000	145,000
Non-Capital Loss Balance		$465,000

If the non-capital loss cannot be used in the year ending April 30, 2005, it will be carried forward and can be deducted against income earned in the same or a similar line of business in future years. However, if there is doubt about LF's ability to use the non-capital loss carry forward balance before it expires, an election can be made to have one or more deemed dispositions [ITA 111(4)(e)] in order to trigger capital gains or recapture, either of which can be used to absorb the non-capital loss.

Net Capital Loss Balance   If the net capital loss balance of $75,000 cannot be used in the year ending April 30, 2005, it will expire on the acquisition of control. However, as noted in the preceding paragraph, LF can make an election to have one or more deemed dispositions in order to trigger taxable capital gains against which the net capital loss balance can be applied.

Possible Elections   Assets with potential capital gains or recapture are as follows:

Asset	Cost	UCC	FMV
Land	$450,000	N/A	$925,000
Class 3	675,000	$515,000	650,000
Class 8	25,000	10,000	15,000

Asset	Maximum Recapture	Maximum Capital Gain
Land	N/A	$475,000
Class 3	$135,000	Nil
Class 8	5,000	Nil
Total Income	$140,000	$475,000

Note that when the fair market value of the asset exceeds its adjusted cost base, the election can be made at any value between these two values. This means that, in the case of LF's Land, all or part of the accrued capital gain can be recognized.

If the election is made on the Land, its adjusted cost base will be increased to the elected value. If the election is made on the depreciable assets, their UCC will be increased to the elected value. However, for purposes of determining future recapture or capital gains, the cost of the depreciable assets will be unchanged. The difference between their original cost to LF and their new UCC is deemed to have been claimed as CCA.

Recommendation - Uncertainty As To Future Income   At a minimum, elections should be made to ensure use of the net capital loss carry forward, as it will not survive the acquisition of control. Further, if there is uncertainty with respect to the ability of OLC and LF to generate income in the same or similar line of business, in amounts sufficient to absorb the non-capital loss carry forward, additional elections should be made to absorb as much of this balance as possible. This would require elections on all of the assets listed in the preceding table. The resulting Taxable Income would be calculated as follows:

Land - Taxable Capital Gain [(1/2)($475,000)]	$237,500
Class 3 - Recaptured CCA	135,000
Class 8 - Recaptured CCA	5,000
Total Income From ITA 111(4)(e) Elections	$377,500
Short Fiscal Period Loss	(145,000)
Net Income For Tax Purposes	$232,500
Net Capital Loss Carry Forward (All)	(75,000)
Subtotal	$157,500
Non-Capital Loss Carry Forward (Maximum Needed)	(157,500)
Taxable Income	Nil

This leaves a non-capital loss carry forward of $162,500 ($320,000 - $157,500).

Recommendation - Expected Future Income   If the Companies believe that they will be able to generate sufficient income to use the non-capital loss carry forward in future periods, they will not want to make elections that will result in maximum pre-acquisition income. If the elections are made, the losses will increase the adjusted cost base or UCC balance of the assets the elections are made on. In the case of the Land, the increased cost will not be of benefit until the land is sold. In the case of the depreciable assets, the increased UCC will only be deductible at the applicable rates of 5 or 20 percent. Alternatively, a non-capital loss carry forward can be deducted in full, as soon as the Companies have sufficient income to absorb it.

In certain circumstances, companies can effectively use a net capital loss balance even when non-capital losses have reduced Net Income For Tax Purposes to nil. More specifically, if an enterprise has net taxable capital gains for the year, they are permitted to deduct a net capital loss carry over from a nil Net Income For Tax Purposes, with the amount of the deduction being added to the non-capital loss balance.

In the case at hand, it would be necessary to elect a value of $600,000 on the Land in order to trigger the required taxable capital gain of $75,000 [(1/2)($600,000 - $450,000)]. The results would be as follows:

ITA 3(a)	Nil
ITA 3(b) Net Taxable Capital Gains	$ 75,000
ITA 3(c)	$ 75,000
ITA 3(d) Non-Capital Losses	(145,000)
Net Income For Tax Purposes	Nil
Net Capital Loss Carry Forward	($ 75,000)
Taxable Income	Nil

This would leave a non-capital loss carry forward from the short fiscal period of $145,000, calculated as follows:

Non-Capital Loss For The Short Fiscal Period	$145,000
Net Capital Loss Deducted	75,000
Subtotal	$220,000
Income Under ITA 3(c)	(75,000)
Non-Capital Loss Available For Carry Over	$145,000

The total non-capital loss carry forward of $465,000 is made up of the $320,000 carry forward from 2003 and 2004, plus the preceding short fiscal period loss of $145,000. There is no net capital loss carry forward.

Using LF's Losses   Without changing the structure of the two Companies, it may be possible to generate income for LF through transfer pricing between the Companies, or by selling some of OLC's profitable assets to LF. Alternatively, to directly apply LF's losses against OLC's profits, it will be necessary to have a wind-up, amalgamation, or other form of corporate reorganization (See Chapter 19).

Solution to Self Study Problem Fifteen - 4

Net Income For Tax Purposes And Taxable Income Before Carry Overs   The income calculations for the four years, before any consideration of loss carry overs, would be as follows:

	2002	2003	2004	2005
Business Income (Loss)	$ 95,000	($205,000)	$ 69,500	$ 90,000
Taxable Capital Gains	Nil	Nil	4,500	5,000
Dividends	12,000	42,000	28,000	32,000
Net Income (Loss) For Tax Purposes*	$107,000	($163,000)	$102,000	$127,000
Dividends	(12,000)	(42,000)	(28,000)	(32,000)
Charitable Donations	(21,400)	Nil	(8,000)	(22,000)
Taxable Income (Loss) Before Carry Overs*	$ 73,600	($205,000)	$ 66,000	$ 73,000

*There is, of course, no concept of a negative Net Income For Tax Purposes or Taxable Income. However, showing the 2003 loss amount as negative is useful in problems involving loss carry overs.

2002 Analysis   The Taxable Income as reported in the 2002 tax return would be $73,600, as in the preceding schedule. There would be a carry forward at the end of the year as follows:

- 2002 Net Capital Loss [($10,000)(1/2)] $5,000

2003 Analysis   For 2003, Net Income For Tax Purposes and Taxable Income are nil. This would leave a non-capital loss carry over of $205,000, a portion of which could be carried back to 2002. This would result in the following amended 2002 Taxable Income:

2002 Taxable Income As Reported In 2002	$73,600
Non-Capital Loss Carry Back From 2003	(73,600)
Amended 2002 Taxable Income	$ Nil

This would leave the following carry over balances at the end of 2003:

- Charitable Donations .... $ 4,600
- Non-Capital Loss ($205,000 - $73,600) $131,400
- 2002 Net Capital Loss [($10,000)(1/2)] $5,000
  2003 Net Capital Loss [($14,000)(1/2)] .... 7,000 .... $ 12,000

2004 Analysis   As shown in the preceding schedule, 2004 Taxable Income before the application of carry overs was $66,000. The various balances carried forward from 2003 could be used in any order that Linden chooses. The following calculation uses the losses in inverse order to their time limits. As charitable donations expire after five years, we have deducted those first. This is followed by non-capital losses, which expire after ten years. As shown in the following calculation, this leaves no room for the deduction of net capital loss carry overs:

Taxable Income Before Carry Overs	$66,000
Carry Forward Of Charitable Donations	(4,600)
Carry Forward Of 2003 Non-Capital Loss	
(Maximum To Reduce 2004 Taxable Income To Nil)	(61,400)
Taxable Income	$ Nil

The order that we have used in deducting losses will generally be preferable, as long as the taxpayer anticipates future taxable capital gains. Note, however, that while net capital loss carry overs have an unlimited life, they can only be deducted against taxable capital gains. If Linden does not anticipate future taxable capital gains, they would probably deduct the maximum $4,500 of net capital losses, and make a corresponding reduction in the non-capital loss deduction.

After the preceding allocation of losses, the following balances remain:

• Charitable Donations ($4,600 - $4,600)		Nil
• Non-Capital Loss ($131,400 - $61,400)		$70,000
• 2002 Net Capital Loss [($10,000)(1/2)]	$5,000	
2003 Net Capital Loss [($14,000)(1/2)]	7,000	$ 12,000

2005 Analysis Using the same ordering of losses as in 2004, the 2005 Taxable Income would be as follows:

Taxable Income Before Carry Overs	$73,000
Remaining 2003 Non-Capital Loss Carry Over	(70,000)
Balance Available	$ 3,000
Carry Forward Of 2002 Net Capital Loss	
(Maximum To Reduce 2005 Taxable Income To Nil)	(3,000)
Taxable Income	$ Nil

The amount of the net capital loss carry forward used in this period is limited to the balance of income available after deducting the 2003 non-capital loss carryover. Note, however, if 2005 taxable capital gains had been less than $3,000, they would have been the limiting factor for deduction of the net capital loss carry over.

At the end of 2005, the only remaining carry forward is the balance of the net capital loss:

• 2002 Net Capital Loss [($10,000 - $6,000)(1/2)]	$2,000	
• 2003 Net Capital Loss [($14,000)(1/2)]	7,000	$ 9,000

Solution to Self Study Problem Fifteen - 5

From the descriptions in the problem, it would appear that each of the provincial warehouses of the Sundean Company would qualify as a permanent establishment. As a consequence, the allocation to each of the five provinces would be based on the following calculations:

Province	Gross Revenues		Salaries And Wages	
	Amount	Percent	Amount	Percent
Alberta	$ 1,873,000	18%	$ 264,000	21%
British Columbia	2,246,000	22%	273,000	22%
Nova Scotia	1,397,000	13%	179,000	14%
Saskatchewan	1,298,000	12%	104,000	8%
Ontario	3,669,000	35%	427,000	35%
Total	$10,483,000	100%	$1,247,000	100%

The province by province average of the two percentages calculated above, and the allocation of the total Taxable Income of $1,546,000 would be as follows:

Province	Revenues	Wages	Average	Taxable Income
Alberta	18%	21%	19.5%	$ 301,470
British Columbia	22%	22%	22.0%	340,120
Nova Scotia	13%	14%	13.5%	208,710
Saskatchewan	12%	8%	10.0%	154,600
Ontario	35%	35%	35.0%	541,100
Total	100%	100%	100.0%	$1,546,000

Solution to Self Study Problem Fifteen - 6

Total Capital   The total capital would be calculated as follows:

Mortgage Payable	$ 97,000,000
Bank Debt (Due On Demand)	106,000,000
Future Income Tax Liability	242,000,000
Common Stock - No Par	60,000,000
Retained Earnings (Note)	192,000,000
Total Capital	$697,000,000

Note   The use of the equity method for the Investment In Mini Ltd. has resulted in $4,000,000 ($63,000,000 - $59,000,000) being added to both the investment account and to Max Inc.'s Retained Earnings. As ITA 181(3) makes clear, the equity method is not acceptable in the calculation of Total Capital. As a consequence, the $4,000,000 difference between the equity value of the investment and its cost, must be removed from both the Investment In Mini Ltd. account and Max Inc.'s Retained Earnings.

Investment Allowance   The investment allowance includes both the cost of the Investment In Mini Ltd. ($59,000,000) and the Loan To Mini Ltd. ($14,000,000), a total of $73,000,000. Note that the loan to the president of Mini Ltd. does not add to this allowance, as it is not a loan to a corporate entity.

Part I.3 Tax Payable   This amount would be calculated as follows:

Total Capital	$697,000,000
Investment Allowance	(73,000,000)
Taxable Capital	$624,000,000
Percentage Employed In Canada	73%
Taxable Capital Employed In Canada	$455,520,000
Capital Deduction (As Allocated Within Group)	(32,500,000)
Amount Subject To Part I.3 Tax	$423,020,000
Rate	.00175
Part I.3 Tax Payable Before Surtax	$ 740,285
Canadian Surtax (Note)	(343,392)
Part I.3 Tax Payable	$ 396,893

Note This amount would be calculated as follows:

Total Corporate Surtax [(4%)(28%)($42,000,000)]	$470,400
Portion Of Income Earned In A Province	73%
Canadian Surtax	$343,392

As the Part I.3 tax exceeds the surtax, there will be no carry over of the surtax credit to previous or subsequent years.

Solution to Self Study Problem Fifteen - 7

Part A By virtue of ITA 256(1)(b), John Fleming and Eric Flame are related by the fact that they are married to persons who are connected by a blood relationship (their wives). Further, under ITA 256(1.5), a person who holds shares in two or more corporations shall be, as a shareholder of one of the corporations, deemed to be related to himself as a shareholder of the other corporation(s). Therefore, Fleming Ltd. and Lartch Inc. are associated under ITA 256(1)(d), as John Fleming controls Fleming Ltd., is a member of a related group (John Fleming and Eric Flame) that controls Lartch Inc., and owns more than 25 percent of the voting shares of Lartch Inc. In a similar fashion, Flame Ltd. is associated with Lartch Inc. under ITA 256(1)(d), as Eric Flame controls Flame Ltd., is a member of a related group (John Fleming and Eric Flame) that controls Lartch Inc., and owns more than 25 percent of Lartch Inc. Fleming Ltd. and Flame Ltd. are associated under ITA 256(2), as they are both associated with a third corporation, Lartch Inc.

Part B Mr. and Mrs. Cuso are a group with respect to both Male Ltd. and Female Inc. [ITA 256(1.2)(a) - two or more persons holding shares in the same corporation]. As a group, they control both Male Ltd. and Female Inc. Therefore, the two Companies are associated under ITA 256 (1)(b). The fact that Mr. and Mrs. Cuso are related is not relevant.

Part C Ms. Jones and Miss Lange are a group that controls Alliance Ltd. However, they do not control Breaker Inc., as Mrs. Kelly (not a member of the group that controls Alliance Ltd.) owns 50 percent of the shares. Therefore, Alliance Ltd. and Breaker Inc. are not associated.

Part D Mr. Martin and Mr. Oakley constitute a group [ITA 256(1.2)(a)] with respect to both Martin Inc. and Oakley Ltd. ITA 256(1.2)(b)(i) indicates that where one person in a group controls a corporation, the group is considered to control that corporation. As the group Mr. Martin and Mr. Oakley control both corporations, the two Companies are associated under ITA 256(1)(b).

Solution to Self Study Problem Fifteen - 8

Only the Canadian active business income would have any eligibility for the manufacturing and processing profits deduction. Neither the investment income, nor the income of the U.S. subsidiary would fall within the definition of adjusted active business income. As the Gladstone Company is a public company, none of its income is eligible for the small business deduction.

The formula for computing the amount of income that is eligible for the manufacturing and processing profits tax deduction is found in Income Tax Regulation 5200 as follows:

$$\begin{bmatrix} \text{Adjusted} \\ \text{Active} \\ \text{Business} \\ \text{Income} \end{bmatrix} \left[\frac{\left([^{100}\!/_{75}] \text{ of Canadian M\&P Labour Costs} \right) + \left([^{100}\!/_{85}] \text{ of Canadian M\&P Capital Costs} \right)}{\left(\text{Total Canadian Labour Costs} \right) + \left(\text{Total Canadian Active Business Income Capital Costs} \right)} \right]$$

Applying this formula to the information for the Gladstone Company provides the following result:

$$[\$2,353,000]\left[\frac{\left(\frac{100}{75}\right)(\$2,986,000) + \left(\frac{100}{85}\right)(\$4,127,000)}{(\$4,618,000 + \$4,923,000)}\right]$$

$$= [\$2,353,000]\left[\frac{\$8,836,627}{\$9,541,000}\right]$$

$$= \underline{\$2,179,288}$$

Solution to Self Study Problem Fifteen - 9

Assuming the net rental income is considered property income, the components to be used in the calculation of the manufacturing and processing profits deduction for Mason Industries are as follows:

Adjusted Active Business Income ($1,556,000 - $106,000)	$1,450,000
Cost Of Labour	$1,940,000
Cost Of Manufacturing Labour	$1,270,000
Cost Of Capital:	
Rent Paid [(75%)($375,000 - $50,000)]	$ 243,750
Depreciable Assets [(10%)($6,850,000)]	685,000
Total Cost Of Capital	$ 928,750
Cost Of Manufacturing Capital:	
Rent [(55%)($375,000 - $50,000)]	$ 178,750
Depreciable Assets [(10%)($5,560,000)]	556,000
Total Cost Of Manufacturing Capital	$ 734,750

Given the preceding, the base for the manufacturing and processing profits deduction is calculated as follows:

$$[\$1,450,000]\left[\frac{\left(\frac{100}{75}\right)(\$1,270,000) + \left(\frac{100}{85}\right)(\$734,750)}{(\$1,940,000 + \$928,750)}\right]$$

$$= [\$1,450,000]\left[\frac{\$2,557,745}{\$2,868,750}\right]$$

$$= \underline{\$1,292,804}$$

The manufacturing and processing profits deduction rate is 7 percent. The federal Tax Payable for Mason Industries Ltd. would be calculated as follows:

Taxable Income As Given	$1,556,000

Base Amount Of Part I Tax [(38%)($1,556,000)]	$ 591,280
Surtax [(4%)(28%)($1,556,000)]	17,427
Federal Tax Abatement [(10%)($1,556,000)]	(155,600)
M&P Deduction [(7%)($1,292,804)]	(90,496)
General Rate Reduction [(7%)($1,556,000 - $1,292,804)]	(18,424)
Federal Tax Payable	$ 344,187

Solution to Self Study Problem Fifteen - 10

The Taxable Income and Tax Payable for the Serendipity Shop Corp. for the year would be calculated as follows:

Net Income For Tax Purposes		$240,000
Deductions:		
Dividends	($20,000)	
Donations	(48,000)	(68,000)
Taxable Income		$172,000

Base Amount Of Part I Tax [(38%)($172,000)]	$ 65,360
Federal Surtax [(4%)(28%)($172,000)]	1,926
Federal Tax Abatement [(10%)($172,000)]	(17,200)
Small Business Deduction (Note)	(21,600)
General Rate Reduction [(7%)($172,000 - $135,000)]	(2,590)
Part I Federal Tax Payable	$ 25,896

Note   The small business deduction is based on the least of the following:

Active business income	$220,000
Taxable Income	172,000
Allocated annual business limit	135,000

The small business deduction is equal to $21,600 [(16%)($135,000)].

Solution to Self Study Problem Fifteen - 11

Part A   The minimum Net Income For Tax Purposes for Borscan Inc. would be calculated as follows:

Accounting Income Before Taxes		$1,375,000
Additions:		
Amortization Expense	$255,000	
Taxable Capital Gain [(1/2)($525,000 - $500,000)]	12,500	
Recaptured CCA ($500,000 - $350,000)	150,000	
Political Contributions	1,500	
Interest And Penalties - Late Payment	500	
Charitable Donations	12,000	431,500
		$1,806,500
Deductions:		
Capital Cost Allowance	($287,000)	
Extraordinary Gain	(125,000)	
Amortization Of Cumulative Eligible Capital [(7%)($85,000)]	(5,950)	(417,950)
Net Income For Tax Purposes		$1,388,550

Part B   The minimum Taxable Income for Borscan Inc. would be calculated as follows:

Net Income For Tax Purposes	$1,388,550
Dividends Received	(25,000)
Charitable Donations	(12,000)
Net Capital Loss Carry Forward (Note)	(12,500)
Non-Capital Loss Carry Forward	(35,000)
Taxable Income	$1,304,050

Note   The net capital loss carry forward can be used only to the extent of the taxable capital gain for the year, resulting in a deduction of $12,500. This leaves a remaining net capital loss carry forward of $17,500 ($30,000 - $12,500).

Part C   The minimum federal Tax Payable for Borscan Inc. is as follows:

Base Amount Of Part I Tax [(38%)($1,304,350)]	$495,539
Surtax [(4%)(28%)($1,304,050)]	14,605
Federal Tax Abatement [(10%)($1,304,050)]	(130,405)
General Rate Reduction [(7%)($1,304,050)]	(91,284)
Political Contributions Credit (Maximum Allowable)	(650)
Federal Tax Payable	$287,805

Solution to Self Study Problem Fifteen - 12

Taxable Income   The Company's Taxable Income would be calculated as follows:

Accounting Income Before Taxes	$523,000
Accounting Gain On Sale Of Shares	(22,900)
Taxable Capital Gain [(1/2)($22,900)]	11,450
Donations To Registered Canadian Charity	18,700
Contributions To Registered Political Party	7,400
Net Income For Tax Purposes	$537,650
Donations To Registered Canadian Charity	(18,700)
Dividends From Taxable Canadian Corporations	(9,400)
Non-Capital Loss Carry Forward	(21,950)
Net Capital Loss Carry Forward*	(11,450)
Taxable Income	$476,150

*Lesser of $11,450 [(1/2)($22,900)] and $13,500 [(1/2)($27,000)].

Part I Tax Payable   The Company's Part I Tax Payable would be calculated as follows:

Base Amount Of Part I Tax [(38%)($476,150)]	$180,937
Surtax [(4%)(28%)($476,150)]	5,333
Federal Tax Abatement (Note One)	(42,854)
General Rate Reduction [(7%)($476,150 - $410,406)]	(4,602)
Subtotal	$138,814
Small Business Deduction (Note Two)	Nil
Foreign Non-Business Tax Credit (Note Three)	(4,845)
Foreign Business Tax Credit (Note Four)	(20,700)
M&P Deduction (Note Five)	(28,728)
Political Contributions Tax Credit (Maximum)	(650)
Part I Tax Payable	$ 83,891

Note One   No income would be allocated to Manitoba as there are no permanent establishments in that province. However, the Manitoba sales would be included in the Ontario total, as the Manitoba customers are serviced through that province. Based on this, the allocation would be as follows:

Gross Revenues	Amount	Percent
Ontario (Including Manitoba)	$5,725,000	91.0
New York	565,000	9.0
Total	$6,290,000	100.0

Salaries And Wages	Amount	Percent
Ontario	$3,540,000	89.0
New York	438,000	11.0
Total	$3,978,000	100.0

Average Ontario Percent [(91.0% + 89.0%) ÷ 2]	90.0%
Average New York Percent [(9.0% + 11.0%) ÷ 2]	10.0%
Total	100.0%

Based on the preceding calculations, the federal tax abatement would be $42,854 [(10%)(90%)($476,150)].

Note Two There is no small business deduction in the calculation of Part I tax, as Mercury Manufacturing Company is not Canadian controlled.

Note Three The foreign non-business tax credit would be the lesser of:

- The Amount Withheld $4,845

- $\left(\dfrac{\text{Foreign Non - Business Income}}{\text{Adjusted Net Income}}\right)$(Part I Tax Otherwise Payable)

$$=\left(\frac{\$32,300}{\$537,650-\$11,450-\$9,400}\right)(\$138,814) \qquad \$8,676$$

The lesser figure would be the actual withholding of $4,845.

Note Four The foreign business tax credit would be the least of:

- The Amount Withheld $ 20,700

- $\left(\dfrac{\text{Foreign Business Income}}{\text{Adjusted Net Income}}\right)$(Part I Tax Otherwise Payable)

$$=\left(\frac{\$64,200}{\$537,650-\$11,450-\$9,400}\right)(\$138,814+\$42,854) \qquad \$ 22,568$$

- Tax Otherwise Payable, Less The Foreign Non-Business Tax Credit ($138,814 + $42,854 - $4,845) $176,823

The least of these three figures would be the U.S. taxes withheld of $20,700.

Note Five The M&P deduction would be equal to $28,728. This amount is 7 percent of $410,406, which is the lesser of:

- M & P Profits (See Following Calculation) $410,406
- Taxable Income $476,150
  Less 3 Times The Foreign Business
  Tax Credit [(3)($20,700)]   (62,100) $414,050

Technically, a second calculation of the foreign tax credit, made without regard to the general rate reduction is required here. However, the result would be unchanged as the credit is based on the actual withholding.

The components used in the M & P profits formula would be calculated as follows:

Adjusted Business Income

Net Income For Tax Purposes	$537,650
Taxable Capital Gains [(1/2)($22,900)]	(11,450)
Dividends From Taxable Canadian Corporations	(9,400)
Interest Income From Canadian Sources	(7,800)
Dividends From U.S. Corporations	(32,300)
Foreign Business Income	(64,200)
Income From An Active Business In Canada	$412,500

Solution to Self Study Problem Fifteen - 12

Cost Of Capital

Gross Cost Of Business Property In Canada	$2,680,000
Applicable Percent	10%
Cost Of Capital Owned	$ 268,000
Canadian Rental Costs	67,200
Total Cost Of Capital	$ 335,200

Cost Of M & P Capital

Gross Cost Of Business Property Used In M & P [(75%)($2,680,000)]	$2,010,000
Applicable Percent	10%
Cost Of Capital Used In M & P	$ 201,000
M & P Rental Costs	67,200
Total Cost Of M & P Capital	$ 268,200
Gross Up Factor	100/85
Cost Of M & P Capital	$ 315,529

Cost Of Labour

Canadian Salaries And Wages (Total Cost Of Labour)	$3,540,000

Cost Of M & P Labour

Canadian Salaries And Wages Used In M & P	$3,250,000
Gross Up Factor	100/75
Cost Of M & P Labour*	$4,333,333

*As this grossed up amount exceeds the actual total cost of Canadian labour, the actual total cost of labour of $3,540,000 will be used in the formula.

Application Of The M & P Formula

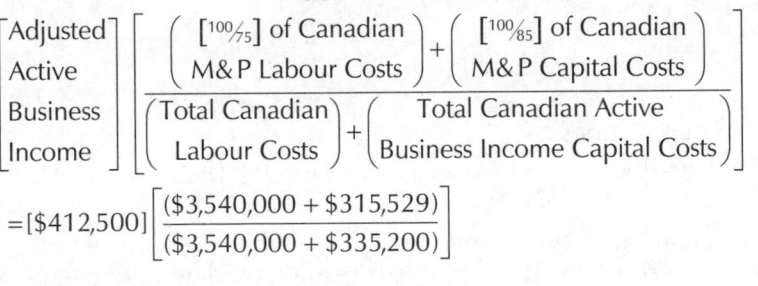

$$=[\$412,500]\left[\frac{(\$3,540,000 + \$315,529)}{(\$3,540,000 + \$335,200)}\right]$$

$$= \underline{\$410,406}$$

Chapter Fifteen Learning Objectives

After completing Chapter 15, you should be able to:

1. Calculate a corporation's Net Income For Tax Purposes (paragraphs 15-1 through 15-3).

2. List the deductions that are available to corporations in calculating Taxable Income (paragraphs 15-4 through 15-8).

3. Apply the treatment of dividends received from taxable Canadian corporations (paragraphs 15-9 through 15-20).

4. Apply the provisions related to loss carry overs when there has been an acquisition of control (paragraphs 15-21 through 15-30).

5. Apply the treatment of unrecognized losses at a deemed year end resulting from an acquisition of control (paragraphs 15-31 through 15-39).

6. Calculate the non-capital loss carry over for a corporation (paragraphs 15-40 through 15-47).

7. Apply the concepts relating to the ordering of deduction of loss carry overs (paragraphs 15-48 through 15-52).

8. Allocate corporate Taxable Income to specific provinces (paragraphs 15-53 through 15-61).

9. Calculate basic federal Tax Payable for a corporation (paragraphs 15-62 through 15-71).

10. Demonstrate a basic understanding of provincial Tax Payable for a corporation (paragraphs 15-72 through 15-80).

11. Demonstrate an understanding of the non-revenue raising goals of the corporate tax system (paragraphs 15-81 and 15-82).

12. Calculate the federal large corporations tax and apply any associated tax planning issues (paragraphs 15-83 through 15-93).

13. Explain the rules for determining which corporations and what amounts of income are eligible for the small business deduction (paragraphs 15-94 through 15-114).

14. Apply the associated companies rules (paragraphs 15-115 through 15-130).

15. Calculate the amount of the small business deduction (paragraphs 15-131 through 15-140).

16. Calculate the reduction in the small business deduction that is applicable to large CCPCs (paragraphs 15-141 through 15-152).

17. Identify personal services corporations and demonstrate an understanding of their tax treatment (paragraphs 15-153 through 15-157).

18. Identify professional corporations and management companies and demonstrate an understanding of their tax treatment (paragraphs 15-158 and 15-159).

19. Identify the types of income eligible for the manufacturing and processing profits deduction and calculate the amount of the manufacturing and processing profits deduction using the ITR 5200 formula (paragraphs 15-160 through 15-189).

20. Calculate the general rate reduction that is available to all corporations and the specific application of the general rate reduction to CCPCs (paragraphs 15-190 through 15-199).

21. Recall the history of the accelerated rate reduction (paragraph 15-200).

22. Calculate the foreign non-business (property) income tax credit for corporations (paragraphs 15-201 through 15-206).

23. Calculate the foreign business income tax credit for corporations (paragraphs 15-207 through 15-210).

24. Apply the general rules applicable to investment tax credits (paragraphs 15-211 through 15-220).

25. Apply the provisions related to refundable investment tax credits (paragraphs 15-221 through 15-226).

26. Apply the carry over rules for investment tax credits, as well as the influence of an acquisition of control on their availability (paragraphs 15-227 through 15-230).

27. Apply the provisions associated with the special incentives for scientific research and experimental development expenditures (paragraphs 15-231 through 15-254).

CHAPTER SIXTEEN

How To Work Through Chapter Sixteen

We recommend the following approach in dealing with the material in this Chapter:

Integration
☐ Read pages 651 (from paragraph 16-1) through 654 (through paragraph 16-17) of the text.

☐ Complete Exercise Sixteen-1. The Exercise is on page 654 of the text. The solution is on page S-212 of this Study Guide.

Shareholders' Equity Under GAAP
☐ Read pages 654 (from paragraph 16-18) and 655 (through paragraph 16-20) of the text.

Paid Up Capital
☐ Read page 655 (paragraphs 16-21 through 16-24) of the text.

☐ Complete Exercise Sixteen-2. The Exercise is on page 655 of the text. The solution is on page S-212 of this Study Guide.

Tax Basis Retained Earnings - Introduction
☐ Read page 656 (paragraphs 16-25 through 16-28) of the text.

Pre-1972 Capital Surplus On Hand (CSOH)
☐ Read pages 656 (from paragraph 16-29) and 657 (through paragraph 16-33) of the text.

Capital Dividend Account
☐ Read pages 657 (from paragraph 16-34) through 659 (through paragraph 16-40) of the text.

☐ Complete Exercise Sixteen-3. The Exercise is on page 659 of the text. The solution is on page S-212 of this Study Guide.

Distributions Of Corporate Surplus
☐ Read pages 659 (from paragraph 16-41) through 661 (though paragraph 16-53) of the text.

Capital Dividends Under ITA 83(2)
☐ Read page 661 (paragraphs 16-54 through 16-56) of the text.

Deemed Dividends Under ITA 84(1) - Increase In PUC
☐ Read pages 661 (from paragraph 16-57) and 662 (through paragraph 16-61) of the text.

☐ Complete Exercise Sixteen-4. The Exercise is on page 662 of the text. The solution is on page S-213 of this Study Guide.

Deemed Dividends Under ITA 84(2) - On Winding-Up
☐ Read pages 663 (from paragraph 16-62) and 664 (through paragraph 16-65) of the text.

☐ Complete Exercise Sixteen-5. The Exercise is on page 664 of the text. The solution is on page S-213 of this Study Guide.

How To Work Through Chapter Sixteen

Deemed Dividends Under ITA 84(3) - Redemption, Acquisition, Or Cancellation

☐ Read pages 664 (from paragraph 16-66) and 665 (through paragraph 16-67) of the text.

☐ Complete Exercise Sixteen-6. The Exercise is on page 665 of the text. The solution is on pages S-213 and S-214 of this Study Guide.

Deemed Dividends Under ITA 84(4) And ITA 84(4.1)

☐ Read pages 665 (from paragraph 16-68) and 666 (through paragraph 16-71) of the text.

☐ Complete Exercise Sixteen-7. The Exercise is on page 666 of the text. The solution is on page S-214 of this Study Guide.

☐ Complete Self Study Problem Sixteen-1. The Self Study Problem is on page 699 of the text. The solution is on pages S-216 and S-217 of this Study Guide.

Refundable Taxes On Investment Income - Introduction

☐ Read pages 666 (from paragraph 16-72) through 668 (through paragraph 16-80) of the text.

Refundable Part I Tax On Income From Investments

☐ Read pages 668 (from paragraph 16-81) and 669 (through paragraph 16-83) of the text.

☐ Complete Exercise Sixteen-8. The Exercise is on page 669 of the text. The solution is on page S-214 of this Study Guide.

☐ Read pages 669 (from paragraph 16-84) through 674 (through paragraph 16-104) of the text.

☐ Complete Exercise Sixteen-9. The Exercise is on page 674 of the text. The solution is on pages S-214 and S-215 of this Study Guide.

Refundable Part IV Tax On Dividends Received

☐ Read pages 675 (from paragraph 16-105) through 679 (through paragraph 16-131) of the text.

☐ Complete Exercise Sixteen-10. The Exercise is on page 679 of the text. The solution is on page S-215 of this Study Guide.

☐ Read pages 679 (from paragraph 16-132) and 680 (through paragraph 16-133) of the text.

Refundable Dividend Tax On Hand (RDTOH)

☐ Read pages 680 (from paragraph 16-134) through 685 (through paragraph 16-159) of the text.

☐ Complete Exercises Sixteen-11 and Sixteen-12. The Exercises are on page 685 of the text. The solutions are on pages S-215 and S-216 of this Study Guide.

☐ Complete Self Study Problems Sixteen-2 through Sixteen-6. The Self Study Problems are on pages 699 through 704 of the text. The solutions are on pages S-217 through S-227 of this Study Guide.

Corporate Tax Return

☐ Review the Sample Corporate Tax Return found on pages 687 through 698 of the text.

To Complete This Chapter

☐ Review the Key Terms Used In The Chapter on pages 685 and 686 of the text. Consult the Glossary for the meaning of any key terms you do not know.

☐ Review the Learning Objectives of the Chapter found on pages S-227 and S-228 of this Study Guide.

☐   As a review, we recommend that you view the PowerPoint Slides for Chapter Sixteen that
     are available on the web site at:

www.pearsoned.ca/byrdchen/ctp2006/

If you do not have access to the Microsoft PowerPoint program, the PowerPoint Viewer
program can be installed from the Companion CD-ROM.

Solution to Chapter Sixteen Exercises

Exercise Sixteen - 1 Solution

If she incorporates, the corporation will pay taxes of $19,000 [(19%)($100,000)], leaving $81,000 to be distributed as dividends. Her individual Tax Payable on these dividends would be calculated as follows:

Dividends Received	$ 81,000
Gross Up [(25%)($81,000)]	20,250
Grossed Up Dividends	$101,250
Tax Rate	45%
Tax Before Credit	$ 45,563
Dividend Tax Credit [(2/3 + 25%)($20,250)]	(18,563)
Tax Payable On Dividends	$ 27,000

The net after tax retention would be $54,000 ($81,000 - $27,000). This compares to $55,000 [($100,000)(1 - .45)] retained if a corporation is not used. The use of a corporation is undesirable because the province's low dividend tax credit rate more than offsets the province's favourable corporate tax rate.

Exercise Sixteen - 2 Solution

The adjusted cost base of the shares would be determined as follows:

	Number of Shares	Cost/Share	Total Cost
1st Purchase	2,400	$1.10	$2,640
2nd Purchase	3,850	$1.82	7,007
Totals	6,250		$9,647

The adjusted cost base per share would be $1.54 ($9,647 ÷ 6,250).

The PUC for the investor's shares would be calculated as follows:

	Number of Shares	PUC/Share	Total PUC
1st Sale	100,000	$1.10	$110,000
2nd Sale	50,000	$1.35	67,500
3rd Sale	30,000	$1.82	54,600
Total PUC Of Outstanding Shares	180,000		$232,100

Number Of Shares	6,250
PUC Per Share [$232,100 ÷ 180,000 Shares]	$ 1.29
PUC For Investor's Shares	$8,063

Exercise Sixteen - 3 Solution

The balance in the capital dividend account as at December 31, 2005 would be as follows:

1987 Capital Gain [(1/2)($123,000 - $98,000)]	$12,500
1996 Capital Loss [(1/4)($72,000 - $86,000)]	(3,500)
Capital Dividend Received - 2004	8,200
2005 Sale Of Goodwill [(3/4)($42,000 - $37,000)(2/3)]	2,500
Capital Dividend Paid - 2005	(16,000)
Balance - End Of 2005	$ 3,700

Exercise Sixteen - 4 Solution

This transaction will result in an ITA 84(1) deemed dividend for all shareholders, calculated as follows:

PUC Of New Shares [(40,000)($12.70)]	$508,000
Increase In Net Assets	(450,000)
ITA 84(1) Deemed Dividend	$ 58,000

This would be allocated to all 166,000 shares outstanding, on the basis of $0.35 per share. This would be a taxable dividend, subject to the usual gross up and tax credit procedures. This amount would be added to the adjusted cost base of all 166,000 shares.

With the addition of $0.35 resulting from the ITA 84(1) deemed dividend to the original issue price of $10.50, the adjusted cost base of these shares is now $10.85. Mr. Uni's sale of 5,000 shares at $13.42 per share would result in a taxable capital gain of $6,425 [(1/2)(5,000)($13.42 - $10.85)].

Exercise Sixteen - 5 Solution

The analysis of the $2,350,000 distribution would be as follows:

Cash Distributed	$2,350,000
PUC Of Shares	(250,000)
ITA 84(2) Deemed Dividend	$2,100,000
ITA 83(2) Capital Dividend	(340,000)
ITA 88(2)(b) Wind-Up Dividend	$1,760,000

The $1,760,000 wind-up dividend would be subject to the usual gross up and dividend tax credit treatment.

Proceeds Of Disposition	$2,350,000
ITA 84(2) Deemed Dividend	(2,100,000)
ITA 54 Proceeds Of Disposition	$ 250,000
Adjusted Cost Base	(250,000)
Capital Gain	$ Nil

As shown by the preceding calculation, there would be no capital gain on the disposition.

Exercise Sixteen - 6 Solution

The redemption transaction would have no tax consequences for Ms. Tandy. The tax consequences to Jesuiah Tandy resulting from the redemption of his shares would be as follows:

Proceeds Of Redemption [(15,000)($11.75)]	$176,250
PUC [(15,000)($8.25)]	(123,750)
ITA 84(3) Deemed Dividend	$ 52,500
Proceeds Of Redemption [(15,000)($11.75)]	$176,250
ITA 84(3) Deemed Dividend	(52,500)
ITA 54 Proceeds Of Disposition	$123,750
Adjusted Cost Base [(15,000)($10.57)]	(158,550)
Capital Loss	($ 34,800)
Inclusion Rate	1/2
Allowable Capital Loss	($ 17,400)

The deemed dividend of $52,500 would be subject to the usual gross up and dividend tax credit treatment. The allowable capital loss can be used in the current period, only to the extent of taxable capital gains realized in the current period.

Exercise Sixteen - 7 Solution

To the extent of the $225,000 PUC reduction, the dividend will be treated as a tax free distribution. The only tax consequence associated with this will be a reduction in the adjusted cost base of his shares to $400,000 ($625,000 - $225,000). The remaining $105,000 ($330,000 - $225,000) of the distribution will be an ITA 84(4) deemed dividend, subject to the usual gross up and tax credit procedures. As it will be taxed as a dividend, this part of the distribution will not be subtracted from the adjusted cost base of the shares.

Exercise Sixteen - 8 Solution

Zircon's Taxable Income would be calculated as follows:

Net Income For Tax Purposes	$281,000
Dividends From Taxable Canadian Corporations	(22,000)
Net Capital Loss Carry Over	(26,000)
Non-Capital Loss Carry Over	(23,000)
Taxable Income	$210,000

Zircon's amount eligible for the small business deduction would be the least of active business income of $198,000, Taxable Income of $210,000, and the annual business limit of $300,000.

Given these calculations, Zircon's additional refundable tax on investment income would be calculated using the lesser of:

Aggregate Investment Income		
Taxable Capital Gains	$46,000	
Interest Income	15,000	
Net Capital Loss Deducted	(26,000)	$35,000
Taxable Income	$210,000	
Amount Eligible For SBD	(198,000)	$12,000

The additional refundable tax on investment income would be $800 [(6-2/3%)($12,000)].

Exercise Sixteen - 9 Solution

If Ms. Nicastro receives the income directly, she will retain $51,000 [($100,000)(1 - .49)]. Alternatively, if the investments are transferred to a corporation, the results would be as follows:

Corporate Investment Income	$100,000
Corporate Tax At 48 Percent	(48,000)
Income Before Dividends	$ 52,000
Dividend Refund ($1 For Each $3 Of Dividends Paid)	26,000
Dividends Paid To Ms. Nicastro	$ 78,000

Dividends Received	$ 78,000
Gross Up Of 25 Percent	19,500
Personal Taxable Income	$ 97,500
Personal Tax Rate	49%
Tax Payable Before Dividend Tax Credit	$ 47,775
Dividend Tax Credit [(2/3 + 42%)($19,500)]	(21,190)
Personal Tax Payable With Corporation	$ 26,585
Dividends Received	$ 78,000
Personal Tax Payable	(26,585)
After Tax Cash Retained With Corporation	$ 51,415

There would be two tax advantages associated with using the corporation. First, as corporate taxes of $48,000 are less than the personal taxes of $49,000, there would be a small tax deferral on income left in the corporation. Second, the after tax cash retained with a corporation of $51,415, is slightly higher than the $51,000 retained on direct receipt of the income.

Exercise Sixteen - 10 Solution

The amount of Part IV Tax Payable would be calculated as follows:

Tax On Portfolio Investments [(1/3)($14,000)]	$4,667
Tax On Subsidiary Dividends	Nil
Tax On Ruby Inc. Dividends [(30%)($15,000)]	4,500
Part IV Tax Payable	$9,167

Exercise Sixteen - 11 Solution

The refundable amount of Debut Inc.'s Part I tax for the current year would be the least of the following three figures:

Foreign Non-Business Income (100 Percent)		$15,000
Taxable Capital Gains [(1/2)($38,250)]		19,125
Net Rental Income		6,500
Interest Income		9,200
Net Capital Loss Carry Forward Deducted [(1/2 ÷ 3/4)($13,500)]		(9,000)
Aggregate Investment Income Under ITA 129(4)		$40,825
Rate		26-2/3%
Amount Before Foreign Income Adjustment		$10,887
Deduct Excess Of:		
Foreign Non-Business Tax Credit	$ 750	
Over 9-1/3 Percent Of Foreign Non-Business		
Income [(9-1/3%)($15,000)]	(1,400)	Nil
ITA 129(3)(a)(i) Amount		$10,887
Taxable Income ($136,700 - $22,000 - $9,000)		$105,700
Deduct:		
Amount Eligible For The Small Business Deduction ($8,000 ÷ 16%)		(50,000)
[(25/9)($750)] Foreign Non-Business Tax Credit		(2,083)
Adjusted Taxable Income		$ 53,617
Rate		26-2/3%
Amount Under ITA 129(3)(a)(ii)		$ 14,298

Part I Tax Payable	$24,752
Deduct: Surtax	(1,184)
Amount Under ITA 129(3)(a)(iii)	$23,568

The least of these three amounts is $10,887, and this would be the refundable portion of Part I tax for the year.

Exercise Sixteen - 12 Solution

The balance in the RDTOH account of QIL would be as follows:

Opening Balance	$12,500	
Previous Year's Dividend Refund	(2,000)	$10,500
Part I Refundable Addition [(26-2/3%)($24,000)]	$6,400	
Part IV Tax On Portfolio Dividends [(1/3)($6,000)]	2,000	8,400
Closing Balance - RDTOH		$18,900

The dividend refund would be $5,000, the lesser of one-third of the dividends paid and the $18,900 balance in the RDTOH account.

Solution to Self Study Problem Sixteen - 1

Part A(i)   There would be an ITA 84(1) deemed dividend calculated as follows:

Increase In PUC - Preferred Shares	$11,000
Increase In Net Assets (Decrease In Liabilities)	(10,000)
ITA 84(1) Deemed Dividend	$ 1,000

This $1,000 deemed dividend is applicable to all 1,000 of the Preferred Shares that are now outstanding. A pro rata share of the dividend, $1 per share, will be added to the adjusted cost base of all of the Preferred Shares that are outstanding. All of the preferred stock investors will be taxed on the deemed dividend of $1 per share.

Part A(ii)   This investor's taxable capital gain would be calculated as follows:

Proceeds Of Disposition		$11,000
Adjusted Cost Base:		
Original Cost	($4,100)	
ITA 84(1) Dividend [(250)($1)]	(250)	(4,350)
Capital Gain		$ 6,650
Inclusion Rate		1/2
Taxable Capital Gain		$ 3,325

Part B   As noted in ITA 84(1)(a), a stock dividend is not considered to be a deemed dividend under ITA 84. However, the $780 addition to Paid Up Capital will be considered to be a regular dividend under the definition in ITA 248(1). The holders of the common shares will have a dividend of $1.30 ($780 ÷ 600) per share, and this will be grossed up to a taxable dividend of $1.63 per share.

Part C   As the increase in Paid Up Capital was less than the increase in net assets, there is no deemed dividend or any other tax consequences in this Part. This is verified in the following calculation:

Increase In Paid Up Capital [(250/500)($11,000)]		$ 5,500
Increase In Net Assets:		
New Assets Acquired	$17,500	
Increase In Liabilities	(7,500)	(10,000)
ITA 84(1) Deemed Dividend		Nil

Part D   The ITA 84(3) deemed dividend would be calculated as follows:

Redemption Proceeds [(100 Shares)($32)]	$3,200
Paid Up Capital [(100 Shares)($26)]	(2,600)
ITA 84(3) Deemed Dividend	$ 600

In addition, there would be a taxable capital gain calculated as follows:

Redemption Proceeds	$3,200
ITA 84(3) Deemed Dividend	(600)
Deemed Proceeds Of Disposition	$2,600
Adjusted Cost Base [(100)($15)]	(1,500)
Capital Gain	$1,100
Inclusion Rate	1/2
Taxable Capital Gain	$ 550

Solution to Self Study Problem Sixteen - 2

Part A   The ending RDTOH balance for FOL would be as follows:

Refundable Dividend Tax On Hand - Beginning	$2,000
Refundable Portion Of Part I Tax [(26-2/3%)($7,000)]	1,867
Refundable Dividend Tax On Hand - Ending	$3,867

As FOL has no foreign investment income or deductions for loss carry overs, the calculation of the addition to the RDTOH for the refundable portion of Part I tax is based solely on the interest income.

The dividend refund would be $3,867, the lesser of:

• One-Third Of Taxable Dividends Paid [(1/3)($75,000)]	$25,000
• Refundable Dividend Tax On Hand - Ending	$ 3,867

Part B   The Part IV tax for SHI would be calculated as follows:

Portfolio Dividends [(1/3)($8,000)]	$2,667
SHI's Share Of FOL's Dividend Refund (100%)	3,867
Part IV Tax Payable	$6,534

Part C SHI's aggregate investment income totals $35,625, the sum of $12,000 in interest income and $23,625 [(1/2)($47,250)] in taxable capital gains. This means that the ending RDTOH balance for SHI would be as follows:

Refundable Dividend Tax On Hand - Beginning	$ 8,000
Refundable Portion Of Part I Tax [(26-2/3%)($35,625)]	9,500
Part IV Tax Payable (Part B)	6,534
Refundable Dividend Tax On Hand - Ending	$24,034

The dividend refund would be $16,667, the lesser of:

• One-Third Of Taxable Dividends Paid [(1/3)($50,000)]	$16,667
• Refundable Dividend Tax On Hand - Ending	$24,034

Solution to Self Study Problem Sixteen - 3

The Part IV Tax Payable for Burton Investments Ltd. would be calculated as follows:

Puligny's Dividend Refund	$12,500
Burton's Percentage Of Ownership	52%
Part IV Tax Payable On Puligny's Dividends	$ 6,500
Part IV Tax Payable On Portfolio Dividends From Bank Of Montreal [(1/3)($13,480)]	4,493
Part IV Tax Payable	$10,993

The end of year balance in the Refundable Dividend Tax On Hand account and refundable Part I tax can be calculated as follows:

Balance - End Of Preceding Year	$22,346
Dividend Refund For The Preceding Year	(7,920)
Opening Balance	$14,426
Part IV Tax Payable	10,993
Refundable Part I Tax On Capital Gain [(1/2)($18,000)(26-2/3%)]	2,400
Balance - End Of The Year	$27,819

As the interest received appears to be related to temporary balances resulting from the Company's normal business activities, it would be viewed as active business income, and would not influence the preceding calculations.

The dividends paid of $22,500 will generate a $7,500 [(1/3)($22,500)] dividend refund, as this is less than the $27,819 ending balance in the Refundable Dividend Tax On Hand account.

Solution to Self Study Problem Sixteen - 4

Part A   The Part I Tax Payable is calculated as follows:

Base Amount Of Part I Tax [(38%)($503,500)]	$191,330
Surtax [(4%)(28%)($503,500)]	5,639
ART [(6-2/3%)($43,250 + $55,000 + $24,500 - $12,300)]	7,363
Federal Tax Abatement [(10%)($503,500 - $38,200 - $98,000)]	(36,730)
Foreign Business Income Tax Credit (Given)	(34,000)
Foreign Non-Business Income Tax Credit (Given)	(8,250)
Small Business Deduction [(16%)($200,000)]	(32,000)
General Rate Reduction For CCPCs	
[(7%)($503,500 - $200,000 - $110,450)]	(13,514)
Part I Tax Payable	$ 79,838

Part B   To determine the dividend refund, the RDTOH balance must first be calculated. This requires the calculation of the refundable portion of Part I tax and the Part IV tax.

Refundable Part I Tax   The refundable portion of Part I tax would be the least of the following three amounts:

Interest On Loan To Subsidiary		$ 43,250
Taxable Capital Gains		24,500
Foreign Investment Income		55,000
Net Capital Losses Claimed		(12,300)
Aggregate Investment Income (Note One)		$110,450
Rate		26-2/3%
Total		$ 29,453
Deduct Excess Of:		
Foreign Non-Business Tax Credit	$8,250	
Over 9-1/3% Of Foreign Non-Business Income		
[(9-1/3%)($55,000)]	(5,133)	(3,117)
Amount Under ITA 129(3)(a)(i)		$ 26,336

Taxable Income	$503,500
Deduct:	
Amount Eligible For The Small Business Deduction	(200,000)
[(25/9)($8,250)] Foreign Non-Business Tax Credit	(22,917)
[(3)($34,000)] Foreign Business Tax Credit	(102,000)
	$178,583
Rate	26-2/3%
Amount Under ITA 129(3)(a)(ii)	$ 47,622

Part I Tax Payable	$79,838
Deduct: Surtax	(5,639)
Amount Under ITA 129(3)(a)(iii)	$74,199

The least of these three amounts is $26,336, the amount calculated under ITA 129(3)(a)(i).

Note One   The definition contained in ITA 129(4.1) excludes income from property that is incidental to carrying on an active business and, as a consequence, we have left out the $5,050 of term deposit interest. With respect to the interest on the loan to the subsidiary, if the subsidiary had deducted the $43,250 in computing active business income eligible for the small business deduction, ITA 129(6) would have deemed this interest to be active business income rather than investment income.   However, the subsidiary was not involved in the production of active business income and, as a consequence, the interest from the subsidiary is included in the above calculation of aggregate investment income.

Part IV Tax Payable   The Part IV Tax Payable would be calculated as follows:

One-Third Of Portfolio Dividends Received [(1/3)($19,600)]	$ 6,533
Share Of Dividend Refund Included In	
Dividends From Subsidiary [(75%)($12,750)]	9,563
Part IV Tax Payable	$16,096

Refundable Dividend Tax On Hand Balance   This balance would be calculated as follows:

RDTOH Balance - End Of The Preceding Year	$23,500	
Dividend Refund For The Preceding Year	(9,600)	$13,900
Refundable Portion Of Part I Tax	$26,336	
Part IV Tax Payable	16,096	42,432
RDTOH Balance - December 31, 2005		$56,332

Dividend Refund   The dividend refund for the year would be $36,333, the lesser of:

- One-third of taxable dividends paid during the year
{[1/3][$25,000 + (3)($28,000)]} = $36,333
- RDTOH Balance - December 31, 2005 = $56,332

Solution to Self Study Problem Sixteen - 5

Part A - Taxable Income   The calculation of Acme Imports' Taxable Income would be as follows:

Accounting Income Before Taxes		$232,300
Additions:		
Amortization Expense	$20,000	
Charitable Donations	25,000	
Taxable Capital Gain On Sale Of Equipment		
[(1/2)($84,500 - $62,000)]	11,250	
Golf Club Membership	2,800	
50 Percent Of Business Meals And Entertainment	3,360	
Share Issue Costs [(80%)($950)]	760	
Costs Of Supplementary Letters Patent	7,000	
Interest On Mortgage For The Land	12,300	82,470
Deductions:		
CCA (Note One)	($38,800)	
Gain On Sale Of Equipment ($84,500 - $27,500)	(57,000)	
Cumulative Eligible Capital:		
Customer List [($183,000)(3/4)(7%)]	(9,608)	
Letters Patent [($7,000)(3/4)(7%)]	(368)	(105,776)
Net Income For Tax Purposes		$208,994
Charitable Donations		(25,000)
Dividends From Sarco Ltd.		(24,000)
Taxable Income		$159,994

Note One   The maximum CCA on the equipment would be calculated as follows:

Opening UCC	$256,000
Disposition (Capital Cost)	(62,000)
CCA Base	$194,000
Rate - Class 8	20%
CCA	$ 38,800

Several of the items in this problem need further comment. These are as follows:

- **Item 4**   With respect to the costs of issuing shares, IT-341R3 indicates that these amounts are deductible under ITA 20(1)(e). However, such amounts have to be deducted over at least five years at a maximum rate of 20 percent per year. With respect to the costs of acquiring supplementary letters patent, they are considered to be an eligible capital expenditure, three-quarters of which must be added to the cumulative eligible capital account, and amortized at 7 percent.

- **Item 5**   As the loan to the shareholder has been included in two consecutive Balance Sheets, it will become income to the shareholder. However, this does not affect the Company's calculations.

- **Item 6**   Only 50 percent of the $6,720 in charges at the local golf and country club are deductible.

- **Item 7**   The cars provided to the principal shareholder and to the manager of the Company will result in their being assessed for a substantial taxable benefit. However, the costs are fully deductible to the Company.

Solution to Self Study Problem Sixteen - 5

- **Item 11** The fees paid to the site consultant are deductible as indicated in ITA 20(1)(dd). ITA 18(3.1) disallows the deduction of interest on financing related to land during construction. The $12,300 interest on the $244,000 mortgage on the land would be capitalized and is not deductible.

Part B - Active Business Income   The active business income of Acme is as follows:

Net Income For Tax Purposes		$208,994
Dividends		(24,000)
Aggregate Investment Income:		
Interest Revenue	($10,000)	
Taxable Capital Gain	(11,250)	(21,250)
Active Business Income		$163,744

Part C - Tax Payable   The calculation of Acme Ltd.'s federal Tax Payable would be as follows:

Base Amount Of Part I Tax [(38%)($159,994)]	$ 60,798
Corporate Surtax [(4%)(28%)($159,994)]	1,792
Refundable Tax On Investment Income (Note Three)	Nil
Federal Tax Abatement [(10%)($159,994)]	(15,999)
Small Business Deduction (Note Two)	(25,599)
General Rate Reduction (Note Four)	Nil
Part I Tax Payable	$ 20,992
Part IV Tax Payable (Note Five)	3,000
Federal Tax Payable	$ 23,992
Instalments Paid (From Balance Sheet)	(28,000)
Amount Payable (Refund)	($ 4,008)

Note Two   Since none of the annual business limit has been allocated to Sarco, the small business deduction is 16 percent of the least of the following three amounts:

1. Active Business Income (Part B) $163,744

2. Taxable Income (no foreign tax credit adjustment) $159,994

3. Annual Business Limit $300,000

The lowest of these figures is the Taxable Income of $159,994 and this gives a small business deduction of $25,599 [(16%)($159,994)].

Note Three   The ITA 123.3 refundable tax (ART) is 6-2/3 percent of the lesser of:

1. Aggregate Investment Income (Part B) $21,250

2. Taxable Income $159,994
    Deduct: Amount Eligible For The SBD   (159,994)   Nil

Since the income eligible for the small business deduction is not less than Taxable Income, there is no ITA 123.3 tax on investment income payable.

Note Four   The general rate reduction under ITA 123.4(2) would be nil, calculated as follows:

S - 222   *Canadian Tax Principles Study Guide 2005/2006*

Taxable Income		$159,994
Amount Eligible For The Small Business Deduction [(100/16)($25,599)]		(159,994)
Aggregate Investment Income (Part B)		(21,250)
Full Rate Taxable Income		Nil
Rate		7%
ITA 123.4(2) General Rate Reduction For CCPCs		Nil

Note Five   Acme would have to pay a Part IV tax equal to its share of the dividend refund received from Sarco Ltd. This amount would be $3,000 [(60%)($5,000)].

Part D - Refundable Dividend Tax On Hand   The ending balance in this account would be calculated as follows:

RDTOH, End Of The Preceding Year		$ -0-
Refundable Portion Of Part I Tax (Note Six)	$ -0-	
Part IV Tax Payable (Note Five)	3,000	3,000
RDTOH Balance - December 31, 2005		$3,000

Note Six   The amount of refundable Part I tax will be the least of the following three amounts. In this problem, the calculation of these amounts is greatly simplified by the absence of foreign non-business income. The calculations are as follows:

ITA 129(3)(a)(i)   This amount would be $5,667, 26-2/3 percent of aggregate investment income of $21,250 ($10,000 + $11,250).

ITA 129(3)(a)(ii)   This amount would be nil, 26-2/3 percent of Taxable Income, reduced by the amount of income that is eligible for the small business deduction [(26-2/3%)($159,994 - $159,994)].

ITA 129(3)(a)(iii)   This amount would be Part I Tax Payable, less the corporate surtax, for an amount of $19,200 ($20,992 - $1,792).

The least of these amounts is nil, so there would be no refundable portion of Part I tax.

Solution to Self Study Problem Sixteen - 6

Part A   Brasco's Net Income For Tax Purposes and Taxable Income would be calculated as follows:

Active Business Income		$171,000
Taxable Capital Gains [($72,000)(1/2)]		36,000
Canadian Source Interest Income		2,200
Portfolio Dividends		15,800
Foreign Source Investment Income (Gross Amount)		4,500
Dividends From Subsidiary		37,800
Net Income For Tax Purposes		$267,300
Dividends Received:		
Portfolio	($15,800)	
Subsidiary	(37,800)	(53,600)
Charitable Donations		(11,900)
Non-Capital Loss Carry Forward Deducted		(25,800)
Net Capital Loss Carry Forward Deducted (Note One)		(36,000)
Taxable Income		$140,000

Note One   Note that the net capital loss carry forward is limited to the taxable capital gains. This will leave a net capital loss carry forward of $28,500 ($64,500 - $36,000) for subsequent periods.

Part B   Brasco's Tax Payable would be calculated as follows:

Base Amount Of Part I Tax [(38%)($140,000)]	$53,200
Corporate Surtax [(4%)(28%)($140,000)]	1,568
Additional Refundable Tax On Investment Income (Note Two)	447
Federal Tax Abatement [(10%)($140,000)]	(14,000)
Small Business Deduction (Note Three)	(20,000)
Foreign Non-Business Tax Credit (Amount Withheld)	(675)
General Rate Reduction For CCPCs (Note Four)	(581)
Part I Tax Payable	$19,959
Part IV Tax Payable (Note Five)	17,867
Total Tax Payable	$37,826
Dividend Refund (Note Six)	(13,000)
Net Tax Payable	$24,826

Note Two   The aggregate investment income of $6,700 is calculated as follows:

Canadian Interest	$ 2,200
Taxable Capital Gains	36,000
Foreign Investment Income	4,500
Net Capital Loss Carry Forward Deducted	(36,000)
Aggregate Investment Income	$ 6,700

The ITA 123.3 refundable tax (ART) is 6-2/3 percent of the lesser of:

1. Aggregate Investment Income		$ 6,700
2. Taxable Income	$140,000	
Deduct: Amount Eligible For The SBD	(125,000)	$15,000

The ITA 123.3 tax on aggregate investment income is $447 [(6-2/3%)($6,700)].

Note Three   The small business deduction is 16 percent of the least of the following three amounts:

1. Active Business Income		$171,000
2. Taxable Income	$140,000	
Deduct:		
[(10/3)($675)] Foreign Non-Business Tax Credit	(2,250)	$137,750
3. Annual Business Limit (Given)		$125,000

The lowest of these figures is the allocated annual limit of $125,000 and this gives a small business deduction of $20,000 [(16%)($125,000)].

Note Four   The general rate reduction would be calculated as follows:

Taxable Income	$140,000
Amount Eligible For The Small Business Deduction [(100/16)($20,000)]	(125,000)
Aggregate Investment Income (See Note Two)	(6,700)
Full Rate Taxable Income	$ 8,300
Rate	7%
ITA 123.4(2) General Rate Reduction For CCPCs	$ 581

Note Five   The calculation of Part IV Tax Payable would be as follows:

Part IV Tax Transfer From Masco [(60%)($21,000)]	$12,600
Part IV Tax On Portfolio Dividends [(1/3)($15,800)]	5,267
Part IV Tax Payable	$17,867

Note Six   The dividend refund would be equal to the lesser of:

- One-third of taxable dividends paid [(1/3)($39,000)] = $13,000

- RDTOH Balance - December 31, 2005 (Note Seven) = $26,399

The lesser of these two figures is $13,000 and that would be the refund for the year. Note that the payment of capital dividends does not generate a dividend refund.

Note Seven   The Balance in the RDTOH would be calculated as follows:

RDTOH Balance - End Of The Preceding Year	$ 7,000	
Dividend Refund For The Preceding Year	Nil	$ 7,000
Refundable Portion Of Part I Tax (Note Eight)	$ 1,532	
Part IV Tax (Note Five)	17,867	19,399
RDTOH Balance - December 31, 2005		$26,399

Note Eight   The refundable portion of Part I tax will be the least of the following three amounts:

Aggregate Investment Income (Note Two)		$ 6,700
Rate		26-2/3%
		$ 1,787
Deduct Excess Of:		
Foreign Non-Business Tax Credit	$675	
Over 9-1/3% Of Foreign Non-Business Income [(9-1/3%)($4,500)]	(420)	(255)
Amount Under ITA 129(3)(a)(i)		$ 1,532
Taxable Income		$140,000
Deduct:		
Amount Eligible For The Small Business Deduction		(125,000)
[(25/9)($675)] Foreign Non-Business Tax Credit		(1,875)
Adjusted Taxable Income		$ 13,125
Rate		26-2/3%
Amount Under ITA 129(3)(a)(ii)		$ 3,500

Solution to Self Study Problem Sixteen - 6

Part I Tax Payable	$ 19,959
Deduct: Surtax	(1,568)
Amount Under ITA 129(3)(a)(iii)	$ 18,391

The least of these three amounts would be $1,532, the amount calculated under ITA 129(3)(a)(i).

Part C If you cannot assume that the foreign tax credit is equal to the amount withheld, the actual foreign tax credit is a complex calculation in this situation. The use of foreign taxes paid as credits against Canadian Tax Payable is limited by a formula that includes the "tax otherwise payable". In the case of foreign taxes paid on non-business income, the "tax otherwise payable" in the formula includes the ART that is assessed under ITA 123.3. This creates a problem in that the calculation of the ART includes the amount eligible for the small business deduction [ITA 123.3(b)]. In turn, the determination of the amount eligible for the small business deduction requires the use of the foreign tax credits for foreign taxes paid on non-business and business income [ITA 125(b)(i) and (ii)].

To solve this circular calculation, for the purpose of calculating the small business deduction, the foreign tax credit for taxes paid on non-business income is calculated using a "tax otherwise payable" figure that does not include the ART under ITA 123.3. This means that in situations where foreign non-business income, the small business deduction, and the ART are involved, the following procedures should be used:

1. Calculate the foreign non-business tax credit using a "tax otherwise payable" that excludes the ART. This initial version of the foreign non-business tax credit will be used only for determining the small business deduction, with the actual credit to be applied calculated after the ART has been determined.

2. Calculate the amount eligible for the small business deduction using the numbers determined in step 1.

3. Calculate the ART, using the amount eligible for the small business deduction determined in step 2.

4. Calculate the actual foreign non-business tax credit using a "tax otherwise payable" figure that includes the ART.

The initial version of the foreign non-business tax credit will be the lesser of the actual tax paid of $675, and an amount determined by the following formula:

$$\left(\frac{\text{Foreign Non - Business Income}}{\text{Adjusted Net Income}}\right)(\text{Part I Tax Otherwise Payable Excluding The ART})$$

$$= \left(\frac{\$4,500}{\$267,300 - \$53,600 - \$36,000}\right)(\$53,200 + \$1,568 - \$14,000)$$

$$= \underline{\$1,032}$$

Part I tax otherwise payable in the preceding formula does not include the ART under ITA 123.3 or the general rate reduction under ITA 123.4. The ITA 123.4 reduction will also be excluded in the calculation of the regular foreign tax credit, as the definition of tax otherwise payable excludes this amount for CCPCs. Adjusted Net Income in the formula is Net Income For Tax Purposes minus deductible dividends and net capital loss carry overs claimed in the current year. In this case, the actual tax paid of $675 will be the credit. As a result, the small business deduction will be the same amount as calculated in Part A of this problem.

The actual foreign non-business tax credit, which takes into consideration the ART, will be the lesser of the actual taxes paid of $675 and an amount determined by the following formula:

$$\left(\frac{\text{Foreign Non-Business Income}}{\text{Adjusted Net Income}}\right)(\text{Part I Tax Otherwise Payable Including The ART})$$

$$= \left(\frac{\$4,500}{\$267,300 - \$53,600 - \$36,000}\right)(\$53,200 + \$1,568 + \$447 - \$14,000)$$

$$= \underline{\$1,044}$$

In this calculation, the actual taxes paid of $675 will again be the credit.

Chapter Sixteen Learning Objectives

After completing Chapter 16, you should be able to:

1. Explain the goal of integration in the design of the Canadian corporate tax system (paragraphs 16-1 through 16-5).

2. Calculate after-tax income retained from dividends received (paragraphs 16-6 through 16-11).

3. Demonstrate how the dividend gross up and tax credit procedures work to implement integration with respect to business income (paragraphs 16-12 through 16-17).

4. Explain the relationship between tax basis Shareholders' Equity and Shareholders' Equity as presented under GAAP (paragraphs 16-18 through 16-20).

5. Demonstrate an understanding of the concept of, and calculate the amount of, Paid Up Capital (paragraphs 16-21 through 16-24).

6. Identify and explain the major components of tax basis Retained Earnings (paragraphs 16-25 through 16-40).

7. List the various types of corporate surplus distributions (paragraphs 16-41 through 16-43).

8. Apply the procedures related to the declaration and payment of cash dividends (paragraphs 16-44 through 16-46).

9. Apply the procedures related to the declaration and payment of stock dividends (paragraphs 16-47 through 16-50).

10. Apply the procedures related to the declaration and payment of dividends in kind (paragraphs 16-51 through 16-53).

11. Apply the procedures related to the declaration and payment of capital dividends (paragraphs 16-54 through 16-56).

12. Explain and apply the procedures related to ITA 84(1) deemed dividends (paragraphs 16-57 through 16-61).

13. Explain and apply the procedures related to ITA 84(2) deemed dividends (paragraphs 16-62 through 16-65).

14. Explain and apply the procedures related to ITA 84(3) deemed dividends (paragraphs 16-66 and 16-67).

15. Explain and apply the procedures related to ITA 84(4) and 84(4.1) deemed dividends (paragraphs 16-68 through 16-71).

16. List the components of aggregate investment income as it is defined in ITA 129(4) (paragraphs 16-72 and 16-73).

17. Demonstrate an understanding of the basic concepts of the Part I refundable tax (paragraphs 16-74 through 16-80).

18. Calculate the additional refundable tax on the investment income of a Canadian controlled private corporation (paragraphs 16-81 through 16-87).

19. Calculate the Part I refundable tax on the investment income of a Canadian controlled private corporation (paragraphs 16-88 through 16-104).

20. Describe and apply the provision related to the Part IV refundable tax on private corporations (paragraphs 16-105 through 16-133).

21. Calculate the balance in the Refundable Dividend Tax On Hand account and the dividend refund (paragraphs 16-134 through 16-159).

CHAPTER SEVENTEEN

How To Work Through Chapter Seventeen

We recommend the following approach in dealing with the material in this Chapter:

The Decision To Incorporate

☐ Read pages 713 (from paragraph 17-1) through 716 (through paragraph 17-16) of the text.

Reduction And Deferral Of Taxes - Public Companies

☐ Read pages 716 (from paragraph 17-17) and 717 (through paragraph 17-22) of the text.

Reduction And Deferral Of Taxes - Active Business Income - CCPC

☐ Read pages 717 (from paragraph 17-23) through 719 (through paragraph 17-33) of the text.

☐ Complete Exercise Seventeen-1. The Exercise is on page 719 of the text. The solution is on page S-231 of this Study Guide.

Reduction And Deferral Of Taxes - Investment Income - CCPC

☐ Read pages 719 (from paragraph 17-34) and 720 (through paragraph 17-36) of the text.

☐ Complete Exercise Seventeen-2. The Exercise is on page 720 of the text. The solution is on page S-231 of this Study Guide.

Reduction And Deferral Of Taxes - Dividend Income - CCPC

☐ Read pages 720 (from paragraph 17-37) and 721 (through paragraph 17-39) of the text.

Tax Reduction And Deferrals - Conclusions

☐ Read pages 721 (from paragraph 17-40) and 722 (through paragraph 17-42) of the text.

☐ Complete Exercises Seventeen-3 and Seventeen-4. The Exercises are on page 723 of the text. The solutions are on pages S-231 through S-233 of this Study Guide.

Using Imperfections In The Integration System

☐ Read pages 723 (from paragraph 17-43) through 726 (through paragraph 17-52) of the text.

Income Splitting

☐ Read pages 726 (from paragraph 17-53) and 727 (through paragraph 17-61) of the text.

Other Advantages And Disadvantages Of Incorporation

☐ Read pages 727 (from paragraph 17-62) and 728 (through paragraph 17-64) of the text.

☐ Complete Self Study Problem Seventeen-1. The Self Study Problem is on page 741 of the text. The solution is on pages S-235 and S-236 of this Study Guide.

Management Compensation - General Principles

☐ Read pages 728 (from paragraph 17-65) through 730 (through paragraph 17-71) of the text.

Salary Vs. Dividends For The Owner-Manager

☐ Read pages 730 (from paragraph 17-72) through 735 (through paragraph 17-103) of the text.

☐ Complete Exercises Seventeen-5 and Seventeen-6. The Exercises are on page 736 of the text. The solutions are on pages S-233 and S-234 of this Study Guide.

Salary Vs. Dividends - Use Of Tax Credits

☐ Read pages 736 (from paragraph 17-104) through 738 (through paragraph 17-115) of the text.

☐ Complete Exercises Seventeen-7 and Seventeen-8. The Exercises are on page 739 of the text. The solutions are on page S-234 of this Study Guide.

Salary Vs. Dividends - Conclusion

☐ Read page 739 (paragraphs 17-116 and 17-117) of the text.

☐ Complete Self Study Problems Seventeen-2 and Seventeen-3. The Self Study Problems are on page 742 of the text. The solutions are on pages S-237 through S-239 of this Study Guide.

To Complete This Chapter

☐ Review the Key Terms Used In The Chapter on page 740 of the text. Consult the Glossary for the meaning of any key terms you do not know.

☐ Review the Learning Objectives of the Chapter found on page S-240 of this Study Guide.

☐ As a review, we recommend that you view the PowerPoint Slides for Chapter Seventeen that are available on the web site at:

www.pearsoned.ca/byrdchen/ctp2006/

If you do not have access to the Microsoft PowerPoint program, the PowerPoint Viewer program can be installed from the Companion CD-ROM.

Solution to Chapter Seventeen Exercises

Exercise Seventeen - 1 Solution

Mr. Slater's combined tax rate on income earned by the unincorporated business is 43 percent (29% + 14%). If he incorporates, all of the $126,000 will be eligible for the small business deduction. This means it will be taxed at a rate of 20.12 percent [(38% - 10%)(1.04) - 16% + 7%]. There is clearly a significant amount of tax deferral with respect to income left in the corporation. His Tax Payable on direct receipt of the $126,000 of business income would be $54,180 [(43%)($126,000)], far higher than the $25,351 [(20.12%)($126,000)] that would be paid by the corporation.

Mr. Slater's tax rate on dividend income is 28.75 percent [(1.25)(43%) - (2/3 + 1/3)(25%)]. This means that the overall tax rate on income that is paid out in dividends is 43 percent [20.12% + (100% - 20.12%)(28.75%)]. This is equal to the 43 percent rate applicable to income from the unincorporated business. As a consequence, there is no tax savings available on income that is paid out as dividends.

Exercise Seventeen - 2 Solution

Mr. Slater's combined tax rate on interest income earned outside the corporation is 43 percent (29% + 14%). If he incorporates, the interest income will not be eligible for the small business deduction or the general rate reduction, and it will be subject to the ART. This means that, if the investments are transferred to a corporation, the interest will be taxed at a rate of 51.2 percent [(38% - 10%)(1.04) + 6-2/3% + 15.4%]. As this is higher than the 43 percent rate applicable to the direct receipt of interest income, the corporation does not provide any deferral on amounts left within the corporation. In this case, incorporation requires prepayment of taxes.

After being taxed at 51.2 percent, the corporation would have $61,488 in after tax funds available. With the available refund, this would allow the payment of a dividend of $92,232 [(3/2)($61,488)]. Mr. Slater's tax rate on dividends received is 28.75 percent [(1.25)(43%) - (2/3 + 1/3)(25%)]. After payment of taxes at this rate, he would be left with $65,715 in after tax funds. If he does not incorporate, the $126,000 in interest income would be taxed at 43 percent, leaving an after tax amount of $71,820. There is clearly a tax cost as a result of transferring the investments to a corporation.

Exercise Seventeen - 3 Solution

Direct Receipt If the income is received directly, the total Tax Payable will be as follows:

Dividends Received ($46,000 + $87,000)	$133,000
Gross Up (25%)	33,250
Taxable Dividends	$166,250
Interest Income	32,000
Taxable Income	$198,250
Personal Tax Rate (29% + 15%)	44%
Tax Payable Before Dividend Tax Credit	$ 87,230
Dividend Tax Credit [(2/3 + 1/3)($33,250)]	(33,250)
Personal Tax Payable	$ 53,980

The after tax retention can be calculated as follows:

Cash Received ($46,000 + $87,000 + $32,000)	$165,000
Tax Payable	(53,980)
After Tax Retention	$111,020

Transfer To Corporation If the investments are transferred to a corporation, the corporate taxes will be as follows:

Part IV Tax On Dividends Received [(1/3)($46,000) + $23,000]	$38,333
Part I Tax On Interest Income	
{[$32,000][(38% - 10%)(1.04) + 6-2/3% + 15%]}	16,252
Corporate Tax Payable Before Refund	**$54,585**

The RDTOH balance prior to the dividend refund would be calculated as follows:

Part IV Addition	$38,333
Part I Addition [(26-2/3%)($32,000)]	8,533
RDTOH Balance	**$46,866**

The cash available for paying dividends would be $110,415 ($165,000 - $54,585). This represents two-thirds of $165,623, a dividend that would generate a dividend refund of $55,208. However, as the balance in the RDTOH is only $46,866, the maximum dividend that can be paid is $157,281 ($110,415 + $46,866). This would result in personal taxes as follows:

Dividends Received	$157,281
Gross Up (25%)	39,320
Taxable Dividends	**$196,601**
Personal Tax Rate	44%
Tax Before Dividend Tax Credit	**$ 86,504**
Dividend Tax Credit [(2/3 + 1/3)($39,320)]	(39,320)
Tax Payable	**$ 47,184**

After tax retention with the use of a corporation would be $110,097 ($165,000 - $54,585 + $46,866 - $47,184). This is $923 less than the $111,020 that would be retained through the direct receipt of this income. You should advise your client not to form or use a corporation to hold these investments.

Note that, as the client needs all of the income produced by these investments, the use of a corporation to defer taxes is not an issue.

Exercise Seventeen - 4 Solution

The client's combined tax rate on direct receipt of income is 45 percent (29% + 16%). If she receives the capital gains directly, the Tax Payable will be $20,700 [($46,000)(45%)]. This will leave her with after tax cash of $71,300 ($92,000 - $20,700).

If the investments are transferred to a CCPC, the aggregate investment income will be $46,000. The applicable tax rate will be 51.8% [(38% - 10%)(1.04) + 6-2/3% + 16%]. Corporate Tax Payable will be $23,828 [(51.8%)($46,000)], leaving cash of $68,172 ($92,000 - $23,828). Of this total, $46,000 [(1/2)($92,000)] can be distributed as a tax free capital dividend. The remaining $22,172 ($68,172 - $46,000) must be distributed as a taxable dividend. This represents two-thirds of $33,258, a dividend that would generate a dividend refund of $11,086. As the balance in the RDTOH is $12,267 [(26-2/3%)($46,000)], a taxable dividend of $33,258 can be paid.

The client's tax rate on dividend income is 31.25 percent [(1.25)(45%) - (2/3 + 1/3)(25%)], resulting in Tax Payable on the dividend received of $10,393 [(31.25%)($33,258)]. The overall after tax retention when a corporation is used would be as follows:

Capital Dividend Received	$46,000
Taxable Dividend Received	33,258
Tax Payable On Dividend Received	(10,393)
After Tax Cash Retained	$68,865

As this is less than the $71,300 after tax cash retained on the direct receipt of the income, the use of a corporation to hold these investments is not an appropriate choice.

Note that, as the client needs all of the income produced by these investments, the use of a corporation to defer taxes is not an issue.

Exercise Seventeen - 5 Solution

If the full $333,000 is paid out as salary, it will be deductible and will reduce the Company's Taxable Income to nil. This means that no corporate taxes will be paid. This salary payment will result in Ms. Broad having Taxable Income of $333,000. Given this, her Tax Payable will be calculated as follows:

Federal Tax On First $115,739	$ 25,109
Federal Tax On Remaining $217,261 At 29%	63,006
Provincial Tax At 10 Percent Of $333,000	33,300
Tax Payable Before Credits	$121,415
Personal Tax Credits (Given)	(3,800)
Total Tax Payable	$117,615

Based on the preceding Tax Payable, Ms. Broad's after tax retention would be $215,385 ($333,000 - $117,615).

Exercise Seventeen - 6 Solution

As dividends are not deductible for tax purposes, corporate taxes will have to be paid prior to the payment of any dividends. While the $33,000 of income in excess of the annual business limit of $300,000 would not get the small business deduction, it would be eligible for the general rate reduction of 7 percent. Given this, the corporate rate on this income would be 39.12% [(38% - 10%)(1.04) - 7% + 17%]. On income eligible for the small business deduction, the rate would be 21.12% [(38% - 10%)(1.04) - 16% + 8%]. Using these rates, corporate taxes would be calculated as follows:

Income Not Eligible For SBD [(39.12%)($33,000)]	$12,910
Income Eligible For SBD [(21.12%)($300,000)]	63,360
Corporate Tax Payable	$76,270

After payment of these taxes, the maximum dividend that could be paid would be $256,730 ($333,000 - $76,270). Personal taxes on this dividend would be calculated as follows:

Dividends Received	$256,730
Gross Up At 25%	64,183
Taxable Dividends	$320,913

Federal Tax On First $115,739	$ 25,109
Federal Tax On Remaining $205,174 At 29%	59,500
Provincial Tax At 10 Percent Of $320,913	32,091
Taxes Payable Before Credits	$116,700
Personal Tax Credits (Given)	(3,800)
Dividend Tax Credit [(2/3 + 40%)($64,183)]	(68,462)
Personal Tax Payable	$ 44,438

The after tax retention would be equal to $212,292 ($256,730 - $44,438).

Exercise Seventeen - 7 Solution

As the available cash is less than Taxable Income, some corporate taxes will have to be paid since there is insufficient cash to pay a salary equivalent to Taxable Income. To determine the maximum salary that can be paid (X), it is necessary to solve the following equation:

$$X = \$18,500 - [(\$21,500 - X)(17.3\%)]$$

$$X = \underline{\$17,872}$$

Given this salary, Mr. Fargo would be subject to the following personal Tax Payable:

Tax Payable Before Credits [(16% + 10%)($17,872)]	$4,647
Available Tax Credits	(3,950)
Personal Tax Payable	$ 697

Given the preceding Tax Payable, Mr. Fargo's after tax retention on salary would be $17,175 ($17,872 - $697).

As dividends are not deductible, corporate taxes would have to be paid on the full $21,500. These taxes would be $3,720 [(17.3%)($21,500)], leaving an amount available for dividends of $14,780 ($18,500 - $3,720). As no individual taxes would be payable on this amount of dividends, the full $14,780 would be retained.

Given these calculations, it is clear that the preferred approach is to pay the maximum salary. Note, however, some combination of dividends and salary may provide an even better result.

Exercise Seventeen - 8 Solution

Ms. Mortell's combined tax rate on additional salary is 45 percent (29% + 16%). In order to have $30,000 in after tax funds, she would have to receive salary of $54,545 [$30,000 ÷ (1 - .45)]. If the corporation pays this amount in deductible salary, it will pay taxes at a rate of 16.5 percent on $143,455 ($198,000 - $54,545), an amount of $23,670 [(16.5%)($143,455)]. The combined cash outflow for salary and taxes would be $78,215 ($54,545 + $23,670).

Ms. Mortell's tax rate on dividends is 33-1/3 percent [(1.25)(45%) - (2/3 + 25%)(25%)]. In order to have $30,000 in after tax funds, she would have to receive dividends of $45,000 [$30,000 ÷ (1 - .3333)]. As none of this amount would be deductible, the corporation will pay taxes at 16.5 percent on the full $198,000 of Taxable Income, an amount of $32,670 [(16.5%)($198,000)]. The combined cash outflow would be $77,670 ($45,000 + $32,670).

As the cash outflows associated with the payment of salary are larger, the dividend alternative would be preferable.

Solution to Self Study Problem Seventeen - 1

Calculation Of Corporate Business Income The business income of the corporation would be calculated as follows:

Management Fees		$82,900
Expenses:		
Mr. Ashley's Salary	($18,400)	
Office Salaries	(25,400)	
Office Rent	(8,180)	
CCA On Office And Dental Equipment	(5,700)	
Other Business Expenses	(2,170)	(59,850)
Business Income		$23,050
Rate On Active Business Income		20%
Tax Payable On Active Business Income		$ 4,610

Tax Payable on the dividends and investment income would be calculated as follows:

Interest Income [(51%)($21,600)]	$11,016
Net Rental Income [(51%)($34,600 - $27,800)]	3,468
Part IV Tax On Dividends Received [(1/3)($13,900)]	4,633
Tax Payable On Property Income	$19,117

Given the preceding taxes on property income, the RDTOH balance is as follows:

Part I Refundable Amount [(26-2/3%)($21,600 + $6,800)]	$ 7,574
Part IV Refundable Amount [(1/3)($13,900)]	4,633
RDTOH Balance	$12,207

Given the preceding calculations, the maximum dividend that could be paid is as follows:

Business Income	$23,050
Interest Income	21,600
Net Rental Income	6,800
Dividends	13,900
Taxes On Business Income	(4,610)
Taxes On Property Income	(19,117)
Balance Before Refund	$41,623
Refundable Taxes (RDTOH Balance)	12,207
Available For Dividends	$53,830

On the basis of their relative shareholdings, this payment would go $32,298 to Mr. Ashley (60 percent) and $21,532 to Ms. Ashley (40 percent). This would result in the following Tax Payable:

Solution to Self Study Problem Seventeen - 1

	Ms. Ashley	Mr. Ashley
Salary	$ Nil	$18,400
Dividends	21,532	32,298
Gross Up	5,383	8,075
Taxable Income	$26,915	$58,773
Tax Rate	47%	30%
Tax Payable Before Dividend Tax Credit	$12,650	$17,632
Dividend Tax Credit [(2/3 + 25%)(Gross Up)]	(4,934)	(7,402)
Tax Payable	$ 7,716	$10,230

This would leave after tax balances available to Ms. and Mr. Ashley as follows:

Ms. Ashley ($21,532 - $7,716)	$13,816
Mr. Ashley ($18,400 + $32,298 - $10,230)	40,468
After Tax Retention	$54,284

Balances With No Corporation   If Ms. Ashley had received all of the amounts involved directly, her Tax Payable and net retention could be calculated as follows:

Business Income (No Salary To Husband)	$41,450
Interest Income	21,600
Rental Income (Net)	6,800
Dividends	13,900
Gross Up (25%)	3,475
Taxable Income	$87,225
Tax Rate	47%
Tax Before Dividend Credit	$40,996
Dividend Tax Credit [(2/3 + 25%)(Gross Up)]	(3,185)
Tax Payable	$37,811

Income Received ($41,450 + $21,600 + $6,800 + $13,900)	$83,750
Tax Payable	(37,811)
After Tax Retention	$45,939

It is clear from these calculations that the use of the management company has had a positive effect on after tax retention of income. Without the corporation, Ms. Ashley would have ended up with only $45,939. This compares to a total of $54,284 for Mr. and Ms. Ashley when the corporation is used, an improvement of over $8,000. Although personal tax credits were not taken into consideration, they would have made only a small difference, as Ms. Ashley would be able to claim the spousal credit in full if Mr. Ashley had no income.

Solution to Self Study Problem Seventeen - 2

Salary Alternative   In order to determine the amount of salary that would be required to produce $10,000 in after tax income, we need to know Ms. Lusk's effective tax rate on additional income. In this regard, her Taxable Income of $44,385 puts her in the 22 percent federal tax bracket. She will stay in this bracket for the next $26,805 ($71,190 - $44,385) of income. Any income in excess of $71,190 would be taxed at a 26 percent federal rate.

When the federal rates of 22 and 26 percent are combined with an additional 10 percent at the provincial level, Ms. Lusk's combined rates are 32 percent on the next $26,805 of income and 36 percent on any additional amounts. As $10,000 in after tax cash would only require $14,706 in additional salary [$10,000 ÷ (1 - .32)], the higher bracket does not have to be considered. With the additional salary of $14,706 being fully deductible to the corporation, the only tax cost associated with this alternative would be an additional $4,706 ($14,706 - $10,000) in personal taxes for Ms. Lusk.

Dividend Alternative   The dividend alternative involves a more complex analysis. The relevant tax rates on dividends would be as follows:

[(125%)(32%) - (2/3 + 1/3)(25%)] = 15%

[(125%)(36%) - (2/3 + 1/3)(25%)] = 20%

With a tax rate of 15 percent on dividends, a dividend of $11,765 would be required to provide an after tax amount of $10,000 [$10,000 ÷ (1 - .15)]. This would create a taxable dividend of $14,706, and a total Taxable Income of $59,091. As this is below the threshold for the next bracket, the 20 percent rate on dividends can be ignored.

As dividends are not deductible for the corporation, any pre-tax corporate income that is used for the payment of dividends will be subject to the Company's Part I tax rate of 21 percent. This means that, in order to pay $11,765 in dividends to Ms. Lusk, $14,892 [$11,765 ÷ (1 - .21)] of pre-tax corporate income will be required.

The total personal and corporate tax cost of the dividend alternative can be calculated as follows:

Personal Taxes On Dividends ($11,765 - $10,000)	$ 1,765
Corporate Taxes ($14,892 - $11,765)	3,127
Total Tax Cost	$4,892

Conclusion   Since the salary alternative would require tax payments of only $4,706, while the dividend alternative would require tax payments of $4,892, the salary alternative is better.

Solution to Self Study Problem Seventeen - 3

Part A   As salary payments can be deducted by the corporation, the entire $27,500 can be paid as salary. Given this deduction, no taxes would be paid by the Company. With a salary payment of $27,500, Mr. Bedford's after tax cash balance would be as follows:

Salary Payment		$27,500
Tax Before Credits [(16% + 9%)($27,500)]	($ 6,875)	
Personal Tax Credits	3,750	(3,125)
After Tax Cash Retained		**$24,375**

Part B   The tax rate for Bedford Inc. would be 19.12% {[(38% - 10%)(1.04)] - 16% + 6%}. As dividend payments are not deductible to the Company, taxes of $5,258 [(19.12%)($27,500)] will have to be paid, leaving a maximum of $22,242 to be used for the payment of dividends. When this is paid, the after tax retention by Mr. Bedford will be as follows:

Dividends Received	$22,242
Gross Up	5,561
Taxable Dividends	**$27,803**

Tax At 25 Percent [(16% + 9%)($27,803)]	$ 6,951
Personal Tax Credits	(3,750)
Dividend Tax Credit [(2/3 + 30%)($5,561)]	(5,376)
Tax Payable	**$ Nil**

Dividends Received	$22,242
Tax Payable	Nil
After Tax Cash Retained	**$22,242**

Part C   While Mr. Bedford's Tax Payable is nil, subtracting personal and dividend tax credits from the tax balance gives a negative $2,175. This means that the all dividend approach leaves unused tax credits. While not conclusive, this suggests that there may be a better solution than either all salary or all dividends.

Part D   To examine the possibility of an optimum solution using both salary and dividends, consider the result that occurs when $1,000 in salary is paid in lieu of some dividends. Because the deductible salary payment would reduce corporate taxes, dividends would only have to be decreased by $808.80 [($1,000)(1 - .1912)]. The tax effects of this switch can be calculated as follows:

Increase In Salary	$1,000.00
Decrease In Dividend	(808.80)
Decrease In Dividend Gross Up	(202.20)
Decrease In Mr. Bedford's Taxable Income	**($ 11.00)**

Decrease In Tax At 25% [(16% + 9%)($11.00)]	($ 2.75)
Decrease In Dividend Tax Credit [(2/3 + 30%)($202.20)]	195.46
Increase In Personal Tax Payable	**$ 192.71**

The rate on a $1,000 increase in salary is 19.271% ($192.71 ÷ $1,000). Applying this rate to the unused credits of $2,175 (see Part C), gives a required increase in salary of $11,286 ($2,175 ÷ .19271).

Based on this payment of salary, corporate taxes and funds available for dividend payments would be calculated as follows:

Pre-Salary Corporate Taxable Income	$27,500
Salary	(11,286)
Corporate Taxable Income	$16,214
Corporate Tax At 19.12 Percent	(3,100)
Available For Dividends	$13,114

After tax retention at the personal level would be calculated as follows:

Dividends Received	$13,114
Gross Up	3,279
Taxable Dividends	$16,393
Salary	11,286
Mr. Bedford's Taxable Income	$27,679
Tax At 25 Percent [(16% + 9%)($27,679)]	$ 6,920
Personal Tax Credits	(3,750)
Dividend Tax Credit [(2/3 + 30%)($3,279)]	(3,170)
Tax Payable	$ Nil
Amounts Received ($11,286 + $13,114)	$24,400
Personal Tax Payable	Nil
After Tax Cash Retained	$24,400

This combination of salary and dividends will produce the maximum after tax cash retention for Mr. Bedford. While it is a significant improvement over the all dividend after tax retention of $22,242, it is only a very marginal improvement over the all salary after tax retention of $24,375.

Part E   Other factors that might be considered include:

- Dividend payments are not Earned Income for purposes of making RRSP contributions.

- Salary payments incur the additional cost of CPP payments and, in some provinces, payroll taxes.

- If he has a CNIL balance, dividend payments will serve to reduce this constraint on the lifetime capital gains deduction.

- Mr. Bedford should consider declaring a bonus (a form of salary) to be paid after the end of the calender year. This would defer the personal taxes without affecting corporate taxes as long as the bonus was paid within 180 days of December 31.

Chapter Seventeen Learning Objectives

After completing Chapter 17, you should be able to:

1. Explain how a corporation can be used to reduce taxes, defer taxes, and facilitate income splitting (paragraphs 17-1 through 17-7).

2. Use various personal and corporate tax rates in the calculation of after-tax retention of earnings flowed through a corporation (paragraphs 17-8 through 17-16).

3. Calculate the amount of tax reduction and tax deferral that is available through the use of a public corporation (paragraphs 17-17 through 17-22).

4. Calculate the amount of tax reduction and tax deferral that is available through the use of a CCPC earning active business income (paragraphs 17-23 through 17-28).

5. Explain the advantages of bonusing down to the owner of a CCPC eligible for the small business deduction (paragraphs 17-29 through 17-33).

6. Calculate the amount of tax reduction and tax deferral that is available through the use of a CCPC earning investment income (paragraphs 17-34 through 17-36).

7. Calculate the amount of tax reduction and tax deferral that is available through the use of a CCPC earning dividend income (paragraphs 17-37 through 17-39).

8. Summarize the tax reduction and tax deferral that is available through the use of various types of corporations earning different types of income (paragraphs 17-40 through 17-42).

9. Identify imperfections in the integration system that allow for enhanced tax reduction or enhanced tax deferral (paragraphs 17-43 through 17-52).

10. Describe and calculate the benefits that can be achieved by using a corporation to implement income splitting (paragraphs 17-53 through 17-61).

11. Demonstrate a basic understanding of other advantages and disadvantages of incorporation (paragraphs 17-62 through 17-64).

12. Explain the principles of management compensation in the context of an owner-managed corporation (paragraphs 17-65 through 17-71).

13. Explain why large amounts of dividends can be received on a tax free basis by individuals with no other source of income (paragraphs 17-72 through 17-80).

14. Describe the basic trade-off between the payment of salary and the payment of dividends (paragraphs 17-81 through 17-85).

15. Calculate the appropriate choice between salary and dividends, taking into consideration all of the relevant factors (paragraphs 17-86 through 17-115).

16. Summarize the various factors that must be taken into consideration in making salary vs. dividend decisions (paragraphs 17-116 and 17-117).

CHAPTER EIGHTEEN

How To Work Through Chapter Eighteen

We recommend the following approach in dealing with the material in this Chapter:

Rollovers Under Section 85 - Introduction
☐ Read page 749 (paragraphs 18-1 through 18-3) of the text.

Rollovers Under Section 85 - General Rules For The Transfer
☐ Read pages 749 (from paragraph 18-4) through 752 (through paragraph 18-21) of the text.

Transfer Prices - Detailed Rules - Introduction
☐ Read page 753 (paragraphs 18-22 through 18-27) of the text.

Transfer Prices - Detailed Rules - Accounts Receivable
☐ Read pages 753 (from paragraph 18-28) and 754 (through paragraph 18-29) of the text.

Transfer Prices - Detailed Rules - Inventories And Non-Depreciable Property
☐ Read page 754 (paragraphs 18-30 through 18-38) of the text.
☐ Complete Exercise Eighteen-1. The Exercise is on page 755 of the text. The solution is on page S-244 of this Study Guide.

Transfer Prices - Detailed Rules - Disallowed Capital Losses
☐ Read pages 735 (from paragraph 18-39) through 757 (through paragraph 18-49) of the text.

Transfer Prices - Detailed Rules - Depreciable Property
☐ Read pages 757 (from paragraph 18-50) and 758 (through paragraph 18-56) of the text.
☐ Complete Exercise Eighteen-2. The Exercise is on page 758 of the text. The solution is on page S-244 of this Study Guide.

Detailed Rules - Terminal Losses Disallowed
☐ Read pages 758 (from paragraph 18-57) and 759 (through paragraph 18-60) of the text.

Detailed Rules - Cumulative Eligible Capital
☐ Read pages 759 (from paragraph 18-61) and 760 (through paragraph 18-65) of the text.
☐ Complete Exercise Eighteen-3. The Exercise is on page 760 of the text. The solution is on page S-244 of this Study Guide.

Detailed Rules - Disallowed Losses On CEC Dispositions
☐ Read pages 760 (from paragraph 18-66) and 761 (through paragraph 18-72) of the text.
☐ Complete Self Study Problem Eighteen-1. The Self Study Problem is on page 781 of the text. The solution is on pages S-247 and S-248 of this Study Guide.

Allocation Of The Elected Value
☐ Read page 761 (paragraphs 18-73 and 18-74) of the text.
☐ Complete Exercise Eighteen-4. The Exercise is on page 762 of the text. The solution is on page S-244 of this Study Guide.

Assets Acquired By The Corporation

☐ Read pages 762 (from paragraph 18-75) and 763 (through paragraph 18-83) of the text.

Paid Up Capital Of Issued Shares

☐ Read pages 763 (from paragraph 18-84) through 765 (through paragraph 18-93) of the text.

☐ Complete Exercise Eighteen-5. The Exercise is on page 765 of the text. The solution is on pages S-244 and S-245 of this Study Guide.

Section 85 Rollovers - Comprehensive Example

☐ Read pages 766 (from paragraph 18-94) through 768 (through paragraph 18-104) of the text.

☐ Complete Exercises Eighteen-6 and Eighteen-7. The Exercises are on page 768 of the text. The solutions are on page S-245 of this Study Guide.

☐ Complete Self Study Problems Eighteen-2 through Eighteen-5. The Self Study Problems are on pages 781 through 784 of the text. The solutions are on pages S-248 through S-252 of this Study Guide.

Gifts To Related Persons - Section 85

☐ Read pages 768 (from paragraph 18-105) and 769 (through paragraph 18-110) of the text.

☐ Complete Exercise Eighteen-8. The Exercise is on page 769 of the text. The solution is on page S-245 of this Study Guide.

Benefit To Transferor - Section 85

☐ Read page 770 (paragraphs 18-111 and 18-112) of the text.

☐ Complete Exercise Eighteen-9. The Exercise is on page 770 of the text. The solution is on pages S-245 and S-246 of this Study Guide.

GST And Section 85 Rollovers

☐ Read page 771 (paragraphs 18-113 through 18-115) of the text.

Dividend Stripping - ITA 84.1

☐ Read pages 771 (from paragraph 18-116) through 776 (through paragraph 18-144) of the text.

☐ Complete Exercise Eighteen-10. The Exercise is on page 776 of the text. The solution is on page S-246 of this Study Guide.

☐ Complete Self Study Problem Eighteen-6. The Self Study Problem is on pages 784 and 785 of the text. The solution is on pages S-252 and S-253 of this Study Guide.

Capital Gains Stripping - ITA 55(2)

☐ Read pages 776 (from paragraph 18-145) through 779 (through paragraph 18-161) of the text.

☐ Complete Exercise Eighteen-11. The Exercise is on page 779 of the text. The solution is on pages S-246 and S-247 of this Study Guide.

To Complete This Chapter

☐   Review the Key Terms Used In The Chapter on page 780 of the text. Consult the Glossary for the meaning of any key terms you do not know.

☐   Review the Learning Objectives of the Chapter found on pages S-254 and S-255 of this Study Guide.

☐   As a review, we recommend that you view the PowerPoint Slides for Chapter Eighteen that are available on the web site at:

www.pearsoned.ca/byrdchen/ctp2006/

If you do not have access to the Microsoft PowerPoint program, the PowerPoint Viewer program can be installed from the Companion CD-ROM.

Solution to Chapter Eighteen Exercises

Exercise Eighteen - 1 Solution

With respect to the inventories, the $125,000 is both the floor and the ceiling, making this the only possible elected value. The transfer would result in a loss of $15,000 ($140,000 - $125,000), an amount that would be fully deductible as a business loss [ITA(23)]. With respect to the land, the floor would be the boot of $150,000 and the ceiling would be the fair market value of $350,000. Electing the minimum amount would result in a taxable capital gain of $12,500 [($150,000 - $125,000)(1/2)].

Exercise Eighteen - 2 Solution

With respect to the Class 1 property, the range would be from a floor of $250,000 (the boot) to a ceiling of $475,000 (fair market value). Election of the $250,000 floor value would result in recapture of $70,000 ($220,000 - $150,000) and a taxable capital gain of $15,000 [($250,000 - $220,000)(1/2)].

The range for the Class 10 asset would be from a floor of $10,000 (the boot) to a ceiling of $12,000 (fair market value). Electing the minimum value of $10,000 would result in recapture of $2,000 ($10,000 - $8,000).

Exercise Eighteen - 3 Solution

The cumulative eligible capital balance at the time of transfer would be $94,163 [($135,000)(3/4)(93%)]. Four-thirds of this amount would be $125,551. However, the floor would be established by the boot of $135,000. The ceiling would be the fair market value of $175,000. With the election at $135,000, three-quarters of this amount would be subtracted from the CEC balance, leaving a negative balance of $7,087 ($94,163 - $101,250). This would result in an income inclusion of $7,087.

Exercise Eighteen - 4 Solution

The adjusted cost base amounts would be calculated as follows:

Elected Value	$62,000
ACB Of Note (Fair Market Value)	(51,000)
Available For Shares	$11,000
ACB Of Preferred Shares*	(11,000)
ACB Of Common Shares (Residual)	$ Nil

*Remainder available as it is less than the fair market value of $53,000.

Exercise Eighteen - 5 Solution

The total PUC reduction would be calculated as follows:

Increase In Legal Stated Capital ($97,000 + $54,000)		$151,000
Less The Excess Of:		
Total Elected Value	($114,000)	
Over The Total Non-Share Consideration	83,000	(31,000)
PUC Reduction		$120,000

This PUC reduction would be split between the preferred and common shares on the basis of their fair market values, resulting in the following PUC values:

- Preferred Shares = $97,000 - [(97,000/151,000)($120,000)] = $19,914

- Common Shares = $54,000 - [(54,000/151,000)($120,000)] = $11,086

Note that the sum of these two figures equals $31,000, the difference between the elected value of $114,000 and the total non-share consideration of $83,000.

Exercise Eighteen - 6 Solution

The required information is as follows:

- Minimum and maximum transfer value = $33,783 [(4/3)($25,337)] and $86,000.

- If the minimum value of $33,783 is elected, there would be no income resulting from the transfer.

- As the PUC of the shares issued ($93,000) exceeds the fair market value of the net assets acquired ($86,000), there would be an ITA 84(1) deemed dividend of $7,000. The taxable dividend of $8,750 [(125%)($7,000)] would be eligible for federal and provincial dividend tax credits.

- The adjusted cost base of the preferred shares will be $40,783, the elected value of $33,783, plus the $7,000 ITA 84(1) deemed dividend.

Exercise Eighteen - 7 Solution

The tax consequences to Mr. Savage and the corporation can be described as follows:

- Mr. Savage will have a taxable capital gain of $20,000 [(1/2)($160,000 - $120,000)].

- Mr. Savage will have recapture of CCA of $22,000 ($120,000 - $98,000).

- Mr. Savage will be holding shares with an adjusted cost base and a PUC of nil ($160,000 - $160,000).

- The corporation will have a depreciable asset with a capital cost of $160,000 and a value, for CCA and recapture purposes, of $140,000 [$120,000 + (1/2)($160,000 - $120,000)].

Exercise Eighteen - 8 Solution

As Ms. Bellows transferred property with a fair market value of $110,000 and received consideration with a fair market value of $65,000 ($50,000 + $15,000), she has made a gift to her daughter of $45,000 ($110,000 - $65,000). The tax consequences for Ms. Bellows and her daughter are as follows:

- The $45,000 gift will be added to the $50,000 elected value, giving Ms. Bellows a total proceeds of disposition of $95,000. This will result in a taxable capital gain of $22,500 [(1/2)($95,000 - $50,000)].

- The preferred shares issued to Ms. Bellows will have an adjusted cost base and a PUC of nil. A subsequent sale of these shares for fair market value will result in a taxable capital gain of $7,500 [(1/2)($15,000 - Nil)].

- The shares acquired by the daughter will have an adjusted cost base and a PUC of $1,000. However, because of the gift, they will have a fair market value of $46,000 ($1,000 + $45,000). This means that on a subsequent sale for fair market value, the daughter would have a capital gain of $45,000 (46,000 - $1,000), with a taxable amount of $22,500 [(1/2)($45,000)].

Exercise Eighteen - 9 Solution

The tax consequences to Mr. Custer can be described as follows:

- Mr. Custer's maximum election value will be the fair market value of $217,000. This election will result in a taxable capital gain of $47,000 [(1/2)($217,000 - $123,000)].

- There will be a PUC reduction of $53,000 [$75,000 - ($217,000 - $195,000)]. This will leave a PUC of $22,000 ($75,000 - $53,000).

- There is an ITA 84(1) deemed dividend of $22,000, the excess of the increase in PUC of the preferred shares ($22,000) over the related increase in net assets (Nil). The taxable dividend of $27,500 [(125%)($22,000)] would be eligible for federal and provincial dividend tax credits. The $22,000 ITA 84(1) deemed dividend will be added to the adjusted cost base of the preferred shares.

- There is an ITA 15(1) benefit of $31,000 [$270,000 - ($217,000 + $22,000)].

Exercise Eighteen - 10 Solution

Miss Cole (an individual) has sold shares of a subject corporation to a purchasing corporation, both corporations do not deal with Miss Cole at arm's length, and the two corporations are connected subsequent to the sale. As a consequence, ITA 84.1 is applicable. Given this, the tax consequences of this transaction to Miss Cole are as follows:

Increase In Legal Stated Capital		$317,000
PUC And ACB Of Subject Shares	($125,000)	
Less: Non-Share Consideration	450,000	Nil
PUC Reduction		$317,000
PUC Of New Shares ($317,000 - $317,000)		Nil
Increase In Legal Stated Capital		$317,000
Non-Share Consideration		450,000
		$767,000
PUC And ACB Of Subject Shares	($125,000)	
PUC Reduction	(317,000)	(442,000)
ITA 84.1 Deemed Dividend		$325,000
Proceeds Of Disposition For Subject Shares		$625,000
ITA 84.1 Deemed Dividend		(325,000)
Proceeds For Capital Gains Purposes		$300,000
ACB Of Subject Shares		(125,000)
Capital Gain		$175,000
Inclusion Rate		1/2
Taxable Capital Gain		$ 87,500
ACB Of New Shares ($625,000 - $450,000)		$175,000

The taxable dividend of $406,250 [(125%)($325,000)] would be eligible for federal and provincial dividend tax credits. In addition, there would be a taxable capital gain of $87,500.

Exercise Eighteen - 11 Solution

A deductible dividend has been paid in conjunction with an arm's length sale of shares, and it would appear that the dividend payment served to eliminate the potential capital gain on the transaction. As a consequence, ITA 55 is applicable and the tax consequences of the transaction are as follows:

Dividend Payment (Tax Free)	$750,000
Safe Income	(225,000)
Deemed Proceeds Of Disposition	$525,000
Actual Proceeds Of Disposition	90,000
Total Proceeds Of Disposition	$615,000
Adjusted Cost Base Of Shares	(75,000)
Capital Gain	$540,000
Inclusion Rate	1/2
Taxable Capital Gain	$270,000

Solution to Self Study Problem Eighteen - 1

Part A   The disposition of a business is a capital transaction and, in the absence of special provisions, any resulting gain or loss must be treated as a capital gain or loss. With respect to the Inventories, a special provision in ITA 23 indicates that, when such assets are sold as part of the disposition of a business, the sale is deemed to be in the ordinary course of carrying on business and any resulting gain or loss is considered business in nature. ITA 23 automatically applies in the disposition of a business and no election is required on the part of the vendor. ITA 22 provides for a similar treatment of Accounts Receivable. However, a joint election by the vendor and purchaser is required before this business income treatment is applicable. In the absence of this election, losses on Accounts Receivable are treated as capital losses.

If the assets are transferred at fair market values, the Taxable Income resulting from the transfer can be calculated as follows:

Inventories - Business Income ($88,000 - $73,000)	$15,000
Furniture And Fixtures - Recaptured CCA ($45,000 - $38,000)	7,000
Goodwill [(3/4)($150,000 - Nil)(1/2 ÷ 3/4)]	75,000
Taxable Income	$97,000

When the $112,500 [(3/4)($150,000)] proceeds for the goodwill is subtracted from the Cumulative Eligible Capital balance, a business income inclusion is created. As no amounts have been deducted under ITA 20(1)(b), this amount is reduced from a three-quarters inclusion to a one-half inclusion, by multiplying the negative balance by (1/2 ÷ 3/4).

There is also an allowable capital loss of $3,000 [(1/2)($51,000 - $45,000)] on the disposition of the Accounts Receivable. However, ITA 40(2)(g) would disallow this loss as the accounts are being transferred to a corporation that is controlled by the transferor. This loss would be added to the tax cost of the Accounts Receivable on the corporation's books.

Part B   The cash can, of course, be transferred to the corporation with no tax consequences. All of the other assets can be transferred at elected values under ITA 85. Under the provisions of this Section, the tax consequences would be as follows:

Accounts Receivable   If the Accounts Receivable are transferred under ITA 85, the maximum value that can be elected is the fair market value of $45,000. This will result in a capital loss of $6,000 (allowable amount of $3,000). However, this loss will be disallowed under ITA 40(2)(g) because the transfer is to a corporation that will be controlled by Ms. Flack.

Inventories   The Inventories can be transferred at an elected value of $73,000, resulting in no Taxable Income on the transfer.

Furniture And Fixtures   The Furniture And Fixtures can be transferred at their UCC of $38,000, resulting in no Taxable Income on the transfer.

Goodwill   The Goodwill can be transferred at a nominal value of $1, resulting in no significant Taxable Income on the transfer.

An alternative with respect to the Accounts Receivable would be to transfer these assets under the provisions of ITA 22. If Ms. Flack and her corporation were to make this joint election, the $6,000 loss resulting from transferring these assets to the corporation would be fully deductible as a business loss. As it is not a capital loss, it would not be disallowed and Ms. Flack would be able to deduct the full $6,000 against any other source of income in the year of transfer. Using the ITA 22 election is the preferable approach to the transfer of these Accounts Receivable.

Solution to Self Study Problem Eighteen - 2

Part A   All of the assets except cash would be eligible for the transfer. However, it is normal to transfer Accounts Receivable under ITA 22 rather than ITA 85, in order to protect the full deductibility of future bad debts. The Equipment has a terminal loss, which will be disallowed on the transfer. We have assumed that the Equipment will be included in the rollover, though there is no tax advantage for doing so.

Part B   The minimum transfer values for the assets to be included in the rollover would be as follows:

Inventories (Cost)	$261,000
Land (Adjusted Cost Base)	196,000
Building (UCC)	103,600
Equipment (Fair Market Value)	32,500
Goodwill (Nominal Value)	1

Note   The Goodwill has been given a nominal elected value to ensure that it is specifically included in the transfer. A failure to do this could result in the Goodwill being assessed on the basis of a transfer at fair market value.

Part C   The tax consequences of the Section 85 transfers with respect to both Ms. Speaks and Speaks Inc. can be described as follows:

Inventories   The cost of the Inventories to Speaks Inc. would be the transfer price of $261,000. As this was the cost of the Inventories, there would be no tax consequence to Ms. Speaks.

Land   The cost of the Land to Speaks Inc. would be the transfer price of $196,000. As this was the adjusted cost base of the Land, there would be no tax consequence to Ms. Speaks.

Building   The capital cost of the Building to Speaks Inc. would be $155,500, and Speaks Inc. would be deemed to have taken CCA in the amount of $51,900. As the net value of the transfer is equal to UCC, there would be no tax consequence to Ms. Speaks.

Equipment   The capital cost of the Equipment to Speaks Inc. will be its fair market value of $32,500. Ms. Speaks will have a terminal loss of $34,500 ($67,000 - $32,500) that she will not be able to deduct. The $34,500 loss will be placed in the same CCA class as the Equipment was, and Ms. Speaks will continue to take CCA on this class until the Equipment is disposed of by Speaks Inc. or there is no balance left in the class.

Goodwill   The cost of the Goodwill to Speaks Inc. will be $1, and three-quarters of this amount will be added to the Company's Cumulative Eligible Capital balance. There would be no material tax consequence to Ms. Speaks resulting from this transfer.

Solution to Self Study Problem Eighteen - 3

Part A As the $1,241,100 elected price was equal to the sum of the capital cost of the Land and the UCC of the Building ($315,000 + $926,100), there would be no tax consequences associated with the transfer of these assets. However, the corporation will be deemed to have acquired these assets at their old tax values to Mr. Dix, not at their fair market values at the time of transfer.

Under ITA 85(1)(f), the adjusted cost base of the non-share consideration is equal to its fair market value of $1,241,100. The problem does not specify whether preferred shares, common shares, or a combination of both were issued. Under ITA 85(1)(g), the adjusted cost base of any preferred shares received is the lesser of their fair market value and the total elected value, reduced by the non-share consideration. As the $1,241,100 elected value is equal to the non-share consideration provided by the corporation, the adjusted cost base of any preferred shares would be nil. Under ITA 85(1)(h), the adjusted cost base of any common shares issued would be the elected value, reduced by any non-share consideration and any amounts allocated to preferred stock. This value would also be nil.

Part B As the debt was paid off at face value, this amount would be equal to Mr. Dix's adjusted cost base, and he would have no gain or loss. However, the shares have an adjusted cost base of nil and, as a consequence, he would have a capital gain equal to the entire proceeds of disposition of $894,000. This would result in a taxable capital gain of $447,000 [(1/2)($894,000)].

It is likely that the corporation is a "qualified small business corporation". If this is the case, Mr. Dix would be eligible for the $500,000 ($250,000 taxable amount) lifetime capital gains deduction. To qualify, the corporation must be a Canadian controlled private corporation with at least 90 percent of the fair market value of its assets being used in an active business operating primarily in Canada. The 24 month holding period requirement would be met as no other taxpayer has owned the business in the preceding 24 months.

Even if Mr. Dix is eligible for the full lifetime capital gains deduction, he would still have to pay taxes on a $197,000 ($447,000 - $250,000) taxable capital gain. Whether or not he can use the lifetime capital gains deduction, he may need to pay alternative minimum tax.

Solution to Self Study Problem Eighteen - 4

Part A The adjusted cost base (ACB) of the shares would be as follows:

Total Elected Value	$467,000
Non-Share Consideration ($122,000 + $128,000)	(250,000)
Adjusted Cost Base Preferred And Common Shares	$217,000
Allocated To Preferred Shares (FMV)	(150,000)
Adjusted Cost Base Of Common Shares (Residual)	$ 67,000

Part B The legal stated capital of the preferred and common shares would be their respective fair market values of $150,000 and $326,000. The PUC reduction required under ITA 85(2.1) would be calculated as follows:

Increase In Legal Stated Capital ($150,000 + $326,000)		$476,000
Less Excess Of:		
Total Elected Value	($467,000)	
Over The Total Non-Share Consideration	250,000	(217,000)
Reduction In Paid Up Capital		$259,000

Note that this total reduction is equal to the deferred gain on the election ($726,000 - $467,000). This total will be allocated to the two classes of shares on the basis of their relative fair market values. The relevant calculations are as follows:

Preferred Shares = [($150,000 ÷ $476,000)($259,000)] = $81,618

Common Shares = [($326,000 ÷ $476,000)($259,000)] = $177,382

The PUC of the two classes of shares after the ITA 85(2.1) reduction is as follows:

	Preferred Shares	Common Shares
Legal Stated Capital	$150,000	$326,000
PUC Reduction	(81,618)	(177,382)
PUC	$ 68,382	$148,618

Part C The tax consequences to Mr. Lardner, if the corporation redeemed both classes of shares at their respective fair market values, would be calculated as follows:

	Preferred Shares	Common Shares
Redemption Proceeds	$150,000	$326,000
PUC (See Preceding Calculations)	(68,382)	(148,618)
ITA 84(3) Deemed Dividend	$ 81,618	$177,382
Redemption Proceeds	$150,000	$326,000
ITA 84(3) Deemed Dividend	(81,618)	(177,382)
Deemed Proceeds Of Disposition	$ 68,382	$148,618
Adjusted Cost Base	(150,000)	(67,000)
Capital Gain (Loss)	($ 81,618)	$ 81,618

Mr. Lardner would have a deemed dividend of $259,000 ($81,618 + $177,382) that would be subject to the usual gross up and tax credit procedures. He has a net capital gain of nil ($81,618 - $81,618).

Solution to Self Study Problem Eighteen - 5

Part A Accounts Receivable could be transferred under Section 85, but are usually transferred to the corporation under the provisions of ITA 22. ITA 22 is used for two reasons. First, it means that any loss on the transfer will be a fully deductible business loss, rather than a capital loss that will be disallowed on a transfer to a corporation controlled by the transferor under ITA 40(2)(g). In addition, the use of the ITA 22 joint election to make the transfer will permit the transferee corporation to deduct any additional bad debts as business losses, rather than capital losses. As a result, the Accounts Receivable should be transferred at $75,000 using the ITA 22 joint election. This will result in a fully deductible business loss of $3,000 for Miss Brock. Although the corporation will have to add the $3,000 to income, any difference between the $78,000 face value and amounts actually collected will be fully deductible.

The values that should be elected under ITA 85 on the other assets in order to eliminate any current Tax Payable on the transfer, are as follows:

Inventory	$174,000
Equipment	234,000
Goodwill	1
Total Elected Value	$408,001

Part B   The total elected value would become the adjusted cost base of the consideration received by Miss Brock. It would be allocated to the individual items as follows:

Total Elected Value	$408,001
Non-Share Consideration ($95,000 + $75,000)	(170,000)
Available For Preferred And Common Stock	$238,001
Adjusted Cost Base - Preferred Stock (Maximum Of Fair Market Value)	(225,000)
Adjusted Cost Base - Common Stock (Residual)	$ 13,001

Part C   The calculation of PUC would begin with the legal stated capital associated with the two classes of shares, which is their fair market value. This would be $225,000 for the preferred stock and $480,000 for the common stock, a total of $705,000. ITA 85(2.1) would require a reduction in this total as follows:

Increase In Legal Stated Capital		$705,000
Less Excess Of:		
Total Elected Value	($408,001)	
Over The Total Non-Share Consideration	170,000	(238,001)
Reduction In PUC		$466,999

This reduction in PUC would be allocated to the two classes of shares on the basis of their fair market values. The calculations would be as follows:

Preferred Stock = [($225,000 ÷ $705,000)($466,999)] = $149,042

Common Stock = [($480,000 ÷ $705,000)($466,999)] = $317,957

Using this allocation, the Paid Up Capital of the two classes of shares would be as follows:

Preferred Stock = $225,000 - $149,042 = $75,958

Common Stock = $480,000 - $317,957 = $162,043

Note that the total PUC of $238,001 ($75,958 + $162,043) is equal to the difference between the total elected value for the assets of $408,001 and the non-share consideration received by Miss Brock of $170,000.

Part D   The tax consequences for Miss Brock on the redemption of the preferred and common shares would be calculated as follows:

	Preferred Stock	Common Stock
Redemption Proceeds	$225,000	$480,000
Paid Up Capital	(75,958)	(162,043)
ITA 84(3) Deemed Dividend	$149,042	$317,957

	Preferred Stock	Common Stock
Redemption Proceeds	$225,000	$480,000
ITA 84(3) Deemed Dividend	(149,042)	(317,957)
ITA 54 - Deemed Proceeds Of Disposition	$ 75,958	$162,043
Adjusted Cost Base	(225,000)	(13,001)
Capital Gain (Loss)	($149,042)	$149,042

Miss Brock would have a deemed dividend of $466,999 ($149,042 + $317,957), which would be subject to the usual gross up and tax credit procedures. This is also the amount of the gain that was deferred through the use of Section 85 ($208,000 + $317,000 + $350,000 - $408,001). There would be a net capital gain of nil ($149,042 - $149,042).

Solution to Self Study Problem Eighteen - 6

Part A In the absence of ITA 84.1, the Section 85 rollover would have resulted in a capital gain of $500,000. This is based on the elected value of $575,000, less the adjusted cost base of $75,000 [(75%)($100,000)]. However:

- There has been a sale by a Canadian resident (Ms. Chisholm) of shares in a subject corporation (DML).

- The purchaser of the subject corporation (Dorlaine Inc.) does not deal at arm's length with the Canadian resident (Ms. Chisholm).

- Immediately after the disposition, the subject corporation (DML) and the purchaser corporation (Dorlaine Inc.) are connected (Dorlaine Inc. controls DML).

As a consequence, the provisions of ITA 84.1 are applicable. This means that there will be a reduction of Paid Up Capital under ITA 84.1(1)(a) as follows:

Increase In Legal Stated Capital Of Dorlaine Inc.		$400,000
Less Excess, If Any, Of:		
Greater Of PUC And ACB Of DML Shares	($ 75,000)	
Over The Non-Share Consideration	500,000	Nil
PUC Reduction		$400,000

The PUC of the Dorlaine Inc. shares would be nil ($400,000 - $400,000).

The transfer would result in an ITA 84.1(1)(b) deemed dividend that would be calculated as follows:

Increase In Legal Stated Capital Of Dorlaine Inc.		$400,000
Non-Share Consideration		500,000
Total		$900,000
PUC Of DML Shares	($ 75,000)	
PUC Reduction Under ITA 84.1(1)(a)	(400,000)	(475,000)
ITA 84.1(1)(b) Deemed Dividend		$425,000

The capital gain on the disposition of the DML shares would be calculated as follows:

Proceeds Before Adjustment Of DML Shares (Elected Value)	$575,000
Deemed ITA 84.1(1)(b) Dividend	(425,000)
Adjusted Proceeds Of Disposition (ITA 54)	$150,000
ACB Of DML Shares	(75,000)
Capital Gain	$ 75,000
Inclusion Rate	1/2
Taxable Capital Gain	$ 37,500

The tax consequences of transferring the DML shares are:

- a deemed dividend of $425,000, which would be subject to the usual gross up and tax credit procedures; and

- a taxable capital gain of $37,500, which would be eligible for the lifetime capital gains deduction as long as DML is a qualified small business corporation.

Note that, if Ms. Chisholm had elected the same $575,000 value, but limited her non-share consideration to $75,000 (the PUC and ACB of the DML shares), there would have been no deemed dividend. Under this approach, she would have realized a $500,000 capital gain, which would potentially be eligible for the lifetime capital gains deduction, and still retained control of her Company.

Part B At Ms. Chisholm's death, there would be a deemed disposition of all of her capital property at its fair market value, $400,000 in the case of the Dorlaine Inc. shares. The adjusted cost base of these shares would be $75,000, calculated as follows:

Value Elected In Section 85 Rollover	$575,000
Fair Market Value Of Non-Share Consideration	(500,000)
Adjusted Cost Base Of Dorlaine Inc. Shares	$ 75,000

Given this, the taxable capital gain on the deemed disposition would be calculated as follows:

Deemed Proceeds Of Disposition (Fair Market Value)	$400,000
Adjusted Cost Base	(75,000)
Capital Gain	$325,000
Inclusion Rate	1/2
Taxable Capital Gain	$162,500

Since Dorlaine Inc. is holding various investments, it would not be a qualified small business corporation. As a result, none of the taxable capital gain would be eligible for the lifetime capital gains deduction.

Chapter Eighteen Learning Objectives

After completing Chapter 18, you should be able to:

1. Describe the type of situation where ITA 85(1) is applicable (paragraphs 18-1 through 18-3).

2. Explain the general rules that are applicable to the transferor and the transferee under ITA 85(1) (paragraphs 18-4 through 18-9).

3. Describe the types of consideration that can be received by the transferor under ITA 85(1) (paragraph 18-10).

4. Describe the procedures required for making the ITA 85(1) election (paragraphs 18-11 and 18-12).

5. Calculate the range of values that can be used in a transfer under the provisions of ITA 85(1) (paragraphs 18-13 through 18-21).

6. Apply the detailed rules for the transfer of accounts receivable, inventories, and non-depreciable capital property under ITA 85(1) (paragraphs 18-22 through 18-38).

7. Describe the rules for the treatment of capital losses arising on transfers of non-depreciable capital property to affiliated persons and associated tax planning issues (paragraphs 18-39 through 18-49).

8. Apply the detailed rules for the transfer of depreciable assets under ITA 85(1) (paragraphs 18-50 through 18-56).

9. Describe the rules for the treatment of terminal losses arising on transfers of depreciable capital property to affiliated persons and associated tax planning issues (paragraphs 18-57 through 18-60).

10. Apply the detailed rules for the transfer of cumulative eligible capital under ITA 85(1) (paragraphs 18-61 through 18-65).

11. Describe the rules for the treatment of losses arising on transfers of eligible capital property to an affiliated person and associated tax planning issues (paragraphs 18-66 through 18-72).

12. Calculate the amount of the elected value that will be allocated to each component of the consideration received by the transferor under ITA 85(1) (paragraphs 18-73 and 18-74).

13. Calculate the amount of the elected value that will be allocated to each of the assets acquired by the transferee under ITA 85(1) (paragraphs 18-75 through 18-83).

14. Calculate the Paid Up Capital of the shares received by the transferor in an ITA 85(1) Rollover (paragraphs 18-84 through 18-93).

15. Apply the ITA 85(1) rules to comprehensive examples involving the incorporation of an unincorporated business (paragraphs 18-94 through 18-104).

16. Identify situations where the ITA 85(1) rules on gifts to related persons are applicable and make the appropriate adjustments that are required by these rules (paragraphs 18-105 through 18-110).

17. Apply the ITA 85(1) rules to appropriately identified situations where there has been a benefit to the transferor (paragraphs 18-111 and 18-112).

18. Explain the GST rules related to transfers under ITA 85(1) (paragraphs 18-113 through 18-115).

19. Identify situations where ITA 84.1 (dividend stripping rules) is applicable (paragraphs 18-116 through 18-123).

20. Apply the ITA 84.1 rules to situations involving shares issued after December 31, 1971 (paragraphs 18-124 through 18-132).

21. Apply the ITA 84.1 rules to situations involving shares issued before January 1, 1972 (paragraphs 18-133 through 18-144).

22. Identify situations where ITA 55(2) (capital gains stripping rules) is applicable (paragraphs 18-145 through 18-151).

23. Apply the ITA 55(2) rules to situations involving capital gains stripping (paragraphs 18-152 through 18-161).

CHAPTER NINETEEN

How To Work Through Chapter Nineteen

We recommend the following approach in dealing with the material in this Chapter:

Introduction
☐ Read page 793 (paragraphs 19-1 through 19-3) of the text.

Share For Share Exchanges (ITA 85.1)
☐ Read pages 793 (from paragraph 19-4) and 794 (through paragraph 19-9) of the text.

☐ Complete Exercise Nineteen-1. The Exercise is on page 794 of the text. The solution is on page S-259 of this Study Guide.

Exchange Of Shares In A Reorganization (ITA 86)
☐ Read pages 795 (from paragraph 19-10) through 798 (through paragraph 19-24) of the text.

☐ Complete Exercises Nineteen-2 through Nineteen-4. The Exercises are on pages 798 and 799 of the text. The solutions are on pages S-259 and S-260 of this Study Guide.

☐ Complete Self Study Problem Nineteen-1. The Self Study Problem is on page 832 of the text. The solution is on pages S-262 and S-263 of this Study Guide.

ITA 86(2) Benefit Rule
☐ Read pages 799 (from paragraph 19-25) through 801 (through paragraph 19-32) of the text.

☐ Complete Exercise Nineteen-5. The Exercise is on page 801 of the text. The solution is on pages S-260 and S-261 of this Study Guide.

☐ Complete Self Study Problem Nineteen-2. The Self Study Problem is on page 832 of the text. The solution is on pages S-263 through S-265 of this Study Guide.

Using ITA 86 - Practical Considerations
☐ Read page 801 (paragraph 19-33) of the text.

Using ITA 86 - Advantages And Disadvantages
☐ Read page 801 (from paragraph 19-34) and 802 (through paragraph 19-36) of the text.

Amalgamations
☐ Read pages 802 (from paragraph 19-37) through 805 (through paragraph 19-52) of the text.

☐ Complete Exercise Nineteen-6. The Exercise is on page 805 of the text. The solution is on page S-261 of this Study Guide.

Winding-Up Of A 90 Percent Owned Subsidiary
☐ Read pages 805 (from paragraph 19-53) through 807 (through paragraph 19-64) of the text.

☐ Complete Exercise Nineteen-7. The Exercise is on page 807 of the text. The solution is on page S-261 of this Study Guide.

☐ Read pages 807 (from paragraph 19-65) and 808 (through paragraph 19-68) of the text.

☐   Complete Exercise Nineteen-8. The Exercise is on page 808 of the text. The solution is on page S-261 of this Study Guide.

☐   Read pages 808 (from paragraph 19-69) and 809 (through paragraph 19-70) of the text.

☐   Complete Self Study Problem Nineteen-3. The Self Study Problem is on page 833 of the text. The solution is on page S-266 of this Study Guide.

Tax Planning - Amalgamation Vs. Winding-Up
☐   Read pages 809 (from paragraph 19-71) and 810 (through paragraph 19-75) of the text.

Winding-Up Of A Canadian Corporation
☐   Read pages 810 (from paragraph 19-76) through 812 (through paragraph 19-89) of the text.

☐   Complete Exercise Nineteen-9. The Exercise is on page 812 of the text. The solution is on page S-262 of this Study Guide.

☐   Complete Self Study Problem Nineteen-4. The Self Study Problem is on pages 833 and 834 of the text. The solution is on pages S-266 and S-267 of this Study Guide.

Convertible Properties
☐   Read page 813 (paragraphs 19-90 through 19-95) of the text.

The Valuation Of A Business
☐   Read pages 813 (from paragraph 19-96) through 816 (through paragraph 19-112) of the text.

Sale Of An Incorporated Business
☐   Read pages 816 (from paragraph 19-113) through 824 (through paragraph 19-149) of the text.

☐   Complete Self Study Problem Nineteen-5. The Self Study Problem is on pages 834 and 835 of the text. The solution is on pages S-268 and S-269 of this Study Guide.

GST Implications
☐   Read pages 824 (from paragraph 19-150) and 825 (through paragraph 19-159) of the text.

Tax Shelters
☐   Read pages 826 (from paragraph 19-160) through 830 (through paragraph 19-184) of the text.

To Complete This Chapter
☐   Review the Key Terms Used In The Chapter on page 830 of the text. Consult the Glossary for the meaning of any key terms you do not know.

☐   Review the Learning Objectives of the Chapter found on pages S-270 and S-271 of this Study Guide.

☐   As a review, we recommend that you view the PowerPoint Slides for Chapter Nineteen that are available on the web site at:

www.pearsoned.ca/byrdchen/ctp2006/

If you do not have access to the Microsoft PowerPoint program, the PowerPoint Viewer program can be installed from the Companion CD-ROM.

Solution to Chapter Nineteen Exercises

Exercise Nineteen - 1 Solution

It would appear that, in this example, there is a share for share exchange that meets the conditions of ITA 85.1. Unless Ms. Alee elects out of this rollover provision in her income tax return, the tax consequences of this transaction for Ms. Alee would be as follows:

- Ms. Alee would be deemed to have disposed of her Aayee Ltd. shares at a value equal to their adjusted cost base of $450,000. As a consequence, there would be no capital gain on the disposition.
- Ms. Alee would be deemed to have acquired her Global Outreach Inc. shares at a cost equal to the adjusted cost base of the Aayee Ltd. shares, or $450,000.

With respect to Global Outreach Inc., they would be deemed to have acquired the Aayee Ltd. shares at the lesser of their fair market value and their paid up capital. In this case, the $450,000 paid up capital amount is the lower figure.

Exercise Nineteen - 2 Solution

The required PUC reduction on the redeemable preferred shares would be calculated as follows:

Increase In Legal Stated Capital		$1,300,000
Less The Excess, If Any, Of:		
PUC Of Common Shares	($1,000,000)	
Over The Non-Share Consideration	1,000,000	Nil
PUC Reduction		$1,300,000

This means that the redeemable preferred shares would have a PUC of nil ($1,300,000 - $1,300,000).

The adjusted cost base of the redeemable preferred shares would be calculated as follows:

Adjusted Cost Base Of Common Shares	$1,000,000
Non-Share Consideration	(1,000,000)
Adjusted Cost Base Of Redeemable Preferred Shares	Nil

The proceeds of redemption of the common shares would be $1,000,000 ($1,000,000 + Nil new PUC), resulting in an ITA 84(3) deemed dividend of nil ($1,000,000 - $1,000,000 old PUC). The proceeds of disposition would also be $1,000,000 ($1,000,000 cash + Nil new ACB), resulting in a capital gain of nil ($1,000,000 - $1,000,000).

Exercise Nineteen - 3 Solution

The required PUC reduction on the redeemable preferred shares would be calculated as follows:

Increase In Legal Stated Capital		$1,300,000
Less The Excess, If Any, Of:		
PUC Of Common Shares	($1,000,000)	
Over The Non-Share Consideration	1,000,000	Nil
PUC Reduction		$1,300,000

This means that the redeemable preferred shares would have a PUC of nil ($1,300,000 - $1,300,000).

The adjusted cost base of the redeemable preferred shares would be calculated as follows:

Adjusted Cost Base Of Common Shares	$1,250,000
Non-Share Consideration	(1,000,000)
Adjusted Cost Base Of Redeemable Preferred Shares	$ 250,000

The proceeds of redemption of the common shares would be $1,000,000 ($1,000,000 + Nil new PUC), resulting in an ITA 84(3) deemed dividend of nil ($1,000,000 - $1,000,000 old PUC). The proceeds of disposition would be $1,250,000 ($1,000,000 cash + $250,000 new ACB), resulting in a capital gain of nil ($1,250,000 - $1,250,000).

Exercise Nineteen - 4 Solution

The required PUC reduction on the redeemable preferred shares would be calculated as follows:

Increase In Legal Stated Capital		$1,100,000
Less The Excess, If Any, Of:		
PUC Of Common Shares	($1,000,000)	
Over The Non-Share Consideration	1,200,000	Nil
PUC Reduction		$1,100,000

This means that the redeemable preferred shares would have a PUC of nil ($1,100,000 - $1,100,000).

The adjusted cost base of the redeemable preferred shares would be calculated as follows:

Adjusted Cost Base Of Common Shares	$1,250,000
Non-Share Consideration	(1,200,000)
Adjusted Cost Base Of Redeemable Preferred Shares	$ 50,000

The proceeds of redemption of the common shares would be $1,200,000 ($1,200,000 + Nil new PUC), resulting in an ITA 84(3) deemed dividend of $200,000 ($1,200,000 - $1,000,000 old PUC). The proceeds of disposition would be $1,050,000 ($50,000 new ACB + $1,200,000 cash - $200,000 deemed dividend), resulting in a capital loss of $200,000 ($1,050,000 - $1,250,000). The taxable dividend would be $250,000 [(125%)($200,000)] and the allowable capital loss would be $100,000 [(1/2)($200,000)].

Exercise Nineteen - 5 Solution

Ms. Reviser gave up shares with a fair market value of $1,280,000 [(80%)($1,600,000)], in return for consideration of $1,100,000 ($300,000 + $800,000). As her daughter holds common shares, it would appear that there is a gift to the daughter of $180,000. This means that ITA 86(2) is applicable.

The PUC reduction on the new shares would be calculated as follows:

Increase In Legal Stated Capital		$800,000
Less The Excess, If Any, Of:		
PUC Of Common Shares [(80%)($250,000)]	($200,000)	
Over The Non-Share Consideration	300,000	Nil
PUC Reduction		$800,000

This means that the redeemable preferred shares would have a PUC of nil ($800,000 - $800,000).

Under ITA 86(2)(e), the adjusted cost base of the redeemable preferred shares would be calculated as follows:

Adjusted Cost Base Of Common Shares [(80%)($250,000)]		$200,000
Deduct:		
Non-Share Consideration	($300,000)	
Gift	(180,000)	(480,000)
Adjusted Cost Base Of Preferred Shares		Nil

The proceeds of redemption of the common shares would be $300,000 ($300,000 + Nil new PUC), resulting in an ITA 84(3) deemed dividend of $100,000 ($300,000 - $200,000 old PUC). Under ITA 86(2)(c), the proceeds of disposition would be $380,000 [$300,000 plus $180,000, less the $100,000 deemed dividend under ITA 84(3)]. Given this, the capital gain would be $180,000 ($380,000 - $200,000). The taxable dividend would be $125,000 [(125%)($100,000)] and the taxable capital gain would be $90,000 [(1/2)($180,000)].

Exercise Nineteen - 6 Solution

As Upton Inc. has a clear majority of the shares in Amalgo Inc., it would appear that they have acquired control of Downer Ltd. As the acquisition of control rules would be applicable, there would be a deemed year end for both Companies that coincides with the amalgamated year end. The non-capital loss carry forward of Downer Ltd. will be flowed through to the amalgamated company, Amalgo Inc. However, because of the acquisition of control, the net capital loss carry over cannot be used. In addition, for the non-capital loss to be used, Amalgo Inc. would have to continue the business in which the loss occurred. Further, the loss carry forward could only be applied against profits in that business.

Exercise Nineteen - 7 Solution

Subsequent to the beginning of an ITA 88(1) winding-up, the parent company can deduct subsidiary losses in its first taxation year beginning after that date. This would be the year beginning on September 16, 2005.

Side's loss is deemed to occur in Park's taxation year that includes Side's year end. This would be the year ending September 15, 2001. This means that it will expire, after seven taxation years, at the end of Park's taxation year ending September 15, 2007 (the winding-up creates a deemed year end which counts as an additional year).

Exercise Nineteen - 8 Solution

Under ITA 88(1), a limited bump-up of non-depreciable assets is available. The basic limit would be calculated as follows:

Adjusted Cost Base Of Lorne Inc. Shares	$1,200,000
Tax Values Of Lorne Inc.'s Net Assets	
At Winding-Up ($500,000 - $75,000)	(425,000)
Dividends Paid By Lorne Since Acquisition	Nil
Excess	$ 775,000

However, this basic amount cannot exceed the difference between the fair market value of the non-depreciable assets at the time of the share acquisition and their tax cost at that time. This amount would be $130,000 ($270,000 - $140,000). The bump-up in the Land value is limited to that amount, resulting in the following tax values for Lorne's assets at the time of the ITA 88(1) winding-up:

Cash	$120,000
Land ($140,000 + $130,000)	270,000
Depreciable Assets - At UCC	240,000
Total Assets	$630,000

Exercise Nineteen - 9 Solution

Given the size of the proceeds, the balance in the RDTOH account will clearly be less than one-third of the dividends to be declared. Given this, the total distribution to shareholders will be $912,000 ($865,000 + $47,000).

The taxable dividend component of the total distribution to the shareholders is calculated as follows:

Total Distribution	$912,000
Paid Up Capital	(88,000)
ITA 84(2) Dividend On Winding-Up	$824,000
Capital Dividend Account (Election Required)	(26,000)
Dividend Subject To Tax	$798,000

The remaining dividend subject to tax will be subject to the usual gross up and tax credit procedures. As a disposition of shares has occurred, we must also determine whether there is a capital gain or loss. The calculations are as follows:

Total Distribution To Shareholders	$912,000
ITA 84(2) Deemed Dividend	(824,000)
Deemed Proceeds	$ 88,000
Adjusted Cost Base Of Shares	(88,000)
Capital Gain	Nil

Solution to Self Study Problem Nineteen - 1

Part A The PUC of the new shares would be reduced under ITA 86(2.1) as follows:

Increase In Legal Stated Capital Of New Shares		$99,000
PUC - Old Shares	($99,000)	
Non-Share Consideration	69,000	(30,000)
Reduction In PUC		$69,000

Given this reduction, the resulting PUC of the new preferred shares would be as follows:

Increase In Legal Stated Capital Of New Shares	$99,000
Reduction In PUC	(69,000)
PUC - New Shares	$30,000

Part B The adjusted cost base of the new preferred shares would be calculated as follows:

Adjusted Cost Base - Old Shares	$99,000
Non-Share Consideration	(69,000)
Adjusted Cost Base - New Shares	$30,000

Part C The proceeds of disposition for the old common shares would be calculated as follows:

Adjusted Cost Base And PUC - New Shares	$30,000
Non-Share Consideration	69,000
Proceeds Of Disposition - Old Shares	$99,000

As the PUC of the old shares is equal to their ACB, this would be the proceeds of disposition under both ITA 86(1)(b) and ITA 84(5)(d).

Part D   As the proceeds of disposition is equal to both the adjusted cost base and PUC of the old shares, there would be no ITA 84(3) deemed dividend and no capital gain for Mr. Farnsworth at the time of the reorganization transaction.

Part E   If the preferred shares were redeemed for $381,000, the tax consequences would be as follows:

Redemption Proceeds	$381,000
Paid Up Capital - Preferred Shares	(30,000)
ITA 84(3) Deemed Dividend	$351,000

Proceeds Of Disposition	$381,000
ITA 84(3) Deemed Dividend	(351,000)
Adjusted Proceeds Of Disposition	$ 30,000
Adjusted Cost Base - Preferred Shares	(30,000)
Capital Gain	Nil

There would be a taxable dividend of $438,750 [(125%)($351,000)], which would be eligible for a federal dividend tax credit of $58,500 [(2/3)(25%)($351,000)].

Solution to Self Study Problem Nineteen - 2

Approach One

Gift   The fair market value of the common shares given up is $810,000 [(90%)($900,000)] and this is equal to the fair market value of the consideration received ($90,000 + $720,000). Given this, no gift is involved in the rollover and ITA 86(1) applies.

Adjusted Cost Base Of New Preferred Shares   The adjusted cost base of these shares is calculated as follows:

Adjusted Cost Base Of Old Common Shares [($360,000)(90%)]	$324,000
Fair Market Value Of Boot	(90,000)
Adjusted Cost Base Of Preferred Shares	$234,000

PUC Reduction - New Shares   The PUC reduction on the new shares would be calculated as follows:

Increase In Legal Stated Capital Of New Shares		$234,000
PUC Of Common Shares [(90%)($100,000)] ($90,000)		
Fair Market Value Of Boot	90,000	Nil
PUC Reduction		$234,000

PUC Of New Preferred Shares Giving the preceding PUC reduction, the PUC of the new shares would be nil ($234,000 - $234,000).

Redemption Of Common Shares For purposes of determining any ITA 84(3) dividend, the calculation would be as follows:

Non-Share Consideration	$90,000
PUC Of New Shares	Nil
Proceeds Of Redemption - ITA 84(5)(d)	$90,000
PUC Of Common Shares Redeemed [(90%)($100,000)]	(90,000)
ITA 84(3) Deemed Dividend	$ Nil

For purposes of determining any capital gain or loss, the calculation would be as follows:

Proceeds Of Disposition - ITA 86(1)(c) ($90,000 + $234,000)	$324,000
Deduct: ITA 84(3) Deemed Dividend	Nil
Adjusted Proceeds Of Disposition - ITA 54	$324,000
Adjusted Cost Base [(90%)($360,000)]	(324,000)
Capital Gain	$ Nil

Net Economic Effect No current income would be assessed to Mr. Long as a result of this reorganization transaction. He would retain the $90,000 note along with the preferred stock with a fair market value of $720,000. The $486,000 ($720,000 - $234,000) deferred capital gain on these shares would be the same as the deferred capital gain that was present on his previous holding of common shares ($810,000 - $324,000). He has accomplished the goal of freezing the value of his estate with no immediate tax consequences.

Approach Two

Gift There is a gift involved in this approach, calculated as follows:

FMV Of Common Shares [(90%)($900,000)]		$810,000
FMV Of Boot	($ 50,000)	
FMV Of Preferred Shares	(660,000)	(710,000)
Gift		$100,000

As Mr. Long's daughter holds the remaining common shares, it is reasonable to assume that this $100,000 in value accrues to her. This means that the provisions of ITA 86(2) will be applicable if this approach is used.

Adjusted Cost Base Of New Preferred Shares Under the provisions of ITA 86(2), the adjusted cost base of the new preferred shares would be calculated as follows:

Adjusted Cost Base Of Old Common Shares [(90%)($360,000)]		$324,000
Fair Market Value Of Boot	($ 50,000)	
Amount Of Gift	(100,000)	(150,000)
Adjusted Cost Base Of Preferred Shares		$174,000

PUC Reduction - New Shares   The PUC reduction on the new shares would be calculated as follows:

Increase In Legal Stated Capital Of New Shares		$40,000
PUC Of Common Shares	($90,000)	
Fair Market Value Of Boot	50,000	(40,000)
PUC Reduction		$ Nil

PUC Of New Preferred Shares   As there is no PUC reduction, the PUC of the new shares would be $40,000.

Redemption Of Common Shares   For purposes of determining any ITA 84(3) deemed dividend, the calculation would be as follows:

Fair Market Value Of The Boot	$50,000
PUC Of Preferred Shares	40,000
Proceeds Of Redemption - ITA 84(5)(d)	$90,000
PUC Of Common Shares Redeemed	(90,000)
ITA 84(3) Deemed Dividend	$ Nil

For purposes of determining any capital gain or loss, the calculation would be as follows:

Fair Market Value Of The Boot	$ 50,000
Gift	100,000
Proceeds Of Disposition - ITA 86(2)(c)	$150,000
ITA 84(3) Deemed Dividend	Nil
Adjusted Proceeds Of Disposition - ITA 54	$150,000
Adjusted Cost Base [(90%)($360,000)]	(324,000)
Capital Loss [Disallowed By ITA 86(2)(d)]	$ Nil

Net Economic Result   No current income would be assessed to Mr. Long as a result of this reorganization transaction. He would retain the $50,000 note along with the preferred stock with a fair market value of $660,000. The $486,000 ($660,000 - $174,000) deferred capital gain on these shares would be the same as the deferred capital gain that was present on his previous holding of common shares. However, the value of his investment has been reduced by $150,000 ($810,000 - $660,000). While he has received $50,000 of this reduction in non-share consideration, there is no corresponding reduction in tax values for the remaining $100,000. In addition, the fair market value of his daughter's shares has increased by $100,000 with no corresponding increase in their tax value. In effect, this approach will result in the amount of the $100,000 gift being subject to tax in his daughter's hands, with no compensating benefit available to either his daughter or himself.

Solution to Self Study Problem Nineteen - 3

Section 87   If ITA 87 is used, the tax consequences are as follows:

- Lynn will have proceeds of disposition equal to the adjusted cost base of the land of $175,000. No capital gain or loss will be recorded.

- Ricon Ltd. will be deemed to have acquired the land at its adjusted cost base of $175,000. As the subsidiary is less than 100 percent owned by Ricon, the bump-up provision from ITA 88(1) is not available if ITA (87) is used.

Section 88(1)   If ITA 88(1) is used, the tax consequences are as follows:

- Lynn will have proceeds of disposition equal to the adjusted cost base of the land of $175,000. No capital gain or loss will be recorded.

- Ricon Ltd. will have a "bump-up" in the tax value of the land that is the lesser of:

Adjusted Cost Base Of Lynn Shares		$380,000
Deduct:		
Cost Of Lynn's Assets	$175,000	
Dividends Paid By Lynn	Nil	(175,000)
Maximum Bump-Up		$205,000

Fair Market Value Of Land When Lynn Shares Acquired (90 Percent)	$351,000
Adjusted Cost Base Of Land (90 Percent)	(157,500)
Maximum Increase In Land Value	$193,500

The amount of the bump-up will be limited to $193,500, resulting in an adjusted cost base of the land of $368,500 ($175,000 + $193,500).

Conclusion   ITA 88(1) is the preferable approach as it adds $193,500 to Ricon's adjusted cost base for the land. This will serve to reduce any future capital gain on an arm's length disposition of the land. Note that this solution does not consider the tax consequences to the minority shareholders of Lynn.

Solution to Self Study Problem Nineteen - 4

The proceeds from the disposition and the taxable capital gains at the corporate level can be calculated as follows:

Asset	Proceeds	Taxable Capital Gains	Business Income (Recapture)
Inventories	$ 43,750	$ Nil	$ Nil
Land	1,553,750	387,500	Nil
Building	1,591,250	248,750	361,250
Totals	$3,188,750	$636,250	$361,250

The taxable capital gains will result in an addition to the Refundable Dividend Tax On Hand account. This will leave a balance in this account as follows:

RDTOH Balance Prior To Asset Dispositions	$ 33,750
Additions [(26-2/3%)($636,250)]	169,667
Ending RDTOH Balance	$203,417

The amount available for distribution to the shareholders, after the payment of all taxes at the corporate level, can be calculated as follows:

Gross Proceeds ($43,750 + $1,553,750 + $1,591,250)	$3,188,750
Tax On Income Eligible For Small Business Deduction [(18%)($300,000)]	(54,000)
Tax On Remaining Active Business Income [(37%)($361,250 - $300,000)]	(22,663)
Tax On Taxable Capital Gains [(50-2/3%)($636,250)]	(322,367)
Dividend Refund (Note)	203,417
Available For Distribution	$2,993,137

Note The dividend refund is equal to the balance in the RDTOH account. As will be shown in a subsequent calculation, the taxable dividends paid on the wind-up are well in excess of the amount needed to trigger the refund of the balance in the RDTOH account.

With respect to the capital dividend account, the final balance is calculated as follows:

Balance Before Dispositions	$268,750
Disposition Of Land	387,500
Disposition Of Building	248,750
Ending Balance	$905,000

Assuming an election has been made to declare the maximum capital dividend, the taxable dividend component of the total distribution to the shareholders can be calculated as follows:

Distribution To Shareholders	$2,993,137
Paid Up Capital	(68,750)
ITA 84(2) Deemed Dividend	$2,924,387
ITA 83(2) Capital Dividend (Balance In Account)	(905,000)
Deemed Dividend Subject To Tax	$2,019,387

ITA 54 indicates that the proceeds of disposition for purposes of determining any capital gain on the disposition of shares does not include any amount paid out as ITA 84(2) deemed dividends. Given the preceding calculation, the capital gain to the shareholders would be calculated as follows:

Distribution To Shareholders	$2,993,137
ITA 84(2) Deemed Dividend	(2,924,387)
Deemed Proceeds	$ 68,750
Adjusted Cost Base Of Shares	(68,750)
Capital Gain	$ Nil

Solution to Self Study Problem Nineteen - 5

Solution to Self Study Problem Nineteen - 5

Sale Of Shares   If the shares are sold for $455,000, the after tax results are as follows:

Proceeds Of Disposition	$455,000
Adjusted Cost Base	(52,500)
Capital Gain	$402,500
Inclusion Rate	1/2
Taxable Capital Gain	$201,250
Tax Rate For Mr. Brock	47%
Tax Payable	$ 94,588

Proceeds Of Disposition	$455,000
Tax Payable	(94,588)
After Tax Proceeds	$360,412

Sale Of Assets   This more complex transaction begins with a calculation of the Tax Payable at the corporate level, subsequent to the sale of assets:

	Business Income	Taxable Capital Gains
Inventory ($109,500 - $105,000)	$ 4,500	$ Nil
Land	Nil	17,500
Building	87,500	7,000
Equipment (Note One)	(21,000)	Nil
Goodwill (Note Two)	82,250	Nil
Taxable Amounts	$153,250	$24,500
Tax Rate	18%	47%
Tax Payable	$ 27,585	$11,515

Note One   There is a terminal loss of $21,000 ($63,000 - $42,000).

Note Two   Business income in the amount of $82,250 [(3/4)($164,500)(1/2 ÷ 3/4)] will have to be recognized on the disposition of the business assets.

Given the preceding calculations, the amount that would be available for distribution to Mr. Brock would be as follows:

Gross Proceeds (Given)	$491,000
Tax Payable ($27,585 + $11,515)	(39,100)
Dividend Refund (Note)	6,533
Available For Distribution	$458,433

Note   The dividend refund would be the lesser of the ending balance in the RDTOH and an amount equal to $1 for every $3 in taxable dividends paid. There was no opening balance in the RDTOH and the only addition during the year was $6,533 [(26-2/3%)($24,500)]. This leaves a balance of $6,533, which is significantly less than one-third of the dividends that will be paid.

With respect to the capital dividend account, the final balance is calculated as follows:

Balance Before Dispositions	$ 70,000
Disposition Of Land [(1/2)($70,000 - $35,000)]	17,500
Disposition Of Building [(1/2)($136,500 - $122,500)]	7,000
Disposition Of Goodwill [(1/4)($164,500)(1/2 ÷ 1/4)]	82,250
Ending Balance	$176,750

Assuming an election has been made to declare the maximum capital dividend, the taxable dividend component of the total distribution to Mr. Brock can be calculated as follows:

Funds Available For Distribution	$458,433
Paid Up Capital	(52,500)
ITA 84(2) Deemed Dividend	$405,933
ITA 83(2) Capital Dividend (Balance In Account)	(176,750)
Deemed Dividend Subject To Tax	$229,183

The gain or loss resulting from the disposition of shares on winding-up the corporation is calculated as follows:

Funds Distributed	$458,433
ITA 84(2) Deemed Dividend	(405,933)
Deemed Proceeds Of Disposition For Shares	$ 52,500
Adjusted Cost Base	(52,500)
Capital Gain	$ Nil

The total cash retained, after the deemed dividends and winding-up of the corporation, can be calculated as follows:

Funds Distributed	$458,433
Tax On Deemed Taxable Dividend [(31%)($229,183)]	(71,047)
After Tax Proceeds	$387,386

As this result is more favourable than the $360,412 in after tax proceeds resulting from the sale of shares, Mr. Brock should sell the assets rather than the shares.

Chapter Nineteen Learning Objectives

After completing Chapter 19, you should be able to:

1. Identify situations where the ITA 85.1 rollover provision is applicable (paragraphs 19-4 through 19-9).

2. Identify situations where the ITA 86(1) rollover provision is applicable (paragraphs 19-10 through 19-12).

3. List the conditions that must be met in order to use the ITA 86(1) rollover provision (paragraphs 19-13 and 19-14).

4. Explain the procedures that are required in implementing an ITA 86(1) rollover (paragraphs 19-15 through 19-18).

5. Apply the ITA 86(1) rollover procedures to specific examples (paragraphs 19-19 through 19-24).

6. Identify situations where the ITA 86(2) benefit rule is applicable and apply the required procedures to specific examples (paragraphs 19-25 through 19-32).

7. Describe the practical factors that must be given consideration in implementing an ITA 86(1) rollover (paragraph 19-33).

8. Describe some of the advantages and disadvantages associated with the use of ITA 86(1) (paragraphs 19-34 through 19-36).

9. Explain the nature of an ITA 87 amalgamation (paragraphs 19-37 through 19-39).

10. Describe the position of the amalgamated company subsequent to an ITA 87 amalgamation (paragraphs 19-40 through 19-42).

11. Describe the position of the shareholders of the amalgamated company subsequent to an ITA 87 amalgamation (paragraphs 19-43 through 19-48).

12. Identify the specific considerations involved in vertical amalgamations (paragraphs 19-44 through 19-48).

13. Explain both the non-tax and tax planning considerations related to ITA 87 amalgamations (paragraphs 19-49 through 19-52).

14. Explain the nature of an ITA 88(1) winding-up of a 90 percent owned subsidiary (paragraphs 19-53 through 19-60).

15. Apply the procedures for recording the assets acquired by the parent company in an ITA 88(1) winding-up of a 90 percent owned subsidiary (paragraphs 19-61 through 19-68).

16. Apply the procedures required for the disposition of shares that occurs in the winding-up of a 90 percent owned subsidiary (paragraph 19-69 and 19-70).

17. Compare the results of applying ITA 87 vs. the results of applying ITA 88(1) and any associated tax planning issues (paragraphs 19-71 through 19-75).

18. Apply the procedures required in an ITA 88(2) winding-up of a Canadian corporation (paragraphs 19-76 through 19-89).

19. Explain the procedures used under ITA 51 when there is a conversion of a corporation's debt securities (paragraphs 19-90 through 19-95).

20. Describe the alternative methods of business valuation (paragraphs 19-96 through 19-100).

21. Demonstrate an understanding of the asset based methods of business valuation (paragraphs 19-101 through 19-104).

22. Demonstrate an understanding of the income based methods of business valuation (paragraphs 19-105 through 19-112).

23. Explain the basic alternatives for the sale of an incorporated business (paragraphs 19-113 and 19-114).

24. Demonstrate an understanding of the provisions relating to restrictive covenants (a.k.a. non-competition agreements) (paragraphs 19-115 through 19-119).

25. Describe the procedures used when the individual assets of a business are sold (paragraphs 19-120 through 19-122).

26. Describe the procedures used when the total assets of a business are sold (paragraphs 19-123 through 19-131).

27. Describe the procedures used when the shares of a business are sold (paragraphs 19-132 through 19-136).

28. Determine the preferable alternative between selling the shares of a business and selling its assets (paragraphs 19-137 through 19-149).

29. Describe the GST implications resulting from the sale of an incorporated business (paragraphs 19-150 through 19-159).

30. Explain the meaning of the term tax shelter and describe the basic forms of organization for these investments (paragraphs 19-160 through 19-182).

31. List the factors to consider in evaluating investments in tax shelters (paragraphs 19-183 and 19-184).

CHAPTER TWENTY

How To Work Through Chapter Twenty

We recommend the following approach in dealing with the material in this Chapter:

Partnerships - Introduction
☐ Read pages 843 (from paragraph 20-1) and 844 (through paragraph 20-6) of the text.

Partnerships Defined
☐ Read pages 844 (from paragraph 20-7) through 846 (through paragraph 20-22) of the text.

☐ Complete Self Study Problem Twenty-1. The Self Study Problem is on page 869 of the text. The solution is on pages S-277 and S-278 of this Study Guide.

Co-Ownerships, Joint Ventures, And Syndicates
☐ Read pages 846 (from paragraph 20-23) through 848 (through paragraph 20-37) of the text.

Determining Partnership Income, Losses, And Tax Credits
☐ Read pages 848 (from paragraph 20-38) through 850 (through paragraph 20-50) of the text.

☐ Complete Exercise Twenty-1. The Exercise is on page 850 of the text. The solution is on page S-275 of this Study Guide.

☐ Read page 851 (paragraph 20-50) of the text.

☐ Complete Exercises Twenty-2 and Twenty-3. The Exercises are on pages 851 and 852 of the text. The solutions are on page S-275 of this Study Guide.

Allocations To Partners And Partner Expenses
☐ Read pages 852 (from paragraph 20-51) through 854 (through paragraph 20-62) of the text.

☐ Complete Exercise Twenty-4. The Exercise is on page 854 of the text. The solution is on page S-275 of this Study Guide.

☐ Complete Self Study Problem Twenty-2. The Self Study Problem is on pages 869 and 870 of the text. The solution is on pages S-278 and S-279 of this Study Guide.

The Partnership Interest
☐ Read pages 854 (from paragraph 20-63) and 855 (through paragraph 20-70) of the text.

☐ Complete Exercise Twenty-5. The Exercise is on page 855 of the text. The solution is on pages S-275 and S-276 of this Study Guide.

Adjustments To The ACB Of A Partnership Interest
☐ Read pages 855 (from paragraph 20-71) through 858 (through paragraph 20-82) of the text.

☐ Complete Exercise Twenty-6. The Exercise is on page 858 of the text. The solution is on page S-276 of this Study Guide.

☐ Complete Self Study Problem Twenty-3. The Self Study Problem is on pages 870 and 871 of the text. The solution is on pages S-279 and S-280 of this Study Guide.

How To Work Through Chapter Twenty

Limited Partnerships And Limited Partners
☐ Read pages 858 (from paragraph 20-83) through 860 (through paragraph 20-93) of the text.

☐ Complete Exercise Twenty-7. The Exercise is on pages 860 and 861 of the text. The solution is on page S-276 of this Study Guide.

☐ Complete Self Study Problem Twenty-4. The Self Study Problem is on page 871 of the text. The solution is on page S-280 of this Study Guide.

Transfers Of Property To And From A Partnership - No Rollover
☐ Read page 861 (paragraphs 20-94 through 20-97) of the text.

☐ Complete Exercise Twenty-8. The Exercise is on page 862 of the text. The solution is on pages S-276 and S-277 of this Study Guide.

☐ Read page 862 (paragraph 20-98) of the text.

☐ Complete Exercise Twenty-9. The Exercise is on page 862 of the text. The solution is on page S-277 of this Study Guide.

Common Partnership Rollovers
☐ Read pages 862 (from paragraph 20-99) through 865 (through paragraph 20-114) of the text.

☐ Complete Self Study Problem Twenty-5. The Self Study Problem is on pages 871 and 872 of the text. The solution is on page S-281 of this Study Guide.

Partnerships And GST
☐ Read pages 865 (from paragraph 20-115) and 866 (through paragraph 20-121) of the text.

If The Appendix To Chapter 20 (Non-Calendar Year Election) Has Been Assigned
☐ Read page 868 (paragraphs 20-124 through 20-126) of the text.

☐ Complete Exercise Twenty-10. The Exercise is on page 868 of the text. The solution is on page S-277 of this Study Guide.

To Complete This Chapter
☐ Review the Key Terms Used In The Chapter on page 867 of the text. Consult the Glossary for the meaning of any key terms you do not know.

☐ Review the Learning Objectives of the Chapter found on page S-282 of this Study Guide.

Solution to Chapter Twenty Exercises

Exercise Twenty - 1 Solution

Net Accounting Income	$146,000
Interest On Partner Capital Accounts	4,400
Salaries To Partners	37,000
Net Income For Tax Purposes	$187,400

Exercise Twenty - 2 Solution

A. Deductible - Office rent expense is deductible if incurred to earn property or business income.
B. Not deductible - Political contributions eligible for the tax credit are flowed through to the individual partners.
C. Deductible - Interest can be deducted if the loan is a bona fide arrangement and the proceeds are used by the partnership to earn property or business income.
D. Not deductible - Donations to registered Canadian charities are flowed through to the individual partners.

Exercise Twenty - 3 Solution

Net Accounting Loss	($71,600)
Qualifying Political Contributions	16,000
Personal Expenditures Of Partner	8,000
Rental Expenses	(12,000)
Net Loss For Tax Purposes	($59,600)

Exercise Twenty - 4 Solution

The required first $40,000 of partnership income should be allocated to Ruth. The remaining negative balance of $5,000 should be allocated equally between Emily and Ruth, as follows:

	Emily	Ruth	Total
Guaranteed income allocation (salary)	Nil	$40,000	$40,000
Share of remainder ($35,000 - $40,000)	($2,500)	(2,500)	(5,000)
Net allocations	($2,500)	$37,500	$35,000

This solution follows the recommendations in the CRA's "Guide For The Partnership Information Form". This is the recommended treatment when salaries are considered as part of the allocation process to partners.

Exercise Twenty - 5 Solution

Alan and Balan will each have a disposition of one-third of their partnership interests for $40,000. The adjusted cost base of each third is $16,000 [(1/3)($48,000)], so Alan and Balan will each have a $24,000 ($40,000 - $16,000) capital gain, of which one-half, or $12,000, will be a taxable capital gain.

Solution to Chapter Twenty Exercises

The partner capital account transactions and ending balances will be:

	Alan	Balan	Caitlin
Opening Capital Accounts	$48,000	$48,000	Nil
Adjustment For Caitlin's Admission	(16,000)	(16,000)	32,000
Ending Capital Accounts (Accounting Values)	$32,000	$32,000	$32,000
ACB Of Partnership Interest	$32,000	$32,000	$80,000

Exercise Twenty - 6 Solution
The ACB of Robert's partnership interest on December 31, 2005 and January 1, 2006 would be determined as follows:

Original Capital Contribution	$12,500
Additional Contribution [(ITA 53(1)(e)]	7,200
Withdrawal [ITA 53(2)(c)]	(4,000)
ACB - December 31, 2005	$15,700
Adjustment For 2005 Income [(40%)($11,600 + $3,100 + $46,700)]	24,560
ACB - January 1, 2006	$40,260

Note that the adjustment to the partnership ACB for 2005 income is not the same amount that Robert would report as his share of partnership income for the year. This amount would be $22,550 {[40%][($11,600)(1/2) + ($3,100)(125%) + $46,700]}.

Exercise Twenty - 7 Solution

ACB Of Partnership Interest		$200,000
Share Of Partnership Income For Current Period		Nil
Subtotal		$200,000
Amounts Owed To The Partnership	($150,000)	
Other Amounts Intended To Reduce Investment Risk	Nil	(150,000)
At-Risk Amount - December 31, 2005		$ 50,000

The loss is only deductible to the extent of the $50,000 at-risk amount. The $25,000 ($75,000 - $50,000) excess is his limited partnership loss for 2005.

Exercise Twenty - 8 Solution

Part A Charles is considered to have disposed of the land for $100,000, resulting in a $33,500 [(1/2)($100,000 - $33,000)] taxable capital gain. LIU will be considered to have acquired the land for $100,000. Charles is considered to have made a capital contribution of $100,000 that will be added to the ACB of his partnership interest.

Part B Charles will have the same $33,500 taxable capital gain as in Part A and LIU will be considered to have acquired the land for $100,000. The capital contribution and the addition to the ACB of the partnership interest is equal to $75,000. This is the difference between the fair market value of the land transferred to LIU of $100,000 and the $25,000 in other consideration received by Charles on the property transfer.

Part C   Charles will have the same $33,500 taxable capital gain as in Part A and LIU will be considered to have acquired the land for $100,000. No capital contribution is made. As Charles withdrew $12,000 ($112,000 - $100,000) more from LIU than he transferred in, Charles will be considered to have made a net withdrawal. The ACB of his partnership interest will be reduced by $12,000.

Exercise Twenty - 9 Solution

ITA 98(2) deems DG to have disposed of the share investments for the fair market value of $94,000, resulting in an $55,000 ($94,000 - $39,000) capital gain. One-fifth of the capital gain, or $11,000, will be allocated to Darlene. One-half of this amount, or $5,500, will be a taxable capital gain that she will be required to include in her income for 2005. Darlene will also be considered to have acquired the share investments for $18,800 [(20%)($94,000)]. The adjusted cost base of her partnership interest on December 31, 2005 and on January 1, 2006 is calculated as follows:

Adjusted Cost Base Prior To The Distribution	$30,000
Drawings	(18,800)
Adjusted Cost Base - December 31, 2005	$11,200
Allocated Capital Gain	11,000
Adjusted Cost Base - January 1, 2006	$22,200

Exercise Twenty - 10 Solution

Mr. Gelato's additional business income for the current year will be $15,088 [($12,300)(184 Days ÷ 150 Days)]. The 184 days is for the period July 1 through December 31, while the 150 days is for the period February 1 through June 30. The total business income for the year will be $27,388 ($15,088 + $12,300).

Solution to Self Study Problem Twenty - 1

The determination of the existence of a partnership is a mixed question of fact and law, based upon the intention of the parties that may be expressed clearly through a valid written partnership agreement or inferred from actions. In Canada, the relevant provincial partnership legislation is applicable to answering this question.

In this case, an analysis of the three elements of a partnership is as follows:

1. **Was a business carried on by the partnership?**

    A business has a beginning and an end. Ongoing profitable activity within the business may actually only occur between these two extremes, but the activity remains a business throughout the period. In other words, profitability is generally irrelevant to a finding that a business exists. In this case, the selling off of store property will likely occur as part of the wind up process of the two stores. Accordingly, there are arguments that support the carrying on of a business.

2. **Was the business carried on in common by two or more persons?**

    The details of the partnership agreement contain many of the necessary ingredients that the courts will look to in support of this element. Accordingly, it appears that this element has also been met.

3. **Was there a view to profit?**

This element will be satisfied if there is a potential for profit even though one may never be realized. The facts clearly lead to a conclusion that there is no hope of profit. The additional fact that the partnership will be terminated once the property is sold and that losses are not only expected, but anticipated, speaks for itself. A tax motivation that predominates, such as this, will not invalidate a partnership as long as there is a profit potential and the other elements are met. This is not the case.

Conclusion: A partnership was not created. As a result, no losses can be allocated to the investors. The losses belong to Wayout Ltd.

Solution to Self Study Problem Twenty - 2

Partnership Net Income The income of the partnership, calculated as if the partnership were a separate person resident in Canada, is as follows:

Net Income As Per Income Statement		$192,100
Additions:		
Partners' Salaries [(2)($44,000)]	$88,000	
Depreciation Deducted	12,500	
Charitable Donations	7,200	
Closing Accounts Receivable (Note One)	56,000	163,700
Deductions:		
Opening Accounts Receivable (Note One)	($27,000)	
Capital Gains On Securities (Note Two)	(14,000)	
Dividends Received (Note Three)	(48,000)	
CCA:		
Class 8 [(20%)($26,000)]	(5,200)	
Class 45 {[45%][$14,000 + ($8,500)(1/2)]}	(8,213)	(102,413)
Net Business Income		$253,387

Note One The addition of closing accounts receivable and the deduction of the opening accounts receivable are required to adjust the cash based income figure to an accrual based income figure.

Note Two The total capital gain is deducted in the calculation of net business income. The taxable one-half of these gains is included on a flow through basis in the income of the individual partners.

Note Three The dividends received are deducted in the calculation of net business income. They are flowed through as taxable Canadian dividends in the income of the individual partners.

Mr. Caldwell's Personal Income   The amount to be included in Mr. Caldwell's personal tax return would be calculated as follows:

Partnership Income [(1/2)($253,387)]	$126,694
Automobile Costs:	
CCA [($13,500)(30%)(75%)]	(3,038)
Operating Costs [($4,000)(75%)]	(3,000)
Net Business Income From Professional Practice	$120,656
Taxable Capital Gains [(1/2)($14,000)(1/2)]	3,500
Dividends From Taxable Canadian Corporations [($48,000)(125%)(1/2)]	30,000
Net Income For Tax Purposes	$154,156

Mr. Caldwell's $3,600 [(1/2)($7,200)] share of the charitable donations can be used as the basis for a credit against his personal Tax Payable. The amount of the credit would be $1,018 [(16%)($200) + (29%)($3,400)].

He is also entitled to a federal dividend tax credit of $4,000 [(2/3)($48,000)(25%)(1/2)].

Solution to Self Study Problem Twenty - 3

The adjusted cost base of Eric Beam's partnership interest on the date he withdrew from the partnership is calculated as follows:

Initial Investment	$225,000
Share Of Business Income [(1/3)($195,000)]	65,000
Share Of Capital Gains (Note One) [(1/3)($66,000)]	22,000
Share Of Charitable Donations (Note Two) [(1/3)($12,000)]	(4,000)
Drawings From The Partnership	(43,000)
Additional Capital Contributions	54,000
Adjusted Cost Base On January 1, 2005	$319,000

Note One   Only one-half of the capital gain is included in the partner's income on the flow through of capital gains realized by a partnership. However, the remaining one-half is included in the assets of the partnership and, in the absence of a special provision to deal with this situation, the realization of this amount would be added to any capital gain realized on the disposition of the partnership interest. ITA 53(1)(e)(i) provides such a provision, indicating that the full amount of any capital gains must be added to the ACB of a partnership interest.

Note Two   Charitable donations cannot be deducted in the calculation of partnership income for tax purposes. Instead, they are allocated to the individual partners to be used by them as the basis for credits against their personal Tax Payable. Given this, ITA 53(2)(c)(iii) requires that these amounts be deducted from the ACB of the partnership interest.

Given the preceding calculation, the gain on the disposition of the partnership interest can be calculated as follows:

Proceeds Of Disposition		$355,000
Adjusted Cost Base:		
From Preceding Calculation	($319,000)	
Legal And Accounting Fees	(1,800)	(320,800)
Capital Gain		$ 34,200
Inclusion Rate		1/2
Taxable Capital Gain		$ 17,100

This amount would be included in Eric Beam's Net Income For Tax Purposes for 2005 as a taxable capital gain. He would not include any partnership income for the period January 1 to February 1, 2005, as he was not allocated any of this income.

Solution to Self Study Problem Twenty - 4

Note The addition of the share of the partnership income amounts to the at-risk balance as at December 31 is intended to ensure that this amount is taken into consideration in determining the amount that is actually at risk on that date. Notice, however, losses are not deducted at this time in the determination of the at-risk amount. We would remind you that in calculating the adjusted cost base of the partnership interest, a partner's share of either a loss or a gain is not added until the first day of the following taxation year.

The required amounts for Melanie's investment in the Cross Your Fingers Partnership are as follows:

Adjusted Cost Base - December 31, 2005		$20,000
Add: Share Of Partnership Income For The Current Period		
[(4%)($12,000 + $17,500 + $20,000)]		1,980
Total		$21,980
Less:		
Amounts Owed To The Partnership		
($16,800 - $2,100)	$ 14,700	
Other Amounts Intended To		
Reduce The Investment Risk	1,500	(16,200)
At-Risk Amount - December 31, 2005		$ 5,780

Allocated 4 Percent Share Of 2005 Partnership Income (Loss)	($ 7,200)
At-Risk Amount - December 31, 2005	5,780
Limited Partnership Loss For 2005	($ 1,420)

Allocated 4 Percent Share Of 2005 Partnership Income (Loss)	($ 7,200)
Limited Partnership Loss For 2005	1,420
Deductible Loss For 2005	($ 5,780)

There is a limited partnership loss carry forward of $1,420 at the end of 2005.

Solution to Self Study Problem Twenty - 5

Cash   With all non-share consideration, the ACB is equal to its fair market value. In the case of cash, the fair market value is equal to the face value. These amounts would be $78,000 for Porter, $222,000 for Quinn, and $422,000 for Roberts.

Preferred Shares   With respect to the preferred shares received by each partner, ITA 85(3)(e) indicates that their ACB will be the lesser of:

• Their fair market value, which would be $180,000 for each of the three partners.

• The ACB of each partnership interest, reduced by the amount of non-share consideration received by the partner.

This latter value would be calculated as follows for each of the three partners:

	Porter	Quinn	Roberts
ACB	$382,000	$526,000	$726,000
Cash Received	(78,000)	(222,000)	(422,000)
Balance	$304,000	$304,000	$304,000

For each of the three partners, the lower figure would be the fair market value of $180,000 and, as a consequence, this would be the ACB of their preferred shares.

Common Shares   Under ITA 85(3)(f), the ACB of the common shares received by each partner would be the ACB of their partnership interest, less the sum of the value of the non-share consideration received and the value assigned to the preferred shares received. These amounts would be calculated as follows:

	Porter	Quinn	Roberts
ACB - Partnership Interest	$382,000	$526,000	$726,000
Cash Received	(78,000)	(222,000)	(422,000)
ACB - Preferred Shares	(180,000)	(180,000)	(180,000)
ACB - Common Shares	$124,000	$124,000	$124,000

Capital Gain Or Loss   As the non-share consideration had a value that was less than the value of the assets transferred, there will be no immediate gain or loss on this rollover. This can be demonstrated with the following calculation:

	Porter	Quinn	Roberts
Proceeds Of Disposition:			
Cash	$ 78,000	$222,000	$422,000
Preferred Shares	180,000	180,000	180,000
Common Shares	124,000	124,000	124,000
Total Proceeds	$382,000	$526,000	$726,000
ACB	(382,000)	(526,000)	(726,000)
Capital Gain (Loss)	Nil	Nil	Nil

From an economic point of view the gain is still present. The partners have simply deferred recording it for tax purposes by placing a value on the common shares of $372,000 [(3)($124,000)]. This is significantly below their current fair market value of $1,080,000. Note that the difference of $708,000 ($1,080,000 - $372,000) is also the difference between the $2,342,000 fair market value of the total consideration given and the $1,634,000 value for the total ACB of the partnership interests.

Chapter Twenty Learning Objectives

After completing Chapter 20, you should be able to:

1. Explain the basic approach of Canadian income tax legislation to the taxation of partnerships (paragraphs 20-1 through 20-6).

2. Define, for income tax purposes, a partnership arrangement (paragraphs 20-7 through 20-16).

3. List the various types of partnership arrangements that are used in Canada (paragraphs 20-17 through 20-22).

4. Describe the difference between partnership arrangements and such other forms of organization as co-ownership, joint ventures, and syndicates (paragraphs 20-23 through 20-37).

5. Explain the basic concepts that are involved in the determination of partnership income, losses, and tax credits (paragraphs 20-38 through 20-48).

6. Calculate partnership Net Income For Tax Purposes (paragraphs 20-49 and 20-50).

7. Calculate the amount of partnership income that will be allocated to each partner under the terms of a partnership agreement (paragraphs 20-51 through 20-62).

8. Explain the concept of the adjusted cost base of a partnership interest (paragraphs 20-63 and 20-64).

9. Apply the procedures related to recording the acquisition of a partnership interest (paragraphs 20-65 through 20-70).

10. Calculate the amount of the adjusted cost base of a partnership interest (paragraphs 20-71 through 20-82).

11. Define a limited partnership arrangement (paragraphs 20-83 through 20-85).

12. Apply the at-risk rules to limited partnership arrangements (paragraphs 20-86 through 20-93).

13. Outline the various types of transfers that may take place between a partnership and its partners (paragraphs 20-94 through 20-96).

14. Apply the procedures related to transfers between a partnership and its partners when no rollover provision is used (paragraphs 20-97 and 20-98).

15. List and apply the common rollover provisions for transfers between a partnership and its partners (paragraphs 20-99 through 20-114).

16. Describe the GST implications related to partner expenses, dispositions of partnership interests, transfers between a partnership and its partners, and reorganizations of partnerships (paragraphs 20-115 through 20-121).

If The Appendix To Chapter 20 (Non-Calendar Year Election) Has Been Assigned

17. Apply the provisions related to the election involving a non-calendar year end (paragraphs 20-124 through 20-126).

CHAPTER TWENTY-ONE

How To Work Through Chapter Twenty-One

We recommend the following approach in dealing with the material in this Chapter:

Introduction
☐   Read pages 879 (from paragraph 21-1) and 880 (through paragraph 21-7) of the text.

Basic Concepts
☐   Read pages 880 (from paragraph 21-8) and 881 (through paragraph 21-19) of the text.

Establishing A Trust
☐   Read pages 881 (from paragraph 21-20) and 882 (through paragraph 21-23) of the text.

☐   Complete Exercise Twenty-One-1. The Exercise is on page 882 of the text. The solution is on page S-285 of this Study Guide.

Non-Tax Reasons For Using Trusts
☐   Read pages 882 (from paragraph 21-24) and 883 (through paragraph 21-25) of the text.

Classification Of Trusts
☐   Read pages 883 (from paragraph 21-26) through 885 (through paragraph 21-36) of the text.

Taxation Of Trusts - The Basic Model
☐   Read pages 885 (from paragraph 21-37) and 886 (through paragraph 21-37) of the text.

☐   Complete Exercise Twenty-One-2. The Exercise is on page 886 of the text. The solution is on page S-285 of this Study Guide.

Rollovers To A Trust
☐   Read pages 886 (from paragraph 21-38) and 887 (through paragraph 21-45) of the text.

☐   Complete Exercise Twenty-One-3. The Exercise is on page 887 of the text. The solution is on page S-285 of this Study Guide.

☐   Read pages 887 (from paragraph 21-46) and 888 (through paragraph 21-49) of the text.

☐   Complete Exercise Twenty-One-4. The Exercise is on page 888 of the text. The solution is on page S-285 of this Study Guide.

☐   Read pages 888 (from paragraph 21-50) and 889 (through paragraph 21-54) of the text.

21 Year Deemed Disposition Rule
☐   Read page 889 (paragraphs 21-55 through 21-57) of the text.

Net Income For Tax Purposes And Taxable Income Of A Trust
☐   Read pages 889 (from paragraph 21-58) through 891 (through paragraph 21-66) of the text.

☐   Complete Exercise Twenty-One-5. The Exercise is on pages 891 and 892 of the text. The solution is on page S-286 of this Study Guide.

Income Allocations To Beneficiaries

☐ Read pages 892 (from paragraph 21-67) through 894 (through paragraph 21-84) of the text.

☐ Complete Exercise Twenty-One-6. The Exercise is on page 894 of the text. The solution is on page S-286 of this Study Guide.

Tax Payable Of Personal Trusts

☐ Read pages 894 (from paragraph 21-85) and 895 (through paragraph 21-93) of the text.

☐ Complete Exercise Twenty-One-7. The Exercise is on page 896 of the text. The solution is on page S-287 of this Study Guide.

☐ Complete Self Study Problems Twenty-One-1 through Twenty-One-4. The Self Study Problems are on pages 908 through 910 of the text. The solutions are on pages S-288 through S-291 of this Study Guide.

Trust Tax And Information Returns

☐ Read page 896 (paragraph 21-94) of the text.

Income Attribution

☐ Read pages 896 (from paragraph 21-95) and 897 (through paragraph 21-97) of the text.

☐ Complete Exercise Twenty-One-8. The Exercise is on page 897 of the text. The solution is on page S-287 of this Study Guide.

☐ Read page 987 (paragraphs 21-98 and 21-99) of the text.

Purchase Or Sale Of An Interest In A Trust

☐ Read pages 897 (from paragraph 21-100) and 898 (through paragraph 21-105) of the text.

☐ Complete Exercise Twenty-One-9. The Exercise is on page 898 of the text. The solution is on page S-287 of this Study Guide.

Tax Planning

☐ Read pages 898 (from paragraph 21-106) and 899 (through paragraph 21-109) of the text.

☐ Complete Exercise Twenty-One-10. The Exercise is on page 899 of the text. The solution is on page S-288 of this Study Guide.

☐ Read pages 899 (from paragraph 21-110) through 901 (through paragraph 21-116) of the text.

Estate Planning

☐ Read pages 901 (from paragraph 21-117) through 905 (through paragraph 21-140) of the text.

GST And Trusts

☐ Read page 906 (paragraphs 21-141 through 21-143) of the text.

To Complete This Chapter

☐ Review the Key Terms Used In The Chapter on page 906 of the text. Consult the Glossary for the meaning of any key terms you do not know.

☐ Review the Learning Objectives of the Chapter found on pages S-292 and S-293 of this Study Guide.

Solution to Chapter Twenty-One Exercises

Exercise Twenty-One - 1 Solution

Case A   While Mr. Black has transferred property, it is not clear that his intention was to create a trust. No trust would be created by his transfer.

Case B   Jane's "friends" cannot be considered to be an identifiable class. As a consequence, there is no certainty as to beneficiaries and no trust would be created by her transfer.

Case C   Robert's "children" would be an identifiable class. It would appear that a trust has been created.

Case D   While Suzanne has signed the agreement, it does not appear that the property has been transferred. This means that no trust has been created.

Exercise Twenty-One - 2 Solution

With respect to Joanne's transfer of her securities to the trust, the transaction would be deemed to take place at fair market value. This would result in a taxable capital gain to Joanne of $10,000 [(1/2)($220,000 - $200,000)]. There would be no tax consequences to Jocelyn or the trust as a result of this transfer.

As the trust distributed all of its income during the year, none of the interest would be taxed in the trust. All of the interest would be included in Jocelyn's income and, because she is an adult, there would be no income attribution to Joanne.

Under ITA 107(2), the transfer from the trust to Jocelyn on January 1, 2006 would take place at the trust's tax cost of $220,000. There would be no tax consequences for Joanne, Jocelyn, or the trust as a result of this transfer.

Exercise Twenty-One - 3 Solution

As there is a rollover available on transfers to a qualifying spousal trust, the accrued $30,000 gain ($90,000 - $60,000) will not be recognized until her husband or the spousal trust eventually disposes of the asset. The spousal trust acquires the asset at an adjusted cost base of $60,000, which will be her husband's adjusted cost base if the trust transfers the asset to him.

Exercise Twenty-One - 4 Solution

Scenario	Taxable Capital Gain (Settlor)	Adjusted Cost Base (Trust)
1. Inter vivos trust for adult child	$300	$1,600
2. Inter vivos trust for minor child	300	1,600
3. Testamentary trust for friend	300	1,600
4. Inter vivos spousal trust	Nil	1,000
5. Testamentary spousal trust	Nil	1,000
6. Joint spousal trust	Nil	1,000
7. Alter ego trust	Nil	1,000

Solution to Chapter Twenty-One Exercises

Exercise Twenty-One - 5 Solution

The required calculations are as follows:

Business Income	$220,000
Preferred Beneficiary Election	(50,000)
Distributions To Other Beneficiaries	(170,000)
Designation Under ITA 104(13.1)	35,000
Net Income For Tax Purposes	$ 35,000
Business Loss Carry Over	(35,000)
Taxable Income	$ Nil

The preferred beneficiary election would mean that the $50,000 would be taxed in the hands of the disabled beneficiary even though the funds are retained in the trust. Since this is an inter vivos trust, the $50,000 would be taxed at the maximum rate in the trust without the election. As the disabled beneficiary has no other source of income, the $50,000 would be subject to tax at lower rates than would be the case if it was left in the trust.

By designating $35,000 as amounts not paid, the trust can absorb the loss carry forward. As a result, the beneficiaries will not pay tax on this amount even though it has been distributed to them.

Exercise Twenty-One - 6 Solution

The Net Income For Tax Purposes of the trust would be calculated as follows:

Dividends From Canadian Public Corporations	$100,000
Dividends From CCPC	30,000
Taxable Capital Gain [(1/2)($20,000)]	10,000
Income Distributions To Bryan	
($60,000 + $30,000 + $10,000)	(100,000)
Gross Up Of Retained Dividends	
[(25%)($100,000 - $60,000)]	10,000
Net Income For Tax Purposes - Trust	$ 50,000

The corresponding calculation for Bryan would be as follows:

Dividends From Canadian Public Corporations	$ 60,000
Dividends From CCPC	30,000
Dividend Gross Up [(25%)($60,000 + $30,000)]	22,500
Taxable Capital Gains [(1/2)($20,000)]	10,000
Subtotal	$122,500
Split Income Deduction - ITA 20(1)(ww)	(37,500)
Net Income For Tax Purposes - Bryan	$ 85,000

Note that the dividends from Canadian controlled private corporations, while not included in regular Net Income For Tax Purposes or Taxable Income, would be subject to the tax on split income. The non-taxable one-half of the capital gain would be received by Bryan on a tax free basis. Both the trust and Bryan will be able to deduct a dividend tax credit against Tax Payable.

Exercise Twenty-One - 7 Solution

Taxable Income and federal Tax Payable for the trust would be calculated as follows:

Income From Dividends	$20,000
Deduction For Distribution To Beneficiary	(15,000)
Net Dividend Income	$ 5,000
Dividend Gross Up [(25%)($5,000)]	1,250
Taxable Income For The Trust	$ 6,250
Federal Tax Rate (Inter Vivos Trust)	29%
Federal Tax Before Credits	$ 1,813
Federal Dividend Tax Credit [(2/3)($1,250)]	(833)
Federal Tax Payable - Trust	$ 980

Taxable Income and federal Tax Payable for the son would be calculated as follows:

Dividend Income From The Trust	$15,000
Dividend Gross Up [(25%)($15,000)]	3,750
Taxable Income For The Son	$18,750
Federal Tax Rate	16%
Federal Tax Before Credits	$ 3,000
Basic Personal Credit [(16%)($8,148)]	(1,304)
Federal Dividend Tax Credit [(2/3)($3,750)]	(2,500)
Federal Tax Payable - Son	Nil

Exercise Twenty-One - 8 Solution

Income on the bonds is subject to the attribution rules to the extent that the income is allocated to Trevor's spouse, Carmen, and to their minor son, Mitch. This means that two-thirds of the interest will be attributed back to Trevor. With respect to the capital gain, the attribution rules do not apply on transfers to minors. This means that only Carmen's one-third share of the gain will be attributed back to Trevor.

	Carmen	Mitch	Rhonda
Interest Income ($27,000 ÷ 3)	$9,000	$9,000	$ 9,000
Taxable Capital Gain ($3,000 ÷ 3)	1,000	1,000	1,000
Interest Attribution To Trevor	(9,000)	(9,000)	Nil
Capital Gain Attribution To Trevor	(1,000)	Nil	Nil
Allocated Trust Income	Nil	$1,000	$10,000

The total amount attributed to Trevor would be $19,000 ($9,000 + $9,000 + $1,000)

Exercise Twenty-One - 9 Solution

With respect to Sam, he has acquired a capital interest for consideration of $190,000. This will be the adjusted cost base of the interest he has acquired.

With respect to Mehrdad, he has disposed of a capital asset for proceeds of disposition of $190,000. Since he did not purchase the interest in the trust, his adjusted cost base as usually determined would be nil. However, for this disposition, the adjusted cost base of the capital interest is the greater of nil and the cost amount as determined under ITA 108(1). The cost amount would be $125,000, one-half of the tax cost of the assets in the trust. The result would be a taxable capital gain of $32,500 [(1/2)($190,000 - $125,000)].

Exercise Twenty-One - 10 Solution

As Sarah's other income places her in the maximum federal tax bracket of 29 percent, her tax savings resulting from transferring the assets to the family trust would be $31,900 [($110,000)(29%)]. The federal tax that would be payable on the additional $55,000 received by each of her two children is as follows:

Jerri

Tax On First $35,595	$5,695
Tax On Additional $19,405 ($55,000 - $35,595) At 22 Percent	4,269
Tax Before Credit	$9,964
Personal Credit	(1,304)
Tax Payable	$8,660

Mark

Marginal Tax At 22 Percent [(22%)($71,190 - $45,000)]	$ 5,762
Additional Tax At 26 Percent [($55,000 + $45,000 - $71,190)]	7,491
Additional Tax Payable (See Note)	$13,253

Note As Mark would be in a position to use all of his tax credits prior to receiving the additional $55,000 in income, they are not relevant to the determination of his marginal increase in taxes.

The total tax paid by the two children would $21,913 ($8,660 + $13,253). This is $9,987 ($31,900 - $21,913) per year less than the amount that would be paid by Sarah without the trust. When combined with a reduction in provincial taxes, the total value of establishing a family trust would be about $15,000 per year. This is more than enough to cover the costs of establishing and maintaining this trust.

Solution to Self Study Problem Twenty-One - 1

A. The following schedule allocates income as per the trust agreement:

Income Allocation	Trust	Spouse	Son
Business Income	$ Nil	$12,000	$ 8,000
Interest	Nil	1,800	1,200
Dividends	25,000	15,000	10,000
Dividend Gross Up (25%)	6,250	3,750	2,500
Net Rental Income (Note)	Nil	2,400	1,600
Net Income And Taxable Income	$31,250	$34,950	$23,300
Federal Income Tax (16%)	$5,000	$5,592	$3,728
Basic Personal Credit	N/A	(1,304)	(1,304)
Federal Dividend Tax Credit	(4,167)	(2,500)	(1,667)
Federal Tax Payable	$ 833	$1,788	$ 757

Note The $4,000 net rental income is calculated as the rent receipts of $12,000, less the operating expenses of $6,000 and CCA of $2,000. The CCA is claimed at the trust level, and is flowed through as a deduction in calculating the income of the beneficiaries.

B. The following income allocation assumes that all of the trust's income will be allocated to Mrs. Rowand and Roger. This means that the Taxable Income and federal Tax Payable of the trust will be nil. The calculations for Mrs. Rowand and Roger are as follows:

Income Allocation	Spouse	Son
Business Income	$12,000	$ 8,000
Interest	1,800	1,200
Dividends	30,000	20,000
Dividend Gross Up (25%)	7,500	5,000
Net Rental Income	2,400	1,600
Net And Taxable Income	$53,700	$35,800

Federal Income Tax		
On First $35,595 At 16 Percent	$5,695	$5,695
On Remaining $18,105 At 22 Percent	3,983	Nil
On Remaining $205 At 22 Percent	Nil	45
Basic Personal Credit	(1,304)	(1,304)
Federal Dividend Tax Credit	(5,000)	(3,333)
Federal Tax Payable	$3,374	$ 1,103

C. The total basic federal Tax Payable in Part B is $4,477, which is $1,099 higher than the total of $3,378 in Part A. This excess tax bill of $1,099 results because, unlike the situation in Part A where all of the income accruing to the three taxpayers was taxed at 16 percent, in Part B, $18,105 of Mrs. Rowand's income and $205 of Roger's income is taxed at the higher 22 percent rate. The $1,099 can also be calculated as 6 percent (22% - 16%) of $18,310 ($18,105 + $205).

Solution to Self Study Problem Twenty-One - 2

Calculation Of Taxable Income The Taxable Income of the two beneficiaries and the trust would be calculated as shown in the following table. With the exception of the recapture on the sale of the rental property, all amounts are allocated 30 percent to Ms. Robinson's son, 50 percent to her daughter, and 20 percent to the trust.

	Son	Daughter	Trust
Interest On Government Bonds	$ 19,500	$ 32,500	$ 13,000
Dividends On Canadian Stocks	75,000	125,000	50,000
Gross Up Of 25 Percent	18,750	31,250	12,500
Rental Revenues	147,600	246,000	98,400
Rental Expenses	(102,600)	(171,000)	(68,400)
Taxable Capital Gain On Land [(1/2)($2,300,000 - $1,430,000)]	130,500	217,500	87,000
Taxable Capital Gain On Building [(1/2)($4,560,000 - $3,840,000)]	108,000	180,000	72,000
Recaptured CCA On Building (Note)	Nil	Nil	460,000
Net And Taxable Income	$396,750	$661,250	$724,500

Note The recapture of CCA on the Building is calculated as follows:

Capital Cost	$3,840,000
UCC	(3,380,000)
Recaptured CCA	$ 460,000

As noted in the text, recapture must be included in the Taxable Income of the trust.

Calculation Of Tax Payable Based on the preceding Taxable Income, the federal Tax Payable of the trust can be calculated as follows:

Federal Tax [(29%)($724,500)]	$210,105
Federal Dividend Tax Credit [(2/3)($12,500)]	(8,333)
Federal Tax Payable	$201,772

Solution to Self Study Problem Twenty-One - 3

The various components of the trust's income would be allocated as follows:

	Daughter	Son	Trust
Canadian Dividends Received	$26,100	$43,500	$17,400
Gross Up Of 25 Percent	6,525	10,875	4,350
British Interest (Gross Amount Of $110,000)	33,000	55,000	22,000
Net Rental Income	18,300	30,500	12,200
Capital Cost Allowance	(13,500)	(22,500)	(9,000)
Net And Taxable Income	$70,425	$117,375	$46,950
British Taxes Paid ($16,500)	$ 4,950	$ 8,250	$ 3,300

The CCA is claimed at the trust level, and is flowed through as a deduction in calculating the Taxable Income of the beneficiaries. Except for the fact that the ITA 118 personal tax credits are not available, income that remains in a testamentary trust is taxed in the same general manner as would apply to an individual. Given this, Tax Payable for the trust would be calculated as follows:

Basic Federal Tax:	
On First $35,595 At 16 Percent	$5,695
On Remaining $11,355 At 22 Percent	2,498
Federal Tax Payable Before Credits	$8,193
Federal Dividend Tax Credit [(2/3)($4,350)]	(2,900)
Foreign Tax Credit (See Note)	(3,300)
Tax Payable	$1,993

Note The amount that can be deducted for the foreign tax credit is the lesser of the amount of foreign taxes withheld and an amount determined by the following formula:

[(Foreign Non-Business Income ÷ Adjusted Net Income)(Tax Payable Before Credits)]
= [($22,000 ÷ $46,950)($8,193)]
= $3,839

As this amount is more than the actual foreign taxes of $3,300 allocated to the trust, the actual foreign taxes paid would be the lesser amount, and would be the foreign tax credit.

Solution to Self Study Problem Twenty-One - 4

Part A   Trust For Daughter   The first trust created is a testamentary trust for the benefit of Mrs. Turner's daughter, Melanie. When there is a transfer of assets at death to any taxpayer other than a spouse or a spousal trust, there is a deemed disposition with proceeds equal to fair market value. Capital gains on all of the assets transferred would need to be realized along with recapture of CCA on the warehouse building.

The principal residence exemption could be used to eliminate the gain on the residence. Melanie will not have a taxable benefit from use of the residence. However, since the trust pays for the upkeep and maintenance of the residence, the trust can deduct the costs and they are taxable as income to Melanie.

The capital gain and recapture on the disposition of the warehouse building would have to be included in Mrs. Turner's final tax return. The taxable capital gain on the warehouse land is $10,000 [(1/2)($75,000 - $55,000)]. As the fair market value of the warehouse is equal to its capital cost, there is no capital gain on the warehouse building. However, there would be recapture of CCA in the amount of $40,000 ($85,000 - $45,000). This amount would have to be included in Mrs. Turner's final tax return.

The trust will be deemed to acquire all of the assets at their fair market values. In the case of the warehouse building, the new UCC will be the fair market value of $85,000.

Part A   Trust For Husband   The second trust appears to be a qualifying spousal trust. Where there is a transfer at death to a qualifying spousal trust, the transfer is deemed to be a disposition with proceeds equal to the deceased taxpayer's tax cost. This would be the capital cost of the cottage and stock portfolio and, as a consequence of using this value, the transfer of assets to the trust will have no tax consequences for Mrs. Turner's final tax return.

The trust will be deemed to have acquired all of the assets at the same capital cost values that were used as proceeds of disposition by Mrs. Turner.

Part B   Death Of Husband   Unless Mr. West has remarried with great haste and can pass these assets on to a new spouse or qualifying spousal trust, his death will result in a deemed disposition of the trust's assets for proceeds equal to fair market value. In the case of the cottage, a taxable capital gain of $5,000 [(1/2)($72,000 - $62,000)] will result, while on the stock market portfolio there will be a taxable capital gain of $3,000 [(1/2)($28,000 - $22,000)].

Chapter Twenty-One Learning Objectives

After completing Chapter 21, you should be able to:

1. Explain the basic concepts of trusts (paragraphs 21-1 through 21-15).

2. Explain the difference between a trust and an estate (paragraphs 21-16 through 21-19).

3. Describe the procedures required to establish a trust (paragraphs 21-20 through 21-23).

4. Demonstrate an understanding of the non-tax reasons for using trusts (paragraphs 21-24 and 21-25).

5. Demonstrate an understanding of the different classifications of trusts (paragraphs 21-26 through 21-36).

6. Explain the basic model for the taxation of trusts (paragraph 21-37).

7. Demonstrate an understanding of the available rollovers to a trust (paragraphs 21-38 through 21-49).

8. Demonstrate an understanding of the available rollovers to the capital beneficiaries of a trust (paragraphs 21-50 through 21-54).

9. Apply the 21 year deemed disposition rule (paragraphs 21-55 through 21-57).

10. Calculate the Net Income For Tax Purposes and Taxable Income of a trust (paragraphs 21-58 through 21-66).

11. Demonstrate an understanding of the provisions relating to income allocations to beneficiaries (paragraphs 21-67 through 21-84).

12. Calculate the Tax Payable for testamentary and inter vivos trusts (paragraphs 21-85 through 21-93).

13. Describe the procedures applicable to the filing of trust tax and information returns (paragraph 21-94).

14. Explain how the income attribution rules may be applicable to trusts and any associated tax planning considerations (paragraphs 21-95 through 21-99).

15. Explain the tax treatment of the purchase of an interest in a trust (paragraphs 21-100 through 21-105).

16. Demonstrate an understanding of tax planning involving various types of trusts (paragraphs 21-106 through 21-116).

17. Demonstrate an understanding of the objectives of estate planning (paragraphs 21-117 through 21-121).

18. Demonstrate an understanding of the objectives of an estate freeze (paragraphs 21-122 and 21-123).

19. Demonstrate an understanding of the estate freeze techniques that do not involve rollovers (paragraphs 21-124 through 21-129).

20. Apply ITA 86(1) to the implementation of an estate freeze (paragraphs 21-130 through 21-137).

22. Demonstrate a basic understanding of the considerations involved in choosing between Section 85 and Section 86 when implementing an estate freeze (paragraphs 21-138 through 21-140).

23. Explain the applicability of GST legislation to trusts (paragraphs 21-141 through 21-143).

CHAPTER TWENTY-TWO

How To Work Through Chapter Twenty-Two

On-Line Survey

We would appreciate your feedback on this text. Your comments will help us to improve it. In addition, students who complete the survey will have their name entered in a draw for a $100 cash prize.

To complete a brief, on-line survey, visit the "Student And General Resources" web page on our web site at:

www.pearsoned.ca/byrdchen/ctp2006/

We recommend the following approach in dealing with the material in this Chapter:

International Taxation - Introduction

☐   Read pages 915 (from paragraph 22-1) and 916 (through paragraph 22-5) of the text.

Fundamental Concepts - Introduction

☐   Read page 916 (paragraphs 22-6 and 22-7) of the text.

☐   Complete Self Study Problem Twenty-Two-1. The Self Study Problem is on page 950 of the text. The solution is on page S-303 of this Study Guide.

Tax Neutrality

☐   Read pages 916 (from paragraph 22-8) and 917 (through paragraph 22-14) of the text.

☐   Complete Exercise Twenty-Two-1. The Exercise is on page 917 of the text. The solution is on page S-299 of this Study Guide.

Source Vs. Residence

☐   Read pages 917 (from paragraph 22-15) and 918 (through paragraph 22-18) of the text.

☐   Complete Exercise Twenty-Two-2. The Exercise is on page 918 of the text. The solution is on page S-299 of this Study Guide.

Relieving Double Taxation

☐   Read pages 918 (from paragraph 22-19) through 920 (through paragraph 22-30) of the text.

☐   Complete Exercise Twenty-Two-3. The Exercise is on page 920 of the text. The solution is on pages S-299 and S-300 of this Study Guide.

The Role Of Tax Treaties - Objectives

☐   Read pages 921 (from paragraph 22-31) and 922 (through paragraph 22-35) of the text.

☐   Complete Exercise Twenty-Two-4. The Exercise is on page 922 of the text. The solution is on page S-300 of this Study Guide.

Double Taxation And Tax Treaties

☐   Read page 922 (paragraphs 22-36 through 22-38) of the text.

Residence

☐   Read pages 922 (from paragraph 22-39) through 924 (through paragraph 22-50) of the text.

How To Work Through Chapter Twenty-Two

☐ Complete Exercises Twenty-Two-5 and Twenty-Two-6. The Exercises are on page 924 of the text. The solutions are on page S-300 of this Study Guide.

☐ Complete Self Study Problem Twenty-Two-2. The Self Study Problem is on pages 950 and 951 of the text. The solution is on pages S-303 and S-304 of this Study Guide.

☐ Read pages 924 (from paragraph 22-51) and 925 (through paragraph 22-51) of the text.

Non-Residents Earning Canadian Source Income - Basic Approaches
☐ Read pages 925 (from paragraph 22-52) and 926 (through paragraph 22-57) of the text.

Non-Residents Earning Employment Income - General Rules
☐ Read page 926 (paragraphs 22-58 through 22-60) of the text.

☐ Complete Exercise Twenty-Two-7. The Exercise is on page 926 of the text. The solution is on page S-300 of this Study Guide.

Canada/U.S. Tax Treaty On Employment Income
☐ Read pages 926 (from paragraph 22-61) and 927 (through paragraph 22-62) of the text.

☐ Complete Exercise Twenty-Two-8. The Exercise is on page 927 of the text. The solution is on page S-301 of this Study Guide.

Non-Residents Carrying On Business In Canada
☐ Read pages 927 (from paragraph 22-63) and 928 (through paragraph 22-69) of the text.

☐ Complete Exercise Twenty-Two-9. The Exercise is on page 928 of the text. The solution is on page S-301 of this Study Guide.

Dispositions Of Taxable Canadian Property By Non-Residents
☐ Read page 929 (paragraphs 22-70 through 22-73) of the text.

☐ Complete Exercise Twenty-Two-10. The Exercise is on page 930 of the text. The solution is on page S-301 of this Study Guide.

Non-Residents Earning Interest Income
☐ Read pages 930 (from paragraph 22-74) and 931 (through paragraph 22-77) of the text.

☐ Complete Exercise Twenty-Two-11. The Exercise is on page 931 of the text. The solution is on page S-302 of this Study Guide.

Non-Residents Receiving Royalties And Rents
☐ Read pages 931 (from paragraph 22-78) and 932 (through paragraph 22-83) of the text.

☐ Complete Exercise Twenty-Two-12. The Exercise is on page 932 of the text. The solution is on page S-302 of this Study Guide.

Non-Residents Receiving Dividend Income
☐ Read pages 932 (from paragraph 22-84) and 933 (through paragraph 22-84) of the text.

Non-Residents Receiving Pension Income And Other Retirement Benefits
☐ Read page 933 (paragraphs 22-85 through 22-88) of the text.

Foreign Source Employment Income
☐ Read pages 933 (from paragraph 22-89) and 934 (through paragraph 22-91) of the text.

☐ Complete Self Study Problem Twenty-Two-3. The Self Study Problem is on page 951 of the text. The solution is on page S-305 of this Study Guide.

Foreign Source Business Income

☐ Read page 934 (paragraphs 22-92 and 22-93) of the text.

Foreign Source Capital Gains

☐ Read page 934 (paragraphs 22-94 and 22-95) of the text.

Foreign Source Investment Income - Foreign Investment Reporting

☐ Read pages 934 (from paragraph 22-96) through 936 (through paragraph 22-105) of the text.

☐ Complete Exercise Twenty-Two-13. The Exercise is on page 936 of the text. The solution is on page S-302 of this Study Guide.

☐ Complete Self Study Problem Twenty-Two-4. The Self Study Problem is on page 951 of the text. The solution is on page S-305 of this Study Guide.

Non-Resident Entities - Basic Issues

☐ Read pages 936 (from paragraph 22-106) and 937 (through paragraph 22-113) of the text.

Foreign Affiliates

☐ Read pages 937 (from paragraph 22-114) and 938 (through paragraph 22-120) of the text.

Controlled Foreign Affiliates

☐ Read pages 938 (from paragraph 22-121) and 939 (through paragraph 22-124) of the text.

Foreign Accrual Property Income (FAPI)

☐ Read pages 939 (from paragraph 22-125) and 940 (through paragraph 22-131) of the text.

☐ Complete Exercise Twenty-Two-14. The Exercise is on page 940 of the text. The solution is on page S-302 of this Study Guide.

☐ Complete Self Study Problem Twenty-Two-5. The Self Study Problem is on page 952 of the text. The solution is on page S-305 of this Study Guide.

Dividends From FAPI

☐ Read pages 940 (from paragraph 22-132) and 941 (through paragraph 22-132) of the text.

☐ Complete Exercise Twenty-Two-15. The Exercise is on page 941 of the text. The solution is on page S-303 of this Study Guide.

Foreign Affiliate Dividends

☐ Read pages 941 (from paragraph 22-133) through 943 (through paragraph 22-140) of the text.

Foreign Investment Entities

☐ Read pages 944 (from paragraph 22-141) through 946 (through paragraph 22-155) of the text.

Transfer Pricing

☐ Read pages 946 (from paragraph 22-156) through 948 (through paragraph 22-163) of the text.

How To Work Through Chapter Twenty-Two

To Complete This Chapter

☐ Review the Key Terms Used In The Chapter on page 948 of the text. Consult the Glossary for the meaning of any key terms you do not know.

☐ Review the Learning Objectives of the Chapter found on pages S-306 and S-307 of this Study Guide.

Solution to Chapter Twenty-Two Exercises

Exercise Twenty-Two - 1 Solution

1. Capital export neutrality.
2. Capital import neutrality.
3. Neither. Under capital export neutrality only the U.S. would have the right to tax the interest. The Canadian withholding taxes are clearly contrary to that approach. Under capital import neutrality, only the source country (e.g. Canada) would have the right to tax the amount, applying tax rates equal to that of Canadian residents earning interest. Although withholding tax ensures that non-residents pay some tax, the tax rates applied to non-residents are different from the rates applied to residents. In addition, the U.S. taxes the interest income of its residents.

Exercise Twenty-Two - 2 Solution

The residence jurisdiction approach applies to Malcolm since it appears that he is a resident of Canada. All of Malcolm's sources of income are subject to Canadian tax regardless of where the income is earned.

From a Canadian point of view, the source jurisdiction approach applies to Melissa. While she is not a resident of Canada, she would be taxed on her Canadian dividends (under Part XIII), as well as on her sale of taxable Canadian property. This same jurisdiction concept would prevent her from being taxed on her employment income as it is not sourced in Canada.

Exercise Twenty-Two - 3 Solution

The Deduction Method

Gross Foreign Income	$18,000
Foreign Tax Withheld	(1,800)
Foreign Interest Income Received	$16,200
Canadian Tax At 44 Percent	$ 7,128
Foreign Tax Withheld	1,800
Total Taxes Payable	$ 8,928
After Tax Retention ($18,000 - $8,928)	$ 9,072
Overall Tax Rate ($8,928 ÷ $18,000)	49.6%

The Exemption Method

Gross Foreign Income	$18,000
Canadian Tax Payable	$ Nil
Foreign Tax Withheld	1,800
Total Taxes Payable	$ 1,800
After Tax Retention ($18,000 - $1,800)	$16,200
Overall Tax Rate ($1,800 ÷ $18,000)	10.0%

The Credit Method

Foreign Interest Received ($18,000 - $1,800)	$16,200
Foreign Tax Withheld	1,800
Taxable Income Inclusion	$18,000
Canadian Tax Payable At 44 Percent	$ 7,920
Foreign Tax Credit	(1,800)
Net Canadian Tax Payable	$ 6,120
Foreign Tax Withheld	1,800
Total Taxes Payable	$ 7,920
After Tax Retention ($18,000 - $7,920)	$10,080
Overall Tax Rate ($7,920 ÷ $18,000)	44.0%

Exercise Twenty-Two - 4 Solution

The *Income Tax Act* and tax treaty are in conflict. Such inconsistencies are always resolved in favor of the tax treaty. Melissa will be subject to a 15 percent Part XIII withholding rate.

Exercise Twenty-Two - 5 Solution

Case 1 As it appears that Dizzy has a permanent home in Los Angeles, the tie-breaker rules would indicate that he is a resident of the United States. As he has been in Canada for more than 183 days, the sojourner rules might have made him a deemed Canadian resident. However, the tie-breaker rules in the international tax treaty would likely override this.

If the boarding rooms and hotels had been considered a permanent home, then the fact that his centre of vital interests appears to be in Los Angeles would still suggest that he should be considered a U.S. resident.

Case 2 As Donna was in Canada for more than 183 days in 2005, she is a deemed resident through the application of the sojourner rule, and therefore a dual resident. The apartment would be considered a permanent home because it was available on a continuous basis throughout her stay in Canada. However, her centre of vital interests is the U.S., as her social, personal, and economic ties are in that country. This suggests that the U.S. is her country of residence. Donna would therefore be considered a non-resident of Canada and would only be taxable on income sourced to Canada.

Exercise Twenty-Two - 6 Solution

Case 1 Article IV(3) of the Canada/U.S. tax treaty provides that Taxco is a resident of Canada since it was incorporated in Canada.

Case 2 Article IV(3) of the Canada/U.S. tax treaty provides that Junkco is a resident of the U.S. because it was incorporated in that country.

Exercise Twenty-Two - 7 Solution

Dawn is an individual who has become a resident of another country, but continues to receive remuneration from a resident Canadian taxpayer. Given that the tax treaty exempts her salary from taxation in Egypt, ITA 115(2) deems her to be employed in Canada and, as a consequence, she would be subject to Canadian taxes.

Exercise Twenty-Two - 8 Solution

Case 1 The employment income is taxable in Canada. The Canada/U.S. tax treaty allows Canada to tax employment income earned in Canada unless either of two exceptions is applicable. The first exception is the $10,000 rule. This exception however does not apply since David earned $11,200 Canadian in 2005 [($2,800)(4 months)]. The second exception is the 183 day rule. Although David was in Canada for only 122 days during 2005 and therefore met the first part of the test, he failed the remaining part of the test since the employer was a Canadian resident and could deduct payments.

Case 2 The employment income is not taxable in Canada. The 183 day rule exempts the income from Canadian taxation because the employer was not resident in Canada, nor had a fixed base of operations in Canada, and could not deduct the payments.

Case 3 The employment income is taxable in Canada. The Canada/U.S. tax treaty would exempt the income from Canadian tax if the amount was less than $10,000 Canadian, or if Sandra spent less than 183 days in Canada. As she earned $50,000 Canadian and spent 238 days at her job in Canada, neither of these exceptions are applicable.

Exercise Twenty-Two - 9 Solution

Case 1 Jazzco is not carrying on business in Canada and would not be subject to Canadian taxes.

Case 2 Jazzco is carrying on business in Canada in a permanent establishment located in Toronto. Therefore, Jazzco is taxable in Canada under ITA 2(3) on the profits attributable to the Canadian factory.

Case 3 The tax treaty allows Canada to tax business income only if such income is attributable to a permanent establishment in Canada. The warehouse constitutes a fixed place of business regardless of whether it is owned or leased. However, since it appears to be used exclusively to maintain an inventory for delivery, it would be an excluded activity and would therefore not be considered to be a permanent establishment. Jazzco would not be taxable under ITA 2(3) on its Canadian profits.

Case 4 In this Case, because the employee has authority to conclude contracts on behalf of a non-resident enterprise, the employee is deemed to be a permanent establishment. This means that Jazzco is taxable in Canada under ITA 2(3) on its business profits attributable to the permanent establishment.

Exercise Twenty-Two - 10 Solution

Case 1 Nancy is not taxable on the gain. As a non-resident, Nancy is only taxable in Canada on the disposition of taxable Canadian property. Shares of a resident public company are only taxable Canadian property if Nancy had owned more than 25 percent of the issued shares of any class of the company in the 60 months preceding the disposition.

Case 2 Joe is taxable on the gain. The condo is taxable Canadian property since it is real property (e.g. land and buildings) situated in Canada. The Canada/U.S. tax treaty gives Canada the right to tax such gains. The property is not exempt from Canadian tax as a principal residence since Joe did not acquire the condo for his own habitation.

Case 3 Joe would be taxable on the gain on the shares. Shares of an unlisted Canadian corporation are taxable Canadian property. In addition, the Canada/U.S. tax treaty allows Canada to tax gains on the disposition of shares if the value of the shares is principally derived from real property situated in Canada.

Case 4 Joe would not be taxable on the gain on the shares. The shares are taxable Canadian property because they represent shares of an unlisted non-resident corporation that, at some time in the 60 months preceding the disposition, derived more than 50 percent of their value from taxable Canadian property. However, the Canada/U.S. tax treaty does not list this as one of the items where Canada is allowed to tax U.S. residents.

Exercise Twenty-Two - 11 Solution

Case 1   Jason's interest would be subject to Part XIII tax. However, under the treaty, it would be taxed at the reduced rate of 10 percent.

Case 2   Such interest would generally be subject to Part XIII tax, however, ITA 212(1)(b) contains an exemption from tax where the interest is earned on government of Canada bonds. The treaty is irrelevant since there is no Part XIII tax.

Case 3   Such interest would generally be subject to Part XIII tax. However, ITA 212(1)(b) contains an exemption from tax where the interest relates to real property situated outside of Canada and the funds are not used in a Canadian business or used to earn any property income except property income from the foreign real property. In this Case, there is no Part XIII tax.

Case 4   The interest would not be eligible for the exception since the funds were used in a Canadian business. The tax treaty would not override Part XIII tax, but would reduce the withholding to 10 percent.

Exercise Twenty-Two - 12 Solution

Case 1   Rentco appears to be carrying on business in Canada through a permanent establishment. As a result, no Part XIII tax is payable. However, Rentco would be subject to Part I tax on its income attributable to the permanent establishment in Saskatchewan.

Case 2   Jack would be subject to Part XIII tax of $10,500 [(25%)($42,000)]. This represents an effective tax rate of 37.5 percent on his net rental income of $28,000. Alternatively, Jack could elect under ITA 216 to be taxed under Part I on the net rental income of $28,000 ($42,000 - $14,000). If we assume that the net rental income represents a small portion of his worldwide income and his marginal tax rate is less than 37.5 percent, the Part I option would be preferable.

Case 3   Jack would be subject to Part XIII tax on the gross rents received for the boats unless he would be considered to be carrying on a business. However, the Canada/U.S. tax treaty reduces the withholding tax to 10 percent of the gross rents received, or $800. Note that Jack would not be eligible to elect under ITA 216 on the boat rents, since this election is generally restricted to real property.

Exercise Twenty-Two - 13 Solution

Simon's total foreign investments of £65,000 (£30,000 + £35,000) push him over the $100,000 Canadian reporting limit [(£65,000)($2.4) = $156,000]. Therefore, he should report foreign investments held during the year by filing Form T1135. He is also required to report any foreign interest income that he earns on the same form.

Exercise Twenty-Two - 14 Solution

Since Forco is a controlled foreign affiliate of Canco, Canco must report its proportionate share of Forco's investment income:

FAPI [ITA 91(1)]	$100,000
Deduct Lesser Of:	
• FAPI = $100,000	
• ITA 91(4) Deduction [(18%)($100,000)(3.2258)] = $58,064	(58,064)
Addition To Net Income For Tax Purposes	$41,936

Exercise Twenty-Two - 15 Solution

Foreign Dividend – ITA 90(1)	$ 82,000
Deduct Lesser Of:	
• Previous FAPI = $82,000	
• Dividend Received = $82,000	(82,000)
Addition To Net Income For Tax Purposes	Nil

Had there been any withholding taxes on the dividend, then Canco would have been eligible for an increased deduction under ITA 113. Withholding taxes on dividends to corporate shareholders of foreign affiliates are not eligible for a foreign tax credit.

Solution to Self Study Problem Twenty-Two - 1

Paragraph 15 of IT-221R3 indicates that, in general, the CRA will view an individual as becoming a non-resident on the latest of three dates:

- The date the individual leaves Canada.
- The date the individual's spouse or common-law partner and dependants leave Canada.
- The date the individual becomes a resident of another country.

As Paul's wife and daughter did not leave Canada, it would appear that the CRA would take the position that Paul did not stop being a resident of Canada.

As he purchased a house in the U.S., it is possible that he will also be viewed as a resident of that jurisdiction. If this is the case, the tie breaker rules that are contained in the Canada/U.S. tax treaty must be applied. As Paul has a permanent home available in both locations, we need to apply the center of vital interests criterion. The personal ties appear to be stronger in Canada, so it is likely that the CRA would conclude that the center of vital interests is Canada. Given this, Paul would not be considered to be resident in the U.S.

Based on this conclusion, Paul should report his worldwide income in Canada, and claim a foreign tax credit for any U.S. tax paid on his employment income while he was living and working in the U.S.

Solution to Self Study Problem Twenty-Two - 2

Debbie will have a deemed disposition of all property except Canadian real estate and RRSPs. The deemed dispositions should result in the following gains, which will likely be capital gains.

Gains On Deemed Dispositions Of Capital Assets

Description	ACB	FMV	Gain (Loss)
Interest in CCPC (10 percent)	$ 90,000	$140,000	$ 50,000
Sports car (Note 1)	18,000	15,000	-0-
Paintings	50,000	175,000	125,000
10 percent interest in Sorrento Co., a Canadian public company	180,000	110,000	(70,000)
Net Capital Gains			$105,000
Inclusion Rate			1/2
Taxable Capital Gains			$ 52,500
Personal Tax Rate			45%
Personal Tax Payable (Note 2)			$ 23,625

Solution to Self Study Problem Twenty-Two - 2

Note 1   Losses on personal use property are not deductible.

Note 2   If Debbie continues to own the above assets, the CRA will accept security in lieu of cash for the related personal Tax Payable. The unpaid tax is due when the assets are eventually disposed of.

Deferred Gains On Real Estate

Description	ACB	FMV	Gain
House	$150,000	$225,000	$75,000
Whistler ski chalet	125,000	185,000	60,000

As the $20,000 ($60,000/3) annual gain on the Whistler ski chalet is much greater than the $7,500 ($75,000/10) annual gain on the house, Debbie should designate the ski chalet as the family's principal residence for 2004 and 2005, thereby eliminating the entire gain on this property (because of the plus one year rule for principal residences, only two years need to be designated to eliminate all three years of the gain). The house can then be designated as the principal residence from 1996 to 2003. This results in only one year of the gain on the house being taxable (again, due to the plus one year rule for principal residences, designating eight years will eliminate nine years of the gain).

Report Of Assets Held

As Debbie owns assets exceeding $25,000, she is obliged to provide a list to the CRA of all assets owned on her departure date and their related costs. Personal use property up to $10,000 can be excluded. The list of assets owned (Form T1161) should be attached to her tax return for the year of departure.

Other Planning Points   The following factors should also be considered:

Non-Resident Date   As Debbie's husband may defer his move for six months, the deemed date of non-residence will be when he finally moves to Hong Kong. This may be undesirable for Debbie, as the Hong Kong tax rates are less than Canadian rates. Until Debbie is officially a non-resident, all of her income will have to be reported in Canada, and will be subject to the relatively high Canadian tax rates. As Debbie's husband will be commuting anyway, it could be more advantageous for him to work from his Hong Kong base, and to wind up his Canadian client affairs. In this way, the non-resident date could be advanced and a tax savings would be realized.

Moving Expenses   The $50,000 moving allowance may be taxable in Canada, depending on the date she ceases to be a resident. It might be simpler for Debbie to be reimbursed for specific moving costs. Such reimbursements are not a taxable benefit and would not have to be included in her tax return, regardless of the date that she ceases to be a resident.

RRSP   Debbie will have relatively high income in 2005, so she should not collapse her RRSP while resident in Canada in 2005. If the departure from Canada is deferred to 2006, she could collapse some of the RRSP early that year, to be taxed at the low personal tax rates. This assumes that Debbie has no other Canadian income in 2006. It may be more advantageous for Debbie to collapse the RRSP after becoming a non-resident. At that time, a 25 percent Part XIII tax would apply in Canada, and there would likely not be any applicable Hong Kong income tax. Alternatively, Debbie can leave the RRSP invested in Canada and withdraw amounts, after withholding taxes are applied, in later years.

Rental Income   If the house and ski chalet are rented, a 25 percent Part XIII tax will apply to the gross rents received. Debbie can also elect to have the rental income taxed under Part I of the *Income Tax Act*. This is may be preferable in that she can deduct expenses against the gross rents if she makes this election.

Solution to Self Study Problem Twenty-Two - 3

A. With respect to the Florida school, the US$7,000 fee is less than the US$10,000 limit for exempting employment income that is specified in the treaty. Therefore, he would be exempt from U.S. taxation on his work in that country. While this is not discussed in the text, there is a separate limit of $15,000 for artists and athletes. As the individual appears to be a Canadian resident for tax purposes, all of the earnings will be taxable in Canada.

B. While we do not know the amount of remuneration, presumably it exceeds the US$10,000 limit. Regardless, the employment is exempt as the total number of days employed in the U.S. is 180 days [(60 days)(3 periods)], which is less than the cut-off of 183 days. While the earnings would not be subject to U.S. taxation, they would be taxable in Canada.

C. First, we determine that the remuneration is not exempt under Article XV, as it exceeds US$10,000. While the text does not cover this point, the $20,000 inducement payment exceeds the US$15,000 limit that is applicable to athletes. Given this, the bonus is clearly taxable in the U.S.

With respect to the royalty payments, they would likely be subject to a 10 percent withholding tax prior to being remitted to the roller blader. This amount, however, can be claimed as a foreign tax credit under ITA 126(1).

Solution to Self Study Problem Twenty-Two - 4

A. The term deposits do not need to be reported because the total amount is less than $100,000.

B. If the Florida condominium is primarily for personal use, then reporting of the asset is not required. On the other hand, if it is rented out to third parties, it would need to be reported, as the total cost amount is greater than $100,000.

C. As the total cost of the Arizona condominium is $102,000, reporting is required if the condominium is not personal use property.

D. No foreign investment reporting is required when assets are used in an active business.

Solution to Self Study Problem Twenty-Two - 5

Operation As A Branch   As a branch, any profits will be taxed in the United States. In addition, they will be taxed in Canada as part of worldwide income earned by the Canadian company. However, any Canadian Tax Payable will be reduced by foreign tax credits for U.S. taxes paid on branch profits.

As the earnings of the branch will not be active business income earned in Canada, no small business deduction will be available to Tritec. However, any loss suffered in the U.S. operation will be deductible in arriving at Taxable Income for Canadian tax purposes.

Operation As A Subsidiary   A subsidiary will be subject to U.S. taxes on its worldwide income and, if the subsidiary earns investment income, the foreign accrual property income (FAPI) rules will result in this income being taxed in Canada as the investment income is earned. Subsidiary losses will not be deductible in Canada and, in addition, the U.S. taxation authorities will assess a withholding tax on any management fees, interest, or dividends paid to the Canadian parent.

Chapter Twenty-Two Learning Objectives

After completing Chapter 22, you should be able to:

1. Describe the principles of international taxation (paragraphs 22-1 through 22-5).

2. Demonstrate an understanding of the concepts associated with tax neutrality (paragraphs 22-6 through 22-14).

3. Demonstrate an understanding of the source and residence jurisdictional approaches to taxation (paragraphs 22-15 through 22-18).

4. Explain the legislative approaches used to resolve source vs. residence issues (paragraphs 22-21 through 22-30).

5. Describe the role of tax treaties in international taxation (paragraphs 22-31 through 22-38).

6. Determine the residency, for tax purposes, of individuals, corporations, trusts, and partnerships (paragraphs 22-39 through 22-51).

7. Demonstrate an understanding of the basic approaches used for taxing non-residents earning Canadian source income (paragraphs 22-52 through 22-57).

8. Apply the appropriate tax treatment for non-residents earning Canadian source employment income (paragraphs 22-58 through 22-62).

9. Apply the appropriate tax treatment for non-residents carrying on a business in Canada (paragraphs 22-63 through 22-69).

10. Apply the appropriate tax treatment for gains realized by non-residents on the disposition of taxable Canadian property (paragraphs 22-70 through 22-73).

11. Apply the appropriate tax treatment for interest income earned by a non-resident (paragraphs 22-74 though 22-77).

12. Apply the appropriate tax treatment for Canadian source royalties and rents received by non-residents (paragraphs 22-78 through 22-83).

13. Apply the appropriate tax treatment for Canadian source dividends received by non-residents (paragraph 22-84).

14. Apply the appropriate tax treatment for Canadian source pension benefits and other retirement related benefits received by non-residents (paragraphs 22-85 through 22-88).

15. Apply the appropriate tax treatment for foreign source employment income earned by Canadian residents (paragraphs 22-89 through 22-91).

16. Apply the appropriate tax treatment for foreign source business income earned by Canadian residents (paragraphs 22-92 and 22-93).

17. Apply the appropriate tax treatment for foreign source capital gains realized by Canadian residents (paragraphs 22-94 and 22-95).

18. Describe the basic concepts behind the taxation of foreign source investment income (paragraphs 22-96 through 22-100).

19. Demonstrate an understanding of the requirements of foreign investment reporting (paragraphs 22-101 through 22-105).

20. Describe the basic issues associated with the taxation of non-resident entities (paragraphs 22-106 through 22-113).

21. Identify situations where the rules associated with foreign affiliates are applicable (paragraphs 22-114 through 22-120).

22. Explain the concept of a controlled foreign affiliate (paragraphs 22-121 through 22-124).

23. Apply the rules associated with, and the appropriate tax treatment of, foreign property accrual income (FAPI) (paragraphs 22-125 through 22-132).

24. Apply the appropriate tax treatment for dividends received from foreign affiliates (paragraphs 22-133 through 22-140).

25. Apply the appropriate tax treatment for foreign investment entities (paragraphs 22-141 through 22-152).

26. Explain the tax treatment for dividends received from non-affiliated foreign companies (paragraphs 22-153 through 22-155).

27. Demonstrate a basic understanding of transfer pricing, including the models used to establish transfer prices (paragraphs 22-156 through 22-163).